Bit of a "Tiff"

Reminiscences of Fifty Years in Aviation

The Author – HMS Eagle – Spring 1956

Former Naval Air Apprentice

Lt. C.S. (Bill) Drake

(R.N.)rtd. C.Eng. MIERE. MBIM.

With a Foreword by Rear Admiral A.R. Rawbone CB, AFC.

CONTENTS

N.B. Photographs and other illustrations follow the Chapter to which they relate

To

Richard and Barbara

With love

Olim Meminisse Juvabit

ACKNOWLEDGEMENTS

I would first like to record my thanks to "author and historian" Graham Bebbington who encouraged me to start this book, identified the locations of the work sites and buildings at Newcastle-under-Lyme and has continued to give advice from his experience whenever I needed it. Regretfully we have never met in person and have conducted our business by letter and telephone.

At the beginning I had no idea just how much I could remember of past events, but with the prompting given by pictures, cuttings and souvenirs, so much has emerged that I have had to be selective and to exercise restraint on some issues simply to keep the text readable. It has been a very nostalgic experience, none more so than during my visit to the Fleet Air Arm Museum at Yeovilton, where I was able to peruse the "Line Books and Diaries" of my old Squadrons. My thanks are due therefore to the staff at Yeovilton who made this possible.

I am especially grateful to Rear-Admiral Ray Rawbone for writing the Foreword. The period on 897 Squadron under his command gave me valuable experience as a newly promoted Branch Officer and I hope that my writing has done it justice.

All but eight of the photographs included have been in my collection for many years before the book was ever a prospect so I am very grateful to Tony Dowland for permission to include the seven photographs taken at Worthy Down during the war by the former Lt.-Cdr. (Air) of Worthy Down Lt.-Cdr. Bill Blake; without these I would have no photographic record of that important period and also to Lionel.A.Smith for the photograph of Sea Vixen XP924. Of the remainder some 240 photographs are my own work whose quality varies with the camera and film available at the time. Regretfully many opportunities for a better record of events were missed by the nature of my work and of course the sensitivity of the subjects at that time. The two photographs of bomb damage in Maidstone are included by courtesy of the Kent Messenger Group of Maidstone.

The Copyright of wartime extracts from both the *Daily Mail* and *Kent Messenger* in chapter 6 is acknowledged.

I have been unsuccessful in tracing the successor to Ian McDonald (Photographs) Ltd whose superb photograph of a Buccaneer over Trafalgar Square appears in Chapter 18 and whose Copyright is acknowledged.

Every effort has been made to trace and attribute Copyright to a small number of pictures whose origin is uncertain. If unwittingly

Copyright has been infringed then the author offers his apology and will correct the error in subsequent editions.

Finally I must record the patience of my wife Margaret over the past year when I disappeared upstairs to my study for hours on end; of course it may just be a relief that I have not been covered in oil and sawdust which is my normal condition.

Bishops Waltham.

FOREWORD
by
Rear-Admiral A.R. (Ray) Rawbone CB, AFC.

The thrill and glamour of aviation has generally fallen to aircrew or great designers, and bookshelves are full of the adventures of heroes who are household names. Rarely does a book appear about the people in the background, the unsung heroes, many of them engineers, who laboured consistently to provide serviceable aircraft and equipment to meet the daily targets so vital to successful air operations.

During World War II, and in the early post war years, the Fleet Air Arm struggled with many aircraft well past their "sell by" date and the introduction of new models rarely meant that they were designed with ease of maintenance in mind. Clear diagnosis, imaginative improvisation and a "can do" attitude was the environment in which Bill Drake spent his early formative years. The story of his career, intelligently written, forceful, engaging and so human in its telling, helps to fill a vacant gap in the jigsaw of service aviation.

The son of a joiner in Maidstone and a teenager during the Battle of Britain, his candid autobiography reveals the full story of a life spanning five decades in aviation in the Fleet Air Arm and as a civilian. A career that shaped strong beliefs, a profound insight into human behaviour and an extensive knowledge of electrical engineering.

Always fascinated by aviation he was disappointed when he joined the Royal Navy in March 1941 that he was too young to be accepted for aircrew training. With typical good grace and almost by chance, he fell into the air electrical branch.

His detailed memory of a long, wide ranging apprenticeship as an artificer, and his role in wartime squadron service is remarkable, and those that served in those turbulent years will relate to many of his observations and comments – straight to the point, sometimes controversial or cynical but always with underlying good humour and common sense.

After the war his long struggle to commissioned rank and his limited promotion thereafter, clearly frustrating for a bright and ambitious young man, are recounted without rancour and with stoic acceptance of the limited opportunities at the time.

With advances in design and the introduction of an increasing amount of highly technical electrical equipment into service it was inevitable that some serious problems would arise. Based on further extensive experience in the front line and various staff appointments in the Ministry of Defence and R.A.E. Farnborough, the author is well placed to outline with great clarity many of the technical difficulties faced by the service as it assimilated jet propulsion and the computer age.

From an engineer's perspective we experience at first hand the complexities of co-ordinating design, supply and operational requirements not always helped by the rigid attitude of some in a service entrenched in tradition.

However, above all it is the story of a typical Navy family, which makes this book so interesting. The human touches, his marriage to Margaret, his devotion to family and the difficulty of balancing a turbulent service career with the stability needed while caring for a wife handicapped by the aftermath of polio.

Meticulous research and the blend of technical narrative and colourful personal recollection so clearly brings to life the atmosphere and environment in which so many young people gave long and unstinting service.

A Bit of a "Tiff" is an impressive and well-written account of one engineer's contribution to aviation.

Halstock Leigh

INTRODUCTION

This is a story centred on Aviation, primarily about the fortunes and misfortunes of the Fleet Air Arm of the Royal Navy as seen from the perspective of Air Artificers of the Royal Navy under training, at war, and in peace. The Air Artificer branch became and remains the centre of technical expertise in the Fleet Air Arm and together with the Air Mechanic and Air Fitter branches who preceded Artificers has kept the Navy's aircraft flying.

Naval Artificers are generally known as "Tiffies" or "Tiffs", and the first entry of Air Artificers started their careers as Naval Air Apprentices in 1939.

During the war the bulk of Naval Air Apprentices were trained at Newcastle-under-Lyme, and the story of this Establishment has been well told by Graham Bebbington in *Ship without Water*. Originally intended as extra information for Graham's book this story has been developed with his encouragement into a natural sequel. A sort of "whatever happened to the likely lads?" tale, but since it was impracticable to cover the experiences of the thousands of people who have served in these and successor branches and whose contribution to the success of the Fleet Air Arm is seldom reported I have chosen to write about my own career, which I hope will serve to illustrate the whole and perhaps provide another dimension to the Naval, Aviation and Social History of our time. The story is therefore dedicated to the Air Engineering branch of the Royal Navy.

My career in the Navy covered thirty years, during which the Fleet Air Arm recovered from the sorry state in which it entered World War II, expanded during the war to over sixty carriers and then began to reduce in size while increasing its capability, only to have its most powerful asset (the large Aircraft Carrier) taken away at the point when it was most effective. I retired before the big carriers were finally scrapped but have continued to watch with interest as the F.A.A. has changed and adapted to new requirements. In many areas the changes appear beneficial, in others it seems that the wheel has turned almost to its starting point. I have attempted to comment on a few of the changes for the sake of comparison with my own experience.

Purely by chance, as with so many other things in life, I spent most of my Naval career working with fixed-wing aircraft, thus my experiences may differ from other ex-Apprentices but I think that they will "ring a bell" with the majority who passed my way. This is not a tale of "derring do" but of men and the work that they do behind the scenes to keep the aircraft flying. Inevitably, the story includes technical matters, and I hope that I have managed to keep the detail to an acceptable level and included sufficient of the funny, silly and downright stupid aspects of Naval life to keep the reader amused.

I have included my career subsequent to retirement from the Navy because that also concerned Aviation in a variety of areas for which my Naval experience played a part.

The story derives from memory stimulated by my collection of photographs, old letters and souvenirs, and I apologise in advance for any errors of fact, although I have endeavoured to check such facts as seemed relevant.

Overall this is a "Warts and All" story (perhaps not all the Warts!) and the views expressed are my own, not those of the Establishment, but will be recognised and understood by my colleagues. To my surviving colleagues, their heirs and successors in the service I send my good wishes.

Nil Carborundum Illegitimi
(This is Navalese for 'Don't let the bastards grind you down.')

Bill Drake at Bishops Waltham – October 2003

Chapter 1 Schooldays

I was born in Maidstone on August 4th 1925. My father was a Carpenter/Joiner and we lived initially in a small terrace house opposite the grey stone walls of Maidstone prison. I remember almost nothing of this time and when I was four we moved to a three bedroom semi-detached house in Bearsted. My only sister June was born in 1930.

I went first to the Thurnham Infant School and then to Bearsted Junior School until I was eleven, when I took and passed the Scholarship exam for Maidstone Grammar School.

In those days Bearsted was decidedly rural, there were fields opposite our house and at intervals along the lane until one passed a thick and productive chestnut wood and a Dairy farm, then Bearsted Station and finally arrived at the village. A shortcut to Thurnham School was via the Golf course where we lingered looking for lost golf balls and tees. Needless to say all the children walked to school, usually alone or with friends once a routine had been established but I recall one day meeting my chum's dad riding home on his bicycle, he then stopped and wheeled us both home perched shakily on the crossbar and I first realised my dislike for heights.

Bearsted School was conveniently opposite the village green and next door to a small row of shops, which comprised "Moss" the butcher, a draper, "Taylors" a paper-shop and Post Office, and "Brooks" the grocer. The grocer's was a delight, loose goods were shovelled from drawers with brass scoops and poured into twisted blue paper cones, and the whole shop reeked of good food. At Christmas there was always a display of Xmas crackers that I have never seen surpassed. The butcher and grocer called for orders and delivered. Our milk was delivered twice daily and the baker, Houghams of Maidstone, called daily in a van labelled "Often buttered never bettered". His loaves included the beautifully crusty Coburg and Cottage varieties.

Compared with the variety of food now available ours was pretty basic but was good quality and I was never hungry. Every Sunday we would have roast leg of lamb and this stretched usually two further days ending with something like cottage pie from the minced remains. Dad's vegetables were of course critical throughout the year. I cannot recall chicken except for Xmas but we often ate rabbit shot or trapped by a friend and this I considered far more interesting even if a few lead pellets appeared during the meal. Very lucky compared with others in the thirties I still managed to have a few dislikes; these did not survive wartime rationing and the Navy.

Next to the shops was a small garage and in due course, when Dad had made an elegant oak cabinet to hold a kit-built 1-valve radio supplied by a friend, it was my Saturday duty to take the accumulator to the garage to be charged. This was not a chore I enjoyed because on Friday night I was dosed with a spoonful of Syrup of Figs and my Saturday morning trip to the garage was spent wondering whether I would make the garage and back without the explosive proof of the efficacy of Syrup of Figs.

School was enjoyable. Thurnham had two teachers, Miss Sage the headmistress wore her hair in a bun and lived at the schoolhouse and, Miss Hutt a well built, comfortable and motherly lady. I clearly remember a general aroma of soft-soap, overlaid, at lunchtime in the classroom, by the egg sandwiches and malted milk brought by my chum. At one stage we were all taught to knit; firstly we made a grubby dish cloth using some sort of string and wielding awkwardly some very thick knitting needles to our mumbled prayer of "in, over, under, off". Our knitting only covered "plain" but not "pearl". The dishcloth was followed by something in red wool, it may have been a scarf, and in any event it seemed to go on forever.

At Bearsted School the headmaster was Mr Sergeant, a tall solid man with a neat moustache, with teachers Miss Pemble and Mrs Housman. I followed Dad's advice on self-defence and "bonked" a couple of offending noses, thus achieving some credibility and the nickname "Bruiser". Later for obvious reasons the name "Tubby" stuck and remained throughout my Naval Apprenticeship until later my wife used "Bill"; this had been coined by my father when presumably he recognised that my Christian names really didn't suit. In all honesty these days "Tubby" may again be suitable.

I found the young ladies good company, Lucy Garrett was nice and I went to parties at her house, but Rosemary Baker was my choice. Alas all contact was lost when I entered the somewhat monastic Boys Grammar. One young lady a few months older was reputed to know where babies came from, but she never told us boys and I remained in ignorance until I joined up.

In my youth there were few restrictions or risks in children wandering around the countryside and with my friends I did my fair share of wandering, birds nesting and occasionally getting into trouble. Our enthusiasms followed the current trend, from hoops to tops, yo-yos and the light or dark blue badges supporting ones choice for the Cambridge/Oxford boat race, and not forgetting cigarette cards. Although Dad smoked only a pipe, he and his workmates provided a good range of cards which, with swaps and the odd one picked up from discarded packets in the road, enabled me to complete most of the John Players sets as they appeared, until of course the war intervened. The cigarettes may well have been lethal to the smokers but the cards were very informative on a wide range of subjects and I treasured my collection and still have them. At one stage blank cartridge pistols were popular, I was lucky to be given a .22 automatic with a six shot magazine by Uncle Jack, it was not quite lethal, but no doubt today would be totally illegal. Both cricket and soccer were played on the Green and we could join cricket coaching sessions. My Uncle Len was a soccer referee and I proudly watched him one Saturday, that is until he gave a decision against Bearsted and I heard a local supporter shout "throw the s—bag in the pond". Nothing it seems has changed! Dear Uncle Len got carried away when playing cricket in our small backyard and knocked the ball with a mighty swipe through our living room window. Dad was not too thrilled!

I had my ration of measles, mumps, chickenpox and the odd unusual bug, but by good fortune missed the dreaded scarlet fever, which was rampant and doomed the afflicted to a spell in the "isolation" hospital One needed to be hardy, because of course our house had no central heating and no roofing felt, so when the winter winds blew over the North Downs we huddled in front of the coal fire in our living room and watched the linoleum lifting off the floorboards. Dad's favourite position was with his feet resting on the mantelpiece so that the back of his legs were often roasted. If it snowed then it was often possible to see the snow slowly filtering under the "sash windows". Going to bed in winter was by candlelight and needed both hot-water bottle and bed socks. The lath and plaster ceiling in my bedroom reached the end of its fatigue life one night when I was asleep and collapsed on to my bed covering everything in dirt and plaster, but the soft board ceiling that replaced it seemed to be even less effective as an insulator. The outside "loo" had no heating or lighting and at intervals Dad would use his skills to "wipe" a frozen and split lead pipe.

By the standards of village society I was accepted as a "nice boy" and went to parties with friends whose parents were certainly better off than my own. One of these owned a local garage and had been a pilot in the R.F.C; his sideboard carried a silver model of a Nieuport 28, which I naturally much admired. Presumably my good fortune arose because I was obliged to go to Sunday school and then join the choir and later became a server. In those days the all male choir sang at three services each Sunday and it was normal also to sing at both weddings and funerals. The sight and scent of daffodils reminds me of the bunches of those flowers in the vestry on those solemn occasions. I also remember looking out of the vestry as the congregation arrived and observing how Mrs Watcham, always considered a village gossip, appeared to be primarily interested in who was present. However we choirboys were not little angels and spent our time during the sermons sniggering at snippets in Isaiah 36 and hoping to avoid the warning glares of Miss Hoare, the choir mistress, who was able to view us in a large mirror. Miss Hoare was genteel impoverished spinster who lived in a rambling old house next to the church and was dedicated to the choir. She gave individual tuition to the new recruits at her house and even in my youth it struck me that since on every occasion that I visited she had obviously just had her evening meal of potato and onion, then her poverty must have been extreme. Occasionally one of us was called on to pump the organ before eventually an electric pump was fitted. Being in the choir had some benefits, for a start we were paid but we also had lemonade and biscuits, in the interval between Eucharist and Matins, at a big house opposite the Church. Bearsted was the home to a number of prominent people and they did their bit in supporting village life. Other celebrities were Les Ames the Kent cricketer and also the surviving brother of the aviation pioneering Short Bros. The school celebrated Empire Day with a gathering at which we sang rousing songs like *Hearts of Oak* and on Ascension Day we were allowed up the church tower. How could this ever change.

Dad never went to Church and Mum went only very rarely, she considered herself working-class and acted accordingly, although she was very bright but had only elementary schooling. Like so many other girls of her class, her first job was in service, but the war changed that and eventually she, her father, and her elder sister and brother were all employed at the Tilling Stevens munitions factory in Maidstone, where she worked in an office. She devoted herself to the family and was very house-proud. Undoubtedly she deprived herself in favour of her children, mostly myself, but of course I was unaware of it at that time. Dad was not well paid, was buying the house with a mortgage from the "Oddfellows" and was very careful with his pennies, so there were periodic battles over money but in fact Mum was a very good manager. Dad was a good craftsman and was never out of work during the Depression. At one stage he was the only carpenter still working in the small building firm in Maidstone and he remained there until it folded after the war. Like others at that time he started work early and worked on Saturday morning. When he was home he made furniture in his small workshop and maintained the house. His workshop was a source of great interest to me and I loved to watch him at work, smell the timber and listen to the "zing" of his plane. Inevitably I tried my hand in his absence and was banned for blunting the tools. He also grew most of our vegetables in the back garden so he had little relaxation.

Dad smoked a pipe with "Afrikander" tobacco, occasionally burning a hole in his jacket pocket when he stowed it away still smouldering, only drank at Christmas and his weekly entertainment was a visit to the Oddfellows on a Saturday evening followed by a visit to his sister. At one stage he joined the Bearsted and Thurnham Rifle Club. He was a good shot and won two silver spoons in competitions before his eyes gave trouble. Sometimes he went to the cinema and would return with some sweets, but we never went with him. Instead my mother spent the evening emptying the accumulated dust and shavings from the turn-ups and pockets of his working suit and polishing his shoes. Following that it was bath-night in the tin bath in the scullery and my Sundays were less than comfortable in winter as I wore a clean flannel vest, which irritated and overheated me beyond endurance, how I loathed it! We used a tin bath not because there was no bath but because the bath also sited in the scullery was not plumbed in and would have required vast quantities of water manhandled from the copper, which was also not used due to its inconvenience. Instead all hot water was heated on the gas stove in saucepans. The gas stove like many others of that vintage was made of cast iron and was black-leaded at intervals to maintain its finish. The bath however had its uses since it was covered with boards, which became Mum's kitchen table and on occasion the bath itself became a store for the potatoes Dad had harvested from the garden.

We seldom went out as a family nor could we afford a family holiday. This was not unusual among my school chums so we certainly did not feel hard done by, although my school chum next-door went annually to Mevagissy. The highlight of our year was the Sunday School outing to Margate by rail from Bearsted Station and I remember seeing ancient Vickers Virginias flying out of nearby Manston airfield. We occasionally visited our relations since most of them lived in Maidstone and in those days families tended to be more supportive of each other.

Dad's mother, Granny Adams, was by now a widow for the second time and lived in a little terraced house surrounded by Victoriana, aspidistras and loads of highly decorated Victorian Christmas cards. She was an avid crossword competition fan and her sitting room smelled strongly of the pungent powder, which she had to set smouldering at intervals due to her asthma. Dad had three older sisters – two were married to publicans, one in Maidstone the other near Bromley, the third had married a miner and was considered below par. She lived in Doncaster. Only Aunt Flo in Maidstone had children. Two girl cousins Joan and Eileen preceded me by some years and with a younger cousin Billy this left me in the position of first grandson in the family and thus somewhat spoiled.

Mum's parents, Granny and Granddad Burns, had three other daughters and a son Jack, who had joined the Navy as a torpedoman, but there were no cousins until 1932. Granny Burns was a thoroughly kind lady but by the time I was aware of them Granddad was largely blind. For most of his working life he had been a coachman to various wealthy families until the arrival of the motor car, and as a result of a riding accident was crippled and spent his time confined to a tiny hard armchair by the sitting room fire. However he still had a sense of fun and told stories of youthful pranks. When I visited, he liked to hide little sugar eggs in the Fuschia bushes along the side of the house. Somehow they managed to grow vegetables in the back garden and besides the Fuschias, grew Calceolarias. These very attractive flowers fascinated me, they are not very common today and I have never managed to grow them. Granny's speciality was a gelatinous haricot stew that she cooked slowly in a large black cast iron pot on the black-leaded range. Thinking of it still stirs my digestive juices.

At Christmas all the family went to Granny and Granddad's for dinner and tea. I cannot imagine how we all fitted into the tiny room but we did. When my sailor uncle was home he took liquid refreshment at the local pub before arriving late and breathing fumes. However he was a fascination to me, as he had brought back souvenirs from his time on the China station and these were a source of entertainment. Among these were opium pipes and scales, daggers, and a black lacquered cigarette box, on which a heron extracted a cigarette when a button was pressed. I was given a model Chinese junk, and later a pair of daggers. Xmas pudding always had silver threepenny pieces hidden inside. After dinner I was allowed into the front room with my presents. On occasions I received books on aeroplanes and these fed my developing interests. A Christmas treat was a visit to the "grotto" in Cheesemans, a big department store, followed by a look into Halfords window where there was always an operating Hornby railway layout. Uncle Jack D. worked in Halfords and I usually got a new Hornby catalogue. This was a source of interest throughout the year, but not in the hope of upgrading my existing clockwork set; that was obviously out of reach. In due course however my dreams did come true when a former employer gave Uncle Percy a Basset-Lowke train, track and station. This was the last word in model railways and would nowadays fetch a large sum from a collector. Just one small snag, our house had no electricity, and the engine quickly exhausted any batteries, so it remained a static exhibit.

Interest in Aviation started early with a rubber-powered Warneford stick model and this was followed by numerous small catapult gliders. However a source of much information was the *Daily Mail*. In the thirties it carried regular articles and pictures of new technical developments. Although I recall the launching of the *Queen Mary* it was the various flying records that caught my interest, Amy Johnson, the "Schneider Trophy", the Westland P.V.7 and Wallace flying over Mt. Everest, but most of all the England-Australia Air Race in 1934. This was won by the beautiful D.H. Comet followed by a Douglas D.C.2 and a Boeing 247D, a little prophetic of the post-war race to build a commercial passenger jet. Later, there was the high altitude record by the Bristol 138. The Bristol Type 142 "Britain First" was developed for Lord Rothermere owner of the *Daily Mail* and was developed into the Blenheim, which was much needed by the R.A.F. These were exciting times, but it was rare to see an aircraft. On one occasion Dad and I went to the Navy Day at Chatham, I clearly remember seeing a submarine v Q ship display in the Basin, but only vaguely recall seeing planes in the hangar of a carrier at Chatham Navy Day, probably H.M.S *Argus*. Sometimes I saw an Imperial Airways machine flying to the Continent and once I dashed from the outside "loo" to see a Pobjoy powered B.A. Swallow fly over. For most of my knowledge I relied upon the *Daily Mail* edition of the *Complete Book of Aviation*, it became my "bible" and I still use it as a reference. When I took the Scholarship Oral Interview in 1936 my interest must have been obvious as the headmaster asked some related questions e.g. how to spell Lympne.

Once I had won the Scholarship my life changed. First I went to visit my aunt and uncle at their pub, the Black Horse in Locksbottom near Bromley. As a birthday present I was given a Skybirds 1/72nd scale model kit of a Fairy Seal. It cost five shillings at W.H. Smiths and I still have the remains. We then went for a cream tea at Lyons. The service was very impressive, the "Nippies" looked smart and we were given glasses of iced water with the meal. Oh, for a similar service today! My cousin Billy joined me for the rest of the holiday during which we went to Croydon airport where I saw aircraft of that era, almost certainly these included the Handley Page HP42 and Junkers Ju52 but at this remove that detail may be due to surviving books and magazines rather than memory. On another day we visited the fascinating Crystal Palace. That evening, there was a fireworks display at which one of the set pieces was the war in Abyssinia. A ditty of that period went ~

> "Roll along Mussolini roll along
> You won't be in Abyssinia very long
> You'll be lying on the grass,
> With a bullet up your a—,
> Roll along Mussolini roll along."

The Crystal Palace burned down later that year, so we were very lucky to see that Victorian structure in all its glory.

My first year at Grammar School passed well enough; I had my lunch at the Fortune of War, the pub owned by Uncle Bill and Aunt Flo, and I met boys with a similar interest in aircraft, but I found difficulty in getting down to homework and was very easily distracted. My parents were unable to help when I had problems and slowly I lost ground in the top class. Outside interests then began to take over.

Annually on August Bank Holiday there was a fair on the Bearsted Green. (It stopped during the war and resumed afterwards long enough for my son to attend before it ceased altogether in the 1950s.) Although swings and roundabouts were supplied by professionals and were a good place to look for lost coins after the event, the village provided most of the stalls and hosted a cricket match at the same time. In addition to the coconut-shy, darts, hoop-la, there were other novelties. One of these was a race using little German Schuco model racing-cars; another was a Rodeo horse mostly made by my father at work. The prize ticket on its head could be won only by climbing over the tail and working across the freely rotating centre-body, without falling off. The small-bore Rifle Club always ran a stall, generally with air rifles but once with bows and arrows. After a visit to the stall in 1937 the team Captain, Arthur Maxted, approached Dad and offered to take me to the Club. Arthur knew Dad from his time at the Club but also knew my mother when she worked at Tilling – Stevens during the war. They had no objection to his offer but I wonder what modern society would have made of it

Arthur was a bachelor who lived with his bachelor brother and a housekeeper at Crismill. They came from a farming family at Barty Farm in Bearsted. Despite a good education he had opted to become a Turner working at Tilling-Stevens during the war, then at Shorts in Rochester. When I met him he was working at a small garage workshop at Bockingford, close to the Bockingford paper mill, which is still in production. He had not served in the Armed Forces but restarted the Rifle Club after the war. It was one of the first in the country. At the club next to the White Horse pub in Bearsted I learned to shoot well and won a spoon for my efforts, and was privileged to fire a pistol and a German repeating rifle at the club's outdoor range at Thurnham. I also learned about photography, using a camera given me by Arthur and much admired a Contax 3 camera owned by a Rifle Club member; its cost in 1939 would have been £63 or some 21 weeks' wages for my father. Arthur and I went for rides through Kent and Sussex on the pillion of his 350cc. Royal Enfield motorbike, especially to Rye and the Romney Marsh. There was not a lot of traffic on the roads and few people in the village owned a car. This was not surprising since a small car like the Morris 8 cost about £120, it sounds cheap today but was one third of the cost of our 3 bedroomed semi-detached house. As it happened three of my uncles did have a car but it was not something we even considered to be possible. Despite this on Sunday evenings in the summer there would a two mile queue of cars on the A20 trying to get through Maidstone. I also started making flying models beginning with a 30 inch Stinson Reliant Arthur gave me. No doubt all this had a bearing on my decision to be an Air Apprentice but it did nothing to help my schoolwork and I had more diversions than ever.

I had saved enough from pocket money and presents to buy a new Hercules bicycle complete with Sturmey-Archer 3 speed gears for the princely sum of £2.13s.6d so I was now able to cycle to school through Mote Park and also explore with my chums.

At school we were expected to join the O.T.C. and were duly kitted out with the pre-war khaki uniform including peaked cap and puttees. I enjoyed rifle drill, shooting practice and the field day we spent in Knole Park near Sevenoaks, but loathed the thick hot uniform and puttees. A route march round Maidstone, complete with rifle and kit, was a rifle too much for my miniature frame. The Army was clearly not for me, and in any case I wanted to fly.

In the three years before the war I remained fascinated by flying. Dad went to the Hendon Air Display and returned with the programme; at this stage various ageing biplanes did most of the flying but the prototypes of the new monoplanes including the Hurricane and Spitfire were there. I saw the first Sunderland at Rochester together with the Short Scion Senior fitted with a Sunderland shaped hull. The old Detling airfield was refurbished for No 500 "County of Kent" Squadron R.Aux.A.F.; originally using Hawker Hind biplanes but later re-equipped with Avro Ansons, which could be seen dispersed into fields on the south of the airfield when we cycled there past the mound of Thurnham Castle. The airfield was open to the public on Empire Air Day 1939 and the visiting aircraft included a Handley-Page Harrow and an immaculate Avro Tutor looking exactly like the example flown at R.A.F. Upavon in 1969. A tour of the workshops convinced me that I could find a home in the air services. By this time, like most of my chums, I was an avid collector of any literature connected with aviation, this included *Air Stories, Modern Boy* which included Biggles and Captain Justice and Professor Flaznagel, *Meccano Magazine, Popular Flying, Flight, Aeroplane, Aeromodeller, Flying, Model Airplane News from the U.S.* The bible for aero modellers was another U.S. book by Frank Zaic. On the outbreak of war Flight and Aeroplane produced a range of aircraft recognition booklets and *The Aeroplane Spotter*. This was a weekly newspaper costing three pence and with the help of my parents when I was away I was able to obtain a complete set from its first issue in 1941 until it ceased in 1948. All these diversions had an effect on schoolwork and I was moved from the A stream to the C stream, which eliminated Latin. Clearly I was not to be a Classical scholar...

In the run-down to the war interesting things were happening, we were issued with our gas masks, an Army unit visited the village with a searchlight and sound detector unit, and in the 1939 summer holiday my school encouraged us to do useful work. Some worked in the school vegetable garden but I, and several others, sorted piles of boots and other kit at Astley House the new R.A.F. Drill Hall in Hastings road nearby. The wages were welcome too!

The probability of war so disturbed our Latin master that he shot himself in the school rifle range. He was one of our O.T.C. officers and had served in the last war. Only those who had experienced it could have understood the shock of another war and after much reading I wonder how any participant could have avoided long-term after effects. Our school caretaker was also ex-Army and acted as Sergeant in the O.T.C. He also ran the tuck shop and lived in the gatehouse. To all of us he was just known as Sergeant.

My father had served in the East Surrey Regiment but was spared the horrors of the Western Front and went instead to India.

The Commander of H.M.S. *Marshal Soult* lived in Bearsted and he invited the boys' choir to a party on board at Chatham. I cannot recall any details of the elderly Monitor from that visit but I do remember once again the smell of "soft-soap". We had a great time. It was to be a long time before I again entered a Wardroom. Around this time my eldest cousin Joan married Otto Shaw. This gentleman had family links with Austria although I never fully understood his background. However he did receive a telegram from Adolf Hitler congratulating him on the marriage. Despite this he suffered no problems once the war started, so presumably the telegram was simply an attempt to involve him in the political issue.

In August 1939 I went on holiday to Eastbourne with Arthur Maxted during which we saw Blackburn Rocs flying out of Lympne but I had then no idea that it was destined to be the first F.A.A. Apprentice training camp, nor that I would join as an Air Apprentice. We also saw the giant concrete sound detectors on the coast. I understand that they are still there.

At around that time Dad started digging an air raid shelter in the back garden and Arthur helped. He had no need, as he had his own in the form of an old deep sawpit. I helped with the shelter and also in applying the adhesive coated netting to the house windows to protect against splinters. Dad also made up blackout shutters for the windows.

By way of light relief our elderly neighbours had acquired temporary lodgers; a lady with a daughter of my age who was an instant hit with all us local lads. I was infatuated and was quite emotional when I heard her singing the current hit — "Down in the meadow in the Iddy-iddy-poo swam, three little fishes and a mummy fish too." She was still there when I heard the Chamberlain broadcast on 3rd September and the sirens for the air raid that never happened. The elderly neighbours put on their gas masks and went down to their cellar!

Shortly after war broke out Arthur decided to take himself out of harm's way, and went to Penrith where found a job in a lead-mine. In due course he returned to war work back in Bockingford and became a member of the Home Guard. Dad was also a Home Guard, did duty at the local air-raid siren, which was mounted on the nearby Laundry, and was often called away for emergency repair work. There was not much rest in those days. Our shelter was never truly habitable and in the event when the night bombing started, we used to hide in the pantry under the stairs. There were plenty of bombs in Kent but those near us were rather random events. The nearest and largest was a doodlebug in 1944 but fortunately there was no serious structural damage.

When the London evacuation started, Bearsted received children from Plumstead and we had a girl of my sister's age. The Grammar school shared its premises and school time with Dulwich so we had a lot of spare time, in theory filled with homework, but in practice rather less usefully.

Once the "Battle of Britain" started I watched events through my father's Dollond and Aitchison telescope. Rifle shooting experience aided quick and accurate location of aircraft, and on one occasion I watched a 500 Squadron Anson from Detling returning fire at a Hurricane that was attacking it. Recent enquiries show that an Anson, side markings, MK-R crashed and burned on 12.7.40. after circling the airfield . There were no survivors and no record of a similar event or loss. I believe that I must have been the only witness of this friendly fire incident. I also watched Stukas attacking Detling where there were a lot of casualties. It was believed that the greenhouses of a large nursery in Bearsted provided a map reference for the attack and certainly the formation turned toward Detling at that point.

I visited the deeply buried remains of a ME 109 at Thurnham and returned with a "damping strut " as a souvenir; when I dismantled it later I found that every small component was stamped with the German eagle, including circlips. A Hurricane, which also crashed at Bearsted, provided a souvenir for my chum Keith and by chance carried the aircraft serial number, I have now discovered that P3201 belonged to 46 Squadron and was flown on 6.9.40 by Sub-Lt. J.C. Carpenter (R.N.) who was killed. This was an Mk 1 Hurricane as is further confirmed by the silver paint beneath the camouflage topcoat of a small section of fabric in my possession.

I watched the contrails on the day when the highest German losses were announced and then watched again when the bombing of London started. The massed formations of bombers seemed to fly unscathed through the shell-bursts over the Thames Estuary and later we could see the smoke from the fires.

With all that was happening, with little school and little interest when there, it seemed time to join up. Although it was my ambition to fly, this could not be achieved at my age and my first attempt was to join as a seaman boy at Chatham; thankfully the Recruiting C.P.O. persuaded me otherwise. The next logical option was to join the R.A.F. as an Apprentice and hope that in due course I could fly. In fact, my family, including an uncle with some knowledge of Naval Artificer Apprenticeships, talked me into taking that route with the objective of getting a good training and qualifications, flying had still to await an opportunity when I was old enough. First, though, I had to take the entrance examination.

Dad with Granny Adams (Drake) circa 1900.

Granddad

Drake.
Granny Burns aged 56.

Dad aged 21 - India
1918, East Surrey
Regiment.

A Bit of a "Tiff"

Granny Burns holding Aunt Margaret with Aunt Daisy on her left
and Mum on right with neighbours. Maidstone circa 1908-9.

Workers at the Tilling-Stevens munitions factory, Maidstone in
World War 1. Mum is in the rear row, fourth from right of picture.

Author and sister June - Bearsted 1931.

Home in Bearsted.

A Bit of a "Tiff"

The Holy Cross Church - Bearsted.

Thurnham Infant School in 2001. It is now a private home.

Bearsted Junior School in 2001. It is now the village library.

The shops, pub and garage in Bearsted in the 1930s.

A Bit of a "Tiff"

Bearsted village green.

Schoolboy – Maidstone Grammar

O.T.C. 1938

Form Group - Maidstone Grammar School 1938.

A Bit of a "Tiff"

Romney Marsh 1937.

Model Stinson Reliant 1937.

Bearsted and Thurnham Rifle Club 1937.

Beneath the Vickers Vimy Science Museum 1937.

A Bit of a "Tiff"

The one that started it all. "Grosvenor House" the D.H. Comet
winner of the 1934 England-Australia Air Race. Seen in the 1960's
at the Shuttleworth Collection.

Avro Tutor. First seen at Detling in 1939.
Photographed at Upavon in 1969.

Hawker Hind. First seen at Detling in 1939.
Photographed at Upavon in 1969.

The shape of things to come. Blackburn Rocs flying out of Lympne in August 1939.

A Bit of a "Tiff"

Vapour trails over Kent. Photographed on the day in 1940 that the highest German losses were announced.

My friend Keith in 1940 with items from Hurricane MK1 P3201.

Private Keith - Home Guard. He later joined the F.A.A. as an Air Mechanic.

Chapter 2 Joining – up

For those seeking a career in the Navy, joining-up entailed taking an examination, which was held twice yearly. As far as I am aware these exams included a common system for entrants to the civil service, dockyard apprenticeships, R.A.F. apprenticeships. The exam held in spring was I believe the more rigorous but which one was taken depended upon one's age. It is possible that the exams differed for each of the openings on offer, but in my case the exam held on October 15th, 1940 was common to all R.N. apprentices. It consisted of two 2 hour papers:- Maths/Practical Maths and Elementary Science and I took mine in an air raid shelter in the school playing field, together with three boys from Dulwich. Apart from falling down the steps on arrival I do not recall any particular event during our time in the shelter but during an earlier visit to school related to the exam I was fortunate to avoid four bombs dropped directly on my route – the last fell into the school playing field. At the time I was just leaving Mote Park quite unaware of any air raid when I heard a whistling noise, it took a few milliseconds to work out the cause, to identify the Dornier flying at about 10,000 ft and then throw my cycle down a bank and lay flat while the bombs exploded. I then continued on my way, passing the first house to be hit, in Hastings Road not far from Astley House. The side of the house had been blown away leaving the bathroom exposed on the first floor, a classic image of the bombing. I was probably the first on the scene from my refuge a couple of hundred yards away, and it shames me now to think that I did not stop to help, or even think of it as anything other than a commonplace event of the time. Later in October during an early morning raid bombs were dropped on Mill St. Maidstone. The small photographic shop that I always used was demolished and the owner Mr Bellefontaine was killed. This seemed ironic since most of his pre-war stock had been German e.g. Agfa.

The exam results were published in December 1940. I was accepted subject to a Medical at Alhambra House on 28th January. My father came with me to London, only my second visit, but certainly not a place he knew either. We passed bombed sites during the day but it was by then not unusual. Evidently I was fit enough, because I was required to join at Lee-on-Solent on 3rd March 1941. By the time I was called to join up, the family had acquired another temporary member in the form of a soldier billeted on us.

My journey via London was also a first and with the "dubious" help of railway staff my trip was a very roundabout one i.e. Aldershot – Alton – Fareham (3 miles from Lee) and on to Portsmouth in company with boys joining from Plymouth. Finally we took the Gosport ferry and then a lorry to Seafield Park at Hillhead. This outstation of Lee-on-Solent was formerly a boarding school, which had been requisitioned for Naval use. It remained in Naval occupation by the Fleet Air Arm until the 1970's, and at one stage was the home of the Safety Equipment School. It also hosted an annual conference of Air Ordnance Engineer Officers. At present most of the grounds are covered with housing and the future of the remainder itself is uncertain but the main building was burned down a few years ago. On the way to Seafield Park we passed the airfield at Lee where the only evidence of aviation was a lonely old Fairey Seafox on the slipway and I do not recall much flying taking place while we were based at Seafield Park but we were well occupied with the novelty of our new life and not paying too much attention. The airfield at Lee had been bombed and other local buildings had been requisitioned e.g. the dentist's was a house on the seafront and our pay office was a house on the undercliff at Hillhead.

For the majority of the 130 entrants this was to be their first experience of communal living and we spent our first night 4/5 to a room in beds with blankets but no sheets, finding out about each other and speculating on our future. At that stage we did not know whether we would be given the trade of our choice but were not bound to stay if unsatisfied with the choice offered. On the following day the 4th March 1941 this was resolved, a few did not get their preference but only one was brave enough to decline and returned home. I was lucky to get my preference and became a budding electrician. With this over, we were mustered to sign on for twelve years from the age of eighteen i.e. until we were thirty and a very long way into the future. My official number was FX82714, but later us F.A.A. men were identified with L for Lee-on-Solent making L/FX82714, a number which will forever be retained in my memory considering the number of occasions at which it had to be used.

It was clear from the "table of results" that well over 310 boys had applied for the 260 apprenticeships on offer and that the Navy had selected the top scoring entrants to be Engine Room, Electrical, and Ordnance Artificer Apprentices. Fleet Air Arm selection started with Engines (E), Electrical (L), Ordnance (O) and finally Airframes (A); An interesting observation of the priorities and state of technology at that period. Evidently over 50 had changed their minds or failed the Medical – one of these who joined at the next six monthly intake was a Dulwich boy, who had been in the air-raid shelter. Another Dulwich boy, Ken Bilney, became my chum and we still correspond.

Although a proportion was from Naval ports, the majority were from every county in the land, including Ireland, Scotland and Wales and had no connection with the sea. A very few however had entered from a training ship e.g. the *Mercury* or the Royal Hospital School at Holbrook. These were very worldly wise and together with capable sportsmen were soon recognised as potential leaders.

The first stage of the induction process was the issue of kit minus our blue serge suits, which had to be correctly sized. All kit was then marked in black or white paint with wooden stamps assembled from $^1/_2$ inch letters to form our names. The whole business was indescribably messy. The stamps formed part of our kit and mine is still stowed away somewhere although I do not remember ever using it again. Our only badge was of course the cap badge and this we had to sew on using the items in our "hussif" (housewife) i.e. needle and thread. I seem to recall receiving a basic safety razor, but at that time few of us shaved, and when this later became necessary, most of us upgraded to a "Valet" from "slops"; this included a strop thus reducing the need for new razor blades, which were in short supply. Eventually this was replaced by a much more up market Rolls Razor, also fitted with a strop and hone which was clacked away routinely to maintain a sharp edge. Until our suits were delivered a week or so later we wore Naval caps and a Navy blue seaman's jersey (even more itchy than my much hated flannel vests) on top of our school trousers (shades of "woolly pullies"). In this unlikely uniform a new found chum Ken Jury and I visited his Aunt in Farlington on the far side of Portsmouth one Saturday afternoon. We saluted all officers en-route, who must have been a little bemused, and saw a lot of bomb damage in Portsmouth. The return journey got us to the Lee Tower (now demolished) marginally before our leave expired at about 1700 (5 o'clock to landlubbers) and we still had about $1^1/_2$ miles to go. By dint of running and walking between alternate lampposts on the seafront we made the deadline. It was a lesson well learned and I was never adrift from leave for the rest of my career.

During the night raids on Portsmouth in March 1941 we were taken to air raid shelters and on the all-clear given "Pussers Kye" (a thick cocoa made from blocks of coarse chocolate) and "Ship's Biscuits". During one raid some newly issued kit was stolen from a room and a rating on the staff was caught because he had also taken "wooden stamp letters" from various individuals, and these together formed an anagram of his name.

The month at Seafield Park was a mixture of parades, squad drill, rifle drill, P.T., some rifle shooting, menial duties and a number of talks and lectures. One of these, by Rear-Admiral Bell-Davies V.C. (at that time Flag Officer Home Air Command at Lee-on-Solent) had as its punch line a tale of time spent in France early in the war. Logic says it was the First World War, but I cannot be certain. Every other issue is now lost but for some reason I do remember that the French landlady needed a headcount of the servicemen on her premises. Since, at that time all were bathing, it was suggested that she should "count the bollocks and divide by two".

The talk by the Padre was definitely much more inhibited, we understood that it was about "sex" but were no better informed at the end. It seemed that I was not alone in my ignorance. Parents had little to say on the subject in those days and in the end much more was gleaned from a little booklet produced I think by the Salvation Army and which was passed around the rooms.

Seafield Park was also the temporary home to some adult entrants and from these and the more worldly-wise of our lads, we soon learned the words of many rude and typically Naval ditties. Until I started to write this story, I was happy to think that I had barely remembered some of the titles e.g. "The keyhole in the door"; "Eskimo Nell", when out of the blue, two verses of "The good ship Venus" popped out of the memory bank. The rest is thankfully still missing but the reader's education would be incomplete if I did not include the following: -

"Twas on the good ship Venus
By god you should have seen us
The figurehead was a w—— in bed
And the mast a rampant p——

The Captain's daughter Mabel
Would f— when she was able
She gave the crew their weekly screw
Upon the chartroom table"

Quite soon the characters appeared in our ranks; the "Skivers" who managed to avoid unwanted duties (a very slight difference between them and those like me who took great care to position themselves in the best place in the three ranks to avoid being picked in the first place); the "Gannets" who were always hungry; the "Skates" who were always in the "Rattle" (trouble). Then there was the "Awkward Squad" who could only march by swinging their arms and feet forward on the same side. Most people find this impossible as it seems to go against a natural balance and it caused our G.I.'s (Gunnery Instructors) a lot of anguish in their attempts to correct the problem. My chum Joe Hannington had a different problem he walked with a "stoop" and his marching was a good imitation of the "Sand Dance". He continued to "shamble" throughout his Naval career.

Our G.I. was "Killer" Kent; he was a fair-minded man unlike most of his colleagues who we learned to loathe. He took us on draft to the Mechanical Training Establishment (M.T.E.) Rosyth on the 4th April 1941 and we were sorry to see him go.

Bomb damage at Hastings Road Maidstone - October 1940.
Copyright - The Kent Messenger Group

Mill Street Maidstone 31st October 1940.
Copyright - The Kent Messenger Group

Chapter 3 Rosyth

We travelled by train to Waterloo; we were fed at the Union Jack Club and eventually boarded the overnight train to Dunfermline, via Edinburgh. We got little sleep and by the following morning no water was left on the train for drinking or washing. Our arrival at the M.T.E. should have been a welcome relief, but as was usual in Bonnie Scotland the sky was grey, there was a cold damp "scotch mist" and the camp was surrounded by barbed wire, presumably to keep us in.

This was the home to large numbers of E.R.A. and E.A. Apprentices and Direct Entry Artificers, the most senior of whom had entered pre-war and started their training afloat on H.M.S. *Caledonia* moored in the Firth before it was accidentally damaged by fire. Their training took about four years so the most senior were clearly men and us new F.A.A. lads were very low on the pecking order. We were also a different species of low life and definitely not to be taken seriously.

On the *Caledonia*, there had been a well-established "fagging" system and this was now ready to operate at our expense. One took a risk in visiting the main block to drop and pick up laundry and if caught was liable to provide entertainment for the senior classes in their recreation room. We were divided into two Divisions for convenience – *Blake* for the L/O's and *Hood* for the A/E's - but were all housed in the same hutted area. In total our 130 lads outnumbered any other division. Numbers paid off when, eventually, a number of senior apprentices decided to raid our huts – they were severely manhandled and one got a good thrashing from D. Hutchins, who was a very experienced boxer. From that point life became easier. Later in 1941 an element of the first F.A.A. Apprentices (1st "Rodney" Division) arrived to complete their craft training, and their arrival further boosted our confidence. Within the divisions there was an unofficial code of conduct, since we all had to live together, and appropriate punishment was meted out to offenders. This happened in my hut quite soon when one of our division was caught stealing and on another occasion a lad was scrubbed with a coarse brush for lack of personal hygiene. Disputes between individuals occasionally ended in a fight and the official line was to arrange a grudge fight in the gym. I cannot, however, remember this happening during my training.

As young lads our food was of some interest, it was not "haute cuisine" but was generally edible, except for the Friday night "special", Pussers Shark. This was fish that smelled rotten and tasted worse. At mealtimes our food was collected from the Galley serving hatch by our duty server and delivered to the mess tables for distribution. Finally, in desperation, one

Friday, all our servers, in agreement, returned our "Pussers Shark" to the Galley and we went unfed that evening. The following morning the two F.A.A. Divisions were paraded and the "Articles of War" read out to impress upon us that we had committed an "act of mutiny". No other action was taken but from then on our Friday supper was always "egg and chips". The remainder of the camp continued to eat "Pussers Shark" and the message was clear – we had won!

At an Establishment as large as Rosyth, with so many young men and teenagers there was a need to control the youthful tendencies of the inmates and to attempt to instil a disciplined response to orders. These days it would be called "brainwashing". So, as a whole, but particularly the junior entries, we were subject to the whims of G.I.'s , P.T.I.'s (Physical Training Instructors), the Master at Arms (Jossman or Jaunty) and his henchmen the R.P.O.'s (Regulating Petty Officers or Crushers), down to the Chief and Petty Officer Apprentices (Hook Boys) and even 3 badge A.B.'s (long serving Able Seamen) who might find themselves temporarily in charge of a marching party. Often this meant that we would be sent "doubling" up and down the hill from the parade ground to the "factory" for some minor misdemeanour. This was not only irksome but the whole ethos of being an Artificer was to have a good education and to be able to think for oneself, or at least that was what we were constantly being told. In other words, we were a cut above the rest and did not expect to do things by numbers. As a matter of principle therefore we automatically despised the representatives of Naval discipline and attempted by all means possible to minimise their efforts – they of course responded!

With the benefit of hindsight it is possible to see us Apprentices as ordinary teenagers striving to be different from the system, just as today, and our tormentors as the upholders of law and order. However I remain convinced that society includes many who get their kicks from exercising power and that they gravitate to positions where this is possible. Sixty years later I, and my contemporaries, recall these people with distaste, because they evidently enjoyed the power they exercised. The hierarchical nature of the Armed services tends to encourage their ambitions because of the nature of the job, but it appears that a much less authoritarian approach is now used because of the emphasis on technology and that more controls are in place to prevent abuse. Great stuff, I just happened to be born too soon!

Our initial training was primarily Basic Fitting with Workshop Drawing and Workshop Practice. At school we had Maths, Science and Mechanics. This was common for all four trades, giving a common standard at the examinations, after nine months, before we went to Newcastle-under-Lyme for trade specialisation for the following two years. Some of the schoolwork was conducted in the evenings, which was not a good time following a hard day's work in the factory, on the sports field or in the gym and I recall nodding off at times. As was usual, at the time, we worked on Saturday morning and on Sunday we attended Divisions and Church parade.

Metalwork started off with the manufacture of a set of Inside and Outside Calipers, Odd-legs, and Dividers from sheet steel and using a riveted joint. These, plus a steel-rule and square were our measuring instruments for the fitting work that followed. We were also issued with a hammer (large), two chisels, a centre-punch, and a selection of files which we were not allowed to use until the work-piece had been chiselled to within 10 thousandth's of an inch of the finished dimension.

The first work-piece was a cast-iron block to be shaped to a 3 by 3 inch square and 1 inch thick, into this we then fitted a 1 inch square section of mild steel. Both items were shaped as accurately as possible and the steel block had to be capable of fitting the matching hole equally well in all directions. The next job was to shape a 3 inch hexagon from a cylindrical bar, aided by a 120 degree gauge made previously. The block was then sawn into equal halves and joined end-on-end by a male and female T-joint. The results were tested by "micrometer" on all dimensions and by "feeler" gauge at the jointing surfaces; ideally the fit would be so accurate that even the thinnest .0015 inch feeler would not enter the gap. Generally the workmanship was quite good and our instructors did a good job, but one or two could only achieve a "ruler fit" or "drop fit" i.e. a ruler or just daylight replaced the feelers. The high quality of our training ensured that the majority of us achieved a feel for precision and materials, which has endured for our lifetime. It is not now usual for similar craft apprenticeships to be available in our society and those of us of the "old school" deplore this trend. It is not necessary for the skilled man to spend his life bashing lumps of metal but that he can do so if required is the important thing. I understand that there is debate on this in respect of current F.A.A training but I am glad to know that, for the present, craft skills are still included in the syllabus.

Further motivation was provided by the displays of Test Job Work-pieces in cabinets in the workshop and by a facility to purchase tools from the workshop store in order to improve ones toolkit. All this was commonplace in industry at that time. Much hero worship attended the more popular members of senior classes when they were tackling their passing-out Test Job.

Efforts to provide extra tools by private purchase were not especially easy as our pay was very limited. Actual cash in hand started at four shillings a fortnight and rose slowly to about fifteen shillings by the end of our apprenticeship, but we received K.U.A. (Kit up-keep Allowance) and this was retained for our purchases of kit from Naval stores and we later received any remaining balance. By comparison the pay of a new entry Artificer Apprentice in 2001 equates to a 1941 wage of about £4 a fortnight. Quite an improvement, and it is also worth noting that my father only received £3 a week during the 1930's.

Over a period I did buy extra tools and these often were a great help but they were only retained with difficulty after I had passed-out from training, because there were no rules to cover this in the F.A.A. and any that were found during periodic toolkit inspection were confiscated; still it was not difficult to hide them away. In the course of time, concern that tools left in aircraft were a serious risk to safety led to the current tool control system in the 1960's, and personal toolkits were withdrawn. In their place specially designed toolkits were provided for each application; this was again not quite perfect because periodically a small item would go missing and an all out search was then necessary before the aircraft could be declared "serviceable". It was impossible to deny the logic of this scheme but it was another nail in the coffin of the professional craftsman.

Apart from craft and schoolwork, we had time for sports, P.T. and swimming. The gymnasium and swimming baths were first class and were available outside official sessions. The ability to swim was an obvious "survival" requirement; those who had yet to learn were given instruction and all were required to pass the swimming test during which we had to stay afloat and swim for several minutes while wearing a heavy white drill duck suit.

Gym was bearable except for "box work" where the un-acrobatic and un-co-ordinated like myself struggled and continually failed. It was no great surprise when, once again attempting the impossible "through vault with after support," I rammed the box with one foot and was rendered "hors de combat". A visit to the Sick Bay followed and limping my way back to work I was grabbed by our Divisional C.P.O. shortly before 0900. "Right I want you to raise the Ensign for colours. I'll give the signal from the office window when the flagship Nelson starts their hoist." "Yes Chief." Duly, he opened the window to check me out, but my instant response beat Nelson by a good margin. As usual the Navy was not amused.

Generally speaking the "sailor" has a well- developed sense of humour, while "officialdom" does not, and this conflict is a source of pride. "Shouldn't have joined chum if you can't take a joke!"

Boxing was an established activity and extra tuition was available in the evenings. My chum, Paddy Doherty, and I used to practise together, although it was he who had the skills. For the "wimps" it should be

A Bit of a "Tiff"

understood that this was more of a character building exercise than an attempt to encourage aggression. The ultimate objective was to run an annual Boxing Competition and in order to select the most able competitors, a system called 100% boxing was enforced. In this system the members of each division were marched into the gym in line, a second line formed from a division of roughly the same age was marched in at the same time. As one arrived at the front of the queue we were paired off roughly by size, and thrust into the ring to fight for just three minutes. The loser was eliminated and the winner went on to the next round. In practice this system worked quite well at Rosyth since the inherent antagonism between divisions ensured that all were prepared to have a go.

Of course except for those at the very top there was a near certainty of being thrashed sooner or later, but by the time the elimination bouts had taken place there was great enthusiasm for the Competition, which we all attended. This was especially true for the heavyweight contestants, taken of course from the senior divisions.

A similar system was tried later at Newcastle but because of small numbers and the age differences between divisions the elimination contents were held between members of the same division. This was an unpopular idea, since very often one's opponent was a chum. As a result there were examples of "muffed" bouts and the contestants had to be threatened to "get on with it". Generally, of course the first blow was sufficient to produce a like response. Q.E.D!

On the whole we were well fed and fit, but inevitably communal living and workshop grime took its toll. The hammer and chisel work produced cuts and blisters, and the grime, particularly from the carbon in cast-iron, was difficult to remove with the "Pussers Hard" (coarse soap). The crowded washrooms had only wet towels to dry with. This led to whitlows (abscesses) and impetigo; the victims of this problem were clearly identified by the liberal application of Gentian Violet over the infected area. I succumbed to a whitlow and an ear infection and ended up being stretchered from Rosyth by boat to the Naval Hospital at Port Edgar. By chance, the Medical Officer who treated me, Cdr. Willy McGregor, was the E.N.T. Consultant for whom my wife worked at the Kent County Ophthalmic Hospital in 1947. He was very popular. Among the inmates of my ward was an air mechanic from a nearby Air Station with burns from an accident on an aircraft. Even in hospital there was a strict regime and I quickly learned the very precise method of making a hospital bed to satisfy the meticulous inspection by Matron prior to the daily rounds, together with the official way of sitting or lying to attention in bed; as soon as one was allowed out of bed we were detailed for various ward cleaning and polishing duties. Since part of the current debate about standards in N.H.S. hospitals is about the need for the old-fashioned Matron with wide-ranging authority, I can say from experience that I heartily agree.

By the time we arrived at Rosyth we had been issued with all but two elements of our uniform and the remnants of our school uniform had been parcelled up and sent home. At Rosyth we were issued with striped blue working shirts with detached collars, and blue overalls. From that point on all our requirements for new or replacement uniform had to be purchased from the "Slops Room" (Clothing Store) using our K.U.A. We were not entitled to Civilian Clothing Coupons nor of course allowed to wear civilian clothes. The "Slops Room" was a very useful asset during the war since it held any number of goods that were virtually unobtainable to civilians. Items such as white linen handkerchiefs, scissors, towels, and cut-throat razors were within my budget and made admirable presents for my family.

Throughout the year we wore our thick single-breasted blue serge suits, blue shirt, collar and black tie, with overalls on top in the workshop. For parades or on leave it was white shirts with starched round detached collars. After a few trips to the laundry the collars would have sawed through armour-plate. If there is one benefit about retirement in the 21st century it must be the freedom to wear comfortable shirts without stiff collars after a working life spent in suits. No matter what the weather, raincoats or overcoats were only worn when "piped" (broadcast on the Tannoy) or if listed in Daily Orders as "Rig of the Day".

One of the proud symbols of the Artificer was a working cap from which the stiffening "grommet" had been removed and the remaining stiffening softened in hot water so that the top and back of the cap could be moulded to the shape of the head. With time, and the daily handling with greasy hands, the cap became utterly unlike the regulations required. This may well have been acceptable in the engine-room but not while training. Many attempts were made to emulate this macho and highly desirable headgear, all failed, the culprits punished and obliged to buy a new cap.

Recreational facilities were provided within the camp and there was a cinema and canteen. At the canteen we could buy Nutty (sweets and chocolate) with coupons and also a range of other goods, which included tinned fruit and "herrings-in" (herrings in tomato sauce). These were also unobtainable ashore and made acceptable presents for home. However, to post such a parcel home it first had pass inspection before it could be secured and stamped and that was very tedious. It is impossible, now, to

A Bit of a "Tiff"

determine whether the procedure was due to wartime security, to prevent smuggling, or simply because the Navy always assumed you were guilty of something unless proved innocent. It was of course of no avail, because although we were not yet entitled to either Rum or Tickler (duty free tobacco) nonetheless tobacco did occasionally appear. My chum, now a retired clergyman, had a tin and parcelled it up for his father. I helped by throwing it to him over the back fence and he posted it in Dunfermline. Recently, he claimed to have no knowledge of the incident!

Because the junior classes were limited to shore leave on Saturday and Sunday afternoons, most of our trips were to "Dumps" (Dunfermline) and that was not then and still is not a hive of activity or cultural pleasure. However it was reckoned that the Glen was a trysting place for female company. I cannot confirm this rumour.

By way of a change I took a trip into Edinburgh by train one Saturday with a pal. We did the usual tourist trip and saw the ancient sights, but on that dank Scottish afternoon it was our arrival at the grey stone walls lining the track to the station that gave me a lifetime aversion to dour Scottish cities. Pity because the Scots are so nice, and because these grey stone cities were the only form of civilisation en-route to, or close to the various Air Stations in Scotland where eventually, I was to find myself. We were also able to use the canteen/billiard room in the Dockyard.

In 1941 Rosyth Dockyard, Inverkeithing on the southern shore of the Firth of Forth and the Firth itself was a hive of wartime activity with ships coming and going. H.M.S. *Nelson* was in dock undergoing repairs for mine-damage and often Destroyers would leave on patrol towards Norway, sometimes taking with them one of our S.B.A.'s (Sick berth attendants). In a cove beyond the Forth Bridge, two Decoy Battleships and a Decoy Aircraft Carrier rested in what I believe was a ship breaker's yard. The Dockyard itself was a wonderland of ship fittings, which included two spare gun barrels labelled *Iron Duke*. These 13.5 inch barrels had no obvious use since the *Iron Duke* was demilitarised in 1931 and used as a training ship.

We used the big basins in the Dockyard for occasional rowing in the large wooden cutters. Mercifully this experience was never needed in earnest, since the large wooden oars were more than a match for my 5 ft $2^1/2$ inch frame and I spent my time having "caught the crab" and trying to wrestle the beastly thing back out of the water.

We were really fairly insulated from the war during our training; mostly news was obtained via an occasional newspaper and the Gaumont British News, which preceded any film show. What was going on, even when as often at first we were losing on all fronts, did not appear to have a bearing on our future and I do not remember having any doubt that in the end we would win. The sinking of the *Bismark* was a high point during 1941 despite the loss of the *Hood*; Arthur sent me a postal order in reflected glory of the F.A.A. role in the sinking. The only visible form of protection at Rosyth was a single multi-barrelled Pom-Pom by the sports field but of course the ship's guns would have been manned as needed. However, during my stay there were no raids on Rosyth. There were air raid warnings when there were raids on Glasgow and, during these raids the Apprentices had various duties; senior divisions were fully armed as defence platoons but the junior divisions acted as A.R.P. units. We were shown how to put out fires and deal with incendiary bombs and this little exercise caused upset when one of our bright boys extinguished the burning dummy bomb using a bucket of water. This was not the approved method but got rid of the problem. During a raid my post was in the workshops where I sat or stood around waiting for the all clear. It was hard to see what good I could have done amongst the mass of steel benches and non-inflammable machinery. Fortunately like so many other duties given in the Navy this one was never put to the test. Among the miscellaneous duties were cleaning, sweeping, polishing, and sometimes this included the P.O's Mess, which offered a minor perk in the form of left-overs from their supper; all gratefully received.

We would normally have received three 14 day leaves a year but of course had missed Easter 1941 and had just summer and Xmas from Rosyth. Our mass departure was mostly south and special compartments were reserved for us; on one leave our train was stopped during the night, when the communication cord was pulled. Nobody was caught but suspicion fell firmly on one Peppiatt, a very lively individual who had started his activities as early as Seafield Park.

We took school exams and completed our Fitting test-job by Xmas 1941 and, following our return to Rosyth after leave, both *Blake* and *Hood* divisions travelled on 14th January 1942 to Newcastle-under-Lyme for the remainder of our training.

The author - 1941

A good soak in boiling water and it'll look a real Tiffie's cap

The Forth Bridge and Rosyth Dockyard from M.T.E. 1941.

M.T.E. Rosyth 1941 - factory foreground, gym and swimming pool beyond.

M.T.E. Rosyth 1941 - admin block, the hill, pillboxes and factory.

A Bit of a "Tiff"

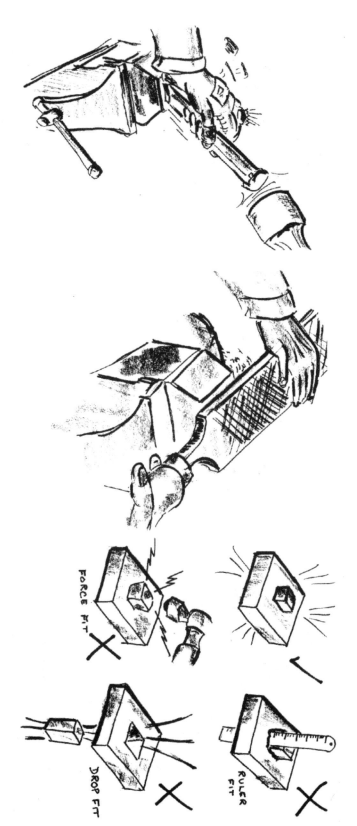

Going at it hammer and chisel

A 14 in bastard (file)

A fitting end!

A Bit of a

I've caught the crab, Chief!

You're the same size – in the ring go!

A Bit of a "Tiff"

Chapter 4 H.M.S. *Daedalus II*
R.N.A.T.E. Newcastle-under-Lyme

When we arrived at Clayton Hall, where the accommodation and administration was based, all 130 apprentices were reformed as Rodney Division and once again, although the junior division, we were far larger than each of the existing divisions. The reason lay in the lack of facilities available for training when the F.A.A. was made independent of the R.A.F. in 1938. Prior to this the Navy did not have responsibility for the maintenance of the aircraft operating from its ships and had no airfields of its own. The first four airfields transferred from the R.A.F. were Lee-on-Solent, Worthy Down, Ford, and Donibristle, but by 1939 Lympne had been added to the list and as already mentioned was operating Blackburn Rocs. The need to move rapidly was made the more urgent by the imminence of war but the Navy had no experienced air engineers to maintain the aircraft let alone train a new generation of apprentices. In these circumstances all options were open. The reasonable similarity between the very basic aircraft electrical and armament systems and ship's equipment enabled the Navy to train the "L" and "O" Apprentices using existing facilities and trade instructors, although they had first to read up on unfamiliar equipment. However the "E" and "A" trades had no equivalent and so initially their training was conducted by the R.A.F. at Halton. The book by Wing Commander Joe Northrop entitled *Joe – The Autobiography of a Trenchard Brat* makes interesting reading concerning the training given to R.A.F. Apprentices in the thirties and reluctantly I believe that those Naval Apprentices trained at Halton by the R.A.F. probably were better equipped technically than most of the wartime trainees passed through the ad-hoc Naval system.

The chosen training base for Naval Air Apprentices was Lympne on the Kent coast and the first three entries of "L" and "O" were already installed when the fall of France made the location unsuitable and the whole facility was moved rapidly to Newcastle. This has been well covered by Graham Bebbington, in *Ship without Water*. By January 1942, the training of "L" and "O" Apprentices had been going on for some eighteen months in requisitioned buildings scattered around Newcastle (see Fig 1) but as 2nd Rodney our numbers included "A" and "E". In fact the arrangements for these trades were still limited and their training was carried in a requisitioned garage at Higherland, I understand that at different stages this held an Albacore, a Swordfish and, an Osprey and Shark from Lympne. Things did not improve until a new hangar was built in Clayton Village in 1943. This had "firing butts" in addition to real live aircraft, which included an Aeronca Jap civilian light aircraft and a Vought-Sikorsky Kingfisher (landplane). Despite this, as an Electrician, I never actually worked on any aircraft during my training and it was left until we had passed out and joined an Air Station for our six-month follow-on experience. In many respects this seemed to suggest that we would spend our time in workshops on the more complex equipment, but of course that was never a sensible prospect and, as aircraft systems have become more and more sophisticated, the need for Artificer skills to diagnose and repair them at the "coal-face" has continued.

Fig 2 gives an outline of the apprentice entries that served at Newcastle. Each division was named after a famous Admiral as at Rosyth but the apprentices who went to the R.A.F. at Halton were identified only by an entry number, thus following the R.A.F. practice. The whole establishment was closed in December 1945 and moved to H.M.S. *Condor* at Arbroath. Further moves have since taken place and at present the Air Engineering training is at H.M.S. *Sultan*, which is the Naval Mechanical Engineering Training Establishment at Gosport. It has to be said that there is a wonderful range of facilities, including aircraft, by comparison with those at Newcastle, but very few trainees.

At different stages the trade structure has changed from the 1939–1945 version. The Radio Electrical Artificer branch was formed, and the Airframe and Engine trades amalgamated. A similar early attempt to merge the Air Electrical and Air Ordnance Artificer trades was short lived, but the Navy has continually adapted to change in both aircraft and weapon complexity, due to integrated electronic control of virtually every system. This has now eliminated the Ordnance branch as a separate entity. This role is now subsumed into the three surviving branches, namely Air Engineering Artificers Mechanical (M), Avionics (L) and Radio (R).

However in 1942 as an early introduction to aircraft the "L's" went to the Airframe school at Higherland for instruction in the "Theory of Flight". This was just a brief introduction and covered the ground I had immersed myself in since 1936 so I found myself dozing through a very soporific training film in which white blobs floated gently over various "aerofoil" shapes.

In the Electrical Technical School yard a skeletal Walrus sat forlornly and minus virtually everything resembling its already minimal electrical installation. It was also minus any accessible bits of Perspex. These had long gone to make brooches for girlfriends. The Walrus was never part of our training.

At Westlands school an ancient Hurricane and a Martlet were sited on the playing field minus engines. Although they still retained some equipment, such as the "Blind Flying Panel" and wiring, their role was only to be viewed and then used for "aircraft handling" practice. This took all of one morning. Gratifyingly, we were well entertained as the undercarriage selector of the Hurricane had inadvertently (or otherwise!) been selected to "UP" and the aircraft began to collapse on to the grass. Order was restored with difficulty after yells of "Two Six" heave, and the struts were finally secured. This was probably the first time that we had heard this age old Naval Command used for real, but it was not the last, as it became an everyday expression whenever co-ordinated manual effort was needed. It is said that it derives from the time when gunnery drill was performed by numbers (i.e. when each member of the team had a numbered role to play) and in typical sailor talk a gunnery instructor dealing with the misfire drill shouted – "If the gun misfires, don't say f— the gun. Numbers two and six will — etc."

In fact the only direct contact that I had with a real aircraft occurred in August 1942 when I was on leave. With a group of A.T.C. Cadets from my old school I visited R.A.F. West Malling. The visit had been arranged to provide them with flight experience in a F.A.A. Fulmar, which had flown in specifically for that purpose. Regretfully the Fulmar went u/s (unserviceable) immediately as a fair prediction of my future. At that point in my training my knowledge of the Fulmar was limited to batteries, lighting, and the deck-hook warning light, so my presence was of no value. West Malling was operating the Douglas Havoc Turbinlight night fighter and used a black painted Airspeed Oxford for continuity training. This aircraft bearing a cartoon like figure labelled "Clutterbuck" gave me my first and only flight during the war. We all clambered aboard wearing parachutes, but they were of course just a formality since we were given no instruction in using them and a safe exit from the cabin at just a couple of thousand feet would have been impossible. I had the luck to fly in the co-pilot's seat.

Clayton Hall was a world apart from Rosyth; although the formal trappings of Naval authority were there, nonetheless the scattered location of the training sites made life less rigid and there was little aggravation between the divisions. When Apprentices first arrived at Newcastle there was no accommodation at Clayton Hall and they were accommodated initially in public buildings in Newcastle until a number of wooden huts were erected. We lived in these until 1943 when the "P" huts were complete. A ballad written by an unknown apprentice had frequent reference to the "Little wooden huts at Clayton Hall" and the chorus was as follows:-

"I'll be there, I'll be there,
When the bugle sounds defaulters I'll be there,
When the bugle sounds defaulters
I'll be sh——— the Admiral's daughters,
When the bugle sounds defaulters I'll be there"

These huts were small and companionable and heated by the inevitable ancient Tortoise stoves, which must have made a fortune for the maker since they provided heating for every new service camp erected during the war. At one end was a toilet but the main ablution block was separate. The huts also had a small room for the resident "Hook boy", in our case a chap from Grenville division. Elderly civilians called "Gobbies" cleaned the huts while we were out at work and ours died of a heart attack one day in our absence.

Our Hook boys were not over dedicated to Naval discipline, at least while living in the wooden huts. We had all learned to sew on badges and repair our uniforms with varying degrees of success and I remember our Hook boy, Dibble, sitting in the hut to repair a suit using the lower half of a pair of old trousers. Unfortunately he discovered too late that he had cut off the leg of his best suit.

Some of our colleagues were able, unwittingly, to entertain us. Pud Coxon came from Middlesborough, and was very proud of Dorman Long (the steel construction firm) and the Yorkshire cricket team. He was easily wound up by a casual remark intentionally critical of his favourites, or, as a change, a suggestion that there were no such thing as "pit-ponies". The resulting outburst was truly explosive and it always seemed to work. Such entertainment was free and, although there was little privacy in the open messes, there was a great deal of good humour and comradeship, which must now be missing in the separate rooms or cabins provided in the modern services. Such is the price of progress!

The "P" huts, when we finally occupied them, were large, cold and impersonal. Essentially, they were surface air-raid shelters and had very small windows. A lot of ingenuity was needed to stay warm in bed on winter nights when the fires were drawn and we resorted to adding our overcoats, raincoats, newspapers and sleeping inside our mattress covers. It never worked and the result was usually leg cramp.

Although I can think of no occasion during squad drill or parades when we were each required as individuals to practise or demonstrate our ability to take charge, nonetheless, unnoticed by the common herd, some selection process was taking place. In due course one of two lads picked out was selected for direct transfer to Engineer Cadet; "Slim" Julian was last heard of as a Commander. The other candidate Percy Morris however did later become a pilot and worked in Naval Intelligence after retiring as Lt.-Cdr. A similar process determined who would become "Hook boys" from the two senior divisions but this was certainly not due to technical merit but some mixture of, size, "presence", and ability at sport. After leaving Newcastle most Hook boys in our division were earmarked for jobs where they were given an opportunity to go for Aircrew selection. A few certainly made the grade. Oddly the system was not seeking candidates for Engineer Officers, although, later, very many ex-apprentices were promoted as officers on the "Branch" or "Special Duties" List and a very few actually made it to the "General" List as Engineers. This required a considerable amount of private study under conditions where there were often no facilities for professional or educational guidance.

By one means or another those ex-apprentices who continued to serve beyond their thirtieth birthday became the backbone of the F.A.A. Air Engineering system as senior artificers or as officers, so perhaps the selection of apprentices and the Newcastle training was effective.

In 1942 there were still no specialised Air Engineer Officers at Newcastle, but by then a few instructors were F.A.A. Petty Officer Air Fitters and we still had one or two R.A.F. N.C.O.'s. The officer in charge of the Armoury was a Royal Marine Major. To us, virtually all the instructors were "old", as, now at seventy-seven, all policemen seem to me to be just boys; but I believe that the long-serving sailor had had a hard life and the prospect of being forced to retire at forty had prematurely aged them. The photograph taken when we passed-out in late 1943 shows our two divisional C.P.O.'s who look elderly to me even now. The transfer to being a pensioner at forty was clearly traumatic to men after twenty-two years of institutionalised life and I saw further proof of this during the 60's when a number of "L" Branch Officers retired at fifty. They were well known and admired as dedicated and "pusser" men; at intervals we would hear that "dear old X" had died of a heart attack on his way to work at his first civilian job. I determined, then, that my own retirement would be treated as a challenge and something to be worked at well in advance.

Although there were serious shortcomings in our training due to the absence of instructors with aircraft experience, in fact the machines were pretty basic and it was only later that equipment became more complex, so that it was simply a matter of reading the manuals (Air Publications), following the rules and working things out from the basic skills acquired in a different environment. During the war most people were faced with a similar problem.

At Newcastle the four trades separated for the first time and not only for technical training. At Westland's school, subjects appropriate to the specific trade replaced the common educational material and the Electrical trade naturally got Electricity, Magnetism, Radio and Valve theory, for which our "bible" was the Admiralty *Handbook of Wireless Telegraphy* in two parts which we were able to purchase, Part I cost 4s. and Part 2 cost 6s.. The theory behind new equipment was also covered, so we got the Velocity

Triangle (for the new Torpedo "F" sight), and Gyroscope principles (for the new Gyro Gun sight). Schoolwork ceased in mid-1943 following a final exam, thereafter all efforts were concentrated on craft skills and technical training.

While the E's, L's and O's were taught metal machining skills the Airframe group spent their time learning the intricacies of fabric repairs and sheet metal work and this latter was a skill that I desired; in the event it was not until I retired and took up silver smithing that I satisfied my ambition.

In the workshops we were introduced to the lathe for the first time. Only a few names stand out from our instructors after sixty years and the first is "Gunga" Puttock, a rather stern man who taught us the rudiments of turning. This was achieved by deliberately offsetting the lathe "tailstock" and then requiring us by measurement, adjustment and, trial and error to reset the tailstock so that the lathe was capable of "turning" between centres a parallel steel bar. In our case the desired result was a nominal 1 inch diameter bar about 12 inches long; in some cases the end result was down to $1/4$ inch before the work was stopped as Gunga took pity on the trainee. For those who succeeded it was a lesson well learned and taught. This was followed by a visit to "Black Mac" in the forge to learn how to make our lathe tools. The nickname was entirely apt.

Progressively other "turning" skills were developed; the most difficult were "parting off" and "square threads". In "parting off", a cut is made straight through the work-piece using a narrow square ended tool; a similar but shorter tool is used to form a screw thread of square section. In both cases the problem lies in the friction at the cutting edge and a slightly blunt tool, badly set up, would often break. The days when this black art was being practised were punctuated by a sharp "crack", a crunching noise, a curse from the unfortunate apprentice and another visit to "Black Mac". Naturally all of the different aspects of fitting and turning were incorporated into our "Passing-out Test Job"; in our case this was a variation of the Swordfish Torpedo Winch and the drawing for this job was done at H.M.S. *Vernon* as the Establishment controlling the Torpedo Branch which was then the branch responsible for Naval Electrical maintenance work.

Part of the problem we faced was that our machines were a mixture of varying quality and age. The newest and therefore the most popular were small American "Atlas" lathes; the majority were the similar but well used British "Challenger". Truly the worst were the "Seabeds", these were large lathes of unspecified make that had, supposedly, been salvaged from a sunken vessel; these ground and rattled away horrifically, and were presided over by a large fairly portly instructor, who sorted out most problems

A Bit of a "Tiff"

using a large hammer. In principle the quality of the machines should have made no difference to skilled craftsmen but we were not yet quite at that level, and so the allocation for our "Passing-out Test Job" was made by lottery. I was lucky and got a good one.

Two other items deserve a mention. The first a very large lathe used exclusively by an instructor; this was used to machine a very long and large diameter Archimedes screw to replace a worn coal feed screw in the boiler house at Westland's school. It was a very impressive piece of workmanship.

The other item was the small group of precision lathes driven by a system of overhead pulleys and belts. One Tommy Yule, who clearly demonstrated the application of skill and initiative, managed these machines. Tommy was a master "Rabbitteer" (producer of private work) and those of us who completed our work-pieces early were likely to find themselves under Tommy's care. This might involve cleaning and polishing model "Spitfires" cast in aluminium, making parts of brass cigarette lighters or Meccano pulley wheels (also in Naval brass), especially, near to Xmas. When apprentice assistance was not available, Tommy would set up work on all the machines and run them on a slow feed, periodically visiting each one in turn, gobbing (spitting) on the work for lubrication and adjusting the feed. We heard that Tommy was brought to book after we had left Newcastle but he was much admired and often emulated later when an opportunity arose.

The Electrical School was a ramshackle old building with rickety wooden floors and doors. Each room was equipped with demonstration equipment and we moved from room to room as the training progressed. At each stage, starting with the simplest circuits and finally ending with the most recent and complex electrical and instrument systems, we were given copious dictated notes and were required to copy diagrams and circuits. I found it imperative to devise much simpler diagrams outside the classroom, since we were eventually required to reproduce or explain these systems in our exams, because the circuits so colourfully produced on blackboards or roll-up drawings were laid out to represent the aircraft layout and therefore had numerous junctions and cross-overs which could be highly confusing to the novice. With a little effort these could be reduced to a circuit so simple that it could be understood and remembered with ease.

One of the more complex items taught was the Link Trainer and this occupied a full fourteen days' instruction, followed by an exam. The Link Trainer had been devised in the U.S. by an organ maker; it was in very wide use in the U.S. and the Commonwealth countries for training pilots in Instrument Flying and Navigation, and was the predecessor of the most complex Electronic Flight Simulators now used by airlines and air forces throughout the world. Even in 1942 it contained a range of novel electronic instruments, but its physical movements were its tour-de-force and derived directly from its inventors expertise with organs. A series of bellows powered by a large electrically operated vacuum pump were activated by sliding wooden valves and variously moved the aircraft structure in pitch or roll, or in yaw when a number of double-acting small bellows worked a crankshaft to rotate the aircraft around its base. To see this turning motor in operation was a real sight. Servicing the mechanical system largely consisted of polishing the sliding valves with graphite powder and patching leaks in the bellows.

In training, the pupils' results were reproduced for the instructor by a moving ink roller on a chart table and the instructor could introduce faults into the flying controls, as is still the case in modern simulators. The most notorious of these was the stall valve, which, when activated, closed yet another small bellows and this made the aircraft rotate on its axis until the correct recovery procedure was followed.

The Link Trainer was of such importance to our exam results that many of us purchased a book, privately, on the subject from the then popular George Newnes *Aeroplane Maintenance and Operation* series at a cost of 7s 6d. As a clear indication of the interest in aviation during the war there were no less than twenty-three books in this series.

The final subjects covered prior to our passing-out exam were the Distant-reading Compass, the Torpedo "F" Sight and the Gyro Gun Sight. All were still classified at some level of secrecy and we were only allowed to make limited notes. Any circuits or sketches that we made were eventually collected and destroyed. The D.R. Compass and Torpedo Sight were ingenious electro-mechanical systems but it was the Gyro Gun Sight that probably had the most long-term benefit to the air war and produced a marked improvement in air-to-air gunnery when it was introduced to both U.S. and British fighters in 1944. By this time our "skates" had found other ways of avoiding boredom in the classroom and used to "skive" off to the local cinema in the afternoon, returning in time to march back to Clayton.

Three names remain in my memory of the Electrical School. The first is "Quasi-Modo"! He was well named for his appearance and was a P.O. Torpedoman with some sort of regulating role at the school. Unpleasant and highly unpopular he tried to proposition a young apprentice. This was a potentially serious offence under the Naval Discipline Act but this was bypassed by the Hook boys and he was warned off. Quasi-Modo was dumped in the Static Water Tank when Grenville division passed-out.

"Jettison Joe" presided over the bombing equipment room. An amiable old boy he was a source of amusement, particularly if he succumbed to requests to tell his tales of life on the China Station. This was a regular tactic to reduce boredom. Periodically Joe would leave the room and during his absence fitting and releasing dummy 25 lb Practise Bombs on the Light series bomb-carriers provided our entertainment. The jettison of four bombs produced a satisfying thump on the wooden floor and Joe would hear this and return to give us a piece of his mind.

The third name is "Li'l Abner". Sid Abnett was an Electrical Artificer recalled to service and his duties seemed to spell out a very comfortable future for us all. Sid's daily round was to repair clocks and watches for all and sundry, but this was occasionally interrupted for a few days by an apprentice class. Sid presided over a collection of watch-making lathes and was required to impart a very minute part of his skills to us. Using only a broken piece of "carborundum" stone and wearing a watchmaker's eyeglass, our task was to shape a flat drill, at the end of a worn out and broken dentists "burr". The drill was to be capable of drilling a 10/1000th inch diameter hole in a piece of sheet-brass, as might be required for a bearing in a watch. Duly I succeeded and although this delicate skill was never required throughout my service career, it nevertheless came home to roost later on. On active service during 1945 I bought a smart "Pierce" Swiss watch in Capetown and after some months in the tropics it failed. The "accredited" Indian watchmaker on the air-station at Trincomalee repaired it, but broke the pivot on the sweep second hand, and this could not be replaced. After my return to U.K. the watch again failed and I found that my grandmother had been a neighbour of Sid Abnett, so I looked him up and he fixed the watch. For some months I went out with his daughter. However the sweep second hand was still inoperative, but by then I was serving at an air-station equipped with watchmaker's lathes. I therefore decided to put my skills to use. I made a 10 thou. Drill and succeeded in drilling the six-toothed sprocket to take a new 10 thou. pivot. The pivot was then made and fitted to the sprocket but it was a little loose and I applied more pressure. The result was that the sprocket split neatly into a six petalled flower. O.K. so the watch would still work without it! Not so! Sid had carefully created extra clearance between two plates by inserting a minute piece of tissue paper and I had already discarded this, so that when I reassembled the watch, the extra tension snapped a further pivot. This was the end of my attempt at watch making, and the watch. It also saved the tedium of searching through the dust and debris beneath the workbench for tiny parts that always seemed to flick out of the tweezers. I decided that I'd better stick to clocks in future.

As usual sport and P.T. was part of our curriculum at Newcastle. P.T. was normally part fun and part "sadism" on the part of the P.T.I. who whacked offenders with a "stonickey" (a rag filled canvas truncheon) and generally dispensed "press-ups" and "up the wall bars go" with gay abandon. The origin of the "stonickey" and even the exact spelling of the name is shrouded in mystery, although I have confirmed that it was in use pre-war. It may well have been derived from the "ropes end" or "starter" used in the days of sail but it was unknown to the Naval Museum at Portsmouth. Enquiries of the P.T. School only confirmed that long retired P.T.I.'s remembered it but that the use of physical force against trainees was now strictly forbidden. Having long since recognised my total inability to vault any box horse, I was much impressed by Wally Brackstone who spent the whole of one session neatly concealed inside the box. This was before the *Great Escape* was published.

On the sports field, as in the gym, my "ducks disease" ensured my continuing ineptitude for team games but there were acceptable alternatives for those like me who would never be chosen for a team. One of these was to skulk in the minute roof space at one end of the "P" huts and hope not to be caught by the prowling R.P.O.'s. The other was to go on a cross-country run. This was not the formal affair when all competitors were monitored and checked in, but a gentle stroll through the pleasant local countryside to Trentham Park, a bit of rowing on the lake with a hired boat, and an equally gentle stroll back to Clayton in time not to be considered adrift.

A further disadvantage of "ducks disease" (although I actually grew two inches during training) was the march back to Clayton Hall from Newcastle. Most of the time we were transported to and from the outlying sites by 3 ton Bedford lorries or "clapped out" buses that had often to be pushed uphill out of the town, but on some evenings we were required to march with our hook boys in charge. Invariably this became a long drawn out straggle with the long-legged "tanking" away in front, anxious to wash and change for supper and a run ashore. The vertically challenged had to "double" in a vain attempt to keep up, but never to succeed.

Despite the low pay and lack of duty-free cigarettes or tobacco, a number of our lads were dedicated smokers. This often meant that non-smokers would be called upon to "lend us a halfpenny till pay day". This repeated five times would provide the price of five Woodbines in a paper packet. The halfpenny was rarely repaid. Personally I was never anxious to take up smoking because the "fug" in the back of a 3 ton Bedford lorry on the way to work was so unpleasant. Regretfully at least one of my contemporaries died of lung cancer after a lifetime of smoking begun as an apprentice. Of course there was plenty of smoke in and around the

A Bit of a "Tiff"

"Potteries" during the war and, coming into Newcastle from Clayton, the view from the high ground showed a long low ridge of black smoke on the horizon lit by the glow of kilns and blast furnaces as the Midlands boosted the war effort.

We youngsters were growing up and, in retrospect, despite all our moans and groans about discipline we were going through that uncomfortable state of being teenagers; true some matured quicker than others but we were only eighteen when we passed-out. Although the idea that Artificers were "God's gift to the Navy" was well encouraged this was something for the future rather than as newly trained apprentices and I remember with some regret my own failings. The Navy in its wisdom, born of experience, imposed its own form of controls, which might nowadays be totally unacceptable in our modern soft and politically correct society but at the time was not so different from the rough existence of many in U.K. both before and during the war and also not too different from the regime in the public schools. What it did in the event was to relieve our parents of the agonies of bringing up a teenager and it eased our passage into an adult world as fairly responsible people. Would that some similar scheme could be made available for our modern youth.

The Navy was investing in us and it took its responsibilities seriously in all aspects of our life as if "in loco parentis". This included the provision of 1/3rd pint of milk and a flat sweet bun each morning at "stand-easy", just like other school children. If all this was directed by our officers, then it must have been behind the scenes, as we seldom had any contact except during formal parades or inspections. Our Divisional Officer was Lt.-Cdr Christian-Smith an Engineer; I chanced across him many years later when he was working for a civilian company. As none of our officers had aircraft experience it is something of a mystery how our syllabus had been generated; probably by ideas from the R.A.F. plus the traditional R.N. Artificer training scheme. I do not know whether the syllabus was laid down or whether local initiatives were allowed from our officers and senior rating instructors, but then as in the future our lives were dictated by the rules in K.R.'s and A.I.'s (King's Regulations and Admiralty Instructions), by A.F.O.'s (Admiralty Fleet Orders) and by a whole range of technical manuals and bulletins in the form of Air Publications covering every last piece of equipment, S.T.I.'s (Special Technical Instructions), S.I.'s (Servicing Instructions) and a range of local orders. In addition to our technical training of course we got the usual odd lectures on other subjects, this included one on Gas Warfare by a weedy lieutenant wearing a pale green ring between his stripes, signifying Special Duties. He contributed little knowledge but for his Scots accent was dubbed "pairr-sistent gasses".

While it was important to understand and observe all the above for our future role, our day-to-day life was dictated by routines promulgated in Daily Orders and broadcast by "Tannoy" (loudspeaker). Failure to read the orders or listen to the broadcasts could lead to trouble. Our day started with the bugle-call for reveille by a duty bugler. One way or another, every division seemed to find in its ranks a qualified bugler, who gained some reward for this task. Ours was Tozer. The bugle-call was followed by the duty P.O. usually banging a dustbin lid and bawling "Wakey Wakey Lash-up and stow". There were other interesting variations on this e.g. "All hands all hands, off cocks on socks" or "Rise and shine the morning's fine, the sun is burning your eyeballs out".

Although there was a fence around Clayton Hall it was impossible to prevent unauthorised exit or entry by Apprentices seeking to avoid the official "liberty boat" for one reason or another, nor was it possible to prevent young ladies from loitering in Clayton Lane by the pond and meeting lads remaining in the camp. Sentries were nominated from the duty watch to prevent this sort of thing happening but were not inclined to take the job seriously. The Orchard sentries who were supposed to prevent pilfering of the officers' garden took a similar view, and the cudgel supplied was found useful in knocking down the apples, which were then stowed in our trousers. On duty we wore gaiters and these held the trouser legs closed and provided a spacious though bulky container. As always, the object was not to get caught.

The problem of course was that once an individual was caught and charged for a misdemeanour then he was likely to be watched and caught for another offence. As a result the worst "skates" were almost always on punishment and rarely allowed shore leave. Two of our worst "skates" fell into this trap and finally in sheer boredom went tadpoling in the pond; once again they were caught, charged and punished. At another stage the same pair were undergoing "rifle drill" one hot evening and were ordered to "Off Jackets". However, they had made their own provision to keep cool; they had trimmed their thick working shirts to leave just a "bib" supporting the collar and tie; the jacket of course normally covered this. Further punishment followed their exposure.

Mostly the punishment awarded was stoppage of leave, but fourteen days No 8a was the norm for the skates as described above. On the punishment scales, as laid down, the most severe was reputed to be No 1, which resulted in the execution of the offender. So perhaps No 8a was just a minor issue to the Navy but it included extra menial duties, rifle drill (Jankers), and a reduction in rations e.g. no pudding, as well as no shore leave. For more serious offences people could be sent to detention camp, dismissed the service, disrated (not too easy when, like us, you were at the bottom of the pile), or given lashes with a cane. For these punishments the "lower deck" would be cleared and we would be paraded to hear the Captain read out the charge and the punishment that he had awarded. In the "Articles of War", which were always part of the preamble to this event, was the statement, "——— shall suffer death or such other punishment as is hereinafter mentioned ———". I do not recall that lashes were given in public. We lost one of our numbers, who was dismissed for persistent misconduct, but during our stay received in compensation a number of "skates" that had been back-classed from earlier divisions for lack of dedication. We eventually lost several of our own people to 2nd Benbow when they failed the Passing Out exams but by Dec. 1943 2nd Rodney division numbered 142 men.

Awareness of the opposite sex, another teenage instinct, had its problems. For one thing the majority of apprentices had entered from single sex Grammar or Technical Schools, so that the day-to-day socialising now a normal part of school life was more difficult before entry. At Rosyth as a junior entry we had so little leave that opportunities were limited. Newcastle was however much more relaxed in that we had more local leave and there was a much greater chance of meeting female company in the bustling "Potteries" towns. Saturday evening "hops" in the "Muni" (Municipal Hall) were a good starting point and a number of lifelong partnerships evolved. At the other end of the scale some young ladies became notorious and the nickname "Toddy" will forever ring a bell with some of my division. Her Christian name was Doris. Another of our division received some "Oral" education from a married lady and had difficulty in climbing into his top bunk on his return. Our Wrens didn't normally figure in our social life; the most visible served in the galley as cooks and servers and this in itself was a deterrent but most were a bit older than us and not particularly attractive; the reverse was also probably true. Our first thought on entering the dining room was food and our second thought if it was edible was more food. The call of the "Gannets" was therefore "Got any gash Ida?" and the most likely response from Ida was "No f——— gash". Even here however anything was possible and one of the least presentable of our division "serviced" an equally unattractive Wren in the "Spud Locker". However with a few exceptions the majority remained remarkably virtuous, much talk but no action. For the lucky few a visit to the Sick Bay provided a little paper packet containing one "Durex".

With the passage of time our moans about food do not seem to be justified considering the rationing in civilian life. We certainly had our share of corned beef, Spam, powdered egg, tinned sausages, tinned tomatoes which with bacon became "train smash", watery yellow custard, and fairly tasteless rice pudding and tapioca. On several occasions we were served "tripe" and this did not appear to be the delicacy claimed by some. One complaint did receive attention, when Johnny Cotton measured the Bread supplied and it proved by micrometer to be less than the perceived standard of $\frac{1}{2}$ inch thick.

I recall little of the camp canteen other than the provision of our "Nutty ration", for which our ration card was endorsed with an ink stamp. With care, an eraser and a mapping pen using Indian ink, the card could be restored to its original state and a second ration obtained. My guilt was limited by the notion that I would then send the extra ration home to my young sister. In fact that decision was very hard to make and I often ended by tossing a coin, several times if I lost first time. I'm sorry to say that I seldom lost.

Once established at Clayton Hall with the other Air Apprentices, it became a matter of pride to obtain and wear on leave a smart No 1 suit with some means of distinguishing us from other similarly dressed non-apprentices. In other words we wanted a "fore and aft" rig equivalent of the sailors "tiddly" suit. The sailors "square" rig was often altered illegally, to give a lower collar, tighter waist and wider flare to the bell-bottomed trousers, and thus enhance the appearance and jauntiness of the wearer. We wanted only to wear a best suit in the style permitted before the war. Such a suit had a double-breasted jacket and was made in "Doe-skin". Normally, it would only be worn ashore, especially if further enhanced by a badge with the initials F.A.A. worn on the left jacket cuff. This was definitely illegal and if worn ashore had to be concealed as we left the camp. Our problem was of course that we had no Clothing Coupons. My coupons came from an aunt and duly on leave I presented myself to a Naval Tailor in Chatham to be measured for the first time for a properly tailored suit. There I was temporarily floored by his question "Do you dress left or right sir?" My suit was very well made and continued in use with different buttons and badges until I was commissioned in 1955. The official passing-out photograph of 2nd Rodney division shows a good number of people wearing double-breasted suits and as usual, being a short-arse, I am largely obscured by the Divisional banner in the middle of the front rank. This position seemed to be my fate over my thirty-year service.

One suit that did not survive was the one that was fumigated during an outbreak of German measles; us sufferers were quickly banished to an isolation hospital outside Newcastle, where the treatment was "nil". Reading matter was rather limited and I was reduced to reading a paperback on the life of Nelson. The stay in hospital was governed by the progress of the sick diet i.e. Liquids–Light Diet–Full Die–Up (out of bed)–Out (back to camp). I then returned to Clayton Hall to pick up my stiff, crumpled and now smaller uniform and proceeded on late Easter leave. Periodically, in a bid to prevent the outbreak of some "bug" or other, we would parade to receive a squirt of carbolic into our throats.

Apart from the camp and social gatherings in the "Muni", there were other possibilities for entertainment and interest. I suspect that the R.C.'s and Non-Conformists, who disappeared from our obligatory Church parade, made social contacts at their church. Various canteens were opened for servicemen in the Pottery towns and I remember eating baked beans on toasted rolls in a Hanley canteen after seeing Bing Crosby in *White Christmas* at a local cinema. Personally I used to attend the meetings of the No 60 Stoke-on-Trent, Spotters club with Oz Rumsby of 1st Grenville Division, and on leave I visited the Observer Corps Post in Bearsted where they held Recognition Books with silhouettes of the latest secret aircraft. On one occasion Oz Rumsby and I went with the club on a visit to the R.A.F. M.U. (Maintenance Unit) at Lichfield, where we saw several fairly rare aircraft, B17c Flying Fortresses, Wellington Mk V/VI (high altitude bombers with a pressure cabin), and Westland Whirlwind fighters. We visited Lichfield Cathedral on our return. On another occasion several of us had a tour of the Spode factory in Stoke; here we were surprised by the quantity of high quality china still being made, mostly for export, and fascinated by the dexterity of the female workers. It was possible to purchase china from a limited range and I bought a tea set in white bone china and had it sent home because it was almost unobtainable. However, the village postman succeeded in destroying most of it by allowing it to bang against his bicycle handlebars, and my expenditure was wasted. It had only been possible to make the purchase since our pay had increased to 15s a fortnight and this was untold wealth.

Normally our local leave was limited to evenings and Saturday and Sunday afternoons and evenings, but on one occasion we had a free weekend, perhaps it was a Bank holiday. Apart from cost, it was generally impractical for most of us to actually get to our homes and back in the time available and many of us took a trip to somewhere in the vicinity; I went to Manchester for the day. With this exception our leave was three 14-day breaks at Christmas, Easter and summer and for these we received a free Railway Warrant. This pattern continued with a few exceptions for the remainder of my career. I was at home in Kent when the Dieppe raid took place and recall seeing for the first time Hurricanes fitted with 3 inch R.P.'s among the armada of aircraft flying to the battle.

At the end of 1943 we took our final technical exams and completed our test job in the workshops. The Technical exam included a practical test for which a number of different test pieces had been assembled and a draw held to select "who got what". To my knowledge none of the test pieces bore any resemblance to the real aircraft maintenance or repair task but such was the shortage of equipment and experience that there was little alternative. The Test job was rather more appropriate and we made a near copy of the Swordfish torpedo release cable adjusting winch. It nicely included most of the features of our training in Fitting and Turning. The results of these were added to the results of our Parts 1 and 2 Educational exams to produce a final grading. Prizes were awarded for both the Technical Exam and also for the Test job. The top scorer in the Test job received a micrometer, the remainder got books, which covered a mixture of technical and naval subjects. My chum Bugsy Spiers, who was an (E) got the micrometer and I picked up 1st for the test job but was 2nd in (L) tech. The real benefit of a top grade was to receive a maximum of six-months advancement to Leading Hand. On passing out we would be rated Air Fitters (L), (E), (O), or (A). and our uniforms would then bear our first official badge, which was a crossed four bladed propeller with the trade letter in the lower segment. The top few could be promoted after our first six-months under supervision.

With our training over we were prepared to enter the outside world and received our full toolkit. The contents of this varied with the trade, and there were one or two surprises. Electricians received a mysterious device called a fan-key, on the false assumption that we would be allowed to work on ships' ventilating fans, and also a device for holding small screws while using a screwdriver. The most practical however was the Electrician's Knife. This had a blade with a screwdriver at the end and a file on one side. For a long time this knife and a single adjustable spanner was the only tool I needed during work in the field. We also received our full kit of clothing. This included tropical whites, cold weather clothing in the form of "Scapa Scanties" (thick knitted long legged pants and long sleeved vests) and a hammock complete with mattress. The hammock was far more to the Navy than a bed, it was the only reasonably private spot in a crowded mess deck and it needed to be kept clean and stowed away when not in use, because the open space in the mess was needed for eating, and recreation such as it was. Hence the reveille call of "Wakey Wakey Lash up and Stow". The hammock was also a life-saver because it could be used to bolster up battle damage and because it could, if correctly lashed up, support a man in the water for some hours. For these very domestic and practical reasons the hammock and its mattress and blankets had to be lashed into a dense sausage bound together with seven loops of rope at equal spacing along its length. Seven knots equated to the seven seas by tradition. This we were taught but although I used my hammock briefly on several occasions and found it comfortable, it was a pain to lug around from place to place and to keep clean. I was glad when they were abolished for bunks. As for the seven knots, I am afraid that the F.A.A. did not care much for tradition and to the disdain of the "Fish-heads" (real sailors) tended to produce a loose and untidy parcel, which fell apart in transit. This was nicknamed a Fleet Air Arm Bundle.

The white tropical kit had a high collared jacket and was thick and stiff. It was difficult to keep clean in shipboard conditions. Mine shrank the first time it was laundered and thereafter was too small. Fortunately it spent all its time in a kitbag because the moment we arrived in the tropics during the war we wore khaki, which was far more practical and comfortable. For all that however the Navy returned to wearing whites after the war, but I never had to wear mine as a rating. The Scapa Scanties were never required either and were eventually converted to knitting wool by my mother. In the meantime going on draft was a "dockyard job" since we carted with us our kitbag, steaming bag (small kitbag for use in transit), large green suitcase, small brown attaché case, hammock and toolbox. It was never much fun.

By the end of our training "2nd Rodney" had won most of the sports trophies (with absolutely no help from yours truly) and considered itself the best, not only for its sporting prowess but also for its general disregard for Naval discipline. Following our Passing-out Parade and Dinner we felt bound to follow tradition by rampaging through the junior huts up-ending beds and generally creating mayhem. It did not produce much response from the occupants and in retrospect seemed rather futile. Just possibly that may have been the first sign of our growing up.

We returned from Christmas leave in January 1944 wearing our badges as Air Fitters and were then sent on draft to our new Air Stations. At that point most of my companions over the last $2^3/4$ years disappeared without trace into the ever-expanding F.A.A. However over the years, even after my return to civilian life, I have by chance met an old acquaintance from those days. I have passed through Newcastle twice briefly since 1944 but never long enough to visit the old sites. I have Graham Bebbington to thank for sending the modern map with the locations marked on it and the advice as to how much has changed.

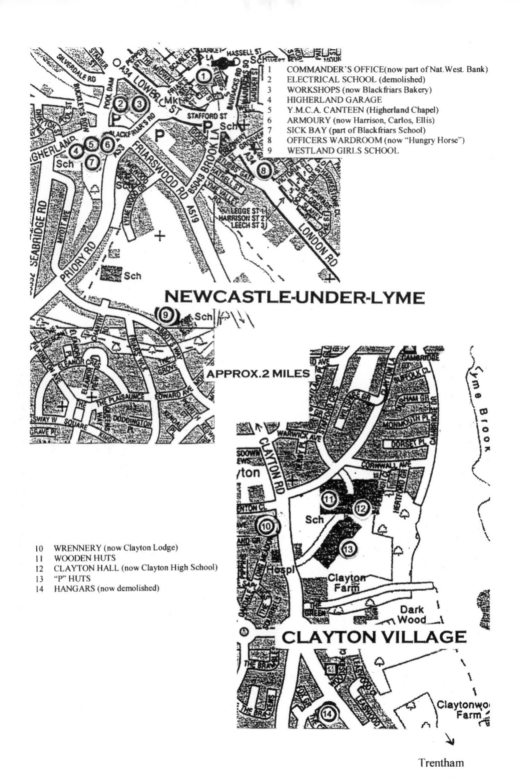

1 COMMANDER'S OFFICE(now part of Nat.West. Bank)
2 ELECTRICAL SCHOOL (demolished)
3 WORKSHOPS (now Blackfriars Bakery)
4 HIGHERLAND GARAGE
5 Y.M.C.A. CANTEEN (Higherland Chapel)
6 ARMOURY (now Harrison, Carlos, Ellis)
7 SICK BAY (part of Blackfriars School)
8 OFFICERS WARDROOM (now "Hungry Horse")
9 WESTLAND GIRLS SCHOOL

NEWCASTLE-UNDER-LYME

APPROX. 2 MILES

10 WRENNERY (now Clayton Lodge)
11 WOODEN HUTS
12 CLAYTON HALL (now Clayton High School)
13 "P" HUTS
14 HANGARS (now demolished)

CLAYTON VILLAGE

Trentham

Fig 1. The layout of H.M.S. *Daedalus II* (1940-1945)
(superimposed on a modern map)

A Bit of a "Tiff"

Figure 2   Newcastle trained Naval Air Apprentice Entries

Division	Trade	Entered	Basic Training	To Newcastle	Passed out
1st Rodney	L/O	Mar.1939	L Rosyth and Lympne / O ?	May 1940 (Mid1941 Rosyth)	Dec.1941
1st Benbow	L/O	Aug. 1939 Portsmouth	L Rosyth / O R.A.F.Cosford/Halton	May 1940	Dec.1941
1st Grenville	L/O	Mar. 1940 Chatham#	L Rosyth and Lympne / O R.A.F. Halton	June 1942	June 1942
1st Anson	L/O	Sept 1940 Ryde	L Lympne / O R.A.F. Halton / Newcastle	May 1940 / Oct. 1940	Dec.1942 / June 1943
2nd Rodney	A/E/L/O	Mar. 1941 Lee	Rosyth	Jan. 1942	Dec.1943
2nd Benbow	A/E/L/O	Sept.*1941 Lee	Torpoint *	Sept. 1942*	June 1944
2nd Grenville	A/E/L/O	Mar. 1942 Lee	Rosyth	Jan. 1943	Dec. 1944
2nd Anson	A/E/L/O	July,1942 Lee	Torpoint &Rosyth	Sept. 1943	June 1945
Hood	A/E/L/O	Mar.1943 Lee	Rosyth	Jan. 1944	Dec. 1945
Raleigh	A/E/L/O	Sept*1943 Lee	Torpoint *	June 1944*	
Effingham	A/E/L/O	Mar. 1944 Lee	Rosyth	Jan. 1945	Transferred to H.M.S.Condor at Arbroath
Keppel	A/E/L/O	Sept.*1944 Lee	Torpoint *	June 1945*	

Freddie Allford remembers being marched into the Dockyard to welcome home the Ajax and Achilles after the Battle of the River Plate.

* In principle the entries and departures should have been at regular six monthly intervals in succession from those for 2nd Rodney, but it is now evident that there were variations such as 2nd Anson of which the Author was previously unaware. It can only be assumed that each entry was adjusted to fit in with vacant slots at Rosyth and Torpoint where the General Service Artificers training was of longer duration. This being the case then the Author apologises for any inaccuracy and would welcome additional information.

The little wooden huts at Clayton Hall.

Inside a little wooden hut.

A Bit of a "Tiff"

What the best dressed "Tiffs" were wearing in 1943. Left Ken Bilney in db. doeskin. Right Alf Norrington in Pussers sb. blue serge.

Two six heave!

Westland's School 1942

Martlet at Westland's School 1942

A Bit of a "Tiff"

Haven't quite got the hang of parallel turning have you
Apprentice Bloggs?

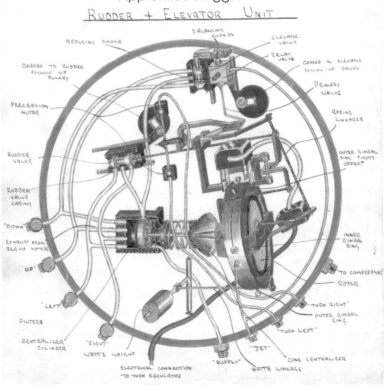

RUDDER + ELEVATOR UNIT

An extract from my notebook showing one unit of the very basic
air operated R.A.E. Autopilot fitted to many large British aircraft
through the war.

Members of 2nd Rodney in the canteen. Tozer our bugler right foreground. Anson hook boy Horney 2nd right foreground.

Wally's great escape!

A Bit of a "Tiff"

Members of 2ⁿᵈ Rodney Division outside "P5" hut in 1943. Resident Anson Division Hook boys are C.P.O. Apprentice Horley and P.O. Apprentice Cathery.

The orchard sentry.

Hutchins and Rennie Sir. Caught tadpoling whilst under punishment.

Hutchins and Rennie. I only ordered "Off jackets. Report to the regulating office, you're in the rattle again!"

A Bit of a "Tiff"

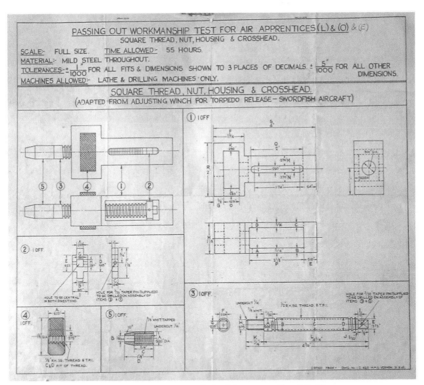

Passing out test job. Newcastle 1943.

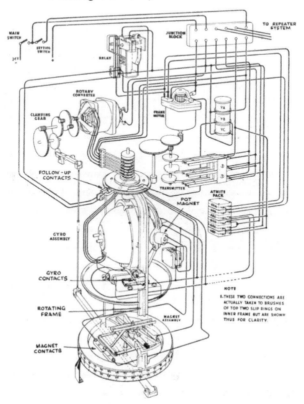

The Distant Reading Compass - very high tech in 1943.
Author's collection.

Now that I had qualified as an Air Fitter (L) I might actually see a Naval aeroplane flying. In fact I had to wait until 1969 at Upavon to see a Fulmar in flight. "The Last of the Few".

2nd Rodney Division Passing Out photograph in front of Clayton Hall - December 1943. Author front row right of centre. Author's collection.

A Bit of a "Tiff"

Chapter 5   H.M.S. *Kestrel* – Worthy Down

Arriving after dark, in a 3 ton Bedford lorry from Winchester station, we were greeted loudly by the Joss-man, who let us know very clearly that he had all-weather vision and that we might expect to see him watching for us day and night. A good start! Had he been warned of our potential for skatish behaviour or was he his normal self? I think the latter and it seemed to confirm that only a small matter of geography prevented men of his nature from being members of the Gestapo. However we kept well clear of him and his R.P.O.'s for safety. Despite this dubious welcome, the group of 2nd Rodney's drafted to Worthy Down considered ourselves lucky not to be at one of the more outlandish spots such as Machrihanish, or Twatt in the Orkneys.

Another feature of arriving at Worthy Down, in common with every other station that I joined later, was the need to collect bedding i.e. mattress, pillows and blankets, from the bedding store. This was always sited well away from the accommodation block and, since trucks, trolleys or other vehicular assistance were not available, then for those with "ducks disease" it was rather a nightmare. It usually rained on these occasions just to help.

Worthy Down was a pre-war R.A.F. station and had been an airfield since 1917. German P.O.W.'s were said to have built the hangars. Living quarters followed a common design evolved during the establishment of the R.A.F. by Lord Trenchard and could be found on many of the pre-war airfields. At Worthy Down the ratings lived in four blocks, two opening on to and facing the parade ground and a further two separated by a road immediately behind. Each block had two dormitories on the ground floor and first floor with an ablution facility in the centre of each floor. The whole was brick built and very solid as was the heating. In each dormitory two solid brick and tiled chimneys ran from floor to ceiling, with a coal burning stove set into the inner face. Even had the stove been burning continuously, which was not allowed for safety and because of the fuel shortage, then the massive chimney would have still absorbed most of the heat. In the event, during our evenings off we used to crowd into the narrow arc of warmth immediately in front of the stove. No heat penetrated to the sides or rear at all. Occasionally we would make a foray to the coal dump near to the back gate to pilfer extra fuel beyond that issued on a daily basis.

For the first time our messmates were a mixed bunch, mostly H.O.'s and from widely different backgrounds. I remember only one, an elderly Irish armourer who had tales to tell of his exploits with the Black and Tans. He demonstrated his skill at blowing petrol from his mouth on to a flame once too often and received some nasty burns. My continuing interest in model aircraft led to experiments with rocket propulsion using Coffman starter cartridges. The first static test from a light fitting in the ablutions was moderately successful and caused no damage.

Leaving the entrance hall, we faced the Ensign on the far side of the parade ground, to the left the galley and dining room, and to the right the admin. block. The objective of the occupants was to organize our lives or to make them a misery (take your pick).

The geography of Worthy Down was as follows. Leaving Winchester station we passed H.M.S. *Flowerdown* on the left (now an Army Training Camp) and continued on the A34 to a junction (now a roundabout). To the left was the B3420, a long straight Roman road leading to the A30 and thence Wherwell. This road, initially well screened by trees, was now closed and contained a solid mass of U.S. Army vehicles including tanks. The open ground between it and the A34 was also filled with vehicles. The entrance to Worthy Down was on the right at the bottom of a hill and this had a barrier. Beyond the barrier on the left was an estate of pre-war R.A.F. married quarters but now used by the Wrens. Here the houses were clearly graded by rank. Small terraced houses were for "other ranks" and embodied the intriguing option of having the adjacent top floor bedrooms in each house with two doors. This enabled families with extra children to be accommodated within what would otherwise have been a two-bedroom unit, simply by opening the second door. House size depended on rank and was seen to get progressively larger until one reached the large detached house of the station commander. Behind the married quarters was an aircraft dispersal site. Continuing toward the main site, with the airfield on the left, one passed large numbers of U.S. Army L5 Sentinel observation planes parked on the grass verge and further on were grassy areas, understood to be part of a pre-war horse racing track. In one of these was a small depression used for ground defence training. At this site we were trained to use the Blacker Bombard, a Dad's Army device firing a form of mortar shell. Before reaching the Main Gate and Guardroom there were aircraft parked along the perimeter and I remember seeing a Skua and Albacores when we first arrived. A gate led on to the main tarmac apron in front of the hangars and control tower but the main road continued past the wardroom on the right and thence to the admin. block and parade ground. A series of wooden buildings were sited behind the wardroom and continued past the main accommodation blocks and on toward the back gate. This led to the Worthy Down railway station and also to a road, which led to Springvale and Kingsworthy. Some of the wooden huts were also used as billets and, when later as a leading hand, I found myself there, my fellow occupants were Leading Radio Mechanics. They were all H.O's and were responsible for Radio and Radar servicing for which there were as yet no ex-Apprentices trained in these black arts despite our educational grounding in the subject. The wartime Radio Mechanics were selected from men who were educationally of a high standard and they seemed to come from a common mould; it seemed that a studious appearance, horn-rimmed glasses, boots not shoes and a pocket edition of Omar Khayyam was the norm.

On the same back road was the gymnasium cum cinema cum theatre. This was almost certainly the best entertainment facility ever found on a Naval Air Station, since in addition to operating as a cinema it hosted a wide range of top shows. During my time these included *No No Nanette,* a circus, and the Boyd Neal String Orchestra. This latter was not quite to the taste of the audience who progressively disappeared and only a mere handful stuck it out from sympathy with the musicians. I am not entirely clear how we came to be so well served, one view favours the involvement of Ralph Richardson and Lawrence Olivier who had been trained as F.A.A. pilots but were now back in the entertainment business. I also understand that both they and Vivien Leigh were living close by. Another view favours our Padre the Reverend Churchill. The assumption of a family link with Winston may not be correct but whatever strings were pulled they certainly worked miracles. If it was the Padre then it is doubtful that "divine intervention" played a part, as his sermons at our compulsory Sunday Church Parade were quite abysmal.

Another on-site entertainment was by the P.O. cook who had a quite remarkable skill as a hypnotist. I do not know whether this was intended to compensate for his shortcomings in the galley, but it was evident that the daily tot of rum issued before dinner (lunch) was of even greater assistance to those entitled to draw their tot i.e. over twenty. To those of a gambling nature the illegal Crown and Anchor board was available, but kept well out of sight by the old salts that ran the game.

Winchester was accessible, mostly on Saturday afternoons when a very infrequent bus service passed the main gate. This was usually filled with people from outlying villages doing their weekly shopping. There were a number of canteens and cafes in Winchester but apart from pubs it was a pretty dozy place in the evening despite the large numbers of British and U.S. servicemen. In many respects this has not changed due no doubt to the stultifying influence of college, cathedral and county. One popular exception was the dance held in the Tearooms, in what is now the top floor of W.H. Smith.

An alternative means of getting into town was to catch the train from Worthy Down Halt; the train from Newbury stopped at Winchester's Chesil Station; now a car park. The return journey was never too easy and one way of making the long slog by road less boring was to follow the railway line. By starting on the main line just North of Winchester main line station one continued on the track (not then electrified) to Headbourne Worthy where the Newbury line crossed beneath the main line. At that point we changed tracks and ended back at Worthy Down Halt, thus eliminating the long walk from the A34 into the camp. The spacing of the sleepers was not conducive to an easy walk in the dark and I cannot recommend railway walking, but I find that an occasional reminder of idiotic acts like that tends to mollify my criticism of modern youth.

To continue our journey around Worthy Down; from the Admin block the road led toward several hangars on the left of the road and stores and other buildings on the right; it continued past these and then looped to the left in a wide sweep around the perimeter past another hutted dispersal site at which Percival Proctors were operated, and thence to rejoin the A34 Winchester to Sutton Scotney road by the water tower thus completing the circuit. At this point barriers were mounted either side of the A34, and crossing the road one entered a very large open space bounded by woods and holding a number of Dutch barn hangars. This was the aircraft storage site.

Anti-aircraft protection at Worthy Down appeared to be limited to a single multiple 3 inch rocket launcher based on the right of the road as it passed the main hangars. At one point I had some role in servicing the electrical system but it was never fired during my stay. Worthy Down was obviously a low priority target but it sat surrounded by such a mass of military hardware in the build up to D-Day that any enemy intruder would have faced a swarm of fighters. In fact I do not recall any air raid warnings until after D-Day when the V1's were being launched against Southern England.

There were effectively six working sites at Worthy Down and we were moved progressively through these sites to obtain practical experience during our six-month continuity training. Until mid 1944 Supermarine operated the first two hangars at the entrance to the hard standing and used the airfield for test flying. We were entertained to some thrilling flying by test pilot Geoffrey Quill using a wide range of Spitfire and Seafire variants and also the Supermarine Type 322 S24/27 variable incidence wing torpedo bomber prototype, nicknamed "Dumbo". Supermarine then moved to nearby Chilbolton at which was also based a unit of R.A.F. "Thunderbolts"; altogether a better airfield this remained as their test airfield for some years after the war.

A Bit of a "Tiff"

My first workplace was the Maintenance hangar where most of the station aircraft were maintained and repaired. This provided me with a first chance to get to grips with the electrical and instrument systems as actually installed. Since the aircraft were all trainers there was no sophistication, but at first sight it was a bit baffling. Most of the work was concerned with carrying out Minor Inspections on Westland Lysanders, which with Blackburn Sharks, Percival Proctors and Curtis Seamews were used to train T.A.G.'s (Telegraphist Air Gunners). The Minors were required every 25 flying hours and were conducted in accordance with a servicing schedule. There was little chance of an error and after six weeks I was made Q.S. (Qualified to sign the Aircraft Servicing Record–Form A700 for work carried out). In those days of piston engine aircraft it was a regular requirement to test the ignition harness following a report of mag. drop. In other words faulty high tension wiring to the spark plugs caused the engine revs. to fall when one of the two magnetos were switched off. The test equipment for this was a portable device, which measured insulation resistance by applying a high voltage from a hand cranked starting magneto. Accidentally, and sometimes deliberately, an engine fitter might still be working up a ladder when the H.T. tester was applied. Tools and often the fitter himself would fall when several thousand volts arrived and the culprit would be roundly cursed. In general the possibility of falling from a ladder when working was a real one. We had been warned against wearing a ring because of the chance that it might snag on some object during a fall and for this reason I have never worn a ring. I understand that in everyday life this accident is still a regular event, and people still lose their fingers.

W.R.N.S. Air Mechanics carried out a lot of work and there were no problems as far as I am aware, but it was a novelty to most of us and I notice that far more photographs were taken at Worthy Down showing them at work than of any other maintenance activity. During the summer two Wrens were killed when a Proctor crashed while taking them on a joy ride. The cause of the crash was found to be failure of the wooden wing main spar due to short grain in the timber. In general there were few opportunities for joy rides, and no compulsion to fly in an aircraft that you had serviced.

From the Maintenance Hangar to the "OOMPH" Den. This was the crew room at the aircraft dispersal behind the Married Quarters, and so named because the old Tortoise stove was ignited with a mixture of any inflammable material to hand; usually this included Cellulose Thinners. The "OOMPH" was the result of applying a match and the cast iron lid was propelled toward the ceiling. This unit had only the Blackburn Shark, an obsolete torpedo biplane used in its B3 version for training T.A.G's. I was now Q.S. and able to carry out Daily Inspections, but since the only electrical gear fitted was lighting and one solitary Aldis lamp this was hardly a technical challenge. The problem was however getting into the aircraft in the first place. The difficulty lay in the canopy fitted to the B3 version; this had to be opened while standing in the footholds. Getting a foot on the first step was a problem to me in any case but if it was the wrong foot then you arrived at the last step with no hand holds while you attempted to unlock and slide back the canopy. The Shark was unique in another respect in having a self-charging compressed air starter for its Armstrong Siddeley "Tiger" engine. Someone in Armstrong Siddley must have liked compressed air because in due course early models of the "Python" propeller gas turbine engine as fitted to the Westland Wyvern also used compressed air starting. In this case a massive trolley with racks of air cylinders was hauled around the flight deck until superseded by a more sensible cartridge system.

Although this was 1944 and running up to D–Day, Worthy Down was only a training airfield and we were not working under pressure; we were well occupied but there was no late work or overtime and it was possible to keep trade demarcations which would not have been possible or sensible on an operational unit. In one example, the ex-apprentices were not allowed to use machines in the station workshop, which was manned by civilians. In general by following this practice we left all tasks not strictly defined as within our trade to someone else, who was allowed to sign for the task. I found the hard way that this was not correct when I changed the battery on a Seamew. A unit of these odd looking U.S. planes was sited at a dispersal beyond the last hangar. The Seamew had a covered cockpit for both pilot and observer and the battery was mounted between the two seats. Access was obtained by removing a long wire from a piano type hinge and then lifting the centre section of the canopy, this was normally the job of an airframe mechanic and he would then replace it on completion and sign for his work. Well I changed the battery and left the canopy to be replaced by A.N. Other; it was still unfitted when a pilot came to fly the aircraft and I got the rollicking I so richly deserved. Another odd job on the dispersal was to replace a nipple on a stainless steel "Bowden" control cable fitted in either a Martinet or Defiant Target Tug; although many joints on aircraft wiring were soldered, this was tricky since it required a lot more heat and the use of "phosphoric acid" as a flux. On a dispersal, soldering required either a battery operated low voltage soldering iron, these were as rare as hen's teeth and incapable of reaching a high temperature in the open air, or one used a "Mox" iron; this fearsome and cumbersome device was heated by igniting a "Thermite" charge fitted in the central body and you hoped that you could finish the job before it had cooled down.

As is still the case, workshops and offices were built along the sides of the hangars and my next job was in the Electrical Workshop attached to the Maintenance Hangar. This was more to my taste, and I was employed in testing electrical and instrument components removed from the aircraft. During this time I encountered I.C.I. Dulux for the first time. These days Dulux is well in evidence on all my working clothes but in 1944 it was being used to correct the defective insulation on the magneto distributors of some U.S. aircraft. The remedy was to boil the distributors in a bucket of caustic soda to remove a layer of wax and then to paint them with Dulux Red. This was an effective insulator. While in the workshop I was told to erect some wooden shelving. In the days before tipped drills, Black & Decker, and Rawlplugs, this was not straightforward so I used a hollow steel tube and cut some teeth in the end. Daylight eventually appeared through the tube after much hammering and twisting and the shelf was erected on wooden plugs banged into the holes. Closer inspection showed however that, on the outside, each hole terminated in a fair sized crater of missing brickwork. Once again there was no cement to do a proper job and the holes were bunged up with "gunge".

I was occasionally sent out from the workshops to service the Proctors on the far side of the airfield. On the first trip I was shocked to find that the flying instruments in the rear cabin had been removed and the pipelines loosely plugged with cotton waste. Full of professional indignation, I proceeded around the dispersal correcting this serious fault. At the same time I reset the Altimeters to zero at the barometric pressure of the day (Q.F.E.) as provided by the Control Tower. That was yet another lesson learned, because the dispersal was some 30 – 50 ft lower than the Tower, and the Proctors would have ploughed holes in the runway had I not been told of my error.

In May and June 1944 I attended two courses, the first was on Barracuda Electrics, the second on American Electrics. The Barracuda was being built in part of a working biscuit factory in Manchester and course members were billeted out in civilian lodgings nearby. It was a very congenial atmosphere, including the ever-present smell of baking biscuits. At the weekend we went to Manchester, went on the Big Wheel at Bellevue and watched cinder track races.

The most significant part of the course related to the Strip wiring System. This was a massive improvement on the wiring in the early aircraft, although it was bulky and crude compared with modern miniature connectors. It was made up of about ten flat strip contacts, each silver-plated and gold flashed, wrapped around a keyed insulation strip. The aircraft wiring was soldered to the contacts, and the installation was made up of many distribution and junction boxes located throughout the plane, into which these strip connectors could be uniquely fitted to form circuits. This enabled the wiring to be readily broken down for faultfinding, modification, or repairs. The Barracuda was the most complex F.A.A. plane at that date because it carried Radar, the Torpedo "F" sight, D.R. Compass, and a bomb distribution system. The new wiring system made our life very much simpler, and I found I was able to find faults with confidence.

The American Electrics course was also an eye-opener. Two technical innovations stood out; the first was the use of circuit breakers in place of the large crude brass capped glass fuses and fuse boxes fitted to British aircraft and the second was the gyro stabilised flux-gate compass. This was not only a major step beyond the D.R. Compass but in fact not matched in British service until the Sperry Mk4 compass appeared around 1949/50. This also used a flux-gate detector. Our course was located at the giant Burtonwood depot near Warrington and we shared our training and billets with U.S. and R.A.F. trainees. I found the U.S. men interesting company as individuals, rather less so in bulk and tending to be loud and brash. After my own $2^3/_4$ yr. training I was astonished to find that many U.S. trainees were not trained mechanics or fitters before they joined the course. No matter what their original occupation they apparently only had to volunteer, attend and pass the two-week course to be reclassified as Electrical Mechanics! We all ate in a common mess with R.A.F. catering but using the then innovative serving tray. With luck and a steady hand sometimes the custard did not spill into the gravy! U.S. dietary habits failed to impress us at breakfast when it was usual for the limited supply of marmalade to be scooped up and slopped over bacon and eggs. However the P.X. store did impress. It was open to us Brits. and my family was the beneficiary of a large pack of Camel cigarettes and jars of Yardley's Lavender Talc, which was unobtainable elsewhere in U.K. Burtonwood was a hive of activity with numerous P51 Mustangs, Lightings, and the new Northrop P61 Black Widow night fighter being uncrated and prepared for service. Burtonwood remained a U.S. military depot throughout the Cold War. We were much less impressed by the work gangs, comprised mainly of coloured U.S. military prisoners under armed guard at all times. It made the R.N. system seem somewhat softer.

In between the two courses I was back at Worthy Down for D-Day. It was not unexpected because the military preparations were all around us, what with aircraft flying in formation overhead and bangs and flashes from nearby fields but we had no role to play except to service any operational aircraft that diverted to our airfield. For a period the training flights were stopped and the aircraft painted with the black and white invasion markings for their own protection. When flying recommenced we had a spate of battery problems, caused by the evaporation of water while parked in the hot sun. For a while travel on leave outside the area was stopped but a chum and I borrowed Pusser's bikes and cycled to Farley Mount to obtain a panoramic view of the armada of shipping in the Solent. We also passed a U.S. field hospital on the downs near Stockbridge at which was sited a large number of U.S. Piper Cub light aircraft. At a later stage I managed a weekend at home in Kent courtesy of a ride to London on the canvas top of a large U.S. Army lorry. While waiting at Victoria station I watched a V1 Doodlebug crash and explode nearby. The V1 attacks continued during my night at home and were engaged without effect by a nearby Rocket battery but I was not at home when one landed in the field opposite. Because Kent was the main route from the Continent to London we had a lot of stuff passing over but we lived in a very rural area and any damage locally was primarily from jettisoned bombs and damaged V1's rather than deliberate attacks.

After I was promoted to Leading Air Fitter in July I spent part of my time at Station Flight; this involved servicing visiting aircraft, although there were several station aircraft as well, including a Tiger Moth. This was also very basic and did not even have a proper airspeed indicator; instead it was fitted with a spring-loaded plate mounted on a wing strut, in flight this plate was moved by air pressure against a calibrated scale. Things could hardly be more basic. An engine fitter swung the prop. to start the engine and on one occasion it backfired and hit his hand; surprisingly it did more damage to the propeller. During this period it was commonplace to arrive at work to find the area in front of the hard standing covered with wholly unfamiliar planes, which had arrived overnight. All of these required a Daily Inspection. They included Wellingtons, Spitfires, and Typhoons, but due to the virtual standardisation of British cockpit instruments and equipment it was possible, safely, to carry out the work without the usual handbooks. One aircraft we never had to service was a rare Cierva autogyro communication aircraft. This appeared, regularly, flown by an R.A.F. sergeant pilot; on departure he swung started the engine himself, entered the cockpit and departed without any help whatsoever. Many aircraft were not so obliging; specifically those having an Inertia starter and these included the Walrus, Swordfish, Oxford, Anson, and the U.S. Avenger. The ground crew wound a starting handle close behind the engine to build up speed in a heavy rotor. As the speed increased the high pitched whine gave an indication of full speed and the clutch was engaged, usually by the crew pulling a toggle; the rotor then rotated the engine via a reduction gear, and hopefully the engine started. Frequently this did not happen and a reluctant engine quickly exhausted the ground crew. Exhaustion was not the only hazard; the Avenger had its starter handle next to the exhaust pipe and as the engine started the mechanic would be enveloped in smoke and sometimes flames if the engine backfired. The Walrus engine was of course mounted between the main planes and drove a four bladed pusher propeller rather too close to where the mechanic was cranking the starter; one slip and he was mincemeat.

On Station Flight the small crew all worked in co-operation but this did not apply to batteries. When these needed charging they had to be humped all the way to the battery room by yours truly. One evening the daily pile included a Trolley Acc. containing two heavy-duty batteries for ground starting and a number of aircraft batteries; I set off with these sitting on top of the trolley and all went well until I reached the steep hill leading to the battery room when of course they slipped and cracked on the road; another black mark!

The job's tour of Worthy Down included a spell at the Storage site; here large numbers of aircraft were stored, some in Dutch barns but mostly in the open and the weather played havoc with the electrical systems in the Barracudas and Swordfish Mk3's. It was normal to have to drain water from lighting fittings but in the Barracuda the insulation resistance of the strip wiring was so poor that it was common to leave the battery switched on, in an attempt to dry out the wiring by heating the leakage path between the positive and negative wires. British aircraft were all fitted with a 2 wire wiring system, based no doubt on the early machines having wooden and fabric structures. The U.S. machines had an earth return system using the metal structure as the return path; this saved weight and proved more reliable; it is now the standard. They also had better quality cables and a metal-cased battery, which reduced the risk of handling damage compared with our plastic ones. The storage unit held two types of U.S. aircraft, the little Stinson Reliant communications plane and the Grumman Avenger. These were brand new and rumour had it that they came equipped with an aircraft clock and a full toolkit; if true then they had been pilfered en route and this was a pity because they used Phillips screws and we lacked the correct screwdrivers in our toolkits. However the Avengers did arrive with Emergency Oxygen Bottles and these came in handy for blowing out the spiders and webs that found their way into the Pitot Heads of parked aircraft. Avengers had an electrically operated rear gun turret and it was necessary, routinely, to give this a functional test. The fitter had to enter the turret and swing up the armoured access door before the test and the access door could not then be reopened unless the turret was correctly aligned. It was my misfortune one day to have as my assistant a Wren, who for some unexplained reason had had no training and was in effect allowed to look around before she decided what trade or other job she would go to. She was therefore of no help at all when the Avenger battery ran flat just as I had raised the turret to the vertical. We were at the far side of the dispersal so it would take ages to fetch help or a new battery; in the event I stayed upside down for about 20 mins whilst the battery regained enough urge to drive the turret back into alignment. In flight a gunner had the option of dropping sideways from an emergency hatch, but this was not an option on the ground.

I spent much of the time doing leak tests on the pitot-static systems of stored aircraft and as this meant tramping around the muddy site it was necessary to wear sea-boots (Wellingtons). Naval stores had of course no rubber boots and instead I got a pair of true sea-boots in leather with steel plate heels. It was difficult to work with them and the heels played havoc with the fabric on Swordfish main planes while working at the pitot head; the port Yagi radar aerial also partially obscured the pitot head and was easily broken while one worked.

Work on Barracudas included modifications to circuitry involving the torpedo camera. A hammer and small chisel was used to cut off four 6 B.A. nuts holding a redundant switch and a new cable loosely passed from the pilot's cockpit via the wing root to the rear cabin. The whole process seems now to be much the equivalent of the work of the average building site electrician. One of the least attractive activities involving the Barracuda was the occasional need to perch a man on each wing tip to act as ballast and as guides around obstacles while taxying; with little handhold and a very uneven taxiway the high wing provided a very precarious ride. The A.S.V. radar sets on the Barracuda and Swordfish were still on the Secret List and one routine duty was to guard the Radar Store. This was the only time in my entire career when I was given a rifle and ammunition for real. Like most similar duties in a non-combat zone, it was only necessary to be vigilant until the duty officer had done his rounds and had been properly challenged. After that the sentry retired to his bunk and slept until early morning, when his final duty was to light the ubiquitous Tortoise stove with the usual materials including cordite from broken down starter cartridges and damp wood.

Getting to and from the storage site was usually in a lorry, sometimes in the back of a Jeep, which was even more hair-raising, but occasionally by walking. To avoid walking the full length of the perimeter track we used unofficially to cross the airfield. There were of course no marked runways on the grass and because of its location and because the field was far from level, then the Control Tower had an incomplete view of the airfield. It was therefore not unusual to be in the middle of the airfield when, with a roar, a Barracuda would appear over the hill heading towards you, and looking for all the world like a great swan trying to paddle off the water. The flaps and undercarriage of that aircraft made it look very ungainly on the ground. One of our Barracudas took off without being fuelled and immediately landed in an adjoining field without damage, so presumably the undercarriage was plenty strong enough.

One unusual unit at Worthy Down operated the R.R. Merlin engined Armstrong-Whitworth Whitley. This was the E.H.U. (Engine handling unit) and its aircraft were fitted out as classrooms; it is not known what had prompted this idea since the Merlin had long been fitted to Naval Aircraft before this unit came into being in 1944. The Whitley of course flew very much nose down and was not a happy sight bearing down on you in the middle of the airfield.

During my time at Worthy Down I had a chance to pursue my career; first I took and passed the Higher Educational Test (H.E.T.) in March 1944. This was the first step to Warrant rank. The subjects were Maths, Magnetism and Electricity, General Knowledge, and Geography. I had not touched Geography since school and did a quick revision using *The World* by Stamp. This was enough and at least as good as my Mag.& Elec. results which should have been higher. I also applied for Aircrew Selection and as far as I knew this went ahead, but no more had been heard by October 1944 when my Draft chit arrived for a squadron. I had embarkation leave and travelled on 24th October to H.M.S *Waxwing*, a transit camp near Dunfermline.

Off on draft

– and the joy of collecting bedding in the rain!

Lt. Cdr. Bill Blake with a U.S. Army L5 Stinson Sentinel. Worthy Down 1944. Courtesy Tony Dowland.

The Lysanders were still there in 1944.

Westland Lysanders at Worthy Down in 1941. Lt. Cdr. Bill Blake on left and Lt. Lawrence Olivier R.N.V.R. on right. Courtesy Tony Dowland.

A Bit of a "Tiff"

"Ignition testing"!

The Oomph Den

Blackburn Shark III of 755 Squadron at Worthy Down 1944. Photo
Bill Blake - Courtesy Tony Dowland.

Curtiss Seamew of 755 Squadron at Worthy Down in 1944. Photo
Bill Blake. Courtesy Tony Dowland.

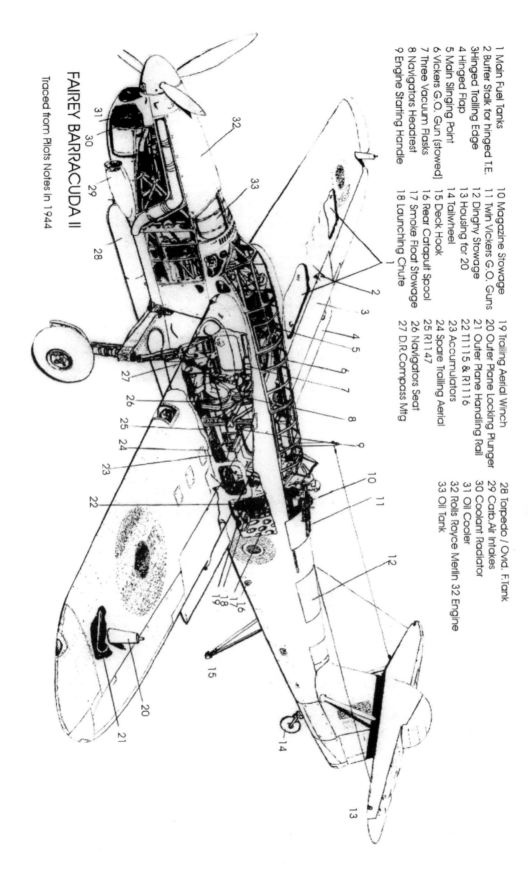

FAIREY BARRACUDA II

Traced from Pilots Notes in 1944

1 Main Fuel Tanks
2 Buffer Stalk for hinged T.E.
3 Hinged Trailing Edge
4 Hinged Flap
5 Main Slinging Point
6 Vickers G.O. Gun (stowed)
7 Three Vacuum Flasks
8 Navigators Headrest
9 Engine Starting Handle

10 Magazine Stowage
11 Twin Vickers G.O. Guns
12 Dinghy Stowage
13 Housing for 20
14 Tailwheel
15 Deck Hook
16 Rear Catapult Spool
17 Smoke Float Stowage
18 Launching Chute

19 Trailing Aerial Winch
20 Outer Plane Locking Plunger
21 Outer Plane Handling Rail
22 T1115 & R1116
23 Accumulators
24 Spare Trailing Aerial
25 R1147
26 Navigators Seat
27 D.R.Compass Mtg

28 Torpedo / Ovld. F.Tank
29 Carb.Air Intakes
30 Coolant Radiator
31 Oil Cooler
32 Rolls Royce Merlin 32 Engine
33 Oil Tank

A short cut across the airfield.

Another hazard. Armstrong Whitworth Whitley of the Engine
Handling Unit. Worthy Down 1944. Courtesy Tony Dowland.

A Bit of a "Tiff"

Grumman Avenger at Worthy
Down in 1944. Courtesy Tony
Dowland.

Starting the Avenger.

Percival Proctor as used to
train Telegraphist Air Gunners
at Worthy Down in 1944.
Courtesy Tony Dowland.

Starting the
Walrus.

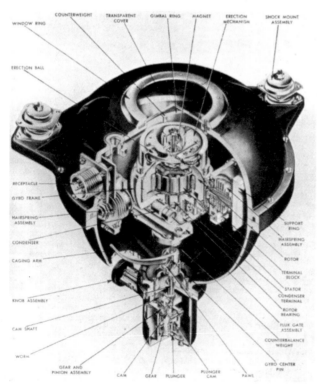

The Bendix Gyro Flux
Gate Compass
circa 1944 from
instructional course
notebook.

A Bit of a "Tiff"

The venerable Swordfish, but not a Mk III equipped with A.S.V. Radar as at Worthy Down - this one was photographed at R.A.F. Upavon in 1969.

Alt, ooh goes there?

My family at home during the war.

Author with dad during embarkation leave - September 1944.

Chapter 6 896 Squadron
Part 1 Going to War

My stay at H.M.S. *Waxwing* was thankfully very short, just twelve days in dank, dark Nissen huts sited in some woods; the showers in the separate ablution block had only two temperatures – freezing and scalding. This required fine judgment to know when to jump in and when to leap out and start again.

We had no serious employment during our stay, since the objective was to prepare us for our next move. To this end we were now issued with khaki tropical kit. Since we already had Whites and Scapa Scanties there was much speculation as to our destination. One possibility was that we were on our way to the South Pole via the Tropics, another that it was a clever ruse to fool the enemy who spent their time looking at the Matelots' Dhobi lines. Whatever, the practical effect was to increase the kit to be dragged around; I had already acquired another kitbag. Our kit was then labelled and marked with a symbol identifying the draft. In the case of 896 Squadron this was a black diagonal cross in a square. This would enable the kit of each group to be identified, assembled, stowed, and recovered at each stage of the journey to our destination. Against the odds, this system worked effectively. At this point we had not been segregated into a unit and were still part of a collection of men some of whom were simply travelling with us to an unknown place.

On the 5th November 1944 we assembled our steaming kit (kit to be used during the journey), which included a steaming bag, our hammock, and in most cases a green suitcase; by good fortune it was again raining, so we were taken by lorry to Dunfermline station instead of marching. Our train proceeded somewhat deviously south; leaving our destination in some doubt and at one point we stopped at a station to be fed by the W.V.S. It has to be said that, by this stage of the war the arrangements for travel and feeding were very well organised. Canteens abounded wherever you went and they were greatly missed when they closed progressively after the war.

We finally arrived at Liverpool, embarked on the S.S. *Monarch of Bermuda* and settled in. Within a day or two we were moved again, this time to the S.S. *Franconia*. This was to be our troopship as far as Port Said. We were at Liverpool for eight days and, during this time watched dockyard workers deliberately damaging crates of oranges to pilfer the contents. Perhaps we were fighting a different war.

Our convoy set sail on 13th November. The ship was full and we actually used our hammocks. I believe the armourers amongst us were found duties manning the defensive weapons, but for the majority we spent our time queuing for meals or washing facilities, otherwise mostly between decks reading books from the ship's library or playing cards. The serious players were a separate gang and one or two had won fair sums by the end of the journey. The weather was normal for November and did not encourage trips to the deck, but because the ship was a large one it was reasonably stable, even in the Bay of Biscay. For most of us this was our first trip to sea and we had expected the worst but it was only a problem for a few. The few, which included my chum Joe Hannington, were ill from the moment the ship put to sea and spent their days on deck rarely coming down for a meal. Poor Joe never overcame his problem and on one occasion later in his career had to be sent from his squadron for this reason.

Early in our journey from Dunfermline the wail of bagpipes proved that our squadron had at least one Scot. Most will agree that the pipes can be very pleasing when played in an outdoor setting, but there was no way of escaping the din on a train or a troopship. For the piper, his pipes were his ticket to better things and he was called to play in more elevated circles than our mess deck, but there was no great sorrow when one day he found that the bag had been punctured. When eventually the pipes were repaired he continued his piping for the benefit of the community in Capetown and elsewhere, but we were spared.

We passed Gibraltar after dark on 17th November, Pantelleria and Malta on 20th and finally docked at Port Said on 23rd November. Obviously there was great interest in seeing a foreign land for the first time but we were denied our first glimpses because the crowding of so many men on to the landward side of the ship caused a marked list and we were then confined to the mess decks. Once the ship had been secured alongside we were allowed on deck and then got the benefit of the smell of the East. This seemed to be largely fuel oil and seawater overlaid with odours that defy analysis. It was sunny, hot and dusty and the bumboats were already vying for custom alongside. Goods were pulled up through open portholes, and not to be outdone our chaps were engaging in some trade of their own by selling off their unwanted cold weather clothes; it was now clear that we had no immediate use for woollens. When we were finally disembarked we joined an Egyptian State Railway train and this became another travelling market. Groups of hawkers moved along the train selling a variety of goods including peanuts, oranges, leather ware and watches. Those daft enough to buy or exchange a watch usually found that it worked long enough for the vendor to escape at the next wayside halt. The tables were turned when sacks of peanuts were found stacked on the trackside at one halt and Jolly Jack took his fill.

Our destination was another transit camp at Fayid in the sandy desert close to the Bitter Lakes. Next door was a Naval Air Station, H.M.S. *Phoenix*. Once again we struggled to collect our bedding and find our kit, which was as usual dumped as far away from the billets as possible. At this time 896 Squadron was told that we would be going to South Africa to form and train as a unit with our aircraft. Other members of the draft would also be going to South Africa but as station staff at Wingfield. This was the Naval Air Station and Air Repair Yard at Capetown. This group included a number of my pals from 2nd Rodney. Once again we had no daily tasks and spent most of our time relaxing. Food was adequate but included sweet potatoes with most cooked meals. The canteen however had stocks of tinned peaches, condensed milk and cornflakes, and this helped to fill any gaps. On one occasion we went swimming in the Bitter Lakes where several decommissioned Italian warships were moored; we returned via a small canteen, possibly Church of Scotland, at which the entrance was made up of strings of folded beer bottle caps and the glasses were cut down beer bottles. Evidently the Aussies had passed that way.

As a Leading Hand I shared a small cabin in the huts used by the troops with a Leading Air Mechanic (L) named Hawkins. The billet was pretty basic with dusty concrete floors. A young Egyptian lad had some sort of employment in the billet, and was keen to explain the rudiments of the currency. On the evening prior to our departure Hawkins and I decided to return our bedding to avoid the mad scramble in the morning. Excepting only the P huts at Newcastle, that was the coldest night of my life and nothing we had in our steaming kit made the slightest difference.

The following day we paraded with our steaming kit as before and were marched carrying our kit, not to the camp railway siding but to Fayid Halt. This wayside stop was over a mile from the camp across soft roasting sand. After a while, a train, consisting only of trucks labelled 4 Chevaux/24 Hommes, pulled up. Cape Coloured soldiers, who we discovered had been prisoners of the Italians, occupied the trucks. This invoked a good deal of sympathy from the lads who then dished out cigarettes and fruit from their personal stocks. After some minutes the train moved slowly forward and stopped. We were herded into more empty wagons at the rear and spent an uncomfortable standing journey to Port Tewfik (The port of Suez). We embarked on the coal burning ex-Polish liner H.M.T. *Kosciusko* on 7th December and sailed on the 8th. This ship was rather less impressive than the *Franconia* and there were problems with food and recreation space. The latter because the presence of the Cape Coloured troops, with whom we had travelled from Fayid, upset the South African contingent on board. Among the one thousand or so servicemen on the ship, only 896 Squadron had a complete command structure, so our C.O. was asked by the O.i.C. troops to help. Our R.P.O. and the cooks out of our 160 strong unit were seconded to help sort out the problems, and the C.O. wrote a lengthy signal complaining about the suitability of the ship. We stopped at Aden for two days without going ashore, crossed the Equator with due ceremony on 20th December and stopped again at Kilindini (the port of Mombassa) on 22nd for coaling. We sailed on 24th and our Christmas day was memorable only for a disastrously burned lunch. In the heat few wished to sleep below and it was the practice to bag a "slinging" space somewhere on deck as soon as it was possible to gain access. I doubt if even the deck chair bagging Germans would have won this particular battle. The favoured spots were based around a number of tall steel stanchions, presumed to be the supports for the deck awnings, which were not fitted. Hammocks were then secured, one above the other, radiating from the stanchion to the nearest deck fitting. Entering one's hammock was a matter of pushing up the occupant of the one above and sliding in beneath. This arrangement was cosy and weatherproof, until one night during heavy rain the occupants of the upper hammocks progressively evacuated and finally I had no choice but to go as well. The heavy weight of bodies eventually caused the steel stanchions to bend to one side. About two days out of Durban the ship's coal bunkers caught fire and we left the convoy, which included the battleship *Valiant*, to proceed into port at our best speed. It was assumed that the fire was caused by badly bunkered coal at Kilindini; this was not uncommon in coal-fired ships and could have had serious results.

Our arrival in Durban on 30th December was greeted by the singing of "The Lady in White" who welcomed every ship in this way during the war. On disembarkation we went to H.M.S. *Assegai* another transit camp; once again the bedding store was up a steep hill, but it was not raining, thank goodness. No question that we were in Africa as the jungle drums beat every night from nearby villages, and we saw chameleons in the bushes. We were at *Assegai* just four days and were able to go ashore to Durban. On one occasion I stayed overnight in a hostel while trying to locate a contact provided by an uncle. On another visit several of us were highly amused to see a Zulu rickshaw driver careering down the main street dangling from the shafts of his vehicle; he had been caught off balance by the weight of a stout passenger climbing aboard and this had lifted him off the ground. Shortly after this we were walking past a bus stop when an Indian lady tripped and fell as she left a bus. When I tried to help her up she shied away in fear. Considering that Durban was probably the most British of all South African cities, this seemed to me quite unbelievable, and caused me to think deeply of the reasons. Later, in Capetown, we observed the separate space for White and Coloured on public transport and the divisions between White English and White Boers. Altogether a beautiful country spoiled by racial tensions and not one in which I would wish to have to live permanently.

We left Durban and travelled to Capetown by train in sleeper compartments over two nights; we passed through Pietermaritzburg, Ladysmith, Bloemfontein, Kimberly, Orange River, and De Doorns. All places familiar to us from school geography and history lessons, and offering fascinating scenery and views of topless African women en route. A German made Henschel locomotive hauled the train and was joined by an extra engine over the steepest gradients, and, despite being fitted with cinder traps on their funnels, they puffed out so much cinder that our compartments were thickly covered with the crunchy stuff by the end of the trip. The locomotives were not the only German equipment used in South Africa, as the S.A.F. were operating a number of Junkers Ju 52 (transports) and Ju 86 (bombers).

896 Squadron was formed and worked up with 24 Grumman Hellcat II fighters from 5th Jan 1945 to 25th April at the Goodwood campsite at Wingfield Air Station. The unit comprised twenty-four pilots including the C.O. plus two Army Officers and some N.C.O.'s who formed the C.B.A.L. team (Carrier Borne Air Liaison). Only one of the pilots Lt Shilcock the Squadron Staff Officer was a regular Officer and he later became C.O. of 809 Sqdn. flying Sea Venoms at Suez in 1956. As already mentioned the rest totalled 160, of the 21 P.O.'s, two were Air Mechanics (L), two were Radio Mechanics, and two were Air Artificers 4th class (A/E) and the majority of these were regulars some of whom I served with post-war ; the junior ratings were mostly H.O.'s (Hostilities Only) and included a writer, officers stewards, Corporal Oxley an R.A.F. armourer, and some aircraft handlers. This fairly new branch had responsibility for fire fighting and aircraft movements on deck, but in the days before mechanical handling gear it was primarily the ground crew who did the pushing and shoving. The representatives of this new branch had one thing in common; they were all a bit thick and could be relied upon to entertain with one daft exploit or another, e.g. the chap who drove his lorry through the wall of the Captain's Office later in our travels.

The large powerful Hellcat was big improvement on earlier F.A.A. fighters It had a max. speed of 380 knots at 23,400 ft. and a normal range of 935 miles. The normal armament was six .5 inch machine guns plus either eight 3 inch rockets or two bombs. We had some teething problems and there was a tendency for the new disc brakes to seize up on landing;

several pilots received back injuries when the aircraft nosed over after brake seizure and the maintenance unit spent much time polishing the discs during night shift. Initially our aircraft were equipped only with a U.S. two breech Coffman starter, which was highly unreliable; the electrical firing contacts were constantly being cleaned and repaired on the flight line. At one point, in desperation, there were plans for hand swinging using a canvas cup on one propeller blade and attached via a bungee cord to a rope. I have no idea if this scheme was actually used on a Hellcat but I have since heard of a similar device used on a smaller plane. The notion of hand starting a 2000 h.p. engine turning a 13 ft. propeller was terrifying and by good luck our aircraft were replaced by a model fitted with an electric starter. This required the use of the dreaded Ground Starter Trolley (Trolley Acc.) but at least it worked. The vibration from the engine did nasty things to the mounting bolts on the starter and the generator, and also sheared off the large condenser mounted on the generator as a suppressor for the British radio equipment. Two men and a length of rope were needed to remove the generator because it was heavy and well buried between the engine and the cockpit firewall. Eventually the condenser was mounted remotely at the cockpit side of the firewall in a local modification. This required the electrician (me) to spend some time head first and upside down among the rudder pedals and control column.

Our 3½ months in Capetown were very pleasant, although we were kept busy and on one occasion toward the end, the Squadron, now fully trained, took part in a joint defence exercise with South African units and demonstrated their skills for local politicians. At first we all worked on the line to get the planes flying but as the flying hours piled up, it was necessary to have a Maintenance unit to carry out the minor inspections and other large tasks outside normal flying hours. The advantage of this was that it was possible to visit Capetown during the day. We finished our shift when the tasks were complete and therefore usually had some sleep before normal reveille, and usually the last task would be a ground run of the serviced aircraft. Rather than secure the tail wheel to a hold down weight, it was normal practice to deploy at least half a dozen "bods" leaning over the tail plane. At full boost we got the full benefit of the 2000 horsepower blast laden with high-octane exhaust and were all folded neatly across the tail plane.

We rarely went to breakfast, instead it was usual to eat bananas, oranges and Cadbury's Milk Chocolate bought on a previous trip ashore; provided that is that the goods had been well protected from the ants. Failure to take precautions would result in a long line of ants appearing from outside and winding their way to the goodies. Our camp food was adequate although it was evident that the Coloured staff were none to happy with their lot; this however did not concern us greatly as we were now in the land of plenty. At the hangar we were serviced by a mobile canteen and by a civilian baker twice each day, and because we were all healthy youngsters they did a roaring trade on each visit.

The shops in Capetown had many goods that were unobtainable in U.K., Swiss watches, some film, and I even bought a U.S. model aircraft engine (an Ohlsson petrol engine) to add to my already bulging kit. The Bioscopes (Cinemas) were intriguingly different and refreshment was automatically included in the entrance ticket and delivered in the interval. We went up Table Mountain, and went swimming at the local resort of Sea Point, and we lost one of our A.M.'s(L), who was found drowned in a pool at Camps Bay on 4th March. Chums on most trips were A.M.(L) Goose and Wilf Honey an ex 2nd Rodney Armourer, but this varied with the jobs we had and our duty watches. Occasionally it was possible to meet other pals from Newcastle who were working in the Repair Yard at Wingfield. However the Squadron and Workshop units were physically well separated and we used the Airfield Shuttle on the few occasions when we visited the Workshop and Administration site. This was an old aircraft crate mounted on a trailer, towed very slowly by a tractor and never stopping on its continual perambulation around the perimeter track.

Unsurprisingly, Capetown had other entertainment for visiting troops and although the notorious District Six was out of bounds it was evidently fairly easy to become a temporary resident of Rose Cottage (the V.D. ward). This despite the warnings, free condoms, and "first aid" centres for the immediate treatment of those who had put themselves at risk. Separate toilets and ablutions were provided for V.D. sufferers and were marked C.D.A. (Contagious Diseases Act). Needless to say there was a great deal of banter about the problem; rumour had it that ratings caught V.D. but officers had "penile catarrh". Among our lads was one who had been physically damaged in a last visit to a "lady" in Dunfermline and another who married just before he left U.K. but found too late that he had been infected by his new wife. The war had made a lot of problems and these were just a sample.

Early in March the squadron was allowed ten days' leave. This was a welcome surprise since we had missed Christmas leave but were not expecting any leave on a front line unit. Accommodation and part of our rail fare to different destinations was arranged by S.A.W.A.S. (South African Women's Auxiliary Service), who also ran service canteens. Many of our number went as far as Johannesburg but a large party including myself and Wilf Honey went to Kimberly, and from there were sent to various families.

Wilf, myself, and, four others went to Warrenton, where we were well cared for by Mrs Weddell, who owned a small private hotel. Our first night was however less than comfortable as we quickly discovered we had been invaded by bedbugs. It took us a while to give our bedding and room a good going over together with a generous libation of neat Dettol. The following night all was well and we were told that it was an occasional problem in the area but the marks of neat Dettol remained. The hotel had a large garden backing on to the Vaal River; this was an exciting place to swim as it was wide and in full spate, and the riverside trees were full of weaver bird nests. Tennis and dancing was arranged at a friend's house where a couple of nice young ladies and several married ladies attempted to provide the social skills I lacked when I left home in 1941. What a different world this was! As a concession to the war we had a meatless day each week amid many apologies, despite this we hardly noticed the difference such was the super food we received. During our stay we were driven into Kimberly, and other Squadron members joined us in visits to the "Big Hole", to De Beers where we were shown diamonds and diamond cutting techniques, and to the Bantu Museum where African artefacts and history were presented. We returned to Capetown as we had arrived in an overnight sleeper, very well relaxed and with little over a month before we joined a ship as an operational unit.

One problem with serving on a squadron at that time was that we had no technical officers and all our day-to-day work was directed by the Petty Officers. Certain pilots were nominated as Engineering and Electrical officers but their technical role was usually nominal. In our case the nominated Sub.-Lt had worked for the Post Office and may well have been professionally qualified but he did not involve himself in our work. While this did not affect our daily tasks, it did mean that there was no one on the unit to qualify me for promotion to Acting Petty Officer Air Fitter when this was due on 1st July. This had therefore to be done at Wingfield before we left and it was arranged for me to remain at Wingfield on the retard party to see the aircraft off, while the remainder of the ground crew travelled to Durban by train.

I had in effect to take two separate boards. The first was to gain a Workshop Supervisory Certificate for advancement to Acting/P.O.A.F. (L). An unusual problem because I had not been and would not be employed in a workshop all the while I was on the squadron. The second was to qualify for Acting Air Artificer 4th class (L), also a Petty Officer rank because this was the intended professional route for ex- Air Apprentices. I have no idea how other ex–Apprentices coped in a similar situation but by luck the key man at Wingfield was Warrant Officer Tommy Orr; the same person who had set up the Air Apprentice training with the very first entry at Lympne. He sat like God in his office in the Electrical and Instrument workshop and overlooked all the work going on in the various bays to keep everyone on their toes. These workshops were part of the R.N. Aircraft Repair Yard at H.M.S. *Malagas* i.e. Wingfield. Under his direction my chums were getting practical experience in all the subjects for which we had received our training. By comparison work on a squadron was technically much less demanding and over a period would put me at a disadvantage. There appeared to be no precedent for this problem but Tommy devised a written exam, several tests and an oral exam, which he conducted himself. One of the practical tests was to check calibrate an A.S.I. (Airspeed Indicator), which was straightforward. Another was to reassemble and test a Sperry Artificial Horizon, which he had had completely dismantled, and which I had never previously seen in this state, let alone reassembled. Thank God for friends! Paddy Doherty had not completely jumbled up the pieces, so it was not difficult to work out the order of assembly and all went well until the two ball races securing the gyro assembly into the main gimbal were offered up. At this point a ball race seized in the soft aluminium housing In the normal event it would have simply been reworked but the practical was time limited and Tommy kept popping round to monitor progress. Paddy therefore slipped me a spare gimbal and I carried on with the new part. At the very last stage I found that the black field plate could not be secured to the new gimbal. It was now evident that this item was not jig built and while two dowel pins fitted, the two screws did not. I had no option but to fit it together as it was, and hope that it would not fall off under test. Well the test started, and although the gyro was not properly balanced, (that would have been a follow up job anyway) it all held together long enough to satisfy Tommy and I was duly qualified.

The final step was to have the certificate signed by the Captain, and it was on his recommendation that I later applied for a Flying Duties Selection Board; this was the only available avenue to a commission. Although this was approved and documents raised, all the records, as in my earlier attempt, were lost when the Squadron was disbanded. With the end of the war this opportunity was gone and, in retrospect even had I qualified, the chance of one's survival to a ripe old age were pretty poor as a naval pilot. So after all I think someone actually did me a good turn!

On 25th April the aircraft were sent off to fly to H.M.S. *Ameer* at Durban and the retard party travelled to Simonstown to join H.M.S. *Relentless* for a sea passage to Durban. This slightly unusual arrangement was needed because troop travel was forbidden by the Orange Free State on a Sunday; we would have faced this ban had we gone by train. What a funny old war!

As passengers aboard *Relentless*, we were dumped in a vacant mess space and required to stay below deck until the ship was under way. By supper time the violent movement as we rounded the Cape of Good Hope, and the lack of fresh air or a visual reference finally took its toll, and to my shame I was seasick for the first and only time. *Relentless* was a destroyer of just 1705 tons but we gathered from our temporary messmates in the stokers' mess that this trip was a doddle, and on earlier trips in the Indian Ocean the mess decks had been awash in bad weather. Hence the well known service banter –"Hardships you b————s you don't know what hardships are!" Thank God for big ships! At one stage during the following day I visited the nearest "heads" (toilet) and discovered the label C.D.A. after I was committed. Fortunately any bugs present on the seat were not contagious, but it was not a pleasant thought.

Like many small ships *Relentless* operated with canteen messing. In this system each mess was responsible for the purchase and preparation of its food, and the ship's galley cooked the meals for collection and consumption back in the individual messes. The messes were of course also the sleeping and recreational space. This was a scheme we F.A.A. lads had not previously encountered but as passengers we helped the off duty stokers prepare the meals. Old salts reckoned this system was better than central messing, which was normal in the bigger ships of the period, because it gave them a choice and they could make economies. However I doubt whether the available supplies and the wartime working conditions allowed a balanced diet. Still we had little time to ponder the issue, as after a day of doing various cleaning duties and another night at sea, we arrived at Durban and rather gratefully transferred to *Ameer* in the hope that size mattered and that this would ensure a more comfortable ride in future.

Chapter 6 896 Squadron
Part 2 At War

When 896 Squadron joined H.M.S. *Ameer* this was only for the trip from South Africa to our intended operational area in S.E.A.C. (South East Asia Command), so we did no flying during our one week trip to Colombo, where arrived on 8th May V.E. Day.

896 Squadron had previously been to war from mid 1943 to June 1944 and had then been disbanded and reformed into the current unit. In its previous life it had operated Wildcats from *Victorious* and later *Pursuer* against the *Tirpitz*, against Bodo in Norway, and as fighter cover during D.Day. *Ameer* had also seen prior service in S.E.A.C. Initially this was limited to trade protection duties in the Indian Ocean using 845 Squadron (Avengers/Wildcats), but during 1945 with 804 Squadron Hellcats had covered the landings on Ramree Island (Operation Matador), on Cheduba Island (Operation Sankey), and as escorts to 888 Squadron for a photographic reconnaissance mission over Kra Isthmus, Penang, and N. Sumatra. This was all part of the progress toward the liberation of Singapore.

Ameer was one of 22 ships of the "Ruler" class Assault Escort Carriers, which were built in the U.S. for the Royal Navy. 9 of these served only as Ferry Carriers to cater for the growing need for aircraft in the war against the Japanese. The design of this class was based upon the U.S. C3 Merchant hull and the incorporation of the hangar and flight deck necessitated expansion joints in each of these decks, and the steel hangar deck curved up fore and aft from amidships. This made aircraft movements difficult in heavy weather. The hangar was 260 ft long by 62 ft wide and 18 ft high with a 42 ft by 34 ft aircraft lift at each end, and could carry a total of 30 aircraft. In our case we normally carried 24 Hellcats and 1 A.S.R. Walrus borrowed from a unit at Trincomalee. The hangar opened directly on to the "sponsons" on the ship's side, and for this reason each access door was fitted with a switch, which cut out all hangar lights and power points when the doors were open at night. This small feature caused endless agony and cursing if a door was left open while we were working upside down inside the planes. Hellcat wings were folded manually by swivelling and rotating backward so that they lay alongside the rear fuselage with the guns pointed downward. In a carrier's hangar this left some headroom into which was stowed various large spares such as mainplanes.

Overall dimensions of the "Ruler" Class were 492 ft long by 108 ft broad, but the wood covered steel flight deck was 450 ft long by 80 ft wide and carried a single hydraulic catapult forward, and three barriers of steel cable that could be raised between this and the nine arrester wires aft in the landing area. The catapult used the U.S. wire strop launch method and this ensured that the new heavier aircraft could still be launched in the light winds often prevalent in the Indian Ocean; British designed Escort Carriers lacked this feature, and could only launch their planes on a free take-off or latterly using R.A.T.O.G. (Rocket Assisted Take-off Gear). With a single screw the 11,200 tons "Ruler" Class managed only 18.5 knots on their 8,500 S.H.P. steam turbines, while the catapult could launch a 16,000 lb plane at 74 knots, thus giving greater capability, but if this failed then the ship was useless in light winds, and would have to steam around searching for more favourable conditions or be withdrawn from operations.

Compared with earlier ships the U.S. Carriers were much better equipped with close range A.A. protection, and *Ameer* carried 8 twin 40mm Bofors, 4 twin and 25 single 20mm Oerlikon guns; and for surface engagement 2 single 5 inch guns mounted astern under the flight deck. These vessels lacked the armoured protection of the large British Fleet Carriers but, clearly, as they were quick and cheap to build, this was less significant, and although the armoured Fleet Carriers continued in use until the demise of the fixed wing carrier in 1978, the wartime Light Fleet Carriers and the present "Invincible" Class are also built to merchant standards and have no primary armour.

Our first carrier was in fact a lucky break for us, because just about everything aboard came with the ship from the U.S., including stores and certainly some of the food. This was served on the ubiquitous aluminium trays in a cafeteria dining space and when we hit turbulent water in the Mozambique Channel the mess tables and their contents were sent flying. The U.S. style toilets were open stalls with a trough flowing with seawater. This did not encourage moments of quiet contemplation and provided opportunities for pranksters with floating paper boats set alight to catch passing "traffic". The U.S. accommodation provided bunks so our hammocks were redundant. Instead each bunk had a mattress inside a waterproof cover, which was opened for use and secured closed over the bedding during the day. Typically American and so much more convenient, it seemed as if we Brits were determined to make our lives hard work. I shared a small 2-bunk cabin off one squadron ratings mess deck with my workmate L.A.M. (L) Hawkins. This was deep in the stern and the sea could be heard lapping the thin steel plates outside; not a lot of protection as we were later to find out. One thing we discovered was that we adapted to the constant hum of machinery and ventilation fans; the ship's chapel was one of the quietest places on the ship, but the real surprise came when for some reason the machinery was switched off and the peace and quiet was uncanny.

We arrived at Madras on 12th May and disembarked to H.M.S. *Valluru*

A Bit of a "Tiff"

at Tambaram, where we spent six hot and dusty weeks living in open sided palm thatched huts. The palm thatch was of course home to a variety of wild life as well as us. We worked tropical routine, so that after a morning's flying we ceased work in the heat of the day and returned for maintenance in the evening. Dozing on one's bunk in the afternoon invariably left the mattress totally soaked in perspiration.

A Portuguese contractor provided meals using local labour as required by the Indian Government. The meals were no great shakes, and numbers of large black crow like birds gathered outside in anticipation of rich pickings from our leavings. Our meals were supplemented by fruit, in the form of mangoes, plantains, and pineapples bought from numerous on-site vendors, and with little iced cakes bought from the Char Wallah. The pineapples were almost certainly the cause of the dysentery that sent me into Fort Madras Hospital for a few days. The walls of the Fort were many feet thick and could have taken a lot of punishment. On being discharged I had to make my own way back to camp by train, and inadvertently got into a 3rd class (Indian) compartment. This was an experience as my travelling companions carried large bundles of goods, laundry, live chickens, and of course children, but they were kind enough to redirect me once we came to the first halt.

Back at camp we travelled to and from the airfield site by lorry past paddy fields and these trips were distinctly dodgy as our drivers were recruited from within the unit and were largely self-taught. Certainly one P.O. had acquired his skill in the desert where there were no roads, and this quickly became obvious. It was here that our aircraft handler savaged the Captain's office. I have only vague memories of visiting Madras itself, however when off duty there was interest from watching the visiting tattoo artists at work; the process looked extremely unhygienic but I do not recall any serious consequences. The chiropodist (the nearest description) was another dubious visitor but also seemed to be effective. He removed boils and corns by applying suction to a hollow bone placed over the spot, and then sealing the end with a piece of well masticated wax. There was no doubt of the efficacy of this treatment; when the bone dropped off, the wound was clean and by some miracle in that climate I do not recall that there were any infections. As expected, our laundry was done by Dhobi Wallahs, usually by the time honoured method of bashing them against a rock in the local stream, it certainly saved us the effort, and the only problem arose when we were about to leave Tambaram and had to try to find the Dhobi Wallah in a hurry.

Early in our trip out we had our normal vaccination and T.A.B.T. inoculations checked, then at intervals we were paraded for the undignified "short arm" inspection. This medical inspection was a common routine during the war, and everyone was lined up, often in full view of spectators. As the M.O. walked past, we each dropped our trousers and bent over. Whether this was justified by the results I have no idea, but it seems to have been discontinued. I have only recently learned that a similar inspection was used for the women's services, presumably not for public viewing! The M.O's continued to interest themselves in our health, we carried standard water bottles, and received a daily issue of "Limers", (lime juice); the two did not however mix, as we found that the juice rapidly attacked the enamel coating of the bottle. We next came in for a series of jabs. against yellow fever, cholera and plague, and were required to wear our long sleeved shirts and trousers at night against the mosquito. Finally, after this, we started to get a daily dose of Mepacrine as a precaution against malaria. This was not simply a local need but intended to protect us in the event that, as an Assault Squadron, we should be landed during an invasion of Malaya to provide shore based air support. The result was that we gradually took on a slightly yellow shade. Another devious means of fooling the Japs?

Back to sea! We found *Ameer* anchored off shore in a fair swell, and I did not enjoy the difficult task of jumping off the lighter and carrying my steaming kit up the rope ladder. I was therefore less than pleased to be detailed, almost at once, to supervise the loading of stores over the after Port Sponson. The overhang on these after Sponsons ensured that halfway up the rope ladder we would be hanging backward at forty-five degrees. Apart from the drop itself, the surrounding water was solid with Portuguese Men of War ready to give a stinging welcome. The stores included sacks of clearly rotting potatoes and some sheets of aircraft aluminium. I was pleased when these were safely hoist aboard using the simplest of knots, "well done the matelot", and even more grateful to be clambering back over the edge of the sponson. We sailed almost at once for Trincomalee and arrived on 30th June.

The "powers that be" had decided not to wait for our designated ship *Empress* to become available and we sailed for our first operation on 3rd July. The objectives of Operation "Collie" were to attack Japanese installations on the Nicobar Islands and to provide cover for minesweeping operations in the area. The task force included our sister ship *Emperor* and the 6th Minesweeping Flotilla, commanded by Rear Admiral Patterson with the 5th Cruiser Squadron in H.M.S. *Nigeria*. We did not have a good start. Our aircraft were loaded with a single 500lb bomb under the port wing and this may have affected the handling, because one of the first to launch veered to port, hit the sea and the pilot was killed. Shortly afterwards a second plane did the same thing but the pilot regained control and landed on after the mission trailing a length of wire cable that he had picked up from the catwalk as he went over the deck edge. Our C.O. Lt.-Cdr. Norris was shot down and killed during the attack on Nancowry Harbour when he made a second strike when the defenders were already alert. Our South African Senior pilot then took temporary command. During the same attack a second pilot was also shot down, but managed to ditch his aircraft off shore and was picked up by the *Eskimo*. On 8th July Sub-Lt. Gregory was also shot down and was recovered from the sea by *Emperor's* A.S.R. Walrus. Our own Walrus did not get airborne as the tail wheel strut collapsed while it was being ranged from the hangar. No less than fifteen Hellcats had protected the Walrus during the rescue. The flight deck party were rather redundant when the Walrus landed, as it flew so slowly that it seemed unlikely to overtake the ship. Take-off was equally straightforward, and with just a few knots of wind over the deck the Walrus lifted off almost at once.

The Hellcats were a different matter, although they used free take-off whenever possible. To achieve the maximum take-off run, the planes were ranged in staggered formation as far aft as possible. Ground crews in attendance, during start up and take-off, had to take great care not to walk into the propeller of one aircraft while working on its neighbour. For a few minutes the flight deck was organised chaos while engines were started, chocks removed, wings spread, and any last minute snags cleared if possible. Prior to this the electricians were involved whenever 3 inch R.P. were loaded. The procedures called for complete insulation checks, and continuity testing of all circuits using test lamps. These were left connected to ensure that no power was present when the final connection was made to the Rockets, and this was done working from inboard to outboard to minimise risk if accidental ignition occurred. We had no accidents but it was not unknown for an unfired rocket to detach on landing and skid across the deck.

On the penultimate day of this operation an aircraft sustained flak damage to a wing, and it was decided to change the wing. Despite the spare wing being to a different modification standard the work was completed overnight and the aircraft flew the following day as part of the C.A.P. detail (Combat Air Patrol). It did not return to the ship and suffered an engine failure and ditched but the pilot was recovered safely. There was little need for routine maintenance during the short operations out of Trinco, since this could be carried out before and after the operation, but of course daily servicing and repairs were carried out as needed, and we did no night flying so we had the night to fix any snags, as long as the hangar access doors were kept closed. In fact it was pleasant at the end of a night's work to stand on the darkened sponsons in the balmy air and watch the phosphorescent water rustle past. My recollection is of a short few days of intense activity before we returned to base. We did receive some brief details of these operations from our Captain, but really very little on the results and on the whole the official news statements printed at home and in the local press were just as informative. I still have a number of cuttings to prove it, but we did hear that a Japanese "Dinah" twin-engine reconnaissance plane had been shot down. In the course of the six day operation we had flown 82 sorties and 142 flying hours but had lost two pilots killed and six aircraft; three to enemy action. We returned to Trinco. on 13th July and transferred to *Empress* on 14th.

We now had a new C.O. Lt.-Cdr. Zegers de Beyl R.N.N. (more accurately Ltz Zegers de Beijil) and replaced our lost planes but it seems that the number was now reduced to eighteen, which included two F.R.Mk II. The F.R. versions had a highly wax-polished finish and carried F.24 Reconnaissance Cameras; for some odd reason they also carried British batteries. The cameras became my baby simply because nobody else had been trained on them, but not before the C.O. had created mayhem by taking one from its hangar side stowage, claiming it was lost, and then mounting a search. This seemed to be part of his idea to instil some sort of control, but it did not impress.

On 19th July we left for our second operation (Operation Livery). Attacks were planned on Phuket Island and on N.Malaya and Siam. Once again these attacks were being conducted in co-operation with minesweeping in the entrance to the Malacca Straits, anticipating eventual landings on the way to Singapore. The minesweeper *Squirrel* hit a mine and had to be sunk by our own ships during this period, and it was a little disconcerting to see a mine floating past us. I believe it was sunk by small arms fire but did not explode. The squadron had better luck and only lost one pilot at Dhung Song in Siam but had lost a pilot in China Bay before we left Trinco. On this three day operation the squadron flew 86 sorties and the Japanese attacked the fleet without success. Two planes were shot down by a cruiser, 1 got away, and a "Sonia" single engine Army light bomber attempted a "kamikaze" attack on *Ameer*, and was shot into the sea. The Gunnery Officer of *Ameer* was Lt. Blamire-Brown who lived only a short way from my parents in Bearsted and he was well pleased. Typically, during this action I was in the hangar with other ground crew, we were aware of the guns but of little else until it was all over, so I can say that I have never seen a gun fired in anger. We heard later that, during this action, the crew of one cruiser were so afflicted with dysentery that the gun crews had operated with "Loo" buckets in their turrets. In retrospect it seems unusual that we never wore protective clothing or anti flash gear, and ground crew spent all their working day in khaki shorts but usually with our inflatable lifebelt and red light tied to our waist. Nor were we trained in any sort of damage control procedure so it was fortunate that we never had a serious incident.

One feature of the intense heat was that our sweaty bodies had little electrical resistance and we found that changing a battery in the rear fuselage could give a mighty "belt" to the unwary; a normally closed circuit discharged via the terminals as they were disconnected. It was difficult to sleep below due to the sticky heat, and although the regular ship's company seemed to manage, quite a few squadron people and I used to lift our bunk mattress with its cover and take it to the flight deck and sleep under an aircraft wing. This worked very well until one night when it started to rain; I then closed up the top and bottom covers and sides until I was cocooned. Unfortunately this was a very heavy and prolonged tropical storm and when water finally crept inside I was forced to evacuate and take the bedding into a space by the funnel casing where the stifling heat dried it out quickly. Another result of the heat was the excessive consumption of fresh water, and because the ship's plant was unable to keep pace with usage it was necessary to ration it by turning on the bathroom supplies for limited periods each day. By this time many of us suffered from "prickly heat", and relief required the afflicted to bath as often as possible using one of two proprietary brands of mercury-based soap. Accordingly we used to make a dash for a quick shower or wash down as soon as the water was on. On one such occasion my haste led to a minor accident.

One problem that had dogged my time since joining up was that washbasins always seemed to lose their plug but the U.S. Navy neatly resolved this by hinging each simple stainless steel basin a little aft of its centre line. Waste disposal was then simply a matter of tilting the basin. This was my undoing, when washing one foot it slipped and tilted the basin. A quick hop back to recover and the basin snapped back on to part of my hanging appendage. I retreated to Sick Bay hanging on to my bleeding anatomy. It was heavily dusted with sulphanilamide powder since a bandage was impractical. I am happy report that all systems are still working at seventy-seven.

We had our share of incidents on the flight deck. On one occasion, four new Hellcats were due to join as replacements as we left Trinco. The first to approach was "waved off" and returned to the circuit when the other three had landed and had been ranged forward. On this approach the aircraft was too high but the pilot failed to respond to the batsman's signals. He eventually cut his engine while still too high to catch a wire, sailed well over the barrier and landed on top of the other three new aircraft. These planes were off-loaded ashore and the new Midshipman pilot followed. It was said that he had been trained in the U.S. and that the U.S. signals were the reverse of our own. I have now been able to confirm this as a fact. British signals were only changed to enable our aircraft to cross operate with the U.S. carriers in the Pacific, and thereafter the batsman directed the pilot, rather than indicated his position on the approach path. There is no doubt that deck landing a large radial engine aircraft like the Hellcat was difficult due to the poor view past the aircraft nose, and landing accidents were common. I discovered a very interesting signal while reading the squadron diary, and it well illustrates the problem of landing accidents and is reproduced as follows: –

Accidents for the Light Carrier Force – July 1945

Decklanding	91.06 %
In flight	5.36 %
Take off	1.79 %
Misc.	1.70 %

A total of 56 accidents were involved, of these 27 were Hellcats, 25 were Seafires, 1 Corsair, 1 Swordfish and one Walrus. The breakdown for each Carrier was as follows : –

Ship	Accidents	Deck landings	% of D.L's
Attacker	14	36	39
Begum	12	101	12
Ameer	9	211	4.3
Hunter	4	47	8.5
Emperor	4	94	4
Khedive	3	132	2.5
Empress	3	153	2
Stalker	3	53	5.6
Shah	3	133	2.5
Pursuer	1	7	14

A rather more serious incident was avoided by pure luck when an Armourer fired a gun of a Hellcat on the flight deck. The wings were folded and the rounds passed through the wood and steel flight deck, through the fin and tailplane of an aircraft in the hangar and through the steel hangar deck into the wardroom. This was proof enough of the power

A Bit of a "Tiff"

of a .5 inch bullet and of the vulnerability of our ship. Fortunately fragments of cupro-nickel casing caused the only minor injuries. When the incident occurred I was just entering the hangar, a few feet from the event. Quite a surprise!

My luck held on another incident. During flying the ground crews had little to do unless another sortie was planned prior to the return of an earlier mission. Normally during this time we would wait forward of the Island by a collection of chocks and trolley accs. ready to pounce on returning planes as they landed and were taxied to park forward of the crash barriers. The pilots were then quizzed as to any defects or repairs needed. One day a Hellcat came in slightly low, the deck-hook hit the round-down, snapped off and the aircraft continued at speed toward the barrier and us ground crew. At this point, evacuation seemed to be in order and I found unexpected agility by leaping clear over the assembled obstacles and into the starboard forward catwalk. At least that was the general subconscious idea; in fact I landed well below the flight deck in a Bofors gun sponson without hitting anything on the way; it could so easily have been straight over the side! The Hellcat ended up on its nose but the pilot was uninjured.

Toward the end of this operation we had ranged one Hellcat fitted with a belly mounted drop tank when, about to take off, the sortie was changed and Cdr. (Air) ordered the removal of the tank over the tannoy from the bridge. This was not straightforward and the calls from the bridge got increasingly irate, "get that bloody tank off". So I gave the order to jettison and it fell to the deck without splitting or leaking. Naturally this caused more panic from on high. As it happened Cdr. (Air) admitted his error. The tank could have been jettisoned after take-off!

Japanese reports of this operation claimed that an attempt to land on Phuket Island was repulsed. Although such a landing would have been inline with earlier landings on the approaches to Singapore it was denied. Post war this has been the subject of controversy and I do not know the truth of the report.

We returned to Trinco. on 30th July and were lucky to get a three day break at the Kinniya Beach Rest Camp. This was reached by landing craft out of Trinco harbour, and the camp was simply a collection of palm-thatched huts set just behind the beach amid coconut palms. We carted all our food rations with us, and a supply of rum for those entitled. Our main meals were half a tin per person of either M&V stew (meat and vegetable) or meat pudding with veg. Despite the heat this typically British food was very good. In effect, this was an extended seaside picnic and we lazed, swam frequently without any serious thought of sharks, or ventured beyond the camp to a muddy creek where there were mudfish and hermit crabs. A little further on was a small Singhalese village of thatched huts, and where the rapid disappearance of women and children showed that visitors were not welcome. We took the hint and left them to their simple existence. Fishermen, probably from the village, used to haul their large net ashore by heaving from both ends until at last a seething pile of fish rolled on to the beach. No doubt some of this would be dried and contribute to the strong aromas always present in the area.

On 9th August we again sailed from Trincomalee for another large air operation in the Malacca Straits but six days after we left we were back again on 15th August V.J. Day without firing a shot. The Fleet celebrated in traditional style by "splicing the main brace", and after dark Trincomalee Harbour was lit up by vast quantities of ready use pyrotechnics. The American Atomic bombs had stopped our war before the really serious task of invading Malaya could start. The scene had already been set by the recent operations and an enormous task force was ready to go. So quick as a flash it was all over, but what was next?

Chapter 6 896 Squadron
Part 3 "Oh, what a luvverly war"!

With the war over, it was a time for reflection. The vast majority of both squadron and ship's company were H.O.'s (Hostilities Only) and looked forward to Demob. at the earliest opportunity. The release dates of some categories had been published since V.E. Day, so for them it was only a matter of time. For the few Regulars like myself, the future promised some change, and I had still another ten years to serve. I was personally pleased that I had at least seen some operational service, however small my contribution. It was very clear what an easy ride we had had when we met some Australian troops back from the front line. In due course our squadron members became entitled to the Burma Star and my pride in wearing it is tempered by unease at the inequality of these awards.

On 25th August I was promoted Acting P.O. Air Fitter (L) backdated to 1st July, and my arrival in front of the Captain's table was somewhat precipitous, as the linoleum had been buffed to the equivalent of a skating rink. The delay was caused by objections raised by the two P.O.A.M.(L)'s who were my superiors in the absence of a qualified Electrical Officer. This was partly pride because, although they had much longer service and experience they lacked the technical knowledge of an ex-Apprentice and this would lower their status. However I can see in retrospect how my evident youth and immaturity would have annoyed them. After the event they accepted the change with good grace. Finally in November I was rated Acting Air Artificer 4th Class (L) backdated to 1st July so I had lost nothing.

As always, it appeared that life was in future to be a question of swings and roundabouts. On a squadron you would always be on the move and see interesting places but would be hard pushed to study and advance for promotion. Ashore in a workshop, life would be more stable with better opportunities for technical experience and study, hopefully with qualified engineers in the wings. With another ten years these distinctions were important, as were the anticipated re-introduction of pre-war "Bull" routines. While I had no option but to grin and bear it, the future seemed very unclear and the joy felt by the H.O.'s in leaving was very unsettling indeed. Jolly Jack had of course an old ditty to cover the general feeling at that time, it was based upon and sung to the tune of a well known hymn *This is my story this is my song* and the first verse went :-

"This is my story, this is my song,
I've been in the Navy too blooming long,
Roll on the *Nelson, Rodney, Renown,*
This whole bloody issue is getting me down"

During my time on the squadron I received mail from home very regularly by the various means then available, including air letters, airgraphs (microfilm), and cryptic cables in which a choice was made of a series of numbers each representing selected phrases of a message. In addition I received printed material, which I now find fascinating, including the V.E. and V.J. Day editions of the *Daily Mail;* both a single folded sheet of just four pages. From these it was apparent that, although we had won the war, life in U.K. was in a desperate state of shortage. In South Africa, India, and Ceylon there was little evidence of hardship among the white population and we servicemen, for all our moans, were well looked after by comparison. As far as possible I sent parcels home, mainly of food, but once I actually sent 3 yds. of knicker elastic and some hairpins. In many cases the goods I sent had been produced in U.K. but still the rations were cut, austerity got worse and my mother sounded in despair.

One way and another from letters and from contact with people from other ships and stations, it seemed that the war had absorbed all the people I had known from school, both pupils and masters, family friends and contacts, and thrown them into the Navy. Very many of them including ex-apprentice chums were now in S.E.A.C. This was evidence of our total commitment to winning the war but how could our life return to normal?

The first priority was the re-occupation of Singapore and Malaya. Operation Zipper was launched with this objective and we set out on 1st September in company with a vast fleet which included the Battleships *Queen Elizabeth, Renown* and the French *Richelieu,* together with five other Escort Carriers; *Khedive, Ameer, Emperor, Hunter, and Stalker.* We were on our way into the Malacca Straits when our catapult broke down and we returned to Trinco on 12th Sept. From then on life was very relaxed, there was little flying and the personal workload was limited as we now had four P.O. Electricians on the Squadron. Almost at once we spent another three days at Kinniya Beach and then sailed to Cochin where the ship was to receive a boiler clean. Prior to this, part of the Squadron had gone to Puttalum in N.W. Ceylon and carried on flying in what were virtually jungle conditions, but I missed that one.

Before we left Trinco I bought a few souvenirs for my family. This included a "sapphire" pendant for my sister. The bargaining required was then, and still is, alien to my nature and when I closed the deal the shopkeeper was so obviously pleased with himself that I concluded that I had been diddled. In the event, it pleased my sister, looked attractive and probably was a bargain. I also attended a concert put on by E.N.S.A. at the Fleet Club, There were a lot of rousing songs including Kipling's *Mandalay*, and the cast had several Anglo-Indian girls who were remarkably attractive, as were some of the nurses at Madras Fort Hospital. For some reason the only liquid refreshment was a local beer. At that time I did not find any interest in alcohol, but, without the option, I found the taste of liquorice in that sample not enough to change my mind. It was in the event pretty innocuous stuff and did not enliven our return to the ship, which was achieved by a tatty wooden landing craft, which picked up returning sailors from "Mustard Pot" jetty and chugged around the fleet at anchor. Censorship had now ceased and there was a little more to write home about but in fact we had had so little information given to us that could have helped the Japs that it had never been a problem in sticking to the rules. On 30th Sept. the Mepacrine issue ceased, our yellow colouring started to disappear and medical interest in our well-being relaxed. We all ate our Emergency Rations; a block of hard coarse chocolate sealed into a flat tin.

At Cochin we had more leave but this time at the hill station of Wellington in the Nilgiri Hills. It was one of four cool summer retreats for the pre-war Army garrisons, the others were Conoor, Ootacamund (Ooty), and Kotagiri. We were accommodated in Wellington Barracks, which had been built in colonial style with wide verandahs in front of the barrack rooms. Although still hot, it was certainly cooler than in the plains at the Naval Air Station at Coimbatore where we had stopped for fuel on the way to Wellington. The bus ride was an experience in itself as we climbed numerous hairpin bends on a road scratched into the hillside, and hoped fervently that oncoming native drivers would obey the local rules of the road and stop for up-going traffic. Although the journey from Cochin was only 190 miles, it seemed much longer and we were none too relaxed about the driving skills of our Indian driver. Wellington was at 5,500 ft. somewhat high by British standards and access to the other hill stations was by bus, or for the more energetic by cycle. One was well rewarded in cycling to Ooty; it involved a ten mile walk uphill for a further 2,000ft. and then a quick two mile glide into town. In reverse the ten mile freewheel into Wellington was exhilarating and a cycle was easily able to overtake motorised transport, which was less able to negotiate the bends. A visit to Conoor and its attractive botanical gardens and wildlife including a glorious 4 inch span Emperor Moth was somewhat diminished by the dreaded Delhi Belly which caused a dash into the roadside bushes en route and a visit to a hole in the ground toilet on the golf course. Our return trip to Cochin was by train; at first this was on a small train using a cogged centre wheel on the steep gradient, and then on to Cochin overnight in carriages with hard wooden seats and a lot of very large cockroaches for company. One of these, or its chum, was still alive in my kit when I arrived home in December.

While still in Cochin, I had to take a Hellcat propeller from the ship to the Naval Air Station. A party of lads loaded it on to a flat top lorry and we drove through Cochin with the 13 ft. propeller overlapping both sides of the lorry. On the way we passed a junction manned by a red turbaned traffic policeman, who ignored our yells warning him of his imminent execution until the very last moment. Jolly Jack was delighted! At the airfield were a number of ex Apprentices, one of whom, "Tich" Habens of 2nd Benbow showed me a captured "Zeke" (the dreaded Japanese Mitsubishi Zero fighter), which was being prepared for flight. A number of its technical features were of interest, including a convenient way of removing the radial engine cowling, the laminated rubber solid tail wheel and a very thin wing skin, which was riveted into flats milled into the edges of the main spar. After the massive build up of aircraft and equipment in the S.E. Asia theatre, it now seemed that the main activity at Cochin immediately after V.J. Day was the disposal of the planes stockpiled there by dumping them out at sea. Not only the U.S. Lease–Lend planes but many Barracudas. Only a few weeks earlier we had been off loading our damaged planes for repair, and had never ditched any overboard on any pretext. During some flying from Cochin another squadron pilot was severely injured with a cracked spine. In the space of ten months we had lost four pilots killed, another three had back injuries and we had lost or severely damaged at least fifteen Hellcats. This was quite a price for such a short period of activity.

When the ship's boilers had been completed we returned to Colombo on the 13th October and the squadron was based ashore at H.M.S. *Ukussa* at Katukurunda. I have recently reread the Summer 1945 number of "Two-Six" the local magazine and discovered the source of both names. Ukussa is a small species of Himalayan eagle and forms part of centuries old Indian legend; Katakurunda derives from two words, "Katus" means thorny and "Kurunda" are Cinnamons thus the thorny cinnamon which once grew in the area. A further gem tells me and those colleagues who served at Ratmalana that it derives from Rathe-mal-rallwa i.e. "The Jungle of Red Flowers". No doubt all the other strange place names that we encountered had descriptive titles that would have made our fleeting visit more interesting had we but known.

Our C.O. had already returned to duty with the R.N.N. and we had no fewer than three replacements in post before we disbanded. At "Kat" we saw the start of a return to peacetime "bull". This included having Sunday Divisions in scorching heat complete with boots, short gaiters, and footless woollen stockings to fill the gap below the knee. It was fortunate that because our Hostility Only ratings had no "whites" we were permitted to continue to wear "khaki". Many of us had earlier bought extra kit from local tailors due to the difficulty of keeping our khaki laundered. Not all of these were to the Naval standard and one of my extra shorts had very wide short legs, which, were cool and comfortable but decidedly not modest and, could not be worn safely in mixed company. The local "cobbler" did a trade in "brothel creepers", quite comfortable to wear but the untanned suede leather had a tendency to stretch, and the "crepe" rubber soles were similarly cut straight from raw rubber sheet and became tacky.

The P.O.'s billets at "Kat" were as usual open-sided palm thatched huts and each bunk had a mosquito net. The huts were on a hill overlooking a flat space in front of a wooded hill occupied by "Gibbons". These remained at a distance, but one night something hurtled through our hut with a blood-curdling scream. There was much speculation after the event, but none of us left our bunks to find out until all was quiet. We assumed that it was a gibbon but the visit was never repeated. The toilets were of the deep-drop bucket variety, and a late night visit was considered a little dodgy in view of the proliferation of creeping, crawling, and biting wildlife. Our evening meal was another experience, and because of the ramshackle electrical system, it was rare that we ate without a power failure. The pattern to the meal was then: - "lights on" with myriads of moths and other flying insects clustering around the lights, dying, and falling into our meal, followed by "lights off" and trying to eat the meal while avoiding the earlier casualties, a pattern repeated several times a night. A slight compensation arose from the presence of glow-worms, which were plentiful as we walked through the camp after dark.

At the airfield one day we found that some enterprising overnight visitors had placed all our trolley accs. on chocks, and removed the tyres and wheels, presumably for the local black market. Considering the open site and the lack of security, this was the only problem we encountered. Quite a few local staff was employed on the station, including the battery room, but were not considered up to much by the British people who worked with them. Deck hockey was the one sport that could be played aboard when the flight deck was free and our Squadron team included Sammy Roe, a P.O. Armourer, notorious for his aggressive style. His tactic was to charge head down thrashing his stick, but eventually he got his come-uppance and the opposition put him into sickbay with a broken bone. We expected good results when our team played a local Singhalese side at hockey but were surprised by the performance of the bare footed players.

For the majority of us youngsters being abroad for the first time had been a confusing as well as an exciting experience. We carried with us notions of fair play and British justice and memories of the third of the world coloured red on our school atlases. From the moment we stepped ashore at Port Said the poverty, squalor and servility of the native populations seemed to support ingrained ideas of our superiority. So we accepted the sight of crowds being controlled by local policemen with "lathis", and reports of political unrest as further indication of the low standards endemic in these places. The immaculate uniform and military bearing of the Indian Sergeant running one of our messes might have served as a clue that we were mistaken, and we conveniently forgot the key roles played by the local armed forces in winning the war. For these reasons we did not appreciate that we were witnessing the first steps in dismantling the Empire that we had failed to protect.

The more relaxed routine gave us opportunities to visit Colombo; where still in search of enlightenment I purchased *Electrical Engineering* by Cotton at the princely sum of 15rs. There were still canteens in operation, and I spent an afternoon at a swimming bath linked with a Church of Scotland canteen. They served a delightful coconut pie; I've still to find the recipe. Reports from chums at Wingfield said that the canteens in South Africa were beginning to close. It rather looked as if we were no longer wanted.

Early in November our aircraft were flown away for disposal and we were again jobless. We were then given leave at the hill station of Diyatalawa in Ceylon. Here we saw tea plantations, visited a rubber plantation, and visited the Diyaluma Falls. At 628ft this was the highest in Ceylon and reputedly the sixth highest in the world. An odd feature of the local climate was that it rained every afternoon without fail, but mornings and evenings were clear and bright. It was beginning to be clear how one lived in the pre-war "Raj", an idyllic existence for the chosen few.

Returning to Colombo we immediately rejoined *Empress* and our return voyage started three days later on 26th November. First call was to Bombay, past the "Gates of India" and a quick trip ashore. Here apart from the poverty, beggars, and crowds, there were shoeshine boys. Stop at one of these and, in no time flat, other service providers would home in, including gentlemen willing to remove the wax from your ears. How we managed to do without these services I'll never know. Yes, I did see snake charmers in India, but never the Indian Rope Trick!

We sailed to Aden, from Bombay and then on to Suez. We passed through on a Sunday morning and obviously attended divisions on the flight deck, but not in "khaki" uniform. We had officially entered the temperate zone, and as it was now winter in U.K. we had to wear our blue serge suits. Never mind the heat, those were the rules. Once again I wondered what had prompted me to join such a daft outfit. We continued from Port Said to Malta and then Gibraltar. We did not have shore leave at any port after Bombay, but at Gibraltar were able to acquire some bananas to take home. Our arrival at grubby and cold Glasgow, on 19th December, did not diminish our joy at getting home for Christmas, and we dispersed as a unit at that point and went on leave.

Empress like the other Lease Lend Carriers was quickly returned to the U.S. and most of these were eventually sold to commercial operators and ended their days as cargo ships, which after all was the basis of their design. During a visit to the U.S. in 1959 I saw a number of escort carriers still berthed at the Boston Navy Yard awaiting their fate.

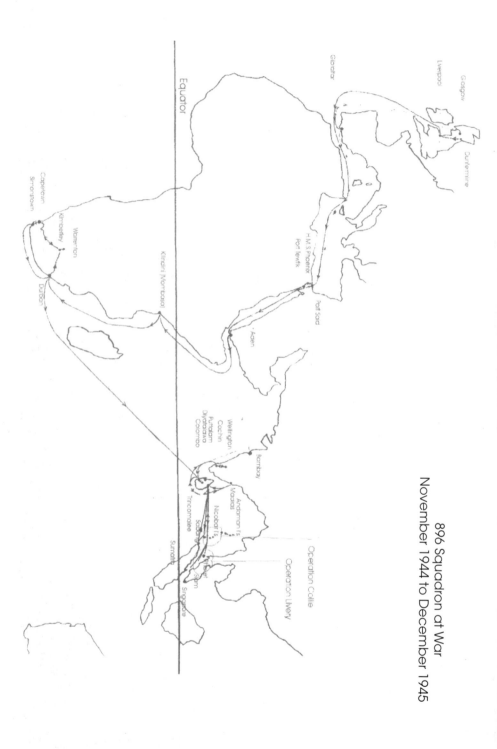

896 Squadron at War
November 1944 to December 1945

A Bit of a "Tiff"

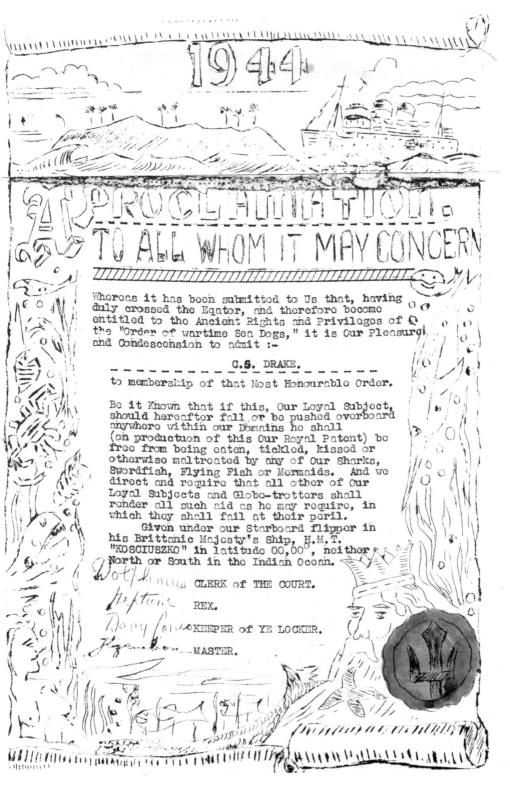

1944

PROCLAMATION.
TO ALL WHOM IT MAY CONCERN

Whereas it has been submitted to Us that, having duly crossed the Eqator, and therefore become entitled to the Ancient Rights and Privileges of the "Order of wartime Sea Dogs," it is Our Pleasure and Condescension to admit :-

-------- C.S. DRAKE. --------

to membership of that Most Honourable Order.

Be it Known that if this, Our Loyal Subject, should hereafter fall or be pushed overboard anywhere within our Domains he shall (on production of this Our Royal Patent) be free from being eaten, tickled, kissed or otherwise maltreated by any of Our Sharks, Swordfish, Flying Fish or Mermaids. And we direct and require that all other of Our Loyal Subjects and Globe-trotters shall render all such aid as he may require, in which they shall fail at their peril.

Given under our Starboard flipper in his Brittanic Majesty's Ship, H.M.T. "KOSCIUSZKO" in latitude 00,00°, neither North or South in the Indian Ocean.

CLERK of THE COURT.

REX.

KEEPER of YE LOCKER.

MASTER.

Admiralty House Port Said 1944. Author's collection.

Surrendered Italian Battleship Bitter Lakes Suez Canal 1944.
Author's collection.

A Bit of a "Tiff"

Crossing the line - H.M.T. Kosciuszko 20/21st December 1944.
Author's collection.

896 Squadron Maintenance Unit - Wingfield, Capetown March
1945. Author 2nd from right front row. Author's collection.

A Bit of a "Tiff"

896 Squadron hardstanding - Wingfield March 1945. Table
Mountain the background. Author's collection.

Wingfield March 1945. Author's collection.

A Bit of a "Tiff"

896 Squadron Hellcat Wingfield March 1945. Author's collection.

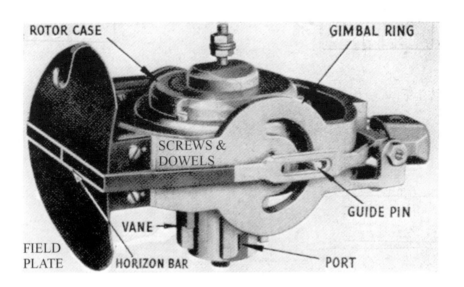

ROTOR CASE   GIMBAL RING

SCREWS & DOWELS

GUIDE PIN

FIELD PLATE   VANE   HORIZON BAR   PORT

Sperry Artificial Horizon minus outer case - Author's notes.

A bungee start! "Jenkins you're supposed to let go
when the engine starts!"

Table Bay from Table Mountain - March 1945.

A Bit of a "Tiff"

"Up homers!" - Archie Pitt and Joe Mutter of 2nd Rodney
Capetown 1945.

896 Squadron party on leave at the Duggan-Cronin Bantu
Gallery in Kimberley. March 1945. Author's collection.

So it's true, they really can jump six feet!

Fireships!

A Bit of a "Tiff"

H.M.S. *Ameer.* Author's collection.

H.M.S. *Ameer* leaving Trincomalee for Operation "Collie".
July 1945. Author's collection.

H.M.S. *Emperor* from *Ameer* during Operation "Collie". July 1945.
Author's collection.

Free take-off H.M.S. *Ameer*. July 1945. Author's collection.

A Bit of a "Tiff"

Landing on. Author's collection.

Emperor's Walrus rescues Sub.-Lt. Gregory. July 1945.
Author's collection.

A very free take-off. *Emperor's* Walrus returns after the rescue.
Author's collection.

Ameer refuels the planeguard destroyer July 1945. Author's
collection.

A Bit of a "Tiff"

H.M.S. *Empress.* Author's collection.

Captain of *Empress* addressing the ship's company before
Operation Livery. July 1945. Author's collection.

One of our Squadron pilots with Cpl. Oxley, and an Armourer with 3" R.P's. H.M.S. *Empress*. July 1945. Author's collection.

Barrier prang. This one had the broken deck hook, *Empress*. July 1945. Author's collection.

Returned u/s. Another repair job at Trinco. Author's collection.

VJ Day group on *Empress*. Captain centre, C.O. 896 second from right. Author's collection.

896 Squadron group on VJ Day with our C.O. Author's collection.

VJ Day fireworks in Trinco Harbour. Author's Collection.

A Bit of a "Tiff"

VJ Day fireworks in Trinco Harbour. Author's collection.

H.M.S. *Nelson* lit up on VJ Day. Author's collection.

Accommodation at the Kinniya beach rest camp August 1945.

Part of 896 Squadron went to Puttalam September 1945.
Author's collection.

A Bit of a "Tiff"

We missed the Japanese surrender at Singapore.
Author's collection.

May 9th 1945 - VE Day

May 11th 1945 - Kent celebrates VE Day.

A Bit of a "Tiff"

SUNDAY SEAC

No. 551   One Anna.
SUNDAY, 15 JULY, 1945.
Printed by Courtesy of
THE STATESMAN in Calcutta.

STARS CUT 'GO-TO-BURMA' PLEA: AIR PRIORITY OFFER

LONDON, Sat.—Lady Leese, wife of Lt-Gen Sir Oliver Leese, Commander, ALFSEA, who wrote an "Open Letter" in the Daily Mail to stage stars appealing to them to entertain troops in Burma, said today: "Although topline stars are wanted desperately by Far East troops, none of them has answered my appeal by writing to me.

She added: "I have received offers from quite a few lesser-known entertainers and these have been passed on to ENSA, so that arrangements can be made for them to entertain the troops.

Lady Louis Mountbatten, wife of the Supreme Commander, S.E. Asia, said: "Troops in S.E.A.C. feel that if they get headline names of radio, stage and screen, they are being treated equally with troops in other theatres.

"They are appreciative of what they are getting, but they want to see famous people of the entertainment world."

Many Promises

Lady Louis, wife of Lt-Gen Sir William Slim, 14th Army Commander, said: "If topline stars went to India and Burma they would be appreciated by the troops who would feel their efforts at winning the war were being appreciated in turn.

"Many promises have been

SIGN OF THE TIMES—A German prisoner paints over RAF markings on a FW190 fighter—one of many fighters and bombers taken at Vaerlose, Copenhagen, after the German surrender.

Good Morning . . .

When the time comes to say "thank you" to civilians for the aid they gave in the defence of India and the liberation of Burma, somebody should remember the tea-planters.

Back at home one of the illusions of fiction-writers is that of the "whisky-swilling planter." This ignores the local difficulty of getting hold of enough of the stuff to swill with; it is also possible that the label arises as from one-nonsense.

Out here many a soldier who served on the Assam-Burma frontier will recall the hospitality of planters who shared their rationed "swill."

And will praise the unselfish work of the planters' wives and daughters who worked in hospitals and canteens to make the soldier's lot a little easier.

Here, we tell another story of the tea-planters—how they built the military roads and airfields which served the front. But for their loyal and undagging effort the front

U.S. NAVY BOMBARDS JAP PORT

GUAM, Sat.—Kamaishi, a port on the east coast of Honshu, a previously unattacked part of the Jap home islands and only 275 miles NE of Tokyo, was battered today by big ships of Admiral Halsey's Third Pacific Fleet.

The ships bombarding include the battleships Indiana, South Dakota and Massachusetts; the heavy cruisers Chicago and Quincy and the destroyers Southerland, Herrman, Erben and Black.

Admiral Chester Nimitz in an earlier communiqué issued from U.S. Pacific Fleet HQ says

NAVY SHIPS, PLANES STRIKE NICOBARS

NAVY SHIPS, PLANES STRIKE NICOBARS

HQ S.E.A.C., KANDY, Sat.—A special naval communiqué dated 13 July says:—During sustained minesweeping operations between 5 July and 10 July in the approaches to the Malacca Straits, ships of the British East Indies Fleet were undisturbed by the enemy.

Combined air attacks and bombardment were also carried out by units of the Fleet against radar installations, airfields and shore batteries on islands in the Nicobar Group, and our carrier-borne aircraft attacked airfields in north-west Sumatra.

The forces, commanded by Rear Admiral W. R. Patterson, C.B., C.V.O., Rear Admiral Commanding the Fifth Cruiser Squadron flying his flag in the cruiser HMS Nigeria, also included the Sixth Minesweeping Flotilla, the aircraft carriers HMS Ameer and Emperor and the destroyer HMS Roebuck.

The first air attack was directed against Car Nicobar and set fire to radar installations on the island. All craft in the area were rendered unseaworthy.

Heavy Flak

Our aircraft were met by heavy flak; and rescue ships and a naval air-sea rescue Walrus aircraft which had to approach close inshore to recover pilots who had been shot down were engaged by ineffective machine-gun fire.

A bombardment and air attack on 7 July against Nan Cowry, another island of the Nicobar Group, were carried out in heavy rain squalls.

Fires and explosions in a camp were observed and two coasters were left on fire.

Two airfields at Kutaraja and Lhonga in NW Sumatra were attacked on 11 July by Hellcats.

One Japanese aircraft was shot down by our pilots returning to the carriers. Only one of our pilots is missing from all these operations.

None of our ships sustained damage or casualties.

'NEW INDIA' PLAN FAILS

SIMLA, Sat.—The official announcement of the failure of the Indian leaders' conference was made by Lord Wavell, the Viceroy, today when he said that the failure was his.

The Viceroy said he had previously adjourned the conference so that agreement might be reached on the composition of the interim Government. All parties had sent their lists for the choice of personnel except the European group and the Muslim League. Mr Jinnah, of the Muslim League, did not agree to the proposal to send a list.

No new move for the solution of the political deadlock was possible at the moment, he added, and as representatives of the various political parties could not be secured for the interim Government, the present arrangement would continue.—API.

CQMS MOGGS MAKES IT CLEAR

LONDON, Sat.—CQMS N. Moggs of Nottingham, who had been expected to stand as an independent candidate for Central

OKINAWA JAPS

Operation "Collie" reported on July 15th.

Navy little ships close in to sniper range

JAP ISLES SMASHED

From **NOEL MONKS**, Daily Mail Special Correspondent

Aboard H.M.S. Ameer, Off Sumatra, Thursday (delayed).

OPERATING nearly 1,000 miles from their base in Ceylon, minesweepers of the British East Indies Fleet have just carried out one of the most audacious minesweeping jobs of the war.

Right under the noses of the Japs, our sturdy minesweepers have cleared passages off the Nicobar Islands, working at times within a few miles of the gleaming white beaches, and never out of sight of the Japs.

They located and destroyed scores of mines without a shot being fired at them, though Jap snipers lying in the jungle that fringes the beaches could have picked off members of the sweepers' crews.

While the sweepers were at work our small task force, including the cruiser Nigeria, the escort carriers Ameer and Emperor, and the destroyer Roebuck, did much to sting the Japs into some sort of retaliatory action, but without result.

The ships raked the islands with broadsides at almost point-blank range and our naval pilots bombed and strafed airstrips and buildings every day, but the only enemy reaction was from light A.A. guns.

For days our task force has not been out of sight of Jap-held land, and Tokio radio has been putting out hourly bulletins about us, elevating the minesweepers to cruisers and the other ships to battleships.

One plane

As a parting gesture, when the minesweepers' work was done, we steamed down here yesterday towards the Malacca Straits and sent off the Hellcats to strike at Jap airfields at Kotaraja and Lhonga, on the northern tip of Sumatra.

Our first attack on Car Nicobar took the Japs completely by surprise and it was not until our pilots were making their third runs on their targets—radar stations and airstrips—that the Japs managed to get a few A.A. guns shooting.

Carriers were sent off on further strikes next morning while we all stood at action stations again. We were so close inshore now that I could see the Hellcats diving on their targets. All this time we could hear Japs gibbering on their radio to Tokio.

Easily the most thrilling moments of our sortie have been concerned with the rescue of pilots who baled out or "ditched" their aircraft in the sea. Three of our pilots were literally snatched from the Japs as they drifted shorewards.

Sub-Lieut. G. Gregory, of Blackpool, was hit by flak on his first operation, and skimming over the tops of trees pancaked his Hellcat on the mirror-like sea barely 10 yards from the beach

The alarm was immediately signalled throughout the Task Force, and everything was concentrated on the pilot's rescue.

Gregory, a powerfully built youth of 20, started swimming out against a strong inshore current, while the rest of his flight ranged up and down the beach at 50ft. with guns blazing to discourage Jap snipers.

The water was too shallow for any of our ships to go in to pick up Gregory, who was losing his fight against the current after half an hour's heroic struggle. A Walrus, the oldest operational aircraft in the British service, waddled off the carrier Emperor like a lame duck and headed for shore. She was escorted by 15 Hellcats

"I think every man in the Task Force said a little prayer. Then came a report that the Walrus was landing near the beach. Our thoughts this time were with the gallant Walrus pilot, making himself a sure target.

Tensely we waited nearly ten minutes for the next report, and when it came we cheered : " Walrus has picked up pilot."

part of the Grenadier Guards during Thursday's ceremony at the Brandenburg Gate, Berlin.

10,000 JAP TROOPS IN BIG TRAP

On Sittang Front, Friday.

THIS roadless, jungle-bound country may be the scene of the greatest single slaughter of the Burma war within the next few days.

Thousands of Japanese, rotting in the relentless rain west of the Mandalay-Rangoon corridor, have orders to get across the swollen Sittang at all costs before the end of the month.

A general to-day put the Japanese force at 10,000.

They have no lines of communication, no supply, no medical kit. Their arms are going rusty from lack of rifle oil, their dead are propped up in waterlogged ditches.

The "hospital" labels are round their necks, their stiff fingers clutch quinine. It came too late to beat the malaria that is killing more Japanese than our shells and bullets.

They have to use scrub and roots for food, bullocks and buffaloes for transport. When they have no animals they turn their own men and the Burmese into beasts of burden.

There is a feeling up here that every water-logged village that a show-down is imminent.

Avoiding battle

The commander of the Japanese remnants strung out along the foot-hills of Pegu Yomas is not likely to accept a battle challenge.

His divisional command has not entirely lost cohesion and co-ordination, but it would be most difficult to assemble a strong striking force with the hope of tearing a gap in the Allied line.

"Put your fingers in your ears while we're passing the bus garage, pet—mummy wants to say a few words about unofficial strikes." —by Neb.

Surprises for 'Big Two'

From COL. 1. PAGE ONE

the United Nations' World Organisation Charter, and the Bretton Woods monetary agreements.

The President will produce these as proof of his good will.

The question to be thrashed out with Mr. Churchill is how the explosive balance of power can be settled between the Eastern and Western Continent. The Russians are creating a cohesive bloc.

According to State department opinion, Britain wants to counter this with a tight Western bloc with France as the key nation.

6,000-Mile airline to Jap war

A FLEET of nearly 300 transport planes will be in regular use by R.A.F. Transport Command in the autumn on their great "air lifeline" between the United Kingdom and India.

It is one of Britain's biggest air transport undertakings, more than 6,000 miles long. Through this great artery are flowing vast numbers of troops and large quantities of supplies.

Towards the end of the year 10,000 men will be flown every month from the United Kingdom to India, and about the same number will be flown home.

PC's powder jar explodes

Police-Constable Thomas Brown, Melbourne-road, East Ham, was showing relatives a small jar containing some powder yesterday, when it exploded.

Brown and his wife and son were injured. Brown said he did not know what the powder was.

Operation "Collie" as reported by the *Daily Mail*.

A Bit of a "Tiff"

NAVY SWEEPING PATH TO SINGAPORE

In a daring, three-day sea and air-strike the task force of British East Indies Fleet has swept a Channel through Japanese minefields as part of a new naval campaign which is steadily clearing a way to Singapore, writes Alan Humphreys, API war correspondent.

The operations took place off Puket Island S. Siam, Lieut-Cmdr W. F. Machin, an eye witness, disclosed after the force, commanded by Vice-Admiral F. T. C. Walker had returned to the base.

Puket Island was mentioned by the Japanese a few days ago when they inaccurately announced that "landings" had taken place (SEAC, 27 July).

The British task force, composed of minesweepers accompanied by a strong Naval escort including escort carriers, carried out its operations in face of "persistent and considerable" air-attacks with warships having to manoeuvre in waters bounded by minefields.

The minesweepers cleared the channel in approaches to the Malacca Strait—the sea gateway of Singapore—and the Royal Indian Navy laid "Dan Buoys" to mark the swept waterways. It was the second minesweeping operation in this area this month.

One minesweeper, H. M. S. Squirrel struck a mine and had to be sunk by gunfire from her sister ships. There was a small number of casualties.

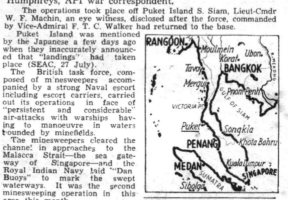

Desperate Measures

The Japanese aircraft, after failing to pierce the screen of defending Hellcat fighters, finally—on the last day—resorted to desperate measures with dive-bombers and suicide planes—first to be seen in the area.

Some dive-bombers got through; but one made off in haze after dropping its bombs into the sea and the second was shot down in flames after a 6,000 foot, nearly-vertical dive at the aircraft carrier Ameer.

Two suicide planes which followed, both failed, in their attempts, one being shot to pieces in its dive at Ameer and the other crashing into the sea.

Activities of the British planes were by no means confined to defence however. Airfields on the mainland from which the Japanese aircraft could attack the force were bombed and strafed and an airfield at Hinluk in Kra Isthmus was left unserviceable.

Fighter Sweep

Fighters also ranged well to the south of the Malayan border attacking, among others, the airfields at Bandon and Sungei Patani, 20 miles NE of Penang.

Altogether eight Japanese planes were destroyed on the ground and five damaged.

Armed reconnaissance craft also flew across Kra Isthmus to Singora on the East coast and set fire to several ships in the Gulf of Siam including a 150 foot steamer and two 200-ton schooners.

In addition, three low-level sweeps were made over almost the whole of Siam's railway system blowing some 60 wagons off the rails and smashing 15 railway engines.

ATTLEE'S FIVE PRIORITIES

Speeding up release from the Services is No. 3 on the list of five priorities which the new Labour Government has decided on, says Globe. Here is the list:—

1—Winning the war against Japan; 2—Intensive house-building scheme in Britain; 3—Speeding up release for Servicemen and women; 4—Building up production for home and overseas markets and; 5—Social insurance and other legislation, including national legislation of key industries.

Mr Attlee, Mr. Morrison and other leaders take the view, for which they are prepared to fight against more eager members of their own party, that the above order of priority must be adhered to.

They argue that there must be peace and contentment in the country before the more sweeping plans of Socialism are attempted.

RUSSIA INVITED TO TANGIER TALKS

British and French diplomatic representatives in Moscow have been instructed to hand invitations to attend the Paris talks on Tangier, international zone occupied by Spain in 1940, to the Soviet Government, says Reuter.

The Paris talks are expected to be resumed on 6 August.

LOST MILLIONS

The assets of some Swiss banks, totalling millions of Swiss francs, have been lost by the fall of Germany, says Globe, and rumours circulating in Switzerland that the Allies will demand this money have caused

Operation "Livery"

No. 563. One Anna.

FRIDAY, 27 JULY, 1945.

Printed by Courtesy of
THE STATESMAN in Calcutta.

Tokyo Radio Reports

NEW S.E.A.C. LANDING

LONDON, Thurs.—The Japanese News Agency reported today an Allied landing on Puket Island, which lies close to the western shore of the Siamese strip of territory which divides Malaya from Burma.

The agency's report, picked up by Reuter in New York, said that some 500 Allied troops landed on the island on Wednesday morning.

"The troops came ashore in nine barges under cover of bombardment by two cruisers," the agency said.

"The Japanese garrison, counter-attacking, pushed the invaders back to the shore line were fighting is now in progress."

Six Transports

Six transports were said to have accompanied the invasion force.

The Siamese island of Puket, also known as Junk Ceylon, is north of the upper entrance to the Strait of Ma'acca, about 600 miles from Singapore and about 650 miles south of Rangoon.

The report, not confirmed from any other source so far, if true, marks the nearest approach to Singapore from the west and adds significance to enemy reports regarding preparations in Singapore to meet the threat of invasion.—Reuter.

Navy prowl at gate to Singapore

Suicide Japs fail

From NOEL MONKS,
Daily Mail Special Correspondent
WITH BRITISH EAST INDIES
FLEET, Monday.

SHIPS of this fleet have had their first brush with Japanese suicide planes and come out on top. They blew one to bits and suffered no damage.

The attack was launched while a Task Force of heavy units, aircraft-carriers, destroyers, and minesweepers was making a daring three-days sea and air strike last week off Puket Island, on the west coast of the Malay Peninsula.

The operations [reported to be part of a new naval campaign which is steadily clearing the way to Singapore] were under the command of Vice-Admiral H. T. C. Walker.

Our ships were picked up by a Japanese "Dinah" reconnaissance plane on the first day, last Tuesday, and from then on they were at constant action stations.

It was on the third day, late in the afternoon, that suicide planes and dive-bombers came in.

Blown to bits

Some broke through our fighter screen and picked out the escort carrier H.M.S. Ameer. One dive-bomber, chased by fighters, cleared off in the haze after dropping its bombs into the sea.

Another dive-bomber was shot down in flames by the Ameer's guns after a 6,000ft. nearly vertical dive at her.

Then two suicide bombers attacked.

Almost every one of the Ameer's guns seemed to hit one suicide plane diving straight for her flight deck, and it was blown to bits, blazing pieces littering the sea.

The second suicide plane crashed into the sea.

During the first day's mine sweeping, H.M.S. Squirrel struck a mine and had to be sunk by our own gunfire. There was a small number of casualties.

Bombing and strafing strikes were carried out in Siam and right across the Malay Isthmus by our carrier-borne aircraft.

Operation "Livery" - the
view from Tokyo.

Operation "Livery" - the
Daily Mail view.

A Bit of a "Tiff"

August 14th 1945 - the Japs surrender.

August 16th - VJ Day.

Joy at last!

"For promotion to Petty Officer, Sir?"

Columbo October 1945. The photographer rather overdid the retouching but at least it shows that I once had some hair.

A Bit of a "Tiff"

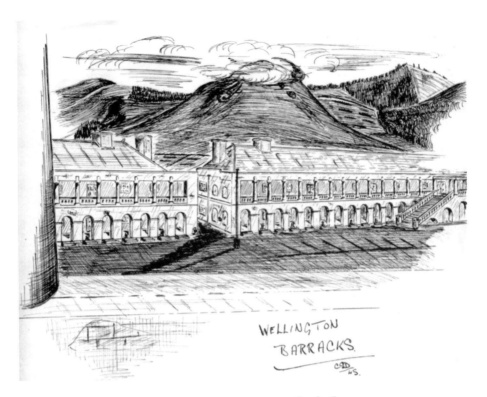

WELLINGTON
BARRACKS.

"Goodness gracious me!" Cochin October 1945.

With the war over the medical interest in us had reduced – and no more short arm inspections!

"No need to stand to attention laddie."

We sent and received our mail by a variety of methods and also received local and British newspapers. Some with good news and some rather worrying.

A Bit of a "Tiff"

Bringing in the Sheaves

"Harvest Wain" 1945 model

FOOD ☆ FACTS

No. 3 IN A SPECIAL SERIES

making the MOST of CABBAGE

No one can afford to waste the food value of anything in these days of world shortage, certainly not mothers who want to see their families growing up strong and healthy. And because it's only too easy to waste the precious vitamins and minerals in green vegetables by incorrect cooking, these simple hints on preparing cabbage are well worth studying. It's easier at this time of year to follow the recommended health plan, "Eat a green, leafy vegetable at least once every day." Here's how to get the full benefit.

GOLDEN RULES FOR COOKING CABBAGE

To enjoy cabbage at its crispest, and full of delicious flavour, follow these rules. Prepared like this, it keeps most of its vitamins and mineral salts, and little of the food value is lost.

1. Use as fresh as possible. If from your own garden, don't gather till needed.

2. Allow 1½ lb. for 4 portions. Remove the dark or coarse outer leaves. Do not throw them away, because they contain more of the vitamins and mineral salts than the more tender inner leaves. Use them shredded in soups and stews. Cut the cabbage in quarters and wash thoroughly. Avoid soaking wherever possible. *Never soak for more than ¼ hour.*

3. Shred with a sharp knife, cutting across from top to stem (*see sketch opposite*).

4. Don't drown it. Allow only quarter pint of water, and about 1 level dessert-spoon of salt for each 2 lb. of cabbage. The water in the pan must be boiling before the cabbage is added.

5. Cook with lid tightly on the pan. If the steam is allowed to escape, the pan will go dry and burn.

6. Boil briskly for 10-15 minutes only. Shake pan occasionally.

7. Drain off any liquid. Use for gravy, soup or sauce.

8. Serve at once. Keeping hot or reheating destroys the vitamin C. Before serving add a teaspoon of margarine if possible, and toss well.

chopped small; a few teaspoons of vinegar and a sprinkling of nutmeg, or perhaps a shake of caraway seeds just before serving, and you have something quite new and interesting.

SUPPER SUGGESTION

Serve cabbage as a main dish, for supper or lunch, combined with cheese. Use *raw*, too, as a sandwich filling, or served in salads with hot or cold dishes.

CABBAGE CREAMED (enough for 4)
Ingredients : 1½ lb. shredded cabbage, ½ pint water, 2 level teaspoons salt, ½ oz. margarine or dripping, 3 level tablespoons plain flour, 4 level tablespoons grated cheese, pinch of pepper. *Method :* Boil half a pint of water, add the cabbage and salt and boil 5 minutes. Add the margarine to this. Blend the flour and cheese with the remaining quarter pin of water, add to the cabbage, stir until it boils, season well, and cook fo another 10 minutes. Serve hot. Suitable for a lunch or supper dish.

FOR VARIETY

All sorts of additions may be made to cabbage or savoys cooked in this way. A few crisped bacon rinds

THIS IS WEEK 4 — THE LAST WEEK OF RATION PERIOD No. 1 (JULY 22nd TO AUG. 18th)
THE MINISTRY OF FOOD, LONDON, W.1. 26

PEACE FIXES RELEASE DATE

THE War Office last night announced dates of releases from the Army beyond Group 11.

These dates they had withheld for reasons "which must now appear obvious."

The programme for men is :

Group 12 : August 13—26.

Group 13 : August 27—September 9.

Group 14 : September 10—23.

Groups 15 and 16 : September 24—October 7.

Groups 17 and 18 : October 8 to 21.

In addition to married women who did not wish to be released in the first period, single women will be released :

Groups 11, 12, 13 : August 13—26.

Groups 14, 15, 16 : August 27—September 9.

Groups 17, 18, 19 : September 10—23.

Groups 20, 21, 22 : September 24—October 7.

Groups 23, 24, 25 : October 8—28.

PLEDGE TO PoWs

THE King in his speech yesterday at the State opening of Parliament said :

"In the Far East my Ministers will make it the most immediate concern to ensure that all prisoners in Japanese hands are cared for and returned to their homes with all speed.

"My Government will continue the orderly release of men and women from the armed forces on the basis of the plans announced in the autumn of last year "

Call-up halts to-day

And 'war' direction ends

By Daily Mail Reporter

CALLING-UP notices to the Forces and directions to "medical" examination will be suspended for seven days as from the official announcement of VJ-Day—that is, to-day.

This "breathing space "—may at the end of the seven days be extended.

Men and women who have already received calling-up notices or summonses for medical examination, or who may receive them during the next day or so, must report as directed.

No more directions to people to work in munition factories or in any factory on war production will be issued. People who have already received directions to report for war work, but have not yet done so, will have their direction notices withdrawn.

Britain, Saturday, July 14, 1945.

More bus services off to-day

2 strikes spread

By Daily Mail Reporter

ROUND London and in the Midlands more busmen have joined the unofficial strikes over revised schedules.

Eight garages and 872 L.P.T.B. workers are idle in Surrey, Sussex, and Kent, and 36 routes are affected.

Men at Chelsham and Guildford came out yesterday.

This stoppage covers also Reigate, Leatherhead, Dorking, East Grinstead, Crawley, and Godstone.

Transport in eight counties is affected in the Midlands strike.

Women's threat

Work stopped again yesterday at the three Midland Red bus garages at Birmingham; employees at Leicester and Stafford came out; and Nuneaton and Swadlincote men are likely to be out to-day.

Leicester Corporation conductresses say they will strike to-morrow unless an alderman withdraws a statement made to the city council that to manage them would turn any man grey-haired.

After nearly six weeks the "go slow" movement among London dockers seems to be ending. Yesterday the men were warned by the Minister of Labour that their action would have to be viewed as an act against the national welfare.

Soldiers have been called out at Grimsby Docks and Immingham to unload perishable cargoes; and also at Glasgow, where 4,500 dockers are striking.

A strike of 1,000 dockers at Swansea has stopped the discharge of general cargo ships. The dispute is over suspension of allowances to men who left work on polling day.

No doubt these images will conjure up mixed emotions. Just look at the prices! And it didn't mean the goods were available!

With nothing to do we had more leave at Diyatalawa, Ceylon.
October 1945.

Finally we left for home, passing through the Suez Canal - the
Anzac Memorial December 1945. Author's collection.

Chapter 7 H.M.S. *Kestrel* Worthy Down

After Christmas leave I reported to H.M.S. *Daedalus III,* a transit camp at Bedhampton. This was originally intended as a camp for evacuees from bombing at Portsmouth. As an emergency home it may have filled a need, but was certainly not an attractive or comfortable place to wait for a draft. First move in these cases was to head for the Education Office and find something to study, thus avoiding odd jobs. Fortunately this was a short stay and I was sent off to Worthy Down to do the Ordnance conversion course, without passing through Lee-on-Solent where the dreaded "Kit Bag Harry" was apt to savage passing draftees with a Kit Inspection. Worthy Down had become a mere shadow of its former self in just fourteen months, it was no longer a busy airfield, and was reduced to a ground training role. The storage site had closed and all evidence of the U.S. Army in and around Winchester had disappeared. Winchester had reverted to its staid old role as a cathedral city.

Their Lordships had decided that it was possible to merge the Electrical and Ordnance Air Artificers into one group as was being done with Airframes and Engines. They were some fifty years too soon in this concept, and this scheme never got off the ground and was cancelled, but not before I had competed my conversion. After some weeks working in the Electrical Training Department, I found myself in a course of just four A.A.4's (L), myself, Duffy Collins, Hoppy Attwood, and Boop-a-doop Jones. All three were senior to me; Jones was a hell-raising 1st Grenville. We formed the penultimate course, but the last course started a little later and consisted of one man, George Carter. Obviously the writing was on the wall for this great new plan, but the system kept on running until we were fully qualified as L/O and then cancelled the scheme and we reverted to being just A.A.4 (L) again.

With such a small group the tuition was pretty personal, and in short order we learned about explosives, the 2lb guncotton demolition charge, bombs and handling equipment, the perils of the highly sensitive exudation from badly stored bombs, weapons store markings, 3 inch rockets, pyrotechnics such as the Signal Distress Two Star Red, the .303 and .5 inch Browning machine guns, the 20mm Hispano cannon and its belt feed mechanism. It was not mind-bending stuff but needed concentration on memorising the nomenclature, without which the armourers were lost. All the tuition was carried out in a cold and very airy partitioned hangar, but we had time out at the firing butts firing the various guns; the demonstration of a 3 inch Maroon Mortar went very well with a double charge, but the Verey cartridges just fell out of the pistol muzzle with a little "fizz". It turned out that they had been made in 1918. In the end the best entertainment took place in the hangar where Connie Upton, an A.A.4 (O) of 1st Grenville, was demonstrating the Aircrew Dinghy operating system. This system had a gas bottle initiated by a cartridge. The cocking system of this cartridge was proving difficult and Connie withdrew to the instructor's room for advice. There was then a loud bang and the instructors evacuated in a great hurry. The firing mechanism had been partly cocked and had then released. The high pressure CO_2 cylinder had then formed a very effective rocket and screamed around the room knocking out half bricks from the wall as it passed. Much was made also of the dangers of the accidental release of two plungers in a buffer assembly on the 20mm cannon. The tension had to be released very slowly since the buffers were under considerable spring pressure, otherwise they would "eject with the speed of a .5 inch bullet." It was never demonstrated.

Once again the course finished with a written exam, an oral exam, and a practical task. Unfortunately all my notes were stolen, but despite this the others and I passed the written and oral exams. Come the practical, and we all failed. The reason was that we had neglected to cover the open-ended pipelines exposed during the work. As it happened no covers had been made available, and we had ignored this omission instead of asking. There was embarrassment all round, so what was to be done? Well, we would be given an extra week's tuition, a weekend, and then we would repeat the practical test. First priority for us was the weekend leave. I nipped up to Maidstone and on my return caught the "milk train" from Waterloo after battling in the solid mass of servicemen to join the train, arriving at Winchester at 02-30 and getting a lift in the G.P.O. van back to Worthy Down. Somewhat weary, I found my practical test was to be the removal and reinstallation of a 20mm cannon into a Seafire. For this purpose a single Air Mech. (O) was allowed to assist with the location of the gun-barrel as directed by the trainee. However the 20mm breechblock was the bit that required manoeuvring and it was extremely heavy. Due to the very restricted space in the Seafire wing, the gun had first to be lifted and then rotated on to its side before removal, and the reverse on replacement. This was totally beyond me, and eventually the invigilating officer did the job himself. I presume that foreknowledge of the demise of the L/O scheme dictated the next move, because we were each awarded a pass at 75% and awaited a draft elsewhere.

As usual I fell foul of the system during the course. On the first occasion I was detected "chuntering" away with my chum while we were on parade after lunch and waiting to be marched to instruction. By that time I had been a P.O. for a year, but had never controlled a squad of men on parade; it had not been necessary and I was more than happy to leave it that way as I detest shouting. However I was given an immediate opportunity to find out, but without the option, as I was hauled out and made to take charge. It was not so bad after the first time.

On the second occasion, I was duty P.O.; another first at Worthy Down. Whatever else was required, the first duty was to lower the Colours at Sunset and the last was to raise them again at the 0900 parade the next morning. None of the duties were written down, so it was a question of enquiry from previous duty P.O.'s. Thus I found that I would wait for and meet the Duty Officer and Bugler just before the appointed time in the "keyboard flat" in the admin. block, and this I did. However time passed with no sign of the Officer of the Day (O.O.D.), and then at the "witching" hour I heard to my horror a bugle sound from the parade ground. Looking out I saw the Officer of the Day hauling the Ensign himself. Obviously I was not going to be very popular, and so it proved. After giving me the expected "rollicking", he advised me to be damned sure to be on time the following morning, and so I was. I arrived in ample time and proceeded to attach the Ensign to the "halyards", prior to the hoist. The parade ground was already full for the ceremony of Colours, but the O.O.D., convinced he had a real live idiot to work with, thrust me aside, saying the Ensign was upside down; a distinct possibility! He then reattached the "cleats" to the "halyards", and at 0900, the bugle sounded and I slowly hoist the ropes, as required, until it became clear that the Ensign had not moved; the O.O.D. had joined the cleats on the Ensign to themselves and not to the halyards, and the halyard cleats were happily rising to the top of the mast with nothing attached. The parade was delayed until I had corrected the O.O.D.'s mistake and nothing more was said.

"If you can't take a joke, you shouldn't have joined!"

Early in 1946 there was an Exhibition of German Aeronautical Developments held in the Science Museum in London. This was open to the public, and followed a much larger event at Farnborough. Normally we were precluded from visiting public displays simply because of the difficulty of travel and naval duties, but on this occasion I was lucky, and visited one weekend. The exhibition was an eye opener due to the range and novelty of devices shown, and subsequently, as more details have been published, then the pre-war view of the quality of German Science and Engineering seems to have been confirmed. However, we had won the war with our U.S. ally, so perhaps we had got our priorities right and had concentrated our efforts on the technology that mattered most. It was nevertheless a surprise to see some of the equipment that seemed to make our stuff look rather dated.

Among the items that caught my eye was the use of "sintered" metal permanent magnets for electrical instruments, miniature electrically driven gyroscopes, and a small electrically driven rate gyro with force feedback to be used for stabilisation. At that time virtually all the British flying instrument gyros had heavy brass rotors, driven by vacuum via a "venturi" tube, and these also formed the basis of both the Sperry and R.A.E. autopilots. Flying with those controls meant setting a datum height or heading, the autopilot maintained the datum but without the benefit of, either, velocity or acceleration feedback to provide a smooth and stable flight path. A report I obtained from Farnborough showed that the German systems incorporated both functions and also used a form of magnetic amplifier. This was completely new to our equipment.

Over the years the information obtained from Germany became incorporated in our own systems; the magnetic amplifier had a brief life before it was superseded by valve and transistor systems, but the very useful German Portable Pitot/Static Instrument Leak Tester was adapted by Bryans Aeroquipment and adopted in place of our locally cobbled-up gear. The rate gyro with force feedback was modified by Louis Newmark and was used in almost every British aircraft fitted with Auto Stabilisation or an autopilot. It was fitted to the Lightning and continued in the Buccaneers S2 until they were phased out after the Gulf War.

We are all familiar with the development of missiles and space flight on the back of the German V2 programme, but not too many are aware that some enormous German radar dishes became part of our post war Radio Astronomy programme, or that the powerful 30mm Aden gun used in many post war British fighters was developed from similar German guns, which used electrically fired ammunition. All these developments were still to come, so in 1946 the German work was a big surprise.

On the social front during in 1946 I finally took the opportunity to learn basic ballroom dancing. Hitherto the prospect of organising my two left feet had been somewhat daunting, and so it would remain, but at least I could now dance the waltz, quickstep, and foxtrot to Victor Sylvester's music, if only the other dancers would stay out of my way! Still it paid off in the long run because in those days a dance was the best place to find female company. However the tango, rumba and jitterbug remained outside my repertoire. Looking back, the dancing was about the only positive achievement in the year, but I had a brief spell of voluntary evening study in Workshop Drawing and started to learn Calculus from *Calculus made easy* by Silvanus P. Thompson. This subject had not formed part of our training, but the book was a delight to use, and assumed nothing on the part of the reader. I particularly remember the use of the quotation from

Dean Swift: -

> "So, Nat'ralists observe, a Flea
> Hath smaller Fleas that on him prey.
> And these have smaller Fleas to bite em,
> And so proceed *ad infinitum*."

As 1946 drew to a close I was drafted North to Evanton, back to "Bonnie Scotland."

"Nine o'clock Sir!"

A Bit of a "Tiff"

The Vertical Gyro Unit of the all-electric 3-axis Auto-pilot fitted to a crashed Dornier 217 in October 1941 and evaluated at R.A.E. Farnborough. Compare with the R.A.E. Autopilot in Chapter 4. Author's collection.

Chapter 8 H.M.S. *Fieldfare* Evanton

I arrived at Evanton shortly before Christmas 1946, and by this time their Lordships had once again changed their minds. Henceforth there would be an Electrical Branch in the Navy and all Air Artificers (L) would become Electrical Artificers (Air). The small matter of a Port Division was resolved after some confusion, when it was decided that all trades of the Air Branch belonged to Lee-on-Solent. I arrived just in time to acquire a fresh chicken from a local farmer and proceeded south on leave with the family Christmas dinner in my luggage.

At the height of its wartime fame, Evanton, on the north bank of the Cromarty Firth between Dingwall and Invergordon, had been an important base for Bomber Command, and it still had excellent workshop facilities, but was no longer operational. Instead under the Navy, it was a store for second line training aircraft, such as Ansons and Harvards, and these were slowly brought forward as required.

My post was in L.R.S. (Electrical Repair Shop) and here I was usually alone. I serviced generators, magnetos, and other gear as required, and used the lathes and engraving machine for a variety of official and private jobs. In the I.R.S. (Instrument Repair Shop) next door, my ex-apprentice colleagues conducted a private watch cleaning and repair service, in addition to occasional work on aircraft instruments. In the absence of a better source of cleaning fluid, they progressively used the carbon tetrachloride in the "Pyrene" fire extinguishers, until the day when someone knocked over a paraffin heater, and was unable to find a working extinguisher.

The workshop was overseen by a Warrant Electrician "Nutty" Burnett, aided by Chief Electrician Randall. Mrs "Mac" a local lady managed the stores. There were of course no Married Quarters on the wartime stations, but a few people managed to find lodgings in the area, and the rest of us lived in the old wartime huts fitted as usual with Tortoise stoves for heating. If there was adequate fuel then our sport was to get the steel chimney red-hot up to the roof, but that did not often happen such was the desperate shortage of everything. Nutty was one of a group of Warrant Electricians recruited to the new branch from the Telegraphist Air Gunner Branch. At one stage these people had been Operator/Maintainers for their own Radio equipment and on the basis of this knowledge of electricity they had been transferred. However Nutty was no expert on the rest of the aircraft systems, but he was a "dab hand" at knots, as you'll find out later.

With the advent of jet propulsion, Aeromodellers were attempting to emulate the full-scale world with variants of the V1 pulse jet engine, and it seemed I was well placed to try my luck. The problem was to obtain suitable materials. At last bits were found or made until the only piece missing was a tail pipe. Then "eureka", I found a beautiful length of chrome-plated steel of the right diameter stowed away in my workshop. A length of this was sawn off and fitted but needless to say my jet failed to work. Somewhat later Chiefy Randall was enquiring about a length of chrome-plated steel tube, which he had failed to return when he had brought his landlady's vacuum cleaner in for a service. Too late, all was revealed, and Chiefy left in a huff!

Early in 1947 I was sent, with others, from Evanton to the P.O.'s Leadership course at H.M.S. *Royal Arthur* at Corsham in Wiltshire. This was in principle a very good scheme, because, until it was introduced, newly promoted P.O.'s had often never needed to handle men outside their professional duties. Like myself, the majority of my class were P.O.'s of several years' standing. Among the course officers was one Lt. Prince Philip, and there were rumours of his mail arriving from Buckingham Palace.

For a month we marched and shouted orders, listened to and gave lectures, but unfortunately the country was under siege in the appalling winter of 1947, and much of the planned outdoor activity could not take place. On one occasion this meant that rifle shooting could not take place at an outdoor range, and instead we were required to mime the target practice indoors. As I reckoned to have some skill in this line, the idea of shouting, "Bang" seemed too ludicrous for words and the poor humourless G.I. was not amused. As I recall, I succeeded in vaulting a box for the first and only time during P.T. but failure would not have been amiss in the collection of P.O.'s, who had long forgotten any aspect of Physical Training and on the whole were unfit having worked in engine rooms and other unhealthy places for years.

If the rail trip down from Evanton had been a bind, then the return journey was impossible. The country was virtually closed down and the trains that were running at all were slow and often diverted because a line was blocked by snow. The train to London had no heating and few windows. We got to Evanton two days after we left Corsham. By 1947 the majority of service canteens had closed and the alternative means of feeding groups of men in transit was to issue "meal chits" individually. In theory these could be presented in lieu of cash wherever food could be found. One day's chits were valued at about six shillings, to cover breakfast, dinner, and supper. On the way down we had stopped at Perth, where the only food in the station café was stale meat loaf sandwiches from under the proverbial "Victorian" glass cover. Although the offerings in London and Edinburgh were better, we had only received 4s 6d in chits from Corsham, which of course did not cover our extended journey, and it was difficult to find restaurants or cafes open by the time our diverted trains had dumped us at each new station on our way north. When we finally arrived at Evanton, we requested payment of our extra expenses, and in due course were each awarded about 5s 6d. This did not seem fair or reasonable, but that we were told was the rule. By chance some years later on *Eagle* I met the former Chaplain of Evanton, and learned that the Paymaster at Evanton had in fact been charged and convicted of embezzlement of, among other things, travel expenses. So justice was done after all.

In other parts of the country spare jet engines (Snow blow) were used for the first time in places to clear snow from airfields and railways, but, due to the Cromarty, the climate at Evanton was warmer and we did not require such drastic measures. Instead the airfield was used as a base for R.A.F. Lancasters that loaded and dropped hay bales to beleaguered highland farmers. The fuel shortage meant that the heating in our huts and particularly in our workshops was inadequate. The lubricant froze in my lathes and we all looked for other ways of providing comfort. I was now entitled to draw "Neaters" (Neat Rum) as a P.O. and for the second time I requested to "draw". On the first occasion when I was at sea I quickly discovered that the "Tot" of "Grog" (Rum diluted with two parts of water) did not appeal, and gave my issue away before I cancelled it. This time was no different, it would have worked very well as paint stripper, and I made myself temporarily popular by giving it away to mates, before I cancelled it yet again. Giving away my tot was of course illegal as was just about every other thing concerned with rum. Rum was a well-established unofficial currency and favours sought and sold, such as an exchange of duty, were graded depending upon the quantity of rum dispensed. At the top was, of course, one or more full tots, followed by "Gulpers" and "Sippers"; both self-explanatory. The Chief and Petty Officers carried out most of the serious exchange because they controlled the issues in their own messes, and the neat rum could be bottled for later use. The ratings' "Grog" did not keep because of the water mixture, and this meant that any extra had to be consumed on the spot; even if the daily issue was made with an officer present it was nearly impossible to prevent this happening. Birthdays or other special occasions were celebrated in a mess by "Sippers all-round" for the "Birthday boy", who would then probably be out for the count for the rest of the day, and be put to bed by his chums. They would of course cover up his absence from duty, but often he would be violently ill, and with nobody else around several sailors died annually from alcohol poisoning or inhaling their vomit following a celebration. C and P.O.'s parties were livened up considerably by their illegal store of neat rum, but the largesse dispensed to invited officers, ensured that the practice was never stopped.

Having disposed of rum as a solution to the cold, I joined the group of people using an electric heater plugged into the lighting circuit, and which of course was then grossly overloaded. In my case I purchased a 500W element in Inverness and fitted it into the bowl reflector of an "Anson" landing lamp, which I then mounted on the base plate of an aircraft generator. Occasionally, it still helps out in my home workshop.

At work there was just enough to keep interest alive. Quite a few aircraft magnetos came in from planes in store and these were invariably thickly coated with red "lanolin" inhibitor. This had to be removed before any work could be done, and the answer was to strip them down and soak them in an "open" bath of lead free petrol; just a few feet away there were magnetos merrily sparking away on the test bench! As was becoming normal in the post war Navy, it was not possible to obtain a spare rubber driving belt for the test bench, and when it snapped I had to make do by splicing together a length of rope. Nutty approved of this idea!

A few odd jobs came my way, and I became an instant expert in magnetic crack detection in the engine bay across the road, and was later involved in an attempt to demagnetise a Harvard, which had been struck by lightning. We took advice from the Admiralty Compass Laboratory at Slough, wound cables round the fuselage and wing stubs, and erected an "Earth field" cancelling coil on a wooden frame at the "Dip" angle for Evanton. Theory suggested that energising the coils from a large ground battery, and successively changing polarity while reducing the voltage tapping should do the trick. It didn't, and the plane was flown elsewhere, possibly Boscombe Down or Farnborough. Although this was not a normal event in the F.A.A., it appeared that in R.A.F. service, there were properly designed "de-gaussing" hangars to perform this function. However, as a result I found that an old Post Office relay connected to the A.C. mains was very handy for wiping (demagnetising) small components.

Another odd job was to rewind the armature of an industrial vacuum cleaner. Quite why this was not simply returned for replacement I never knew, but these were odd times. In this case not only had the armature been completely burned out, but the commutator had disintegrated. So it was back to first principles; first new mica commutator segments were made on the engraving machine, and the commutator rebuilt, then individual armature coils wound on a former and tape insulated. Following assembly the whole had to be impregnated with varnish and baked to harden. This was the purpose of the impregnation plant fitted in one corner of the workshop, but never used. This was absolutely new ground, and all went well until the motor was assembled and switched on; it ran perfectly, but the varnish in the centre of the windings had not hardened and was ejected leaving the coils less rigid. Nutty then lent a hand, and decided to lay a "whipping" around the rear of the armature. This produced a "bun" like bulge and this fouled the casing. The motor was abandoned!

The lack of official work, and chronic shortages outside the camp, allowed the entrepreneurs in the Station Armoury to set up shop. A short "scouser" toughie, Willy Wynne and his mate Pete Grieve, both 1st Rodney's, had detected a need for motor car half shafts and toy soldiers in the local economy. Half shafts were turned from mild steel and flogged to unsuspecting car owners. These only lasted a short time but kept the car going for a while. The toy soldiers were a different matter altogether. Having discovered piles of abandoned (?) lead ballast weights, they purchased some toy soldier moulds, and then turned the whole Armoury into a production line. At one end the lead was melted into the moulds by a very large petrol brazing torch, and at the other the castings were cleaned up and painted by the "bods". They had also discovered a quantity of filled mattresses in old accommodation huts and had plans to flog these. I joined chums in the Armoury one Saturday on a rook shooting expedition using .22 rifles over which there seemed to be little control; I'm bound to say that we were singularly unsuccessful whether this was due to marksmanship, poor ammunition or the ability of the birds to withstand injury. I did not enjoy the experience. Another chum built a sizeable rocket using Coffman starter cartridges; on test the nose cone was the weak link and blew off; the rocket was driven backward and promptly buried itself deep into the soil.

Initially our entertainment was somewhat limited due to the distance between the camp and Dingwall our nearest town, or Inverness. A rail trip to Inverness on a Saturday was fine, but like Cinderella, our dancing at the Caledonian Ballroom had to be cut short to catch the train back. This was a pity because the "Eightsome Reel" and similar Scots dances were better suited to my style and the local lasses were good fun. Dingwall probably offered the best food in an Italian café and had little else of note, but it was a convenient coach stop on evenings when we went swimming in the Inverness Baths. Evanton was just the main street passing through the village on the way to Invergordon, but had two attractions. The first was "Sadie's", a little wooden shack at the Dingwall edge of the village. Sadie offered on Saturday evenings a replica of our Sunday morning breakfast i.e. bacon and eggs, with baps and marmalade. It was a very popular place, but the food was no replica; it was the real thing supplied illegally by a member of the supply staff to our detriment. The other attraction was the "Church of Wads" (Church of Scotland) canteen. Here was a source of tea and buns on a Sunday morning when we cycled to the village for a newspaper. A "Pussers" bike was a necessity for life at Evanton, and as a P.O. working in the L.R.S. at a distance from the billets I was able to get one on loan and there was no ban on using them outside the camp.

As if in answer to a matelot's prayer, their Lordships decided to reintroduce Wrens as Airwomen and to send them to Evanton for their technical training. The majority of those arriving at Evanton were well-educated young ladies from good families and the father of one of these girls was a test pilot for A.V. Roe; he died testing an Avro Tudor in which the flying controls had been incorrectly fitted. The first course included a very few older Wrens who had re-entered after wartime service. One of these was Hank. She was a character who smoked a pipe and played the bugle in the station band. She betrayed her femininity, briefly, on one occasion, when she cried at a funeral at which she was playing her bugle. One or two others copied her example and took up smoking a pipe, and although the femininity of the majority was unquestionable, there were rumours of a lesbian relationship between one lass and a P.O. Wren.

The Wrens provided a much-needed social dimension to our life at Evanton. They went with us, usually on the crossbars of our bikes, to the camp cinema (out of the main camp), to fish and chips at Invergordon after the cinema, and swimming in the Cromarty Firth. This latter was possible until October due to the exceptionally warm water. Access to the water was through a storage park full of redundant Ansons awaiting the scrap dealer, and through private woods. The going was rough, and with two up the bikes took a serious battering. Another option was a walk through the forest above Evanton eventually arriving at "Fyrish". This was one of two similar stone monuments reputedly erected by a local laird in memory of a son lost in India years before. They were said to represent the "Gates of India" in Bombay.

Tea dances were held in the N.A.A.F.I. at the weekend. Even to mention that now is to admit to being a dinosaur! However the major social event was the monthly station dance. This took place in one of the hangars and each station department took its turn to organise it. It was the turn of the Electrical Department for the Christmas dance in 1947, and Nutty Burnett was determined to have a Christmas tree. He accompanied "Dutch" Holland and I, with the workshop handcart and some "Bods", across the Airfield to the private woods to steal a fir tree. I was on Dutch's back hacking at a tree, when a shot was heard and Dutch collapsed into the mud with me on top. However we eventually emerged with a large tree. In the absence of a very large tub, Nutty then decided to lash it from the hangar roof. He loved his knots! The problem of non-flammable candles was solved by experiment, and a number of candle sized aircraft U.V. lighting tubes were attached and wired to an aircraft high-tension boost coil. This provided some 12,000 volts for engine starting, and as a power source for our candles it needed only to be wired to one end of the tubes, the return circuit was via the foliage, the floor and anyone foolish enough to get too close.

As a slight diversion, I was sent to Chatham in July 1947 to attend an A.B.C.D. (Atomic, Bacteriological, and Chemical Defence) course, and following that to train in Cinema Equipment maintenance. This was to support the ancient 16mm Gebescope projectors used in the Wrens' training. Chatham was my idea of hell and held large numbers of all those people whose sole intention was to cause grief to the rest of us. As usual the F.A.A. was something that didn't fit their bill, and so the walk-through joining routine organised for General service didn't apply, and I had some extra shuffling to do. The P.O.'s barracks accommodation had three tier bunks and the stone stairs leading to the first floor were hollowed by many years of sailor's boots. Fortunately I was able, mostly, to sleep at home in Bearsted and quickly got to grips with the delicate business of organising the end of the working day to ensure that I arrived at the main gate for the first liberty boat, so as to catch one of the first of the waiting buses.

As usual in Barracks, the "barrack stanchions" had organised duties to suit themselves and thus I found myself as Duty P.O. i/c Electrical Party one Saturday. I was required to sling a hammock overnight above the M.T. batteries in the battery room, but the remaining duty was a mystery. All was revealed at the 1130 Duty Watch muster on Saturday. My task, with the assistance of six duty stokers was to illuminate the scene of a fire. For this purpose an ancient iron wheeled handcart was provided. On this was mounted a large grey wooden box, and a reel of cable attached to a bowl reflector carrying a number of 100W light bulbs. On the instruction "Fire in Xyz building", the stokers would run with the cart to the site, followed by Joe Bloggins. At the site we were told to expect to find the duty civilian pensioner, who having previously been primed as to the location of the exercise would show us where the nearest electrical socket could be found. After this exercise in futility, I had no doubt that the popular radio show *The Navy Lark* was not fiction. It was unbelievable. Payday fell during my stay, and vast hordes gathered in the drill shed by the parade ground. Since most like me were in transit, there was no easy way of finding one's place in the order of payment. It was therefore a scene of utter chaos as we each tried to find our place, and listen for our name to be called in the din.

Life back at Evanton continued on its pleasant course, until it was announced that it was to close down. The first two months of 1948 were spent crating up the various facilities in the camp. I had an idea that one of the crates would be handy, so when I had sketched the design needed, I added one to the total required. I had the fond belief that the shipwright would make handsome wooden chests, and one would be mine. Not so, the end product looked as rough as my freehand sketch and all stayed at Evanton.

Despite a quite relaxed and pleasant time at Evanton, there were rumblings from afar that led me to wish myself elsewhere when I left. For example, at neighbouring Lossiemouth across the Moray Forth, everyone wore gaiters to work quite unnecessarily; a sure sign that "bull" was back in force, and the continuing moves of conscripts back to civilian life was unsettling. As a result when an A.F.O. asked for volunteers for the Royal Australian and Canadian Navies, I applied for both. I could not wait to get away from U.K. and test the waters elsewhere.

In the event, when I left Evanton for Culdrose, my draft to the R.C.N. arrived and I spent only six weeks there. As far as work was concerned I found myself in a hangar working on aircraft; at least some of these were Sea Mosquitoes but the memory I retain is when one of these had its wings folded after an engine run. Like most British Naval aircraft of that era the Sea Mosquito was folded manually, but in this case the wings were hinged to fold vertically and this required a wooden bar several feet long and about four inches square which, when secured into slots on the mainplane, provided the ground crew with the leverage to heave it into position. On this occasion the lever slipped and the wooden wing fell with a damaging crunch. Such a system would have proved disastrous at sea in rough weather. Culdrose was home to at least one Firebrand squadron and these used to takeoff using R.A.T.O.G. in a spectacular display.

I didn't take to Culdrose; while I was there our main meals were invariably served with dehydrated cabbage and, dehydrated potatoes or sweet potatoes. Why was this I wonder, was it yet another big swindle by a supply officer or was it an attempt to get rid of a wartime stockpile, or both? I was very glad to be on my way.

However just at this point my life started a new phase. On Easter leave I met Margaret (now my wife) at a dance in the Star Hotel at Maidstone. She was then a nurse in the Kent County Ophthalmic Hospital, and over a few days then, and later before I left for Canada we decided to stick together and I looked forward to my return to U.K. for an entirely different reason.

Messmates Evanton 1947.

Luxury
accommodation
for the Petty
Officers at Evanton
in 1947.

A Bit of a "Tiff"

P.O.'s Course No 7, Kingsmoor, Corsham March 1947.
Author far left rear row.

Instrument Repair
Shop Evanton 1947.
Oxygen Rig on left.
Gyro Test Table on
right.

Gunboat at Invergorden 1947.

Chums with a Harvard. Evanton 1947.

A Bit of a "Tiff"

Swimming party. Evanton summer 1947.

"Fyrish" Another popular spot for the Wrens. Evanton 1947.

Evanton Winter 1947.

Nutty's
Xmas Tree.

"Darling –
I get a
tingling
feeling
when you
hold me!"

A Bit of a "Tiff"

Air Day Lossiemouth 1947 Captain's Hellcat flanked by Seafire 46 (left) and Firefly 1 (right). The Hellcat survived to rest in the F.A.A. Museum.

Air Day Lossiemouth 1947 Sea Hornet F20 and Sea Fury.

Air Day Lossiemouth 1947. Visiting R.A.F. Meteor III.

Air Day Lossiemouth 1947 Seafire 46, with Hellcat, Sea Otter and Swordfish behind.

GIVE US A LIGHT CHUM

Electrical Fire Party R.N. Barracks Chatham.

A Bit of a "Tiff"

Margaret – 1948

Chapter 9 Royal Canadian Navy

I joined and commissioned H.M.C.S. *Magnificent* at Belfast on 7th April 1948 together with a batch of other R.N volunteers. We were all C.P.O.'s and P.O.'s, Artificers and Mechanics of the Air Branch, and our initial task was to set to work the ships Air Maintenance facilities. The ship and its aircraft were however manned by Canadians. I was detailed to organise the Battery Room and Oxygen Charging Plant, the latter deep down in the bowels of the ship, and filled with racks of high-pressure transport cylinders. To begin with the Battery Room had a few problems, as there was no means of safely decanting concentrated sulphuric acid from the large "Carboys" to a smaller container for dilution, and also no acid resistant "Fearnought" suits or aprons had been supplied. Batteries had to be carried by hand to and from the battery room with the result that my new Canadian issue of denim working clothes rapidly disintegrated. Even before we got to sea I managed to trip and drop an M.T. battery down a hatch; result one smashed battery, lots of spilled acid, and a pile of soda in an attempt to neutralise it.

Magnificent was the second carrier loaned to Canada, and like the *Warrior* was using R.N. staff to bolster up the Canadian personnel, she was eventually replaced by *Bonaventure*. All three ships, together with *Melbourne* and *Sydney*, which went to Australia, *Vikrant*, which went to India, and *Leviathan* which was never completed, formed the wartime Majestic Class of Light Fleet Carrier. None was completed during the war. The basic design was a 15,700 tons ship capable of 24.5 knots from two steam turbines providing 40,000 s.h.p. It had a steel flight deck 690 ft long by 106 ft wide, a single twin track catapult able to launch a 20,000lb aircraft at 56kts, 9 arrestor wires and 2 barriers. Two 54 ft by 34 ft lifts served the 275 ft main, and 57 ft extension hangars. It could carry up to 37 aircraft of the current types, and had a total of 8 twin and 14 single 40mm Bofors guns. The only armour was to protect the torpedo warhead store, although by then torpedo carrying aircraft were out of fashion. The ship carried a complement of 1,350.

After a month at Belfast we sailed for acceptance trials, and flying trials off the Isle of Wight using various R.N. aircraft, and then stored ship at Portsmouth. I managed a weekend leave from Spithead, but not before I'd knocked my cap into a bucket of Sulphuric Acid, and pondered the chances of actually landing safely in the old steam pinnace used as our "liberty boat". It was secured in such a way that one apparently had a choice of dropping down the tall brass funnel, or over the side. Luckily the third option worked, and I took off home to Margaret. Arriving back on board I heard that one of my 2nd Rodney colleagues had deserted. He had volunteered for Canada with desertion in mind and he was not caught because it was at first assumed by the R.C.N. that he was simply adrift from leave. He eventually reached New Zealand. Our sympathies were with him, as our contract with the Royal Navy was very one sided, and could not be broken. Very many people were disillusioned with the post war system.

The R.C.N. was not immune from R.N. "bull" however, and Cdr. Debbie Piers the Executive Officer introduced morning P.T. and Evening Quarters, the latter routine normally associated with *Nelson* and sailing ships. However the spirited Canadians had other ideas, and the Commander's prized Dartmouth telescope disappeared from his cabin. All leave was stopped and a search carried out; the telescope was not found, and was said to have been seen floating away in the Solent.

Once again we used our hammocks, and had the uncomfortable experience of waking to a fire alarm. This was the result of one of our number smoking in his hammock, and falling asleep. The confusion from this minor event showed the serious problem of fire on board, and one that I hoped to avoid in future. Although we ate in a central P.O.'s mess, the accommodation space was used for our recreation, so when families were invited aboard one afternoon the remainder had to clean, change, and get out to avoid embarrassment. Before we left Portsmouth, one Canadian P.O. decided to marry. He had special leave one morning to marry, and was back aboard by "tot" time with his bride to celebrate. As usual the carrier had a lot of space available when it was party time, and when the officers had a farewell party (I think this was in Belfast), they flooded the after lift well, decorated it as a pond and included live ducks. Our last weekend in U.K. was spent off Bembridge, I.o.W. and I went ashore; the return trip by ships boat took place in rough weather, but we were heartened to know that some senior officers aboard took the brunt of the water.

On completion of trials and storing we returned to Belfast and embarked our aircraft alongside at the R.N.A.Y. at Sydenham, Belfast. These were Sea Furies, and Fireflies Mk 5, which were to form 19th C.A.G. (Carrier Air Group). The Sea Furies replaced the R.C.N. Seafires of 803 Squadron and the unit continued as 803 Squadron until later the R.C.N. Squadrons were renumbered and 803 Squadron was repatriated to the R.N. We also carried the R.N. 806 Squadron Aerobatic Team of 2 Sea Hornets, 2 Sea Furies and a Sea Vampire F 20 (VF315); these were to go on to the opening of New York's Idlewild Airport in the U.S., after flying in Canada. This took until 25th May when we left U.K. and arrived in Halifax a week later.

There were no problems of integration although every now and again we were referred to as "Kippers" (two-faced limey bastards). The food aboard was to Canadian standards, so that we were hardly likely to complain when compared with the "pussers" grub we had been used to, and what was available ashore under continued rationing, but our Canadian shipmates insisted that it was so much better in Canada. "Just you wait, T-bone steaks and ice cream!" When we arrived and at last tried to eat a T-bone steak, it proved too much.

On arrival in Canada, most of us "Kippers" were moved to the Air Station at Dartmouth, Nova Scotia, where we manned various workshops, and I found myself in the L.R.S. under Lt. Steve Darbyshire, a Canadian Electrical Officer. A small number of our colleagues joined the C.A.G. and stayed aboard *Magnificent* as it continued to work up as a unit and as a result succeeded in visiting a bit more of Canada. Steve was very unlike his British counterparts, did not stand on ceremony, and could be spoken to in every day conversation. He was a keen photographer, and, when he became aware of my own interest, he introduced me to the local camera club and camera shop. The L.R.S. was not very busy, and I constructed a generator test rig from a collection of Swordfish tail plane struts found in an old hut. It always paid to investigate such places, and they usually had some useful treasures for conversion to a new role. Later there was a shortage of distilled water for the battery room, and I made a small still using electrodes immersed in slightly salted water. Then, with a need for someone to man the station machine shop, I moved in as the sole occupant. Again there was little official work, and I started to build a photographic enlarger. The bellows were made from a Naval black silk scarf, and the lamp-house from a Firefly 20mm gun muzzle cover. In its Mk 3 version, it is still in occasional use.

Continuing on the photographic line, my chum and I set up a small Developing and Printing business in my cabin, and, I began to take colour transparencies using Ansco colour film using my new Agfa Isolette camera; this material was still not obtainable in U.K. The shops in Halifax held goods that we would not see in England for many years, and it seemed odd to us that the Canadians looked over the border to the U.S. and saw goods that they could not buy due to exchange rates, and currency rules. At that time the exchange rate was £1 = $4 U.S. and the Canadian Dollar was slightly weaker. Halifax was the main port of entry serving commercial ships from U.K. particularly during the winter when shipping could not enter the St Lawrence; when their sailors came ashore they exchanged their currency unofficially in Halifax. This was helpful to us when we returned to U.K. because we got very favourable terms for our dollars at the same shops. We were paid at the Canadian rates; this was much higher than the R.N. pay and enabled me to put some aside for my eventual return. It also showed the possibility of living in Canada with material goods, such as cars and washing machines that were impossibly expensive or actually unobtainable in U.K. The majority of local cars were naturally American, and the model we most fancied was a Studebaker, lots of chrome, fins, and very racy. Even the price looked reasonable. The only British cars seemed to be the Standard "Ensign", and these could not stand the local climate with its extremes of weather and salty atmosphere; they simply rusted away. The C&P.O.'s block had a Bendix washing machine with a power wringer; I promised myself that when I married I would buy a similar machine for my wife, but so much for our dreams! It was a very long time before I was able to afford one back in U.K.

Dartmouth was a joint R.C.N. and R.C.A.F. station when we first arrived, and it also served as the Civil Airport for Halifax. Attendance at the monthly Senior N.C.O.'s mess meeting was compulsory, and always took place after lunch i.e. after "tot" time and after the mess bar had been open during lunch. It was a foregone conclusion that this would be a long drawn out event, and that a previously rejected agenda item would be tipsily proposed, discussed and rejected for a second time, after the bar had reopened at the halfway stage. This could not continue even by the local relaxed ideas, and it was stopped. Our occasional station duties involved a linguistic feat when we attempted to call a duty watch muster, as about half of the Canadian sailors were of French, Canadian Indian, or East European origin, and their names were unpronounceable

It was no surprise that we lived in wooden huts with shingle roofs, as many buildings in Halifax were also of wooden construction, some in an obvious poor state of repair after the war. At least our billets were well heated, with central heating that groaned and creaked as it expanded and contracted through the wooden frames. We had single cabins, which was a great luxury compared with U.K. The only thing lacking in convenience was a light switch by my bed. Running a cable to an aircraft switch sunk into the soft-board wall easily solved that, and the cable was secured to the wall by a frieze of 2 inch wide masking tape, which matched the cream paint. All went well until Captain's Rounds; in my absence at work the central heating had softened the tape adhesive, so that the cable was left hanging like a Christmas decoration. The Captain had seen this as he entered the room, but all that happened was that I got a message to "kindly remove it", or words to that effect.

Our runs ashore were always to Halifax, past the reeking "Imperoyal" Oil refinery, and on to the ferry at Dartmouth. This was the only practical way of crossing, since the modern bridge had not then been built, but unlike the dreadful Gosport ferry, it was spacious and carried cars. This fore and aft loading ferry operated in the most brutal way possible; as it approached the terminal, the bows for the time being were simply driven between two converging piers and bounced and rattled between them until it finally arrived. Vehicles were loaded by a similar method; each driving forward until it hit the car in front, and when the last one came aboard there was a succession of bumps as each vehicle shunted its neighbour. My chum Tubby and I used to eat at Lowndes a little Halifax restaurant, where we were always well served by an attractive red haired young lady of German origin called Vida. Tubby had however married just before we left U.K. and I had promised to wait for Margaret, so we simply chatted with "Ginger", and tried to think of other things.

At that time Nova Scotia was virtually "dry", and alcohol had to be taken home for consumption. We were not much bothered by this in any event, but lack of practice may have been partly to blame when Tubby and I attended Harry's wedding. Harry had met a Canadian girl soon after we arrived in June, and they married in the winter. At the party Tubby took a fancy to rum and coke, which tasted rather innocuous. He was not very steady when we left for camp. By the time he got off the ferry we had no option but to share a taxi with two coloured men and on the way back to camp had to stop the taxi to let him be ill. Surprisingly, neither the driver nor our companions were at all concerned by this, and one said to me "He doan' feel no pain!" The taxi was allowed to take us right to the entrance to our hut, but it was all I could do to get Tubby out of the cab and propel him by the only safe method, "bum's rush" (collar and seat of his trousers) through a gap in the high bank of snow to his bunk. I put him to bed surrounded by newspapers against the inevitable result.

We found that spring and summer in Halifax was warm and there were plenty of "midges" in the humid climate; in autumn and winter snow fell early and thick, so we were grateful for our Canadian issue greatcoats with high collars and for the duffle coats we wore to work. However while it was more intense than in England, it was certainly less than in the centre of Canada; snow-blowing machines cleared the roads leaving great piles on either side but this did not seem to affect the traffic as in U.K., nor did the airfield stay closed for long despite a layer of ice. Attempts to skate on a large frozen pond on the airfield were as ever wishful thinking on my part, but of course the Canadians were happily playing ice hockey as if born on skates. The area around the airfield had little to offer but scrubby woods and some isolated dwellings, worth an occasional walk if the midges weren't biting, and provided that it was not

A Bit of a "Tiff"

the hunting season. Once hunting had started, the papers were routinely reporting shooting accidents, as the hunters fired upon anything that moved; even the recommended red checked shirts were no guarantee of safety. It was possible to sail a dinghy from moorings just below the camp into Halifax harbour. Tubby and I did that one day as he lived on the Isle of Wight and had grown up with boats.

It is hard to recall anything of significance in Dartmouth itself except for a church, which Tubby and I occasionally attended. That church was at least conventional; on the radio there were broadcasts by some alarmingly evangelistic churches that were alien to my conventional C.ofE. philosophy, but one of our number became an instant convert after attending a Church "bun fight". This was a regular reprobate, who now became a regular bible thumper; it seemed to good to be true, and the dedication was frightening.

Halifax is of course an isolated outpost, far removed from Canada proper, and it was galling to realise that we were unable to see the rest because of the great distances involved. It was an issue even for native Canadians, who could not reach their families with the same relative ease that was possible in England. Tubby took a week's leave and travelled inland by Greyhound coach, but quickly found that, even on Canadian pay, he could not afford the expense and returned early without seeing anything worthwhile. Presumably the arrival of low cost air travel has made a big difference since then.

We were surprised to discover that the R.N. was making deductions from our pay, supposedly to pay for our pension entitlement, which of course was non-contributory in U.K. After a lot of moaning among the expatriates, I found myself our spokesman in a request to see the Captain to represent our complaint. The complaint was upheld and the deductions stopped.

By late 1948 it had been seven years since I had worn a civilian suit; it was not yet unacceptable to be seen in uniform while ashore but the Navy argued that there would be insufficient space to stow civilian clothes aboard ships and so they were banned for the lower deck. The continuing austerity in England meant that it had not been easy to buy new clothes, and my entire wardrobe was a pair of grey flannels and a sports jacket. I decided to buy a suit in Halifax with the prospect of returning to U.K in mind. This suit was fine in Canada but when I at last got back home I found that the cut and padded shoulders did not equate to the more conventional style then current, and the suit took a back seat in my wardrobe.

As our first year came to a close, we were given the option of staying on in Canada. Most remained in Canada for good and were very successful.

Briefly I considered bringing Margaret over and marrying in Canada, but I rejected that as too big a step, and I decided to return to U.K. By that time I had been rated C.P.O. as an E.A3 (A) and I returned in great luxury on the *Empress of France* to Liverpool. I travelled with Tubby and just one other C.P.O. from the original group. Our arrival at Liverpool was far from a welcoming sight and seeing the grey and grimy city and railway I doubted my wisdom in returning, and wondered what would be my next move.

H.M.C.S. *Magnificent* 1948 Author's collection.

A Bit of a "Tiff"

Not yet commissioned and still wearing the Harland and Wolff flag. Lots of big ships in 1948. Author's collection.

Alongside at Harland and Wolff Belfast. Author's collection.

Commissioning Ceremony 7th April 1948 Belfast Canadian High
Commissioner speaking. Author's collection.

The Honour Guard. Author's collection.

Hoisting the new Ensign 7th April 1948. Author's collection.

The Ship's Crest. Author's collection.

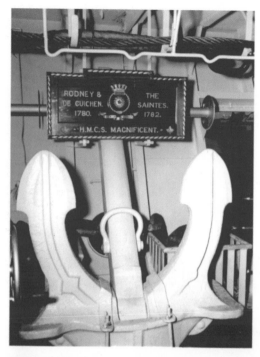

Ship's Mascot. Author's collection.

A Bit of a "Tiff"

Testing the catapult with a water weighted load Belfast 1948.
Author's collection.

Acceptance Trials. Author's collection.

Deck Trials with Barriers rigged. Author's collection.

Deck Trials R.N. Avenger landing. Author's collection.

A Bit of a "Tiff"

Deck Trials R.N. Sea Fury leaving the catapult. Note the strop falling away. Author's collection.

Deck Trials Sea Fury and Firefly IV ranged and ready to start up. Author's collection.

Deck Trials R..N. Seafire from Ford on forward lift. Stbd. wing is being spread manually before being moved aft to catapult, seen to Port. Author's collection.

Deck Trials Firefly IV taxiing to catapult. Shuttle and strop can be seen forward of stbd wing root. Author's collection.

A Bit of a "Tiff"

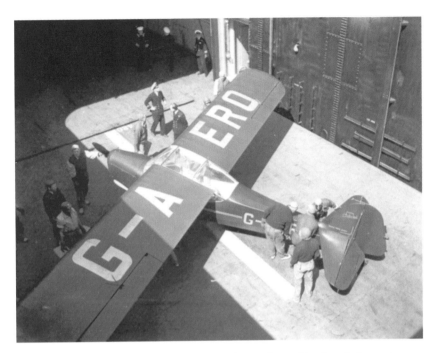

Visiting Auster Autocrat from "The Aeroplane" being taken down
on the lift. It didn't need a Deck Hook to land!
Author's collection.

Aircraft being loaded aboard H.M.C.S. *Magnificent* at
Sydenham, Belfast May 1948.

R.C.N. Sea Fury stowed aboard H.M.C.S. *Magnificent* May 1948.

Canadian Fireflies filling the flight deck aft.
The nearest aircraft is a Trainer.

H.M.C.S. *Magnificent* fully loaded at R.N.A.Y. Sydenham, Belfast. May 1948. Author's collection.

Coming alongside the Starboard Bow. H.M.C.S. *Magnificent* at Spithead May 1948.

Sea Hornet of 806 Squadron being hoist aboard at Sydenham
May 1948.

Sea Vampire F20 VF315 of 806 Sqdn.
Aboard for the trip to Canada.

A Bit of a "Tiff"

Deep maintenance on a Firefly at Dartmouth Nova Scotia 1948.

Visiting U.S.A.F. A.S.R. Fortress Dartmouth 1948.

Visiting U.S. PBY5A Catalina Dartmouth 1948.

Visiting U.S.N. PBM5A Martin Mariners Dartmouth 1948.

A Bit of a "Tiff"

Visiting R.A.F. Lancaster "Libra" Dartmouth 1948.

R.N. 806 Squadron Sea Fury VF 932 and Sea Vampire VF 315 at Dartmouth in 1948.

Maritime Central Airways Dakota Dartmouth 1948.

Beechcraft Model 18 Expediter at Dartmouth 1948.

A Bit of a "Tiff"

Three "Kippers" in
Canada 1948.

Just a small slip -
Dartmouth 1948.

Goodbye Canada! *Empress of France* March 1949.

Homeward bound *Empress of France* March 1949.

A Bit of a "Tiff"

Chapter 10 H.M.S. *Siskin* Gosport

As far as possible I spent my six weeks' leave with Margaret, and during this time was being paid by the Canadians from H.M.C.S. *Niobe*, which was their London Headquarters. This, and my savings, enabled me to get engaged and to buy a nice diamond solitaire ring for Margaret. On completion, I returned to Lee-on-Solent to be drafted next door to H.M.S. *Siskin* at Gosport for duties at N.A.R.I.U. (Naval Air Radio Installation Unit). I stayed there for $2^1/_2$ years and it proved to be a very important period in my life.

Siskin held a number of miscellaneous units as well as N.A.R.I.U. The R.A.F. had the A.T.D.U. (Air Torpedo Development Unit) at Fort Grange, and both the R.N. and R.A.F. separately operated a Planned Maintenance Development Unit. This latter scheme was intended to reduce the downtime of aircraft caused by routine maintenance, and among other things, it determined the occupancy and timing of work, in the restricted spaces on each aircraft type, in a form of work-study. The Avro Lincoln was one of the aircraft under study by the R.A.F. The scheme critically depended on the availability of aircraft spares to enable all work to be conducted on time. In the post-war cut backs, these spares were not normally forthcoming, and the scheme died. As examples of the shortages, it was necessary to exchange a dud light bulb for a new one, but that didn't work if the original had been stolen. Once an S.I. required an equipment to be marked with some identification using a small pencil brush, but all "brushes paint, sailors for the use of" were controlled by the "buffer" (Chief Bosun's Mate), who was averse to let any out of his personal store, and kept us at bay.

A.T.D.U. had a number of aircraft, but mainly operated Bristol Brigands over the torpedo range at Stokes Bay, just as they had been doing pre-war with their ancient Vickers Vildebeest biplanes.

N.A.R.I.U. was responsible for designing the installations and fitting new radio equipment to a range of Naval aircraft. Some of the equipment was wholly experimental, and used "black-boxes" designed and built at R.R.E. Malvern for flight trials, and others were standard gear fitted in a prototyping scheme for a Naval Service Modification. My personal "History sheet" shows that I worked on Anson, Mosquito, Sea Hornet, Sea Fury, Firefly Mk 6, Meteor T7, Harvard, Dominie, and Expediter. Of these, Anson MG231 stands out for several reasons.

It was intended that the cabin of the Anson be fitted out as a flying classroom with the new equipment going into the Firefly A.S.7, before the Firefly entered service. The Firefly A.S.7 was an interim anti-submarine aircraft for use before the Gannet arrived, and was fitted with A.D.R.I.S. (Automatic Dead-Reckoning Instrument System), the new Sperry Mk4b Gyro-magnetic Compass, a prototype Plotting Board, and the new Mk4 Directional Sonobuoys. The new compass used a remote flux–gate element and finally got away from the weird and wonderful devices used during the war. The Plotting Board was the only model in existence and was being shared for trials with a Sunderland and other R.A.F. planes. Ken Wheeler who is now a longstanding chum was in charge of it, and it was basically a captured German design modified by Farnborough to suit the British systems. This rather slow process was yet another example of our use of captured equipment, but the work did in the end result in an entirely British Plotting Board.

The equipment involved a lot of multi-core wiring, and used the new Plessey Mk4 plugs and sockets. This system was a major improvement on any system we had before; it had been developed at Farnborough, and was very flexible and also reliable until relaxed tolerances in production caused problems. It still used soldered joints and to cope with the many 25 pin connectors used in this installation we installed a small production line, which we fitted with a solder bath, a locally designed cable stripper for the new P.V.C. cable, and a carbon–bit contact soldering tool both of which used the Actograph low voltage transformer.

The Anson was not ideally suited for such a large installation, and because the fuselage was a metal frame with fabric covering, there was no suitable structure on which to mount the heavy cables. It was therefore decided to construct a cable tray along the side of the fuselage, but the first was foolishly made of mild steel, until common sense prevailed and aluminium was used. At one stage, while the mass of wires were installed, there was found to be an extra cable until it was realised that a "lead-lamp" had been accidentally included. After the job was complete and tested, the aircraft was weighed and found over-weight; as a result it would be unable to carry an Instructor, Pupils, and Sonobuoys at the same time. The subsequent fate of the aircraft is not known, but the Firefly A.S.7 was itself never fully operational, and although 137 were built, most were sitting and mouldering away in leaky cocoons at Anthorn when I later went there.

Several jobs required the fitting of experimental submarine radio homing gear, These involved a cavity aerial, to be faired into the leading edge of each wing and connected via a co–axial cable to the receiver in the fuselage. It was never easy to thread a 30 ft cable through an enclosed space, and doubly difficult when it became necessary in one case to cover the entire 30 ft with an extra layer of insulation and braided wire screening.

We were required to work to Air Ministry technical regulations, and to use a range of standard fittings from the A.G.S. (Aircraft General Stores) range. Following wartime experience when inadequate packaging destroyed many stores, it was now the practice to supply even the simplest components in full "Tropical" packing. So we received our nuts, bolts, and washers, firstly covered in thick grease, then wrapped in greaseproof paper and placed in a cardboard box. This was then wrapped in paper, labelled, and the whole dunked in molten wax. We used a lot of small items, so this meant that it was a major task to unpack and degrease them before use. At first we used an open bath of carbon tetrachloride, itself now considered a dangerous substance, but when this became unavailable we turned to the nearest alternative. We ordered and received a 60 gallon drum of trichlorethylene. This powerful anaesthetic was very effective as a grease solvent, and also in its primary role as it permeated around our group of M.O.N.A.B. (Mobile Naval Air Base) workshop huts. Its use was discontinued at once. As usual we found that the rules were not realistic; in the case of the S.D.M.'s (Standard Design Memoranda) we were supposed to allow one extra inch of cable for every twelve inches used in a wiring loom, which was intended to allow a small surplus at each end for future repairs and to provide stress free connections. When we applied this rule to the planned T.R.1935/6 installation on a Meteor T7 we had so much spare cable that the rule had to be ignored. The Rolls Royce Derwent jet engines on the Meteor were started by electric motors, and these drained our trolley accs. very quickly, even when they were double banked.

We still used wood in our work, mainly multi-ply boards, but of course the De Haviland aircraft were still of composite wood construction, and so we employed a solitary Leading Airman Woodworker. Jock Thorpe had been a pre-war employee of Imperial Airways and had a reputation from his time in the desert with F.A.A. units during the war. With some equally notorious colleagues he had become a confirmed alcoholic using all possible means of providing "booze", including boot polish. In his N.A.R.I.U. workshop he used one of the new resin based adhesives; this needed a mixture of methylated spirits and dilute sulphuric acid as a hardener. This in his view was a perfectly usable drink, as was any other liquid with the remotest trace of alcohol, including a bottle of medicine found when he visited a C.P.O. in his cabin. He was unlikely to be much use after "tot time", but despite his drinking he retained remarkable co-ordination and could pluck a fly out of the air. He had a number of less attractive party tricks. Presumably he had a talent for his trade, which outweighed his other minus points, and he had spent his career in the Navy being promoted to P.O. and then quickly being disrated for yet another misdemeanour. At an Admiral's Inspection his workshop was unusually neat and tidy, until he was asked to open a cupboard door and the contents fell out.

Admiral's Inspection called for special measures in any event, and one trick used on airfields was to gather up all the rubbish and odds and ends and load them into a lorry; this would then precede the Admiral's retinue on its general tour of the airfield, and return when the coast was clear. My own ploy was to dismantle and reassemble a pair of aircraft voltmeters and ammeters, because by the nature of an inspection it was impossible to carry out normal work, but one had to look busy. My meters served for many inspections, and are now retired to use in my home workshop. Usually these inspections called for some sort of flying exercise, often at night; it was not unusual for a real aircraft accident to occur during this flying and when this happened there was often great confusion until it was clear that it was not just another exercise.

We had various diversions in our daily task, and one of these was a visit from the station rat-catcher; he appeared on his bicycle with his very grubby terrier, which would then set to work rushing in and around the hangar and huts until it found its quarry. With luck the rat would then be chased into the hangar, where the dog would pursue it to loud applause and with the assistance of any loose objects hurled by Jolly Jack.

Our hangar was sited a few yards from the Fire Station and the duty crews used to sit in the tenders watching us at work. They were doing this when we had a real fire on a Harvard. This plane had been sent for us to investigate a problem with radio-interference; during the investigation the ignition had been advanced too far, and this led to a rich mixture, which ignited. In true Navy Lark fashion the duty crew watched until they were called, the fire truck arrived after a very short ride and then the hose was run out and foam pumped out. Not over the burning engine but over the crew, the truck, and the tarmac, as the hose burst! Eventually a new hose was fitted and foam was pumped over the aircraft, but still the fire burned on, and was still burning when the Gosport Fire Brigade turned up and put it out with a quick application of a $C.O.2$ extinguisher.

We watched one day as a Walrus landed safely but unintentionally with his wheels up and on another day saw a Westland Dragonfly crash nearby as it lost control in ground effect. Bits of the rotor blades were thrown around as they hit the ground. I had my second ever flight, in an Anson, to deliver some stores to the Naval Air Station at Culham; sitting in the co-pilot's seat I had to retract the undercarriage manually by winding a small handle with my left hand. This took nearly all the way to just about raise it, before it was time to lower it again and it was clear that it had a defect, so we returned with the wheels down.

One of the pilots at Gosport was Lt.-Cdr. Sproule. He owned and flew a pre-war Hillson Praga light aircraft, and was the inventor of the "Sproule Net". This was a scheme to enable injured aircrew to be scooped out of the sea by helicopter. I believe he was also involved in flying a sailplane to assess the wind-flow over an aircraft carrier. At Gosport he had a nice line in flying a liberated German "Kranich" sailplane at air shows. To enhance the spectacle he acquired a stockpile of red and green smoke grenades from the Army and asked if we could arrange to ignite these electrically, one at each wing tip. Never one to refuse a challenge I became involved and soon devised a method; this replaced the mechanical fuse with an electric fuse from the base of a cut down Coffman Starter cartridge, plus a celluloid gunpowder coated disc and some loose black powder from Verey Cartridges. This was then secured in the fuse cavity by a double thickness of standard electrical insulating tape, no more and no less as proved by several smoky tests, so that on firing the cap was blown free after igniting the smoke mixture. On the sailplane a thin enamelled wire was secured to the main-plane by masking tape and powered by a 4.5 volt battery in the cockpit. In no time flat my workshop became a grenade production line. Lt.-Cdr. Sproule was delighted but my boss was not. Probably the next request for help was prompted by the grenade job, and I was asked to repair an officer's Kodak cine camera, this I did, but cracked the viewfinder glass during assembly. Since this was irreplaceable I made a spare from Perspex, but it was not quite perfect, and I was not bothered again.

The peacetime Navy was developing new tricks, and I found it necessary to buy a cap to use when wearing civilian clothes ashore. Its only function was to enable it to be doffed to the Officer of the Day as I passed the Guardroom, once outside it could be stuffed into one's pocket. In another inspired move the Commander decided to have a "Muster by the Open List" at a Pay Parade. This ancient procedure was used in the past to enable the Captain to actually see and recognise his ship's company. In 1949 this was a practical impossibility at stations as large as *Siskin*. At the parade, several senior officers each stood in front of a desk above which had been displayed a list of items to be reported by each man in turn as they arrived at the desk e.g. name, rank, number, badges and medals, and then each man moved on to be paid. On the day it was chaos as many of us were tongue tied and omitted or reversed the order of reporting. Far from being a formal business most stood in front of the officer gazing up to read the list, it was pure comedy. This good idea never resurfaced. We also attended a current affairs lecture on paydays; these could be quite interesting, and one talk was by Col. Popski who commanded "Popski's

Private Army" in the desert. Another talk given by the R.N.B.T. (Royal Naval Benevolent Trust) representative was greeted with disbelief, when he gave examples of payments made to some of our feckless shipmates. As I recall, we contributed to the fund by compulsory deductions from our pay, and here were people taking the welfare system for a ride. It sounds like the present Social Security fiddles; human nature can be very perverse!

I discovered another problem when I went to the Sick Bay to arrange a routine dental check-up; I was asked if I was in pain and when my answer was "No" then I was told that since Siskin no longer had a resident dentist I could not go to the dentist at Lee unless it was an emergency. I retired in disgust and filled in a request to see the Captain to state a complaint; the result was that I was sent to a private civilian dentist for inspection and treatment. What happened to other people stationed at Gosport in that period I do not know but on that occasion the procedures worked in a fair and logical way.

Whenever I could get away at weekends, and during Easter and summer leave, I was back home to see Margaret; at that time she lived in the nurses' home attached to the Kent County Ophthalmic Hospital in Maidstone so we said our fond goodnights in the churchyard next door to the hospital to ensure the maximum time together before the doors closed for the night at 1030. This was the era of formidable matrons but in this case Matron Stevens was a person who cared for the welfare of her young nurses and always took her dog for a walk around the vicinity at around lock-up time; she always announced her imminent arrival by calling "Marcus" to her black Labrador, so we were able to straighten ourselves up and say "Goodnight Matron" as she walked past.

We were married on 28th December 1949 at Rochester and Matron attended the wedding. I now had new responsibilities, and the first was to find accommodation; our first lodgings lasted just one night when we discovered that our room was infested with fleas. We then spent several months at Eastney with the aunt of my best man, before a married quarter became available at Siskin. Siskin was another ex-R.A.F. station built to the "Trenchard" standards, and the married quarters had the same adaptable upstairs doors for the accommodation of large families. The kitchen equipment made a similar assumption by including an enormous oval frying pan capable of making bacon and eggs for a dozen. It did not however include a pastry board, and a section of multi-ply from Jock Thorpe was an obvious solution. I fetched this from the airfield under cover of my raincoat, but when I jumped off my bike at the gate, the board slid down my side, and it was with great difficulty that the bicycle, the pastry board, and I passed the watchful policeman. The bicycle was my undoing when I intentionally rode over an old "matelot's" cap on the hard standing, as I passed over the cap the grommet sprang back and up between the mudguard and the front wheel, and I went "base over apex".

Our time in married quarters was enlivened every now and again by the sight of our station firemen, who had been called to put out a chimney fire in one of the houses. It was their treat to sit astride the roof and pour buckets of water down the chimney unconcerned at the chaos inside. Sometimes this happened when the occupants were out, and the scene on their return can be imagined.

Margaret was soon pregnant, but we had an enjoyable spring and summer with visits from friends and family and we both had a ride in a glider flown by Lt.-Cdr. Goodhart during a weekend of flying by the Gliding Club. My chums used to call around to play Monopoly or cards; we only used to play for pennies, but one day, on a winning streak, we found to our horror that we had won our friends' "gas money" for the next week; such was our mutual penury at that time! Rationing was then still in force and did not stop until 1953. Many other goods were still in short supply.

Our son Ian was born on 14th November, and was found to have "pyloric stenosis", which prevented him from feeding and he died in hospital a month later. At one point I was travelling nightly between the Portsmouth hospital and nursing home with "expressed" milk, and was nearly washed overboard from the Gosport ferry one evening during extremely rough weather. For a very short while we had Ian at home, and I felt quite helpless dealing with such a sick baby. It seemed that we were destined to mature quickly, and our problems continued. I had been recommended for Upper Yardman (L), and had been studying for the exam. I then developed "sinus" trouble, which was very debilitating; I took the exam but missed the mark by three places, and shortly after was admitted to R.N.H. Haslar. For reasons of their own, the medics dumped me into the isolation ward, which meant no visitors, and the treatment with one of the new antibiotics required a high liquid intake. I actually refused a daily "Guinness" in favour of "Ribena", but even that palled after several pints a day. I was deemed fit on a Friday after just over a week in hospital, but due to the system I could not be discharged until the following Monday, nor could I have weekend leave since that had to be requested on a Thursday. That was too much to bear, and on Saturday I broke ship and went home, returning later over the sea wall into the hospital grounds with a boost from the taxi driver. Purely by coincidence of course, my son Richard was born nine months later just two months after I had left Gosport, and in the meantime to add to my woes, I had taken and failed my Chief E.A.'s exam.

In anticipation of a move, and with our baby expected, we had to think of a permanent home as it was unlikely that there would be married quarters readily available elsewhere. The chance of even applying for a council house in my village in Kent was quickly dashed, because we were not then residents and had no permanent address. In other words as a service family we could never qualify. Finally we decided to buy our own house and found one in Strood in the Medway towns. The price was £1500 and the interest rate on our mortgage was 3.5%. This at least was within range of our friends and families. We bought furniture without the need for hire purchase, moved in, and I began the never-ending task of decorating and maintaining the house. Most of our furniture was from the utility range, each piece stamped with twin circles with a segment removed, but, despite this, was probably as well made as most of the goods now sold by the large furniture chains. My father gave me some help on the first attempt at decorating using a double-knotted distemper brush, which weighed pounds when loaded with oil-bound distemper. The curtain pelmets were secured into concrete lintels, but every hole was made by hammering on an old fluted Rawlplug chisel, and every hole made allowed a steady trickle of sand as if from an hourglass since the plasterwork was over a lime and sand screed. I can assure those who have missed the experience that it was very hard work compared with the materials and tools now available.

I left Gosport for Anthorn with some confidence that I had made the best possible provision for Margaret, and could look forward to the future with a secure base for my family.

"L" Section
N.A.R.I.U. with
Mosquito
Gosport 1950.

A Bit of a "Tiff"

N.A.R.I.U. Gosport 1950 by Author.

N.A.R.I.U.'s winning soccer team Gosport 1950.

Wedding Day Rochester 28th December 1949.

Home Air Command Fire Fighting Competition Gosport 1950.

A Bit of a "Tiff"

Firefly returning the Captain of Yeovilton after the Firefighting
Competition. Gosport 1950.

"- the Captains and the Kings depart -" (in Fireflies) Gosport 1950.

Margaret getting airborne. Gliding Club Open Day. Gosport 1950.

Gosport from a glider 1950. Foreground a Brigand of A.T.D.U. centre right. Airfield gate leading to Main site and M.Q.'s top right. N.A.R.I.U. Hangar top left.

This Swordfish was still flying at Gosport in 1950. Probably NF389 belonging to A.T.D.U.

A replacement for the Swordfish?
Westland Wyvern TF2 prototype flying at Farnborough 1950.

Chimney Fire in
M.Q.'s.

"One more
bucket Jack and
I'm off for my tot."

"Contra props were all the rage in 1950" Fairy Gannet prototype
flying at Farnborough.
in this case each unit of the Double-Mamba drove one propellor.

A Bit of a "Tiff"

"- also on the Bristol Brabazon seen at Farnborough 1950."

"but quite unnecessary on a glider."
Lt.-Cdr. Sproule flying the "Kranich" sailplane with smoke
grenades operating. Gosport 1950.

Early Sikorsky Whirlwind HAR21 at Gosport 1951.

The shape of things to come Supermarine Type 508
at Farnborough 1951.

A Bit of a "Tiff"

English Electric Canberra at Farnborough 1951.

Avro 707B at Farnborough 1951.

Vickers Valiant prototype at Farnborough 1951.

Vickers Valiant prototype at Farnborough 1951.

A Bit of a "Tiff"

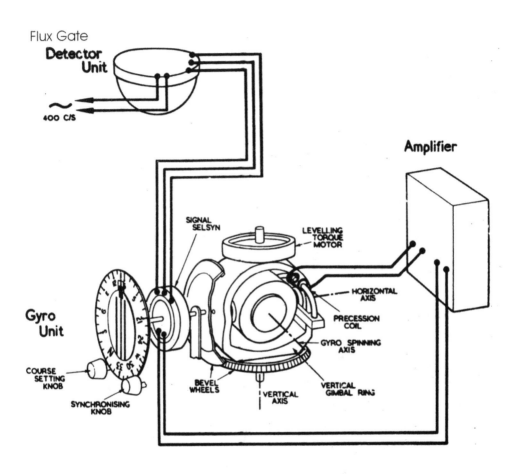

Flux Gate
Detector Unit

~
400 C/S

Amplifier

SIGNAL
SELSYN

LEVELLING
TORQUE
MOTOR

HORIZONTAL
AXIS

Gyro Unit

PRECESSION
COIL

GYRO SPINNING
AXIS

COURSE
SETTING
KNOB

BEVEL
WHEELS

VERTICAL
AXIS

VERTICAL
GIMBAL RING

SYNCHRONISING
KNOB

A schematic diagram of the Gyro-Magnetic Compass Mk4F as fitted to single seat fighter aircraft. The Mk4B fitted to larger aircraft had an Observer's Display which incorporated Correction settings.

Chapter 11 H.M.S. *Nuthatch* Anthorn

I arrived at Anthorn early in November 1951 and almost at once it was Christmas leave, and I was at home when Richard was born in our house on 30th December. I returned to Anthorn well pleased with my lot after our earlier misfortunes. Both Margaret and Richard were well, happy, and comfortable in our house; although I was a fair distance away I expected to be at Anthorn at least two years. With three leaves a year this seemed an acceptable alternative to being constantly on the move each time I had a new job, particularly as there was no provision for married quarters for men serving at sea. Margaret came from a Naval family and accepted this option also.

The air station at Anthorn was about fourteen miles from Carlisle on the edge of the Solway Firth. It was not an operational station, but had large numbers of aircraft in storage. Many of these were Fireflies, and Sea Furies, which were being readied for service in the Korean War, but others, including many of the Firefly A.S.7's mentioned earlier, were stored outside in silvery-coated cocoons. This was the latest idea, but it did not prevent moisture getting inside, and a tour around the dispersal showed that many cocoons were bulging with accumulated water. Very occasionally there was a flap to meet a deadline for delivery, but on the whole the pace was relaxed. In "Operation More Skill" an attempt was made to improve the effectiveness of some of the lower grade technical tasks, such as manning the "Battery Room" by employing Artificers instead of Mechanics, but the scheme was naturally unpopular, and was discontinued.

I found myself in the L.R.S. under Lt. "Harpic" Harpum, (quite unfairly named, as being right round the bend) who was a lively and pleasant character. In the New Year I was detailed by "Harpic" to rig the electrical system for a S.S.A.F.A. ball (Soldiers, Sailors, and Airmen's, Families Association) to be held in Carlisle Castle. No doubt the tickets purchased by the local bigwigs made a nice contribution to S.S.A.F.A. funds but the cost to public funds was high. Essentially, the Army provided most of the labour force, their gymnasium was the ballroom, and a courtyard was converted into a heated covered space for catering; the Navy wired up a large electric cooker for on-site cooking e.g. breakfast after the ball, and extra decorative lighting; the R.A.F. M.U. (Maintenance Unit) at Carlisle arrived with large sheets of aircraft ply, and rolls of foil coated sheet packaging with which the entire gymnasium was coated. They also brought along a glider, which was hung from the ceiling. One of the problems I faced was to find suitable power points near the gymnasium. This was at last solved when I found an apparently empty first floor office without windows, which formed one wall of the gym. It was not too difficult to chisel a hole through the brickwork, and a cable was channelled through to supply the "mirror ball" and its spotlight. It later emerged that the office was used for recruitment interviews, and the owner was not too happy when he returned. He was only a "Pongo" after all, and the deed was done. The ball was a roaring success.

Back again at Anthorn, I was transferred to the Armoury, and for most of my stay I occupied a large workshop containing all the weapons electrical gear from the stored aircraft. With a little initiative I built test rigs, which gave an effective and speedy production line for the Gyro Gun sights, G45 Cameras, Bomb Release Units, and Gun Firing Units, that were required as each aircraft came out of storage. However I was also made responsible for the Link Trainer, the Cinema, and the Typex machines (British equivalent of the German "Enigma" cipher machine). This gave me a lot of freedom on my roving mission.

Warrant Officer Sid Avery, an ex-Newcastle apprentice, was O.i.C. Armoury. He owned a large pre war Chrysler "Airflow", and was adept at finding odd jobs for his workshop i.e. those which would enhance his image with the hierarchy. When a crack appeared in the cast iron soup cooker used to boil pigswill for the Commander's favourite project (the pig farm), Sid volunteered to fix it but failed miserably. Lacking the means of raising the temperature of the whole structure, he attempted to braze or weld the crack with the remainder cold. He chased the ever-enlarging crack around the cooker until even he had to admit defeat. I had a similar experience, when I offered to repair a large engraved brass fruit bowl for Margaret's aunt; this had at one time been dropped and well bent, and the obvious remedy was to anneal the brass before reworking it. Regrettably, the Chinese craftsman must have beaten the brass without annealing it and had converted it to a crystalline state; the whole bowl disintegrated into small pieces with the application of heat and had the strength of a cream cracker. Poor aunty!

Like the cinema, the Link Trainer was a nice diversion when I gave it a routine servicing, but was seldom used by the small number of pilots at Anthorn. However, I was in the cockpit running through the checks one day when there was banging on the outer door of the temperature controlled room, and I tried to level the trainer before getting out to open the door; every attempt to lean outside the cockpit to insert the ground locks stalled the device and sent the machine into a spin and as it rotated I could see the increasingly irate pilot at a window. After several tries, and with the banging getting louder, I switched off the power and let it subside on to its bellows. The pilot was pretty miffed when finally he was admitted.

The "Typex" machines were really very simple in construction, even if their coded output was nearly insoluble, and I had been servicing them happily, removing an electrocuted mouse and lots of cigarette ash in the process, on the basis of their manuals for some time before I was told I was to go on a one week course at H.M.S. *Collingwood* near Fareham. This was to complete just before Easter 1952, and I then found that I could take a Moral Leadership course at Cheltenham in the preceding fourteen days. This would give me three weeks away from Anthorn, with at least two weekends at home, followed by Easter leave. All went well initially at Cheltenham, since I was still a committed Christian, but in the end the reality of service life did not fit the theory, at least in my view, and so on to Collingwood. I found myself in a mixed class of General Service E.A.'s, and EA. Apprentices, whose working routines were out of phase with the remainder e.g. parts of their day were spent elsewhere, and they had a sports afternoon in midweek. The rest of us carried on without interruption and thus completed by Wednesday. Here I thought was another chance to gain an extra day at home, only to discover that my railway warrant to Strood had been incorrectly made out at Anthorn, and could only be reissued with the blessing of the Warrant Master at Arms. This one, the only one I ever came across in my career, was the epitome of every beastly M.A.A. that I'd ever met; instead of going home early on leave I was sent back to Anthorn just in time to about turn and go back south on leave. In the words of another ditty: -

"Oh, I wonder yes I wonder
Did the jaunty make a blunder?
When he made this draft chit out for me?"

Perhaps I got my just deserts, and God in his wisdom had seen through my clever ploy!

Life at Anthorn was bearable and I had found an outside interest in the Carlisle Camera Club. The beautiful Lake District was ideally suited for the photographer and I was soon busy. My name finally appeared at the top of the list of volunteers for loan service to the Royal Australian Navy, but since 1947 my priorities had changed, and I turned it down. However disaster again struck in a flash when I received a telegram saying that Margaret had polio and that Richard was in the care of my mother. I was granted immediate compassionate leave and spent the next three months in a state of turmoil and uncertainty until we were able to discern the degree of Margaret's disability. At first it seemed unlikely that she would be mobile, and that a continuing Naval career would be impossible. I spent a long while, looking for civilian work in or around the Medway towns and writing for interviews in other accessible locations. Several interesting possibilities emerged, including one with a leading Society Photographer in London; oddly the opportunities that most closely matched my technical experience were the least well paid, and this was particularly true of Chatham Dockyard, which was keen to have me. My family responsibility demanded that I receive at least as good a salary as I was getting in the Navy and I was torn as to my next move. At the end of Margaret's stay in hospital, it became clear that the residual disability lay in her left leg, and that using a surgical boot with a leg brace would give her mobility and might in due course become unnecessary after continuing physiotherapy and this gave us hope. The Navy made a M.Q. available to us at Anthorn, and we sold our first home at slightly more than we had paid.

After a long spell of regular therapy in Carlisle the boot was made redundant, although the weakness remained and caused occasional embarrassing falls and still does. Margaret has bravely led as full a life as possible and our children were never disadvantaged by her disability. In my absence some years later, she learned to drive and passed the extended driving test for the disabled. She has only recently given up driving for other reasons. However that was all in the future.

At Anthorn, we happily settled into M.Q.'s and considered ourselves fortunate that they were all new houses, and so much better than our first one at Gosport. It then became essential to simplify our travel arrangements, and some sort of car seemed needed to get us around as a family, even though prior to this it had seemed well down our list of priorities. First I took driving lessons in Carlisle in an old Morris 8 without heating in the first few cold months of 1953 and passed the test. New cars were not only hard to find and also out of reach by cost, but we found two options; locally there was a 1934 Singer with a freewheel device for £120, and the other a 1939 Jowett 8 at £90. The latter belonged to a friend of Margaret's aunt in Glasgow, and this seemed the obvious choice.

Off to Glasgow I went and returned precariously in the car, which had mysteriously just developed a number of faults. The steering was erratic, the exhaust leaked into the cabin, the passenger door catch had broken and was held to the steering column by string from the window winder, the winder had no friction and the window dropped slowly when it was raised, neither the speedometer, trafficators, nor brake lights were working. In other words it was a complete wreck. With all three months of driving behind me I was escorted out of Glasgow on to the A74; at that point the window was open and the exhaust fumes escaped, but later on the April chill prompted me to close the window, I was then between a group of heavy lorries. The window then began to open, and as it dropped, the door handle rotated and the string extended opening the door. With no means of signalling I spent a hazardous few minutes until finally the lorries overtook me and I was able to stop. The last part of the journey between Carlisle and Anthorn was a doddle because the winding country roads absorbed all the lost motion in the steering. After a fair amount of repair work in the road outside the house, and work by Jobby Jeffries in his Kirkbride garage we became mobile again.

An early visit to Carlisle showed the wisdom of A.A. membership, when one of two bolts fell from the drive shaft universal joint, and the resulting vibration left behind a great pile of mud and rust when we were again mobile. We then discovered that the Lake District was not the most suitable place to be driving a 2 cylinder horizontally opposed Jowett 8. Despite the record-breaking hill trials in the 1930's, our particular car lacked punch and on many occasions we failed to make a steep hill, and there was no shortage of these. The worst sort stared downhill with an S-bend, and then having lost all momentum the upward gradient could only be achieved by going up in reverse with Margaret and Richard walking behind. Once we realised the problem, we planned all our trips with the A.A. route map in which the hill gradients were listed and simply avoided any marked as greater than 1 in 8. Trouble was never far away with such an old banger, and I filled the boot with tools and a range of bits and pieces for repairs, as well as plenty of oil and water. We made good time to Kent and back on leave but burned out a clutch while we were there. When friends stayed during the Coronation celebrations in 1953 we followed the family Zephyr 6 around the Lakes and finally boiled dry; even my spare bottle proved insufficient and I paid some small boys a small fortune to fetch enough water to top up the radiator. On another occasion we took a trip to Ullswater, and on the way I replaced a bolt that had dropped from the brake rods, only to find that the starter would not work when we came to leave. No problem, we had a starting handle; unfortunately it was the source of the bolt used in the earlier repair, and we had once again to call the A.A.

Our stay at Anthorn progressed, and with the resilience of youth we began to forget our earlier misfortunes. We watched the Coronation Review on television for the first time in the C.P.O.'s mess, but were not at all impressed by the "Box". When the film of the Coronation arrived at Anthorn it was to be a special event at the camp cinema, and so it was, as a projector failed, and we had to continue on just one, which meant breaks to change reels, and music in the intervals. Some of the officers in the audience were not impressed by the choice of the usual popular music for this solemn occasion! Once, the Solway flooded the road to the airfield and we went to work by old D.U.K.W.'s (amphibious vehicles). Other light entertainment was provided by the noise from the Officer's M.Q.'s, when during a mess ball a Lt.-Cdr. was discovered at home with the baby sitter, at some point the wife was locked out and smashed the glass door to get back in. This was worth a good chuckle. I continued to attend the Camera Club, earned the odd penny taking portraits, and repaired cameras for the Naval photographers. On two occasions I rashly joined Fell walking expeditions organised by the Padre, the first to Scafell and the next to Scafell Pikes; except for the horrendous weather, the lack of suitable clothing, and the Padre's ability to get lost, it was quite an experience.

I was now within two years of completing my twelve years service and needed to decide my next step. My instincts were to avoid the hassle of service life and to be full time with my family as a civilian but the recent experience had been unsettling, and on that occasion the Navy had shown itself to be a caring employer. I therefore decided to keep my options open and again try my chances at gaining a Commission. This time, the objective was Branch rank, and after study I was recommended, took the exam, and qualified in 1954. That year the vacancies were over subscribed and I was drafted to join the Electrical Apprentices training workshop at H.M.S. *Collingwood* for the next year to await promotion.

My boss by now was Bill Wellman, a long serving Commissioned Electrical Officer, he congratulated me and told me not to expect too much from the system, which did not much care for Branch Officers. I discounted this at that time, but later came to find the truth behind his comments.

By this time Margaret was again pregnant following an enjoyable Christmas dance in the C.P.O.'s mess, and so we left Anthorn minus the car, thankfully sold after yet another major problem, without a house and with no hope of a M.Q. at Collingwood. We had $2^{1}/_{2}$ year old Richard and another baby on the way, so we had no choice but to move temporarily to my parents until the baby was born.

Scafell Pikes. The Padre's fell walking Expedition Anthorn
Spring 1953.

Coronation Fireworks Anthorn June 1953.

A Bit of a "Tiff"

Supermarine Attacker WA475 from Eagle. Anthorn Air Day 1953.

Margaret and Richard in the Fells Anthorn 1953.

Chapter 12 H.M.S. *Collingwood*, and promotion

H.M.S. *Collingwood* at Fareham was, and still is, the Naval Electrical School. I understand that Jack Jones (Builders) of Maidenhead, who was my grandmother's brother, had built it during the war.

I arrived at the start of the Apprentices' three-week summer leave, but it was quickly clear that I would not be partaking. I was left with a long list of tasks, which were a challenge to my skills, but which in fact brought me up to speed with machines that I had not previously used. By the time the new term started, I was ready to go, but preferably not as a lecturer. In fact after a few weeks I was placed in charge of workshop maintenance. It was a full-time job to keep up with the damage caused by the trainees, but for major jobs and overhauls a team of Dockyard experts would be called in, and would take the machine back to Portsmouth Dockyard. All the spare parts were ordered through the Dockyard by quoting the description of the machine part, the page number and year of issue of an old "Buck and Hickman" catalogue; this was an Aladdin's Cave of a catalogue and it was always effective.

The raw materials used in the workshop were also my responsibility, and had to be ordered well in advance. On one occasion the repairs needed to a mechanical saw required roughly a 6 inch length each of 4 inch square mild steel bar, and 5 inch round brass rod. Imagine my surprise therefore when the year's stock of material was delivered one lunchtime, and included a complete billet of each item, both over 14 ft. long. I cannot remember how the small lengths were cut for my job, but for a long time errant apprentices were made to saw off a length by hacksaw as a punishment.

As always the workshop was disturbed by the graunching noise of tools breaking and gearwheels being damaged by the trainees; whilst I had ample machinery to machine new gear teeth, the problem was getting them brazed or welded in the first place. Soon while poking around in an old store behind the workshop, I uncovered a number of brand-new and still packaged U.S. welding sets. In a matter of days, and with a bit of practice with the Blacksmith in another workshop, I was fully equipped to tackle all our welding and cutting problems. From then on we were fully independent. The same store yielded other treasures, such as new and unopened sets of numbered drills down to No. 80 in size. These, together with the extra welding gear, enabled the Chief Instructor to introduce extra test pieces to the curriculum e.g. a small gas torch, also handy at home, and a number of Engineering Models, such as Beam Engines, which were built by the most advanced apprentices for display. I scrounged compressed air pumps from the aircraft dump at nearby R.N.A.Y. Fleetlands to power these models.

For the good of my future I was nobbled as i/c Workshop Staff on Friday Divisions; not a problem, but Collingwood had a very large parade ground, and the Gunnery mob had with their usual careful planning managed to require each squad to be dressed from one direction but marched off from the other. Inevitably this meant that chaos ensued as a squad marched off, if a blank file was created by one or two absent men and the blank file rippled back to the other end. It only needed one extra order to solve this difficulty, and thereafter all was well. Divisions were never popular, and we always hoped for rain, but on one Friday the Gunners had taken advice from the Met. Office at Lee-on-Solent, and the rain stopped precisely when the parade fell-in, and started as we were dismissed. We considered that a misuse of science.

As duty C.P.O. one task was to carry out the nightly rounds and to clear and lock up the large canteen and recreation hall. This had the largest bunch of unlabelled keys that I've ever seen, and so many doors that it was easy to get nearly to the exit only to find it was necessary to go into reverse in the dark and go back through a door that had just been locked. A fire drill was called one evening during duty watch muster, and this was yet another Navy Lark of the sort I had seen so many times before. A stack pipe was connected to the hydrant and a fire-hose attached; when the hydrant was turned on the stack pipe separated under full pressure and a mighty fountain appeared. To the delight of most of the duty watch, the deluge continued until a volunteer had braved the water and entered the pit to get at the stopcock. Many were already wet, but "not me Chief", I kept well clear.

My daughter, Barbara, was born at the West Kent Hospital in Maidstone on 13th September, and in order to be with my family at weekends I bought a small motor bike for the 100 mile journey each way, and started to look for a house in the Fareham area. Fareham was still the small market town it had been in 1941, but building had recently started in an area of old strawberry fields at Catisfield. Due to the clay subsoil the majority of the houses were to be bungalows, and these were ideally suited for Margaret's problem. We were able to afford a three bedroom semi-detached bungalow, and eventually lived there for nine years until we needed to expand. It was conveniently sited for access to ships at Portsmouth, to Lee-on-Solent, to Gosport, and other Air Stations in the south. Since then we have moved to several other houses, but always in Hampshire, which is now our adopted county.

The 150cc. two-stroke Royal Enfield Ensign was not a total success, although it served its purpose until we could afford a car. The choice between it and the similarly priced B.S.A. Bantam equivalent was made on the swinging arm rear suspension, which in logic should have reduced chain wear, but the invisible clutch mechanism was the weak link. Cork pads ran in an oil bath, and were reluctant to re-engage after a rest, usually at traffic lights. After a while, the only answer was to run in very thin oil or totally dry, and to accept a high rate of wear. To counter this problem, I made a clutch extractor, and carried this, a spare set of corks, and tools in my toolkit. I was then able to repair the clutch quickly at the roadside, as well as de-whiskering the spark plug, and changing the main chain. We finally bought a car in 1957 but the bike remained in use until 1960.

In 1955 I again took the board and passed for C.E.A. and applied to re-engage for pension i.e. until aged forty, but as hoped for on 27th August I was selected for promotion to Acting Commissioned Electrical Officer (Air Electrical) and drafted to H.M.S. *Ariel* at Worthy Down for the transfer.

Worthy Down under its new title was the Air Electrical School, and I arrived as an E.A.2(A), one of 9 promotees, 4 (L), 4 (R), and 1 R.A.N.(L). For the first month we were given quick instruction in the other half of our now dual trades i.e. both Electrical and Radio. During this period we were briefed on the uniform requirements, measured by Naval Tailors, and kitted up with the remainder of our uniforms at *Collingwood*. We were finally promoted on 29th September 1955.

At this point we were off to H.M.S. *Victory* at Portsmouth Barracks, all freshly rigged out for the barest minimum of officer training and "knife and fork drill" i.e. etiquette, which included attendance at the Trafalgar Night Dinner. The civilian mess staff, and stewards had seen all this many times before, and had a daunting air of superiority when dealing with us greenhorns. We had lectures, in great haste, on the duties of a Divisional Officer and other subjects, and parade ground work including sword drill with Cutlasses in lieu of Officers' Swords. The latter experience convinced me that however nice a sword might appear above my mantlepiece on retirement, it would be of more value to me as a crutch or a walking stick, and would be a great inconvenience on any occasion when it was worn due to my limited height. In fact, I never bought a sword and was only required to wear one on two occasions over the next sixteen years.

After *Victory* we returned to Worthy Down for additional technical briefing. We were now living in the Wardroom and as newly promoted officers were each detailed to be the Assistant to the regular Duty Officer in turn. I quickly blotted my copy book when, on my first day of duty, there was an unusual bugle call on the tannoy during lunch, followed by a terse statement "Bosun's Store". This was a total mystery, and my chum Jan Ingram, who had been stationed at *Ariel* before promotion, had no better advice than that it had nothing to do with the duty watch. How wrong he was! I soon discovered that about half the duty watch and I had failed to attend at a fire in the Bosun's Store Paint Locker. I therefore learned at once how to draft an official letter of apology to the Commander, ending with the formal: -

I have the honour to be sir,

Your humble and obedient Servant.

The introduction of bugle calls was another misguided return to old Naval routines, after that I never again heard the bugle used in this way. For such a practice to be effective it had to be in general use, so that recognition of each call was automatic.

A classmate Fred Allford was on duty one morning as assistant to a rather kindly and elderly Branch Officer. After muster, the Duty Watch was required to plant some greenery around the Admin. Block. When the party was assembled, the Duty Officer said: - "Now we have to plant these shrubs, and this is how to do it." He then dug a hole, planted the first bush, but then continued until all the shrubs were planted, while the duty watch stood back and watched. We had a good laugh about that.

Very quickly our first appointments were announced, and three of us were posted at once to join Squadrons due to work up and embark on H.M.S. *Eagle*. The remainder were sent to H.M.S. *Phoenix* to do the Damage Control Course i.e. to learn how to cope with Fire, Smoke, and Flooding Emergencies on a ship. I much regretted the omission of this training during the rest of my service, and particularly when we were called to Action Stations, for real or as an exercise.

For Exercise Fire. "Well don't just stand there, do something!"

Promotion Class. Commissioned Electrical Officers "AL" and "AR"
October 1955.

A Bit of a "Tiff"

Chapter 13 897 Squadron

Part 1 H.M.S. *Goldcrest* Brawdy

Jan and I left Worthy Down for Brawdy late in October 1955 and arrived on a Saturday evening. We were both to be the Air Electrical Officers of newly forming Seahawk squadrons. I had 897 Squadron and Jan had 899. The commissioning ceremonies for both were to be held the following morning and at that time we had met none of our fellow officers, or our ratings. On parade, and after a deal of shuffling around, I found myself in charge of a group of men whom I supposed to be my Electrical and Radio staff, and with minutes to go before the ceremony commenced I was required to buckle on a sword borrowed from an unattached officer. First attempt was a failure when the sword was placed on the wrong side of the leather sling and, I had then to remove it with a great flourish. My doubts about the sword were being quickly realised, and continued the next day when we were each required to dress up again to be formally introduced to the Captain.

Brawdy near Haverfordwest, was another outpost of the F.A.A. empire. Its merits must be presumed to be the proximity of Milford Haven, which was suitable for large ships, and a nearby weapons range at Castlemartin. The disadvantages were the old wartime accommodation, the distance from civilisation even if Haverfordwest is included, and a tendency for the "Haar" (sea fog) to arrive over the airfield and stop flying.

As officers, we were no better accommodated than the "troops"; small paraffin stoves heated our little wooden cabins, and muddy paths led from the huts to the ablution blocks and to the wardroom. I recall having a washstand, basin and jug of water, as the only concession to en-suite facilities. As we had arrived in winter, the heating was an immediate issue, but the paraffin heaters could not be left unattended even for a short while, and the cabins were always cold when we arrived back from work. Jan's cabin was quickly covered in soot when the heater started smoking while he was absent for a few minutes. The ablution block was heated, or more accurately stopped from freezing by a coke stove, the fumes from which formed a distinct layer about two feet above the floor. Only desperation for a call of nature prompted a visit, no question of lingering as asphyxiation was a possibility. The water supply was uncertain as the local people tended to leave their taps running in cold weather to prevent the pipes from freezing.

It was now ten years since I had served in a front line squadron, and although we were still living in what were basically wartime conditions, there had been other changes. Each squadron now had an Air Engineer Officer (A.E.O.), usually a "Manadon" trained Lieutenant, and an Air Electrical Officer (A.L.O.). The latter were mostly Commissioned Electrical Officers, like myself, and because the electrical equipment at that stage was rather less complex than it was later to become, then the A.L.O. was regarded as a supernumerary, and the orders and requirements from the C.O. and Senior Pilot tended to be relayed through the A.E.O. and his side-kick the Chief A.A. if they remembered to do so. However both ashore and in carriers the A.L.O.'s were supported by a Commander (L); certainly Cdr. (L) Tippetts monitored Jan and I for our first few months at Brawdy. Squadrons also carried E.A.'s (A), and R.E.A.'s (A), but these were primarily used to support the squadron by operating in the electrical and radio workshops. The Armourers were as always a special case, and they worked closely with the squadron's A.W.O. (Air Weapons Officer), with support and guidance from the ship or station Air Ordnance Officer. Wherever the squadron went, a small number of our trained Mechanics were detached for communal duties, such as the ship's laundry, as well as the usual mess deck cleaning. This was unpopular with the men, and also to us engineers when we would have to detail some of our best men as the roster progressed. On the other hand it was sometimes possible to lose a troublemaker in a semi permanent detachment.

The C.O. of 897 was Lt.-Cdr. (later Rear Admiral) Ray Rawbone, his Senior Pilot Lt.-Cdr. (later Captain) Keith Leppard, the A.W.O. Lt. (later Captain) Lyn Middleton, and the A.E.O. Lt. Jimmy James. The complement was 14 aircrew, A.E.O., A.L.O. and 82 ratings. After a while Jan and I settled into our new jobs, and there was a comfortable relationship between the two squadrons. At an early stage Ray Rawbone decided to paint the noses of our 12 Seahawks with the very distinctive head of a "Caspian Tern" derived from that on the Squadron crest; the use of rather flashy insignia was a fairly common practice among the Seahawk units and the paint was supplied by the squadron officers' fund. By the time we disbanded at least thirty original and replacement aircraft had been decorated in this way, so the cost of tins of "Humbrol" enamel was considerable. With or without such decoration, the Seahawk was a very pretty aircraft, and I can think of few comparable in appearance, with the exception of the Spitfire. It was the Seafire that was used by 897 Sqdn. when the unit was operational during the war aboard H.M.S. *Unicorn* in July 1943 at Salerno and later on H.M.S *Stalker*. Thereafter the Squadron seems to have been stood down until 1955.

So what of the Seahawk compared with the Hellcat of my last squadron? It had gained nearly 200 knots in top speed, and another 10,000 ft in altitude, but had about only half the range of a Hellcat. The Seahawk had four 20mm cannon compared with the six .5 inch guns of the Hellcat, but carried a similar weight of bombs i.e. two 500lb. In the F.G.A. (Fighter Ground Attack) versions, which could be fitted with "zero" length R.P. launchers, it was possible to carry up to eighteen rockets in six triple tiers, as opposed to the eight on the Hellcat. However, the Seahawk carried a gyro-gun sight unlike the Hellcat, which had the old reflector sight.

The R.R. Nene engine was a direct descendant of the "Whittle" design with a double-sided centrifugal compressor and, because of this, air was sucked into a plenum chamber from flapped openings in the upper fuselage during start up and at low speed. The engine was started by cartridge, not now the little shotgun sized "Coffman", but something not far removed from an artillery shell case, however it was very reliable. Instead of petrol, the fuel was now kerosene, but the tanks were still topped up by hand held hose. This was a messy process, and the ground crew used cumbersome anti-kerosene suits; but with economy in mind the Navy did not provide sufficient to allow a personal issue, nor had provision been made for a secure stowage of these and other dirty and stinking flight deck clothes away from the crowded mess decks. This caused endless problems, which could have been resolved with a little more thought and cash.

The quantity of fuel now carried in jet aircraft raised the need to pump the fuel in such a way that the weight of fuel remaining continued to be evenly distributed. Various methods were used, but in the Seahawk this was controlled by a system using polarised relays; the contacts in these gave trouble as did the aircraft wiring system. In the Seahawk, Plessey "Breeze" plugs carried the circuits between numbers of large junction boxes, and this system, which pre-dated the Plessey Mk4 mentioned earlier, caused problems with intermittent contact after some use. The 897 Squadron aircraft were the F.B.3 version and had already seen service, while 899 Squadron had new F.G.A.6's. This made a vast difference in reliability, and our solution was for my Chief Electrician "Jumper" Cross and I, to select one aircraft each night and sit on the mainplane dismantling, cleaning, polishing, and generally closing up the contacts on each plug and socket of the main junction boxes. It was a never-ending task.

Two smallish D.C. generators worked together to supply the total load of the electrical systems, and charge the batteries. Each was driven by a quill drive from the engine gearbox; these drives had a waisted section to absorb torque changes, but often a drive would shear, the electrical load then fell on the remaining generator, and unless load was shed rapidly this drive would then also fail, leaving only the battery to power the aircraft for a short time. The "domino" effect on aircraft generating systems was to lead to the loss of an R.A.F. "V" bomber, and the lesson was then learned; in later generations of aircraft the generating capacity was much increased, and the risk of losing an aircraft from a single generator failure was virtually eliminated.

On the Seahawk most equipment such as undercarriage, flaps, and wing fold was electro-hydraulically operated, and the best diagnostic tool for a faulty system was a hide-faced hammer applied to the faulty valve. If the system started working after a quick whack, then it had been sticking and was changed. The instruments had improved by the introduction of the Sperry G.M. Mk4f compass, an electrically driven Artificial Horizon, and a Mach meter, but the instrument panel layout was no longer based upon the standard pre-war "Blind Flying Panel".

Radio equipment included a Xtal controlled V.H.F. radio in the T.R.1934/5/6 range, an improved I.F.F.set, and a U.S. Z.B.X. homing receiver, which worked in conjunction with shore based Y.G. Beacons. All these units used thermionic valves, and reliability depended upon how many shocks they had received; usually all failed quickly when returning to a ship after a spell ashore, then gave a period of serviceability before they failed again. The bashing given by carrier landings quickly found any dodgy gear.

However we learned to cope with these and other foibles as the squadron worked up at Brawdy, and progressed to Weapon training before going to H.M.S. *Bulwark* for deck experience. This was cancelled after two of 897's old F.B.3's suffered from a collapsed undercarriage on landing, and we returned to Brawdy for modifications. On *Bulwark*, Jan and I found ourselves in the Warrant Officers' Mess for the first and only time, i.e. we messed separately from the pilots, who continued to use the wardroom. This concept discriminated between General List Officers and the Commissioned Officers who had come from the lower deck. Although some Senior Commissioned Officers preferred to be separate for good reasons, it was only possible on ships large enough to have the space available but did not apply at Brawdy or any other Air Station at that period. The coloured bands within the gold rings on their sleeves had easily distinguished the specialisation of officers other than the Executive or Seaman branch; thus it was Purple for Engineers (Plumbers), Green for Electricians (Greenies), Red for Doctors, Orange for Dentists (Toothies), White for Supply (Pussers and Paybobs), and Blue for Schoolmasters (Schoolies) and there were other lesser known ones. In one respect it separated out those in commanding roles (Executive Officers), from the remainder who at that time would never be placed in command of a ship or station, but it did have one beneficial result because it was a very easy way of identifying the functions of individuals, particularly when one had just joined a large ship or establishment.

However change was in the air and the new democratic system abolished the coloured bands, and more importantly allowed the possibility of specialist officers taking an executive post in certain roles. In 1956 former Commissioned Officers now became Sub. Lieuts., and Senior Commissioned Officers became Lieuts on the Special Duties List, and all messed in the Wardroom. The immediate effect of the loss of the coloured bands was that everyone wore name tabs, and went around peering at these to identify to whom one was speaking.

For newly promoted officers the range of uniform options became yet another matter to put to memory. No less than eight different options are listed in a little booklet issued by J. Baker - Naval Tailors of Portsmouth, and these did not include the white overalls used by engineers or the blue Action Working Dress (R.N. equivalent of denim jeans). Five were variations of white and navy blue used in hot or tropical climates, and except for white shorts and shirt all were hot and uncomfortable if used in less than fully air-conditioned spaces. The worst hot weather rig was No.10's, White Undress; the high-necked starched tunic and trousers were normally only used for ceremonial duties, particularly when a ship entered harbour.

On carriers, the flight deck made an ideal open space for such a ceremony, and most often involved all non-duty ratings lining each side in their best "whites", while the officers mustered forward in a line across the deck, with its centre behind the "jack staff". Well in advance and before attempting to dress, the "whites" had first to be cracked apart to separate the thick layer of starch applied in the ships laundry. Even before reaching the flight deck the heat in the passageways would have created discomfort, at least we could expect some breeze to help cool us once up top, but there were other snags ahead. Officers were paraded "tallest on the flanks, shortest in the centre", and the centre was of course yours truly; so I usually found myself immediately behind the Ensign, which flapped away in the wind and threatened to knock my cap off on every pass. The other hazard of this position was from the tugs secured to our bows for the final entry to harbour; almost invariably, but particularly in Malta, the tugs would belch clouds of soot and coal dust and we would get the full benefit. The only advantage of being on parade was that it was possible to get a decent look at the new port as we arrived, and sometimes to get a photograph or two, but the moment we were dismissed we were off back to our cabins to strip off and put our sooty whites back in to be laundered.

With all these uniforms and our civilian clothes, which were essential for shore going officers but forbidden for ratings, there was a considerable pile of kit to be carted around with us. No longer the kitbag, but an Officer's tin trunk. Thank goodness we had stewards to do the lifting and shifting. As before, every squadron carried its officers stewards; the service provided by our stewards was of course limited to around one steward to six junior officers; they served in the mess and gave a personal service e.g. by cleaning cabins and dealing with laundry. As usual in these circumstances the little extra services were rewarded, and by the time our young pilots had dispensed their flying pay rather more generously than newly promoted Jan and I, then we received the barest minimum support; that had been our lot for years and so did not create a problem.

J. Baker's little booklet "Come aboard to join Sir!" not only dealt with uniform and etiquette, but mentioned pay; in Jan 1954, the newly promoted Warrant Officer received £1. 3s. 6d. per day, although this depended upon his lower deck rating on promotion. For example, a C.E.A. already received a similar level of pay, and since there had to be some pay incentive to seek promotion, then an increment of 4 shillings was given to such people. The increment could never be removed until further promotion finally overtook the difference, and it created an anomaly in which a newly promoted C.E.A. could be earning more than a Warrant Officer with 8 yrs. seniority. This was obviously a cause of resentment, but was never corrected during my service.

A large part of our normal duties was to act as Divisional Officer for the Junior and Senior ratings working under us; in other words we acted "in loco parentis". We counselled on family matters, pay, promotion, debt, and virtually any other problem that could be created by sailors ashore and afloat. Often the outcome was that the individual had to see the Commander or Captain for the matter to be actioned at the routine Requestmen and Defaulters parade. The Divisional Officer's role was to represent the individual concerned by giving a statement of the facts, a character reference and a recommendation. At Defaulters however the role was to advise the alleged defaulter and give a statement of his conduct, with a plea in mitigation if this was sensible. It was not however an opportunity to do a "Perry Mason" act in order to get the man off the charge. This was soon pointed out to me forcibly, when my Captain at that time said "He wouldn't be here if he wasn't guilty". I had no answer to that, since it was evident that the "Jossman" and the Commander, prior to the parade, had already determined the outcome of the charge. Of course on occasion the sheer novelty of a rating's excuse gave an opportunity for leniency and sometimes hilarity.

The life of all sailors was recorded on a collection of documents enclosed in a blue card cover, which held the "Service Certificate". The records listed his performance, conduct, training courses, qualifications, and work record etc. These were held by the ship's secretarial staff and maintained by them with the Divisional Officers input. Annually a written assessment was required from the D.O. and countersigned by his superiors. These assessments amplified the cryptic words Superior, Satisfactory, Average, or Below Average on the back of the Service Certificate, and any derogatory remarks were underlined in "red", and had to be read out to the rating at his annual interview. Designed to help the ratings improve their performance, or at the very least understand why they had been downgraded, it could on occasion be an unpleasant task for the D.O. as well.

Officers on the other hand had no personal interview. The Officer's Annual Report was produced on Form 206 and this was never shown to the officer concerned but at the end of each appointment or on change of Captain, then a small paper, 4 inches by 6 inches called a "Flimsy" was issued. In principle this gave the Captain's assessment of the individual during the period under his command; actually of course he was merely the signatory. There were two elements to the terse document, and it was the first that was critical. This was written in the form: – "This officer has served under my Command from date x to date y to my satisfaction." The word "satisfaction" was meant to indicate an average performance, and could be changed to suggest a worse or better result; usually "entire satisfaction" was reckoned as a good recommend when promotion loomed. Notoriously a few clocked up the classic "to his own entire satisfaction"; this was a black mark by any standard! A few cryptic phrases then followed in amplification but gave no helpful hints as to how the officer might improve, and very oddly there was never any personal interview or appraisal by one's line manager. It was as if they could not face up to dealing with a colleague, and a complete contrast to the treatment given to the ratings. Similarly the recourse that all ratings had in requesting to see the Captain or higher authority on any disputed matter was not readily available to officers, and stirring up a problem was not popular. The other services appeared to be better organised in this respect.

If I thought that my previous twelve years' service had given me an insight into human behaviour, then it did not take long as a Divisional Officer to learn otherwise. Perhaps the first surprise came at Brawdy when one of my lads was charged by the police in Haverfordwest with "Entering and attempting to drive away a bus". The rating's excuse was certainly plausible; he had missed the last bus back to camp, and had simply got into the bus scheduled for the first run the following day, to sleep overnight as was a common practice. I attended the civilian court to give a statement as to his conduct and character, and sat through the usual Licence applications and a local man charged with poaching on a Sunday. He had been found with two ducks and a quail, both still warm, so his fate was settled. When it was our turn, the Police Sergeant said that he had followed the sailor round the town to the bus station where he entered the bus and started the engine. The door had been locked and he could not enter to turn off the engine but had had to call out a bus company engineer. The outcome was then in no doubt whatever plea my lad had made, and justifiably so, but I failed to understand why the policeman had not simply stopped and questioned the lad before any offence had been committed. When later my colleagues and I were detailed as Shore Patrol Officer, and particularly in foreign ports, it was our practice to gather up the drunks and potential troublemakers before they had a chance to give trouble. Usually a lift back to the ship was welcomed and it saved a lot of problems.

The incident rather confirmed a suspicion that we English were none too welcome in Wales, and I was pleased when it was time to move to *Eagle*.

Chapter 13 897 Squadron

Part 2 H.M.S. *Eagle* The Med. and Suez

In early April 1956 both 897 and 899 squadrons joined *Eagle* at Devonport and sailed for Gibraltar on 20th.

Eagle was then the largest carrier in the fleet at 41,200 tons, but was later matched by her sister ship *Ark Royal; Eagle* was scrapped in 1972 and *Ark Royal* in 1978 after extensive modernisation, which gave each a fully angled flight deck, steam catapults and mirror landing aid; this brought the tonnage to 43,000, but with 152,000 s.h.p. from their steam turbines could still manage 30.5 knots. Since then there have been no carriers of this size in the Royal Navy, but if present plans continue, then in 2012 the first of two new carriers each about 50,000 tons will enter service. None of these compare in size with the largest U.S. ships which are about 100,000 tons. It is worth noting that throughout this book I have quoted only the standard tonnage of each ship, to avoid confusion with the fully laden weight, which includes fuel and other commodities e.g. fuel on *Eagle* amounted to some 5,500 tons. For this reason many references give different tonnages for the same ship.

Eagle was laid down in 1942 as H.M.S. *Audacious*, and was renamed in 1946 but not completed until 1951; she was the 21st ship of the Royal Navy to bear the name, and her predecessor, also a carrier, was sunk in August 1942 during a convoy run to Malta. *Eagle* was well protected by armour and her armoured flight deck was 800 ft by 112 ft; this was fitted with 2 catapults, 16 arrester wires, 3 barriers, and 2 lifts. The flight deck was arranged to give an interim angle of 5.5 degrees. The lifts served both the upper and lower hangars; one was 54 ft by 44 ft, the other 54 ft by 33 ft. The upper hangar was 364 ft by 67 ft, with a 45 ft extension forward of the lift, while the lower hangar was shorter at 172 ft by 54 ft., and in total this gave a potential capacity to carry 100 aircraft The complement was now 2750 men. During this commission, the normal complement of aircraft was as follows: –

897 Sqdn. Seahawk F.B.3
899 Sqdn. Seahawk F.G.A.6
830 Sqdn. Wyvern
892 Sqdn. Venom
812 Sqdn. Gannet
849A Flt. Skyraider A.E.W.
Ships Flt. Whirlwind A.S.R

Ship's armament followed the wartime pattern, with 8 twin 4.5 inch gun turrets and a total of 57 40mm Bofors guns, but these were rarely used. On the only occasion when the gunners had an opportunity to show their worth, they failed miserably. Their practice target was a radar reflective balloon which drifted slowly past the ship; the 4.5 inch gun turrets tracked rapidly toward the balloon, hunted back and forth for a brief moment and then continued on past and opened fire into empty space.

Jan and I were initially bunked in with our young squadron Sub.-Lt. pilots but after a few days of living amid a jumble of discarded flying clothing and smelly "immersion suits" we were found a two berth cabin one deck lower in 6Z. i.e. six decks below the flight deck and Z the last compartment counted from A at the bows. The outer and rear bulkheads literally formed the starboard aft corner of the ship, just above the screws. This was our cabin for the whole of our appointment. There was obviously no porthole, and normally blue guard lights gave some illumination in the cabins and passageways after dark; when on one occasion the guard lights failed, I awoke without any visual reference and was completely disoriented. I could then understand how deprivation of visual reference had been used during prisoner interrogation.

The visit to Gibraltar was the first at which I was able to go ashore; there appeared little on offer for the sightseer but a wealth of bars, and shops selling goods like cameras at much below the U.K. price. With some of our pilots I had a run across the border into the nearest Spanish town of La Linea but this had little more than a rather sleazy run-down bar for our entertainment so I did not envy the British servicemen their postings to this outpost of the Empire.

From Gibraltar we made our way to Malta and the start of the summer cruise. However before entering Malta, *Eagle* spent a weekend off Pozzallo in Sicily. Banyans (picnics) were arranged on the beach, where we were landed with food and drink and wearing informal dress by ship's boat. I joined the C.O. and pilots of 897 and after our lunch we wandered inland; not strictly part of the agreement and despite the presence of the local "carabinieri". Shortly after passing through the vineyards that fronted this hot and sandy beach we came across a wrinkled old farmer with a horse and cart, and following a somewhat unintelligible conversation were invited to jump aboard the cart, which smelled strongly of horse pee and progressed slowly towards the little metropolis of Pozzallo. Before we arrived we were transferred to the crossbars of a group of bicycles and on arrival were entertained royally with wine and Amaretto biscuits in the grand walnut furnished bedroom of a house on the main street. At the end of our visit

A Bit of a "Tiff"

we were carried back to the beach in convoy on the back of "Vespa" scooters. Having subsequently experienced much official and unofficial entertainment around the world, I remember this as the most spontaneous welcome I have ever received; the more surprising since this was a poor agricultural community with whom we had been at war only twelve years before.

Malta was as usual the base from which the fleet operated during the summer cruise, and we were there for a period every month. On occasion the Squadrons disembarked to Hal-Far, and we then lived ashore in Nissen huts bereft of furniture, next door to a U.S. Navy "Neptune" squadron VF24, whose air-conditioned buildings we could only dream about. One thing was evident; the permanent residents of R.N. Air Station Hal-Far did not welcome the interruption to their highly relaxed existence. Many had families with them, and in another anomaly of the system, it was possible for wives of shore based officers to obtain an "Indulgence" passage in one of the R.F.A.'s (Royal Fleet Auxiliaries) that accompanied us on the cruise. They then lounged around on the tankers or supply ships, and could be seen watching us slave away from their deck chairs while our own families were still in U.K.

The pattern of our lives during the cruise was a period of about a week to ten days flying, and generally exercising with our support fleet or as part of a specific N.A.T.O. exercise, followed by a similar rest period in one port or another on our voyage around the Mediterranean. Each visit had a purpose, that of showing the flag, and was a well established way of achieving both official and unofficial liaison between Senior Officers and their military and civilian counterparts at each port visited. With luck the ships and their crews would impress the local people, provided that "Jack" behaved ashore and did not cause incidents by bad behaviour. On the whole it worked well, and we all enjoyed the break.

The pattern set years before was for the senior ship on the first night in port to host an official cocktail party, to which foreign dignitaries and businessmen would be invited together with British residents, and Embassy or Consular staff who had helped arrange the visit and the guest list. *Eagle* was of course the largest vessel and carried the Flag Officer Aircraft Carriers – Rear Admiral Manley Power (later Vice Admiral), so we had the honour of hosting the party. All officers were on duty in best uniforms to welcome and attend the guests, and the stewards would dispense vast quantities of food and drink. On these occasions our chefs worked miracles in producing a wide range of cocktail snacks, some of which included such delicacies as caviare. Naturally there was a well-known ditty on that rarity: -

Caviare comes from the virgin sturgeon,
Virgin sturgeon's a very rare fish,
There aren't many virgins among the sturgeons,
That's why caviare's a very rare dish.

The alcoholic content of mixed drinks such as gin and tonic, and "Horses Neck" got gradually stronger as the evening progressed and the stewards entered into the spirit themselves and this ensured that the junior officers were well supplied. The evening ended when the Royal Marine Band "Beat Retreat", and this was always guaranteed to impress the visitors. At this point, the effectiveness of our prowess as hosts was put to the test and the "Baron Stranglers" were guaranteed a good stay. The "Strangler" set out to impress a guest or guests with his undoubted charm and grace in the fond expectation that he would find himself invited to spend his stay with an individual or a family ashore (the Barons). Some were of course totally successful in their efforts, but generally it was quite unnecessary as the host country or port invariably arranged other social events, official receptions for the senior officers and other events for the remainder. The arrival of the fleet always led to a rush of private invitations to the ship's officers, not all of these from British nationals, and it was open to any of us to take up the offers; in fact in extreme cases where the invitations were in abundance, it was our duty to ensure that all invitations were fully booked. There were exceptions to the rule; in France the official return cocktail party was short and had a defined start and finish, after which it was "Adieu". People outside our knowledge made our own guest list, but I visited Toulon in *Eagle* in 1956 and again in 1959 in *Victorious* and was surprised to recognise many of our guests from the earlier visit. What a hard life for the great and good! It was generally recognised however that the small ships, which could actually come into a harbour and lie alongside, held the best parties, and so did the R.F.A's, in which the R.N. protocol did not apply. It was rarely possible for a ship the size of *Eagle* to enter harbour, and all the coming and going was carried out by ship's boats. A strict protocol applied in the officers' boat and the senior officer always entered last before the boat pushed off.

Malta was of course no stranger to the Royal Navy and no special arrangements were needed. People did their own thing, but for those anxious to be involved in the local social whirl the trick was to sign the visitor's book at Government House, and if the stay were long enough then eventually their name would be added to the invitees at some reception or other. It was not reckoned to be a good option for those hoping to chat up the local hot totty, as it was reported that the females attending were generally well past their sell by date.

A Bit of a "Tiff"

In only a few locations were there any major social events for the lower deck, who made their own contacts with the local population via the bars and other local entertainment centres; hopefully without conflict, because they were obliged to wear uniform ashore and were instantly obvious wherever they went. Nonetheless the ship managed in most places to arrange coach tours for those interested. On the other hand the ship's company always pulled their weight if the ship laid on an open day or a party for local children and their efforts contributed a great deal to the success of a visit. Despite their reputation few sailors fell foul of the local law, or got themselves involved with the local and often well-infected "talent". Compared with my earlier experience, only one of my lads, a C.P.O., came to grief. Generally, it seemed that peer pressure maintained the fidelity of the vast majority of the crew, and during these fleeting visits there was rarely time for any serious liaisons.

Prior to and at the end of each visit several groups came to the top of the luck stakes. The first an officer, probably a Lt.-Cdr., who was appointed liaison officer for the visit, and went ashore to make arrangements for the ship itself, but also for the social events. He would return with quantities of literature and maps of the places to visit, and if he had done his job correctly, then he would have established where all the hot spots and dodgy dives existed, and compiled a full list with recommendations. A typical extract from a much later visit to Hamburg follows: –

" Inter alia on the "Reeperbahn - Allekajuti- this place should be out of bounds but isn't. Pop your head in the door and revolting females literally drag you inside. Drab and dingy, revolting, and rather amusing. One of the female Amazons has a tremendous future ahead of her. Not recommended except for the connoisseur."

The author of this extract clearly had taken his duty seriously and had left nothing to chance.

The ship's photographers were another favoured group who always took to the ship's helicopter to record the arrival and departure of the ship for publicity purposes. They were obviously well placed to obtain more photogenic pictures of the ship than was possible by the dozens of "happy snappers" aboard, and also took some excellent shots of the place as a whole. The result was a "nice little earner" for the photographers, who spent most of their days and nights producing and selling 6d postcard prints using private materials, at least in theory; they also developed and printed private films for a charge. However on this trip I carried my own processing gear and chemicals, and after converting to 35mm, with a new camera purchased in Malta where the prices were attractively low, I made a fixed focus postcard size enlarger from sheet balsa wood and the 2 inch lens from a G45 gun camera. With Jan's blessing, and mostly when he was elsewhere, I was able to do my own D&P. This was my hobby, but I could only carry on with it as a result of Jan's forbearance and because of the space and privacy available as an officer. Traditionally sailors have relaxed with more portable hobbies such as sewing and carving but many other ingenious hobbies existed among us. Tony Ashmore, who was Jan's A.E.O., always carried with him a folding 00 gauge train layout in the form of a shunting yard. He then constructed locomotives and rolling stock from, mainly, sheet brass and used these to produce operational timetables for the layout.

The third group to make a killing in a new port were the caterers. They needed to restock on fresh food and vegetables and the local traders keenly sought their custom! In particular the Wardroom Mess caterer was in a position to benefit as he had virtually a free hand and it was always held out! On *Eagle* he was a Chief Steward, and from his little office he was in a position to offer a variety of useful services to officers, for a fee of course, but his main function was to provide our food. Except for special occasions the main meals followed a predictable and below average pattern. One could readily imagine that the ship's freezer had been filled in advance to the pattern of the meals, e.g. mutton with broad beans each Thursday, and fish with peas on Fridays, and that these were then carved out of the ice blocks in order. The mess suggestion book regularly had complaints about food, but the Commander as Mess President always ignored them. He after all had no complaints because the caterer ensured that his food was noticeably better.

After Malta we went next door to Syracuse in Sicily; colourful, grubby, and scruffy in places, but the "Teatro Greco" was a fascinating place. With few people present when Jan and I visited, it was easy to feel transported back in time as we walked down tracks deeply rutted by chariot wheels and breathed the scent of wild thyme. On another day Lyn Middleton and I walked round town and ended our evening at the Ristorante dell'Orologio in the Piazza Archimede. With our "Pasta on the Piazza", we enjoyed the spectacle of the evening "promenade" in front of the Fountain of Diana. On those occasions doubts about our jobs in the "Grey Funnel Line" were put to one side and we enjoyed being paid tourists. By this time all the Mediterranean ports were geared up for the tourist trade and, from Gibraltar on, every place we visited offered racks of tourist trash, a lot of which were the brightly painted (by numbers) pictures of local scenes, and many embroidered hangings. For some reason these latter always included the old classic scene of Highland Cattle; they are still around, but now in England, and have the same artistic merit as the plaster casts of flying ducks. However as tourists we also had a duty to our families to return with some souvenirs, and eventually I returned with a cameo brooch and earrings from Naples, a music box from Sorrento, and a trinket box from Beirut, but the prize worth having was a silver saltcellar in the form of a donkey with panniers. This came from Istanbul, and was a bargain due to the favourable exchange rate.

Istanbul was our next stop, and had all the sights and attractions one could wish for, the Blue Mosque, St Sophia Mosque, Dolmabahce Palace, the Seraglio Palace, the covered market, and so on. We took a ship's boat up the Bosphorus and went sailing on a large yacht owned by an English businessman. On three evenings we wound up at the Taksim Casino on Taksim Square (Freedom Square). This provided good food and a floor show with belly dancers; by the third visit even the belly dancers took second place to food, and we proceeded en masse to a less salubrious location; here the "girls" were less discreet, but I still do not know whether they were male, female or neuter. I strongly suspect the latter. The local taxi drivers drove at speed and with no regard to any rules, on one journey we were weaving through tram lanes on the wrong side of the road.

Immediately followed by Beirut where Jan and I were invited to spend a weekend as the guests of a German businessman and his wife. They lived in great comfort in a complex of luxury flats, and owned three cars, a Jaguar, a Mercedes, and a Bristol. They took us to the beach, and one evening to a restaurant high in the cedar clad hills above Beirut, where we had a magnificent meal.

Back in Beirut we received other invitations, including one from our taxi driver after the official cocktail party; he wished to introduce us to his daughter. Can't imagine why! We had already stuffed our money in our socks, but he did take us safely to a pleasant Arab restaurant outside Beirut, where we had a meal followed by the thick, gritty, and sweet little cups of coffee. Our fellow diners smoked "hookahs". Beirut had so many benefits for business that it is difficult to imagine how the religious and political problems could have resulted in so much hardship and destruction for all concerned in the years that followed.

Shortly after we returned to Malta, we exercised with the U.S. 6th Fleet and cross-operated our aircraft. We lost two of our Seahawks, which ran out of fuel in bad weather during Exercise Thunderhead; "Horse" Williams ditched into the sea off La Spezia, and the other flown by Lt.-Cdr. Leppard crashed into a house in Genoa having reversed course after he had ejected safely; on their return the Senior Pilot told me that he had removed the I.F.F. controller from his plane before leaving Genoa. The I.F.F. set was the only piece of classified equipment on the Seahawk, but it was the Tx./Rx. that held the sensitive circuits rather than the controller. My pursuit of the fate of this box led to some interesting signals from and to *Eagle*, and the outcome of this was that I had a nice "Jolly" to Rome and

Genoa complete with a new Maltese issued passport. My instructions were to fly out of Malta from R.A.F. Luqa by British European Airways, and I would be met at Ciampino Airport by the duty B.E.A. officer, who would direct me to my hotel. I was to expect a visit from the Naval Attaché Rome on the following day. Arriving at Rome there was no evidence of a duty officer or of any other person who was in the least interested in my arrival. Phone calls to the Embassy eventually led me to a huge expensive room in the Hotel Quirinale, and there the following morning the Assistant Naval Attaché collected me. I spent most of the morning sipping Campari in the Embassy while the system decided the next move; in the meantime the source of the confusion on the previous evening had been found, it emerged that a little scruffy old fellow passenger, in a shabby·raincoat and carrying two game bags over his shoulder, was Sir Millington-Drake K.C.B. etc. He was the diplomat who had played such a large part in keeping the German pocket battleship *Graf Spee* in Montevideo before she was scuttled. With that in mind and facing two Drake's on the passenger list, the duty officer had made the obvious choice, and Sir Millington-Drake was directed to my hotel. Before he left Rome to continue his "butterfly expedition" (the two game bags!) he phoned to thank the Naval Attaché for his courtesy. At least the room had gone to a more deserving cause than my own.

After further delays, when it was found that the local Communist Party offices faced the Consulate in Genoa, arrangements were made for me to go there by train. In the meantime I obtained Italian currency from the Embassy and was booked into a slightly cheaper hotel off the Piazza Navona and close to the Pantheon, where a Sub.-Lt. Hawkins from Hal-Far joined me. He was repairing a Naval Sea Devon aircraft at the airport. We took the grand tour of Rome on foot, including the Coliseum, the Castel St. Angelo, and St. Peters. At St. Peters we had to surrender our cameras before entering, which seemed perfectly reasonable, despite some very photogenic locations once we were inside; when I took Margaret there in 1971 our guided tour was interrupted by the click and flash of tourist cameras even during a funeral service in a chapel and I felt that the whole religious mystique had been degraded. We ended our day at the Caracella Baths where we saw *T. Pagliacci,* and *Cavalleria Rusticana* in the marvellous open-air theatre. The next day I travelled by rail, first class, to Genoa, and this initiated me to the art of coping with the enormous bowl of spaghetti that started the lunch. A friendly Italian couple noted my struggles, and gave me a few tips. In 1956 it was not yet commonplace to eat pasta in U.K., but after that I could slurp with the best of them.

Arriving in Genoa, I was met by the Consul General Harry Stenbock, and spent the evening dining with him and his wife at a nearby Italian Riviera resort. Any doubts I may have had at taking second place to my diplomat namesake in Rome were abolished rapidly when I found myself being addressed as Commander Drake. Of course honesty prevailed, more or less, but I had at the very least to keep up the standard. The following morning we proceeded to the dockside where the battered Seahawk was lying. The rear radio hatch was accessible, and I was able to quickly don my white overalls and, using the few tools brought with me, remove the I.F.F. set, several other "black boxes", and all the V.H.F. radio crystals, as I intended to use these as spares to offset the occasional losses from my permanent loan list. The other alternative to coping with losses was adding them to the list of accountable gear fitted to an aircraft that had crashed and thus written off charge; there were examples of this practice in which the aircraft concerned would have had difficulty in flying with all the extra stores added to its inventory. I spent the rest of the day "goofing" around Genoa with my camera and left for Rome carrying all the bits and pieces in a Diplomatic Bag. Met once again by the Assistant Naval Attaché, I spent the night at his apartment, where he seemed to have acquired an attractive Countess as company. The next morning during a further car trip to see other highlights of Rome, we visited her luxury apartment set above a courtyard with a fountain and I was even more impressed. It looked as if there were better things to do than mending Seahawks! Intriguingly, the Asst. Naval Attaché had duties outside Italy; he kept his eye on the armaments industries in Switzerland, Austria, and Czechoslovakia, and was equipped with a little Minox spy camera for this role.

Arriving back at Luqa the next day I was obliged to share the only available taxi with a group of Maltese and then rather bemused when they saw a priest and insisted on cramming him in as well. Needless to say he did not help pay the bill. The Diplomatic Bag stayed in Rome, and was to have been delivered to the ship when we later called into Naples. In fact it never arrived, but then neither did the Embassy charge its petty cash payment of Italian currency to my pay account; the paymaster insisted that it was an entirely separate issue and paid me full travel expenses for the trip. I got a few "brownie" points for the work and had a real five day holiday with a nice cash bonus to boot.

Naples held plenty of interest, and we visited Pompeii, Amalfi, and Sorrento. There was evidence that the former inhabitants of Pompeii had had an interesting sex life and had few inhibitions, but in the streets of Naples the latter day haggard representatives of the oldest profession failed utterly to attract.

The loss of two aircraft was not the first suffered by our Seahawks. One at least had crashed at Malta, but two were lost on take-off on *Eagle* when I was present. At each launch and recovery both Jimmy James and I were present on the flight deck. As the aircraft started, and assuming there were no snags, they were taxied forward in turn to one of the *Eagle's* twin catapults, and by this time Jimmy and I were crouched behind the retractable Catapult Control Station ready to deal with any last minute problem. The aircraft was then attached firstly to the catapult shuttle itself by a wire strop with loops on to a hook either side of the fuselage, then the tail was secured to a fixed hold back device carrying calibrated steel break out rings. Tension was then applied and the aircraft run up to full power. The signal to launch was given as appropriate to the ship's motion, the initial movement broke the hold back rings and the aircraft accelerated to the bows, with the wire strop falling into the sea ahead of the ship

On one launch, the aircraft of "Jock" Campbell merely trickled forward and fell into the sea but "Jock" was recovered unharmed. The investigation focused on the possible failure of the wire strop, but which I had seen clearly intact as it fell forward into the sea. Since neither the strop nor the aircraft were recovered my evidence was ignored, but some years later I discovered that several other Seahawks had been lost due to the hooks on the aircraft breaking, and clearly this had been the case on our aircraft.

I was also present when a Seahawk flown by "Lyn" Middleton was launched; as the plane accelerated a gush of fuel from the fuselage filler cap entered the plenum chamber and ignited, we watched in horror as the aircraft continued to fly alight aft of the cockpit, until it ditched several miles ahead of the ship. "Lyn" was underwater as the ship continued ahead to his rescue, and was dragged out aft of the ship saturated but safe. Evidently there was a weakness in the filler cap, which could then be forced open by the extra fuel pressure surge as the aircraft was launched. From then on "Jimmy" personally climbed on every aircraft and checked the filler cap before launch, and we had no further trouble. However our accident was not unique and in time all aircraft were modified.

The aircraft with the shortest endurance determined the cycle of flying, and this meant the fighters were first off and first to land on, giving a cycle of about one hour. The Wyverns, Gannets and Skyraiders followed in succession once the Seahawks and Sea Venoms were airborne, and in most cases the propeller driven aircraft used a free take off, rather than the catapult, since by that time there was ample deck space ahead of them. In the short gap between take off and landing our job was to ready aircraft for the next launch, arrange for and progress the repair of defects and the movement of aircraft to suit, and finally, if time allowed, to snatch a quick meal in the aircrew mess below the flight deck. The constant running between flight deck and hangar should have made us very fit, and there was rarely time to wait for the aircraft lift. At recovery stations, we positioned ourselves in or close to the Island and its A.C.R.O. so that we could quickly debrief the returning aircrew as to the state of their aircraft and then make our dispositions for refuelling, rearming, rectification of defects and movements before the next launch. Just occasionally it was possible to watch the landings from the "goofers" position on the Island, but following an accident with a "Wyvern" in the first commission, all "goofers" were banned when the "Wyverns" were landing; the contra props had caused havoc when they disintegrated on striking the Island.

In July and August, we spent most of our time in or around Malta and a Fleet Regatta was held. At one time for some reason, I remained on board while most of the planes and crew were at Hal-Far, and on Saturday decided to visit Mosta to see the famous Mosta Dome, and this I did followed by a visit to Johnnies Bar. Johnny had evidently built his reputation on his "John Collins". Two tall glasses of this cool refreshing and very tasty concoction quenched my thirst admirably, but was literally an alcoholic time bomb, and I floated on air in the Maltese bus back to Valetta. Once aboard I took a quick snooze; that lasted until the following day, and I missed dinner completely.

I was never entranced with Malta; mostly I remember the heat, the squeal of tyres as vehicles skidded around the streets of Valletta even at slow speed, and the smelly drains, particularly those on the streets leading away from the landing stage where we picked up a ships boat or were rowed out by a passing "Dghaisa" similar to the Venetian gondola, and painted in bright colours. The alternative route from the centre of Valetta was via the Baracca lift, which ran from the Baracca Gardens to the landing stage, and this tall open sided structure had some fascination for me as my brother-in-law had climbed it on an earlier visit. The brightly decorated buses carried religious "motifs" to ward off the accidents that always seemed likely, and the drivers sat away to the side of the steering wheel. According to those who had been to Malta before and during the war, the "Gut" was a den of iniquity, but it did not live up to its reputation while we were there. The island was both short of water and of arable soil, so the water was highly chlorinated and any food or drink that involved water had a taste that I can only describe as of "cardboard". All land used for building had to be cleared of soil, which was then used elsewhere. There were plenty of bars and places to eat and I remember the rows of highly coloured bottles and liqueurs that sat behind every bar. Bell's Whisky had a bottle containing a ballerina, and gold leaf flakes, while another bright yellow liqueur in a tall bottle contained a twig of some herb encrusted in crystalline sugar. I enjoy most liqueurs but the opportunity to sample that one never matured, by the time we arrived at such a bar it seemed that the inner man would not take any more punishment.

In September more of Sicily, I joined three other engineers and we hired a little Fiat to drive to Mt. Etna; just as well we were all engineers as the Fiat had fuel problems and needed our roadside attention. We did not reach the main crater up the loose gritty slopes, as we reached the visible peak ahead there was always another beyond. We did begin to appreciate just how volcanic this area was; from the slopes in every direction we could see the humps of extinct volcanoes reaching to the horizon and pondered how anyone could begin to scrape a living in such an inhospitable area.

By the end of summer, the crisis in Egypt had been building up and although we were not informed as to the intentions it became obvious that at least we were making military preparations. Malta again became an armed camp and airfields unused since the war were being reinstated, additional R.N. ships appeared and French aircraft were seen, including the unusual Hurel-Dubois paratroop transport which had a very high aspect ratio wing. The Seahawk was a day fighter, which carried no radar, and did not normally operate at night from a carrier, but in order to have a capability of making strikes at dawn from a night take off our pilots started to practise. Until then they had done very little night flying since the units had formed and we lost one of our young pilots who flew into the sea.

As Flag ship *Eagle* attracted a lot of extra staff for the operation and, as the ratings were still using hammocks, each transit through the crowded "slinging" spaces in passageways on the way to the flight deck at night was a case of ducking under slung hammocks; I claim that my present baldness is the result of abrasion from the undersides of hammocks! The slow build up of a formation of Seahawks on take off at night wasted a lot of time and used up fuel; the solution was found by Lt.-Cdr. Clarke of 899 Squadron who proposed a rear facing light. This was a 500w retractable landing lamp fitted in the rear fuselage to face aft; it served its purpose well, although the mechanism was working in reverse and often failed to take the strain. Thereafter, when our two squadrons took off at night a stream of lights could be seen heading toward their objective.

Eagle then visited Toulon and we exercised with the French Aircraft Carriers *Lafayette* and *Arromanches* (ex-Colossus) which carried "Corsairs" and "Avengers". As the carrier force was being organised for an expected, but still undefined action, the "Gannets" of 812 Sqdn. were disembarked, and the SeaVenoms of 893 Sqdn. replaced them; by a stroke of genius 897 Sqdn. replaced its Seahawk F.B.3's with the F.G.A.6's from 895 Sqdn on *Bulwark*, since at that time *Bulwark* was to have returned home with our older planes. In fact this did not happen and 895 Sqdn. had to use our planes during the operations ahead. From my point of view the new planes were very much more reliable, but we were now able to fire 3 inch R.P.'s, and our pilots, who had not previously used R.P.'s, had to undertake a period of intense training. On the 29th October Lyn Middleton was again dunked into the sea when the Stbd. catapult broke up as he was being launched, he was rescued unharmed but the catapult remained unserviceable throughout the Suez operation, and was not repaired until *Eagle* returned to Malta on 7th November.

Immediately prior to the start of "Operation Musketeer" we were informed that the intention was to keep open the Suez Canal by operating to keep Egyptian and Israeli forces apart. An early objective was to prevent the Egyptians from sinking prepared cement filled blockships in the Canal once air opposition had been eliminated. We had no difficulty with the proposition considering the recent history of attacks against British troops in the Canal Zone, and the similar problems prior to the establishment of the Israeli state, and our lads worked with a will when we were required to paint our planes with the "Invasion Stripes". Late on the night of 31st October 897 Sqdn. was required to fit F24 reconnaissance cameras to some aircraft; this was something not previously used by us, and while this was being carried out I found Green one of my Leading Electricians working extremely well. Until then he had been a "pain in the arse" with a gripe about everything, but now with an incentive he was pulling more than his weight. A very clear lesson on the art of man management!

The pilots were now issued with their escape and evasion kit in the W.W.2 style, this included silk maps, mini compass, and a packet containing gold sovereigns; in theory these would bribe the locals to provide assistance and minimise the risk of being castrated by an angry mob. Fortunately this was never put to the test. Aircrew also received personal weapons; most were content with a pistol, but a few also carried a Sten gun, which was hardly designed to fit into a Seahawk cockpit. Our aircrew meanwhile were feeling a degree of apprehension at the possibility of encounters with Egyptian M.I.G. 15's and 17's; it was by no means certain that our aircraft were a match for them and we still were not fitted with a radar-ranging version of the Gyro Gunsight, which had made a big difference in Korea when the U.S. F86's encountered the M.I.G.15's. Not for the first time our forces went to war with outmoded gear, and success would depend once again on superior training and motivation. In the event luck helped out as well; the Egyptians did not use their aircraft effectively, some were flown south out of harm's way, while many were destroyed on the ground. British, French, and Israeli aircraft dominated the air over the battle zone. The general opinion of our pilots was that it was carrier borne aircraft that were most effective in the operation, and the much-publicised attacks by R.A.F. Canberras and Valiants were largely discounted.

897 Sqdn's first attack came at 0520 on 1st November, when six aircraft attacked Inchas airfield using 20mm guns; at 0845 six aircraft attacked the blockship *Akka* and scored one hit with a 500lb bomb, and a further strike at 1200 also hit the ship and split it in two. However whilst the blockship was sunk this did not prevent the Canal being blocked; one pilot reported that prior to the attack the ship's crew had taken to the water and swam away, only to return after the attack and enable the ship, which was down by the stern, to be dragged athwart the waterway. Some fifty vessels blocked the canal eventually, and these took years to remove. Our pilots reported that during their attacks on vehicles and tanks the populace did not take cover, apparently they were confident that since the leaflets and broadcasts had described the attacks as being against military objectives, then they would be safe. It would be wrong to create the impression that the assault was one-sided, there was a lot of well directed A.A. gunfire and a total of six naval aircraft were lost, but by good fortune no pilot was killed during the six day action. Lt. "Don" Mills of 897 Sqdn. was one of the aircrew who had a lucky escape when his Seahawk was hit and crashed in the desert; he was picked up unharmed by the ships *Whirlwind* while other planes deterred ground forces from approaching. "Lyn" Middleton reported that a lone Egyptian gunner in the middle of one airfield had fired on him, and he was so impressed by his bravery that he had not returned fire.

Our new 3 inch R.P's were a mixed blessing. The "zero length" launchers were each capable of accepting three rockets in a triple tier, and each rocket was fired electrically via a pigtail cable attached to one of three sockets on the rear of the launcher. If the armourers had not correctly matched the "sockets" to the "rockets", or if the surplus cable to the lower two rockets was carried away in the slipstream, then the result was that when eventually one of the rockets was ignited, then it carried away all three, which then fell uselessly to the ground. For the first time at Suez, a number of different warheads were used in addition to the standard 60 lb H.E. head as used during W.W.2. Each warhead had a different role i.e. High Explosive, Semi-Armour Piercing, Anti-tank Squash head, but absolutely no provision had been or could now be made to select which of these specialised devices would be fired. In the event, pure chance determined whether any selection of rockets fired against a tank would include a hit using the Squash warhead. Then there was the question of what could be loaded in time for a particular mission. Probably for the first time our squadron armourers were working their socks off. First the rocket motors minus warheads were fitted to the aircraft, and then a relay team of armourers would begin to screw on the warheads as they were conveyed to the deck. Frequently arming could not be completed before take off, and aircraft would be flown with a part load. My enduring memory is of the ship's Air Ordnance Officer chasing his men along the deck, each carrying a warhead of some sort or another to be fitted at random to the nearest aircraft.

The heaviest bomb used by the F.A.A. aircraft was the 2000lb, and this could only be carried by a Wyvern, however the Wyverns failed to destroy the very solidly built Gamil Bridge, which was being used to bring Egyptian reinforcements. Five Seahawks of 897 also failed to destroy it with 500lb bombs and finally Seahawks of 899 Sqdn. using delayed action 500lb bombs destroyed the Bridge, while Seahawks of 897 Sqdn. attacked local A.A. defences.

Aboard *Eagle* our only contact with events was from sketchy reports from our pilots, and the carrier force, which now included *Bulwark*, *Albion*, plus the French *Lafayette* and *Arromanches*, stayed well offshore. Once at night we were called to action stations when ship's radar picked up signals believed to be from Egyptian Naval vessels and after a tense wait the considered opinion was that we had detected a flock of migrating birds. The Egyptians best chance of hitting the ship had been shortly prior to the operation, when an Egyptian destroyer had left Malta after a refit, and had passed *Eagle* on the way out, but other vessels had carefully screened *Eagle*.

When the sea borne landings took place the Royal Marine Commandos were air lifted ashore by the Whirlwinds and Sycamores from the carriers H.M.S. *Theseus* and *Ocean*, in what is believed to be the first operation of this kind. Later the helicopters were used to ferry injured of both sides to our ships for treatment and for the first time we saw the other side. i.e. the "enemy", and the results of our actions.

Eagle did not escape unscathed however, because it had only the port catapult throughout the operation and returned to Malta for repairs on 7th November once the ceasefire had been declared. Returning later to the general area we spent some time off Cyprus but still with our aircraft fully armed and it was during this period that an armourer of 893 Sqdn. fired about 30 rounds of 20mm ammunition from a Venom in the lower hangar; these killed one person working on the aircraft, damaged other aircraft, and started a large fire. The fire was extinguished with the facilities provided including the water sprinklers but when this happened most officers were finishing their dinner and were away from their normal duty stations. This meant that we were effectively trapped on the wardroom flat by the hatches and doors that were secured at "Action Stations". My recollection is that one person, at least, was injured by a hatch that was closed on him, and we stood around feeling useless while the deck got gradually warmer from the fire. The Seahawks operated from the upper hangar, so when after the fire I made a point of visiting the lower hangar I was surprised to find that much damage had been caused to a vast pile of air stores occupying one side of the hangar; among these were a number of items clearly identifiable as belonging to the "Firebrands" which had been aboard during the first commission in 1951, and which had never been removed.

Eagle's Sqdns. had contributed 621 out of the 1,130 sorties flown by R.N. aircraft during seven days of operations, and 897 Sqdn. had flown 169 of these.

In this period the total munitions expended were : –

72 1000lb bombs

157 500lb bombs

1,4483inch rockets

88,00020mm rounds

From 7<th> Nov. 1955 to 31<st> Dec. 1956, 897 Sqdn. had flown 3,888 sorties (422 at night) and roughly half of these were at sea, giving a total flying time of 3,679 hours. In the course of this we had lost a total of eight Seahawks with one fatality. Although the loss of aircraft is substantial it is worth noting that, compared with the experience of the 896 Sqdn. Hellcats, no serious incident resulted during the 1,994 deck landings. It is to be presumed that better pilot vision over the nose, and a tricycle undercarriage, together with the angled deck had made this a much safer operation.

At the end of hostilities the aircrew had to return their escape maps and sovereigns. This did not happen perfectly, as most had opened their packet and secreted the gold coins in various places about their person and some were now lost. One packet however incredibly had held a double issue so honour was satisfied, but one wonders at the lack of control of this valuable coinage.

As expected we had very little reported unserviceability during the operation, and all the pilots were raring to go; come the ceasefire it was a different matter and all manner of aircraft defects were reported, some of which erroneously included failures of shore based beacons. Other defects were reported just prior to take off and, when our checks found no problem, were clearly merely an excuse to avoid flying on a particular day. I did not blame the pilots for this, after their earlier work they deserved a break, but it kept the ground crews busy.

As the papers began to arrive from U.K. it became clear that it was not only the U.S. and Russia that had wanted the invasion stopped but also a very large number of the British public including the Labour Party. Already aware that our briefing had been less than truthful and that there had been collusion between U.K., France and Israel, the news was a kick in the teeth for those who had been killed or injured and for the rest of us, who had worked hard for success and had virtually completed the objectives when the ceasefire was called. It is impossible to guess the outcome had we fully reoccupied the Canal Zone but in the event we retreated in the face of the international opposition. First thoughts were to blame the U.S. and then to think of the Labour Party as traitors, but it was only when the first books were published that one realised how the personal animosity of one person had led us to the debacle. Since then I have never believed the words of any politician.

The Suez action was the last at which the Royal Navy could deploy such a large carrier force, thereafter as Naval aircraft became larger and more powerful only the larger strike carriers *Eagle, Ark Royal, Victorious* and *Hermes* were equipped to operate them and the light fleet carriers *Albion* and *Bulwark* were converted to the Commando role using helicopters as first proven at Suez by *Ocean* and *Theseus*. Inevitably maintenance and refits prevented all the strike carriers being operational at any one time and progressively they were scrapped. Of the old style strike carriers only *Hermes* was left by 1982 when although converted to the Commando role it played a key role in the Falklands and operated the Sea Harriers of 800 Sqdn. Its Captain was then Lyn Middleton.

Eagle remained in the Eastern Mediterranean during Xmas 1956, when there was a ships concert as part of the on board festivities. Keith Leppard organised a "barbershop" chorus from the 897 officers, in which I was well and truly lathered and we rendered a modified version of the Hippopotamus Song using Nasser and the Nile in place of the original words, together with the chorus of "Mud, Mud, Glorious Mud". The usual rumour went the rounds blaming our lost Xmas to delays in completing *Ark Royal,* all due to the notoriously slow Dockyard Matey's at Devonport. Probably quite untrue, but "Jack" loves to sling mud.

We called briefly at Gibraltar over the New Year and arrived at Plymouth on 7th January, and dispersed to our homes with the Squadron now disbanded. The spell on 897 Squadron was a good introduction to my new role and in fact a very enjoyable period of my life. I arrived to find Barbara now fifteen months old and very uncertain who I was. She took a while to accept me, so I was very pleased to find that my next appointment was to Ford in Sussex, and that I could continue to live at home with my family.

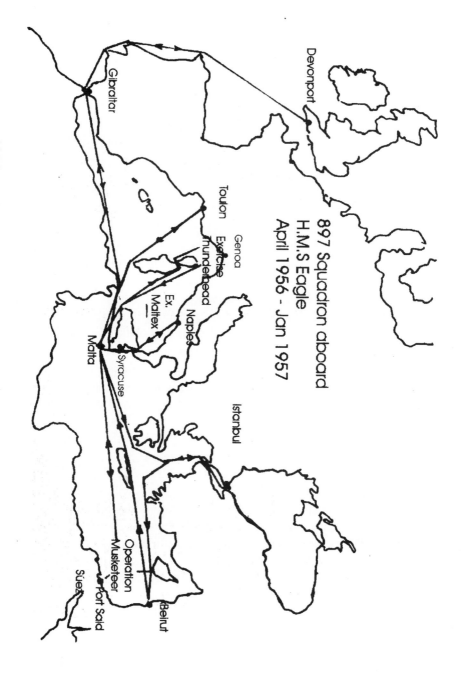

897 Squadron aboard
H.M.S Eagle
April 1956 - Jan 1957

Devonport

Gibraltar

Toulon

Genoa

Exercise
Thunderhead

Ex.
Maltex

Naples

Malta

Syracuse

Istanbul

Operation
Musketeer

Beirut

Suez

Port Said

897 Squadron aboard H.M.S. *Eagle* - Spring and Summer 1956.

A Bit of a "Tiff"

897 Squadron's used Seahawk FB3's before being given nose cone markings Brawdy Winter 1955/6.

897 Squadron Flight Line Brawdy Winter 1955/6.

897 Squadron Line hut Brawdy Winter 1955/6.

897 Squadron Night flying Brawdy Winter 1955/6.

A Bit of a "Tiff"

Arming up a 897 Squadron Seahawk Brawdy Winter 1955/6.

899 Squadron Seahawk FGA6 being refuelled Brawdy Winter 1955/6.

H.M.S. *Bulwark* leaving Devonport February 1956.
Author's collection.

Preparing to launch. H.M.S. *Bulwark* February 1956.

A Bit of a "Tiff"

899 Squadron Seahawk FGA6 about to land.
Bulwark February 1956.

This Seahawk had a collapsed undercarriage.
Hangar Deck *Bulwark* February 1956.

A Bit of a "Tiff"

Another undercarriage collapsed, so we went back to Brawdy.
Bulwark February 1956. Author's collection.

Leaving *Bulwark* in Milford Haven February 1956.

A Bit of a "Tiff"

H.M.S. *Eagle* Autumn 1956. This shows almost all the ship's aircraft after 812 Squadron Gannets had been disembarked prior to the Suez operation. They are made up as follows: 15 Sea Venoms of 892 and 893 Squadrons. 11 Seahawks of 897 Squadron. 10 Seahawks of 899 Squadron. 8 Wyverns of 830 Squadron. Author's collection.

Lt. Tim Samler, Lt. Jimmy James A.E.O. and Author. *Eagle* Spring 1956.

Gibraltar from *Eagle* Spring 1956 Aircraft are 899 Squadron
Seahawk FGA6 fitted with rocket rails.

Eagle being refuelled by the R.F.A. Wave Sovereign Spring 1956.

A Bit of a "Tiff"

"Entente Cordiale" 897 Squadron Aircrew on a Banyan at Pozallo, Sicily. C.O. Lt.-Cdr. Ray Rawbone far right. Spring 1956.

Social Duties (Baron Strangling). "My dear Baroness I would be delighted to visit your Chateau!"

"Pasta on the Piazza" Lyn Middleton et al by the Fountain of Diana, Syracuse, Sicily Spring 1956.

Eagle at Istanbul Summer 1956. Author's collection.

A Bit of a "Tiff"

Refuelling H.M.S. *Corunna* Summer 1956.

H.M.S. *Birmingham* at speed. Eastern Med. Summer 1956.

Eagle, Birmingham and *Corunna* at Beirut Summer 1956.
Author's collection.

USN Grumman F9F-8 Cougar performing a "touch and go"
landing on *Eagle*. Summer 1956.

A Bit of a "Tiff"

USN Chance Voight F7U-3 Cutlass doing a "touch and go" on
Eagle. Summer 1956.

USN McDonnell F2H-2 Banshee doing a "touch and go" on *Eagle*
Summer 1956.

USN Douglas AD-6 Skyraider doing a "touch and go" on *Eagle* Summer 1956.

897 Squadron starting up. *Eagle* Summer 1956.

A Bit of a "Tiff"

1221.

 C E R T I F I C A T O

Si certifica che il Signor C.S. Drake munito
di passaporto britannico No. 91288 rilasciato dallo
Ufficio Passaporti, Malta, il 6 Luglio 1956, è uffi-
ciale tecnico della Portaerei Britannica "Eagle"
facente parte della flotta britannica del Mediterra-
neo. Egli proseguirà oggi da Genova per Roma portando
3 sacchi indirizzati all'Ambasciata Britannica in Roma
contenenti apparecchi e pezzi radio ricuperati dal
relitto dell'apparecchio della Marina Britannica pre-
cipitato a Genova il giorno 25 Giugno scorso.

In fede,

il Console Generale di S.M.
Britannica f.f.,

Harry Stenboeck;

Rilasciato al
Consolato Generale Britannico,
Genova,   addì 9 Luglio 1956.

O.H.M.S. and a nice little jolly to boot! July 1956.

" - a nice little trip via Rome and Genoa." By the Castel St. Angelo, Rome July 1956.

B.E.A. Airspeed Ambassador from Rome, Luqa Airport Malta July 1956.

A Bit of a "Tiff"

Eagle at anchor in Valetta Harbour Malta Summer 1956.

H.M.S. *Birmingham* leaving Malta for home Summer 1956.

A Plumbers' day out to Mt. Etna. Sicily Summer 1956.

897 Squadron Seahawks in formation over Malta. Summer 1956. Author's collection.

A Bit of a "Tiff"

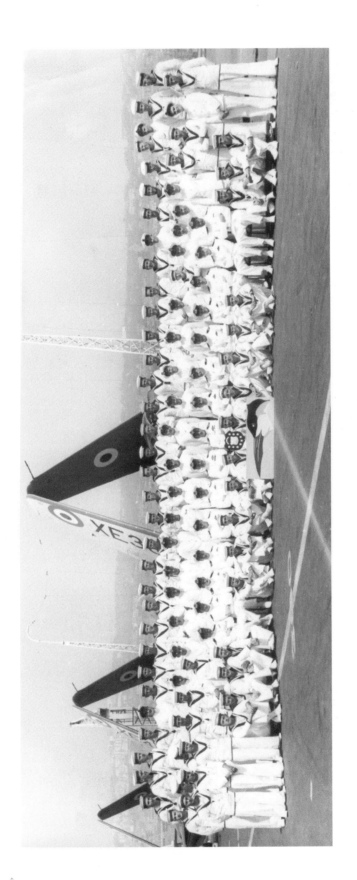

897 Squadron Group Photograph. H.M.S. *Eagle* Summer 1956. Author's collection.

A French Chance Voight F4U-7 Corsair getting the feel of *Eagle* before Suez Autumn 1956.

"Those were the days" *Eagle, Albion* and *Bulwark*. Autumn 1956. Author's collection.

A Bit of a "Tiff"

897 Squadron Seahawks in "invasion markings" *Eagle*. Suez
November 1956.

Flight Deck scene on *Eagle* off Port Said, Suez. November 1956. Two of the ships four AEW Skyraiders of 849 A Flight can be seen at the stern.

830 Squadron Wyverns each carrying a single large bomb taxi for take-off. *Eagle*, Suez. November 1956. Author's collection.

Servicing a Squadron Seahawk. *Eagle,* Suez November 1956.

A Bit of a "Tiff"

One of many blockships on the Suez Canal. November 1956.
Author's collection.

Air Attack on the Gamil Bridge, Suez. November 1956. Author's
collection.

Landing craft approaching Port Said. November 1956. Author's collection.

Naval Whirlwinds ashore by the statue of Ferdinand de Lesseps. Port Said. November 1956. Author's collection.

A Bit of a "Tiff"

Admiralty House. Port Said. November 1956. Author's collection.

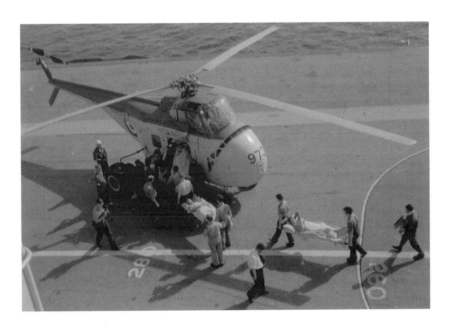

"The losers!" Casevac from *Eagle* to Theseus. Suez.
November 1956.

Chapter 14   H.M.S. *Peregrine* Ford

Ford, located close to Littlehampton in Sussex, was one of the first airfields taken over from the R.A.F. in 1938. Its name derived from its use by the Ford Motor Company when they operated an airline using the Ford Trimotor from a hangar still sited on the far side of the airfield. Nowadays Ford is well known as an open prison, a sad change!

My appointment was to take charge of the Electrical Workshop initially under Cdr. (L) J. Holt who was later relieved by Cdr. Ken Needham. This was an altogether relaxed existence and I was able to commute daily the forty miles each way from our home in Fareham, either by motorbike, train, or later in my old Ford Popular. It was great being with my family and we were close enough for Margaret and I to attend mess functions. Occasionally her leg gave way on the dance floor, but she coped very well, and it wasn't the result of the "Pimms" fountain at the entrance to the mess, which was always pumping out a seemingly inexhaustible supply of the apparently innocuous but lethal mixture, courtesy of an aircraft fuel pump.

At home it was possible to get back to serious D.I.Y. in the house, and the first job had been to replace the clothes posts that I had so carefully erected before leaving for 897 Sqdn. and which had rotted and collapsed within a few months. Certainly one of the hazards of Naval life was the need to ensure the security of your family during your absence; that attempt had been a failure, but fortunately it did not cause further damage. My woodwork around the house started with a minimum of tools, some of which were purchased after I sold two copies of Jane's Aircraft books, and using oak that could only be obtained by mail order, as good quality timber was still in short supply. D.I.Y. chimney sweeping was practised by most of my Naval neighbours, and most have a tale to tell of their experience; in my case the upper cane became detached halfway up the chimney and I spent Sunday morning sitting astride the roof fishing for the brush with a garden hoe and being steadily covered in the soot drifting up the chimney. In the middle of this a civilian neighbour passed the house, looked up and politely said "Good morning." We still lacked a washing machine and made do with a gas boiler; as we needed more space in our tiny kitchen I arranged with the gas company to move the gas point into the conservatory and this had all the elements of farce that were familiar to me in the Navy. At one stage the fitter was chiselling a hole through the wall but had not noticed that the adjoining wall was set at an angle and, until I pointed this out to him, continued chiselling along the length of this wall for some distance; he then lost the fittings he had taken off and placed in his tool bag.

In some respects our estate was much like married quarters since a high proportion of our neighbours were in the Navy, and the wives supported each other when the husbands were away, but there was not quite the same rank consciousness that applied in M.Q.'s and this helped. Our children were growing up and attending the local schools, and as a result we made friends with the parents of their friends. We still meet some of these and have a chuckle at events of that time.

One Christmas we were invited to a party by some Australian Naval neighbours who were in U.K. on a long course; arriving we were given a half pint glass filled with a brown liquid, this tasted pleasantly familiar and I polished it off and was invited to have a refill. "Well, yes please, but what is it?"— "Sherry mate!"

The Home Air Command was at that time in the grip of a campaign to encourage sport, and all departments at Ford were expected to provide a sports team, with every member of the department taking part to earn points, on the basis of a graduated scale of scoring for each activity. The totals were entered in the Home Air Command competition and the best men were entered to represent their department at the station Sports Day. Clearly someone was needed to organize the team in each department, and by the law that governs Naval life (Sod's Law) I got the job for the Electrical Department. At that time I was neither the youngest, largest, nor had I a reputation as a sportsman but there I was, perversely, nominated to attend the R.N. P.T. School at Pitt Street Portsmouth for a fourteen day P.T. Officer's Course.

I had the gravest misgivings on the first morning, when the other "volunteered" and I found ourselves trotting around the cinder track after a course of young and very fit P.T.I.'s, but by the end of the week I actually felt a bit fitter. Swimming and Lifesaving were a doddle but I foresaw trouble as we queued up to do trapeze work over the swimming pool. I understood the effect of gravity only too well and, since I was unable to avoid my turn, the resulting "splash" was inevitable. We continued our lectures, an attempt at Judo, and on the last day carried out Circuit Training. This was a series of exercises capable of being carried out in the confined spaces of ships. The final item was weight lifting lying on one's back; by this time all energy had long since disappeared and the weights simply pinned me to the floor. I was knackered!

However all was not in vain, I had learned a few tricks and the Electrical Dept. went on to win the Station Sports, beating our arch rivals the Armourers. The Armoury had a large ex-apprentice C.P.O. Valentine; he played rugby and was an Olympic standard shot putter among his many athletic achievements. He was much in demand for Naval and national sports and rarely worked as an armourer, but of course he was the inspiration and mentor of the Armoury team, and it was expected that his team would certainly win the Tug of War. However brute force was not the answer as I had learned at Pitt Street, and I soon had a team of the largest of my staff hauling around the collective remains of the workshop group until it became clear that we could not afford to close down the workshops while we practised Tug of War. Instead a solid looking tree behind the workshop provided the anchorage against which we heaved; that is until one day the tree snapped off at the base. This was a big laugh of course, but the tree faced the Control Tower which was the lair of Cdr. (F) Eric (Winkle) Brown A.F.C., who was very proud of his airfield, the grass, and all growing objects. The tree was therefore quickly sawn up and lost. Our team won the Tug of War by the application of elementary science.

"Winkle" had made his reputation as a test pilot at Farnborough during the war, when he had tested many of the captured German aircraft; later he had test flown a converted Vampire 1 on to H.M.S. *Ocean* in Dec. 1945 in the first ever deck landing and take off of a jet aircraft. Although he had not originally been a career officer, he was nonetheless a martinet. He had been Cdr. (F) at Brawdy when I was with 897 but I did not cross his bows until the Annual Assessments at Ford when he questioned my award of Supr. to two C.P.O.'s in my division. His view was simple, if their Lordships had declared that statistically only 5% of ratings could be granted a Supr. assessment then it was impossible for me to have two in my division. He had obviously not studied statistics, and I stuck to my assessment.

The sports enthusiasm continued, and a new idea of having a sports afternoon emerged. Notionally this was meant for the team players who already did quite well in time off for sport, and I felt this only shifted the workload on to the rest. For the Electrical Dept. therefore my rule was that any sport was valid, including golf and rifle shooting, and all had a chance to take part in a sport of their choice. For my part since I had no other leanings I took a place in the station rifle team; we did well in the Air Command competition at the Browndown range near Lee on Solent, and the three officers involved won the Officers' "Tiles" shoot. However, like all good ideas, the emphasis on sports and fitness didn't last because as the work pressure increased it became impossible to spare time for general sport. The R.A.F. however continued, certainly until 1965 when on a visit to Cranwell with some Buccaneers I found the station completely closed down for its Wednesday sport. The R.A.F.'s apparently relaxed style did not much impress the Navy or the Army when they worked together in places such as Borneo.

In 1957 the R.N. still employed a number of conscripts under the National Service scheme and I had several in my workshops. In my experience they had been well selected and many had professional skills from "civvy" street that we lacked and this proved very helpful. One of them, an instrument maker, copied the chemical balance we were using and thus allowed the original item to be returned to stores and off my permanent loan list; another designed and built a "noughts and crosses" machine using only electrical relays which was programmed so as to be virtually impossible to beat, and was a great attraction at our Air Day. These odd jobs were welcome distractions in the unit as our workload was low and they kept boredom at bay. It was obvious that National Servicemen would have preferred to return to being civilians but problems only emerged just before they left, and with freedom in sight they then tended "to let the end go". I also had a couple of Indian Artificers who were gaining experience prior to rejoining the Indian Navy, which was about to receive "Seahawks". These gentlemen were rather less dedicated than all the others and I was glad when they departed.

At intervals I was nobbled for odd jobs, which all officers took in their turn. One was the audit of the Wardroom Bar, and another was the pig farm. Pig farms were run by the Commander at most stations and provided funds for the camp. Needless to say the management of the farm was left to a civilian who knew something about pigs, and very little about financial management. The Audit therefore had somehow to justify income and expenditure based on the evidence of scruffy bits of paper as receipts for a transaction and counting the actual livestock present on the day compared with births, sales, and the premature deaths of piglets, which were of course never seen alive by an auditor. We dared not suggest that perhaps these latter had been consigned to the pot of somebody nameless.

Once again I visited Magistrates Courts with members of my Division. The first of these was held at Dartford under a Mrs Ling, and she and her bench had gained a reputation of hating motorists. On this occasion most of the accused including my lad were up for driving offences, and I watched appalled as the members of the bench sat in discussion among themselves while solicitors tried to plea for their clients and were totally ignored. One solicitor actually had a good case but ended his plea by saying "if the bench has made up its mind?" This was enough to ensure that his client was penalised for the maximum offence and no consideration was given to the possibility that this was unfair. I wondered if the magistrates had received Naval training.

The second visit was to Lewes where a Leading Electrician was charged with indecent assault with threats using a fruit knife. The man was committed for trial and later sentenced to eighteen months; that seemed rather better justice.

Ford had an R.N.V.R. unit (Weekend Flyers Club) operating until 1957 and several other units including 813 Sqdn. with its Wyverns. During my stay the Wyverns received a long outstanding modification to fit very large long range drop tanks; by exceptionally good planning these were fitted just in time for the Wyvern to be scrapped! This was not unique as in 1968 some nine years after the Sea Vixen entered service a modification was introduced to re-orientate several instruments on the pilot's panel. The modification had been recommended during early service trials but by the time of the introduction of this major and expensive change our pilots had become used to the original system and it was probably no longer justified.

I was one of many officers attending a talk at Lee on Solent describing the future plans for the F.A.A. and we heard about the N.A.39 (Buccaneer), Sea Vixen and Saro S.R.177. This latter aircraft would have been a mixed power rocket and turbojet interceptor for the fleet, with two Firestreak missiles and a Mach 2.2 performance. Two prototypes were flown as the S.R.53, but our interest had barely started when in the 1957 Defence Review by Duncan Sandys major cuts were to be made, and the S.R.177 was lost. The "Sandys" plan changed much of the Defence planning in favour of a missile based future, but in the meantime my future had arrived at Ford in the form of 700X flight with Scimitars. This was the Scimitar I.F.T.U. (Intensive Flying Trials Unit) and it remained at Ford from August 1957 until June 1958 when it transferred to Lossiemouth and reformed as 803 Sqdn. During its stay at Ford, the I.F.T.U. operated from the old "Ford" site, and was largely self-supporting with the help of the S.M.P. (Special Maintenance Party) and Contractors, so I learned very little about the machine but did carry out trials of the new "Jetcal" thermo-couple testing set and potted up the electronic gun-firing units with a resin compound to prevent their disintegration when the big 30mm. Aden guns were fired.

The presence of the Scimitar was always with us during 1958, from the shattering noise of its twin R.R. Avon engines, to the constant traffic of visiting delegations for meetings on every subject related to the aircraft. Reputedly the largest of these meetings was held to decide the paint colour for a new range of ground equipment and some fifty or more attended in demonstration of the weight of bureaucracy in our system.

By way of a change the closure of Ford was announced, and when the Scimitars departed the station was quiet and only the local mink farmer cheered. Evidently pregnant minks tended to abort when the Scimitars flew over, and Air Traffic was regularly bombarded by complaints. The progressive run down required each of us to check our Permanent Loan Lists, and it was no surprise when items were found missing after long use on the camp. I was able to help several colleagues by boxing up collections of odds and ends resembling a missing item as dropped from a great height; these were then labelled "Damaged and Irreparable" and resolved the problem.

Unrecognised at the time the F.A.A. ashore was never to return to the relaxed state that had been the case until 1958. When the Scimitar arrived it demanded virtually 24-hour maintenance and repair, as did its successors, so sports days disappeared. National Service finished and the R.N.V.R. Sqdns (weekend flying clubs) also disappeared. Thereafter it was noses to the grindstone. I never again managed a workshop and therefore was deprived of ready access to workshop machinery. As a result over the years I have acquired my own well-equipped workshop and this has kept me happy and creative.

However no sooner had we settled to a nice quiet run down than I received my marching orders. I was off to a few days course at Vickers Armstrong at South Marston near Swindon (now the home of the Honda car plant), and shortly after joined 803 Sqdn. at Lossiemouth.

My family in 1957.

"Good morning, lovely day!"

A Bit of a "Tiff"

Staff outside the Electric and Instrument Workshops. Ford 1958.

"The winners" Electrical Department Sports Team. Ford 1958.

The Ford Shooting Team with their Trophies. Home Air Command
Shooting Competition 1958.

Sanders Roe SR 53. Cancelled in the Sandys 1957 Defence
Review. Flown at Farnborough in 1958 it showed what might have
been.

A Bit of a "Tiff"

Chapter 15 803 Squadron

H.M.S. *Victorious*

I arrived at Lossiemouth to be the Deputy Electrical Officer of 803 Sqdn. My welcome interview at Lossiemouth by Commander (L) took a long time as he unburdened himself on the subject of how Lossiemouth was on the outer circuit and how the idiots in Admiralty hadn't a clue about his problems. He was probably correct but I didn't have time to find out, as within days we were to join *Victorious*, and the waiting was done, when we finished work, in the old wartime wooden huts that continued to serve as accommodation thirteen years after the war had finished.

803 Sqdn. was one of the oldest F.A.A. units having operated Ospreys on *Eagle* and *Hermes* during 1933-4; from 1939-40 it operated with Skuas on *Ark Royal* and *Glorious* but in 1946 it reappeared as an R.C.N Sqdn. flying Seafires from *Warrior*, then Seafuries from *Magnificent* between 1948-50. Once again as an R.N. unit it flew Attackers from *Eagle* from 1952-4, and Seahawks from *Centaur* in 1956. Now it had the honour of flying the largest, heaviest and noisiest naval aircraft to date and it was also the most complex embodying very many new and novel features. The complement was just ten Scimitars, and to keep these flying we had 184 ratings, which of course included the usual cooks, stewards and miscellaneous men, one of whom was now a maintenance data recorder in the hope that useful data could be collected for the benefit of spares provisioning, future modifications, and new design. It was now recognised that the Scimitar needed much more maintenance than any previous naval aircraft, and that some form of shift work was needed to keep it flying. The A.E.O was Lt-Cdr. Don Titford and the A.L.O. Lt.-Cdr. "Rigor" Mortimer and they dealt with the normal daily flying operations and daytime maintenance, while the Deputy A.E.O. Lt. Colin Orpe and myself were to be the second team and work the unsociable shifts as long as we were at sea. The ratings worked a complicated shift system so that no one was on permanent night shift. I joined as the most junior officer on the unit and also certainly the least knowledgeable about the aircraft, as most aircrew, the other engineers and ratings had been on the I.F.T.U. and knew the problems, or at least thought they did until we went to sea when a few surprises were in store.

The Scimitar F1 was as usual a multi role aircraft capable of operating as a day interceptor up to 46,000 ft with four 30mm Aden guns and a Radar-ranging Gun sight, and with the 22,500 lb thrust of its two R.R. Avon engines it could reach 45,000 ft. in 6.65 mins but its main role was as a Low level Strike fighter carrying four 1000 lb. Bombs, Rockets, or a single 2000 lb. H.E.M.C. nuclear bomb, and could achieve about Mach 0.97 (747 m.p.h.) at sea level, with a normal range of 1422 miles. It was able to extend its range by carrying two or four 200 gall. drop tanks, could receive fuel from a tanker aircraft and using a "Buddy" pod could itself act as a tanker, which was the role in which it ended its fairly brief service. By changing the hinged nose cone with the radar-ranging unit, to a new nose containing F95 cameras it was equipped for Photo Reconnaissance, and was later equipped to fire four Bullpup air-to-ground missiles, which was first tested in service by 803 Squadron at Lossiemouth in early 1960, or four Sidewinder air-to-air missiles in a much later change. As a necessary aid to operations away from base it could carry a "Palouste" low-pressure engine starter on one under wing pylon. With all these optional goodies its loaded weight was 34,200 lb. and therefore over twice the weight of the 15,225 lb. Seahawk. With such an impressive performance and with such a range of options it was evident we were in for a busy time.

When it was time to leave Lossiemouth, Colin and I took the ratings plus several tons of ground equipment by train via London to join *Victorious* at Portsmouth. This was our job on most embarkations and disembarkations and needless to say gave us a headache on every occasion. Once aboard and semi-organised, *Victorious* put to sea to receive the aircraft and at once we lost our C.O. Cdr. "Des" Russell in an accident that should never have happened. His Scimitar went over the side at low speed and was still afloat as it passed down the port side; the pilot was seen attempting to release the canopy and harness but failed to do so. The investigation, that followed the salvaging of the plane, made a number of recommendations to prevent a similar problem in future but it was a sad beginning. Lt-Cdr (later Captain) Geoffrey Higgs was now appointed C.O. and remained for most of my time with the Squadron.

Victorious had a distinguished wartime career; laid down in 1937 as one of three Illustrious class fleet carriers she was completed in March 1941 and was immediately involved in the search for *Bismarck* before she had a chance to work up; but her Swordfish of 825 Sqdn. scored one torpedo hit. Later she attacked *Petsamo* and *Kirkenes*, covered a Russian convoy, and attacked *Tirpitz* before moving to the Mediterranean and supporting operations *Pedestal* and *Torch*. From Nov. 1942 to Sept. 1943 she was a part of the U.S. CinCPac's Fast Carrier Task Force using U.S. aircraft, equipment and procedures; on completion of the loan period she returned to U.K. for a refit and was part of Operation Tungsten against the *Tirpitz*. She then joined the 1st A.C.S. (Aircraft Carrier Squadron) of the British Pacific Fleet, which attacked targets in South East Asia before moving into the Pacific in 1945 as Task Force 57 in support of the landings on

Okinawa. She was then hit by two "Kamikaze" aircraft, but due to the protection provided by her armour was able to continue operations after some temporary repairs. She ended her war as part of Task Force 37 with the U.S. Third Fleet against the Japanese homeland until this was curtailed by fuel shortage. Post-war she had no operational role and spent time in reserve and as a training ship until in 1950 she was taken in for a major modernisation at Portsmouth.

The ship that emerged from this work in 1958 was not our largest carrier but the most modern, being equipped with a full 8 degree angled deck, a mirror landing sight, and two steam catapults, all of which were British inventions and came to be adopted as standard for carriers elsewhere. She was also equipped with the Type 984 3D Air Direction Radar, which was itself a world-beater. Beneath all the changes the ship was much as before, weighed 30,300 tons and its three steam turbines delivered 110,000 s.h.p. to give 31 knots. The armoured steel flight deck was 775 ft. long by 145 ft. wide and now carried unstretched nylon emergency barriers, which were better able to limit damage to aircraft. The single hangar had been raised to provide an extra accommodation deck and was 360 ft long with a 52 ft. extension forward of the forward lift, and 62 ft. 6 inches wide. Since the Scimitar was 55 ft 3 inches long (slightly less with its nose folded back), and 20 ft 6.5 inches wide when folded, there was little room for manoeuvre in the hangar, particularly as she also carried 893 Sqdn. Venoms, 849B Skyraiders and 824 Sqdn. Whirlwinds. The original gun armament of eight twin turrets had been reduced to six using U.S. 3 inch guns to accommodate the angle deck, and as in *Eagle* the gunners did not get much practice. During this commission their chance came at last when a small radio controlled target plane was flown round the ship allowing each turret in turn to blast away; in the end it fell to one turret to finally shoot it down after all the others had missed and an investigation was held to determine what had gone wrong.

The combination of new aircraft and on board systems made *Victorious* potentially a very powerful ship and it was obvious that we were to work up, and then demonstrate our capability to our European and American allies. It was easier said than done and we were worked to a frazzle trying to keep up with endless demands for role changes while at the same time trying to actually keep the planes serviceable, a task that could never be successful. It was little comfort that other departments were also overstretched; as usual the flight deck engineers had a full-time job, and the Type 984 Radar needed a lot of t.l.c., which meant that wholesale replacement of electronic components was needed at intervals. The Whirlwinds of 824 also had engine problems and were sent ashore at one stage. As far as 803 Sqdn. was concerned we were unable meet the unrealistic demands for the daily flying programme and there was no hope of improving our ability to do so as long as the pressure continued. Typically the day would start with a call for six aircraft at first light, but in different roles from the previous day, followed by 4, 6, and 4, in succession throughout the day. It was rare that even the first launch was complete due to earlier unserviceability and the time it took to complete a role change, particularly on a camera nose; thereafter, as the day progressed and unserviceability increased with every landing, there were times when no aircraft could be provided. At this point Command then demanded that aircraft already struck down for repair should be brought up to fly out of role, in other words they could not perform any operational function but merely provided flying training experience. However much this was justified, it merely deferred the work already started and the backlog increased, making success even less likely on the next day. Unsurprisingly the maintenance crews became disgruntled and, instead of working till the end of their shift on a particularly lengthy job, would slow down and leave it to the next shift. The next shift would come on duty being only partly aware of progress made by their predecessors and would start from scratch, and so the cycle continued. It did not help when in the middle of work during a non-flying day our men would have to stop and move the aircraft on the flight deck so that off-duty ship's company could play deck hockey. Despite our representations Command seemed unable to recognise the problem even when the first attempt to arrange a Sqdn. group photograph was spoiled deliberately. This was uncomfortably close to mutiny. Eventually a Squadron photograph was taken and this appears in the ship's records but I was never able to acquire a copy. No doubt the C.O. was himself under pressure and, since the demands placed on us were rarely satisfied, he glowered at us whenever a set back occurred. After a while I jokingly developed a mental slate board on which every glower got a black mark; on the rare occasions when he actually smiled the board was wiped clean and I started again.

We encountered a few new problems. Before leaving Lossiemouth an incident occurred when a light series bomb carrier was launched across the hangar by firing the E.R.U. to which it was attached; this was blamed on finger trouble by an electrician. The Scimitar was the first Naval aircraft to be fitted with E.R.U.'s (Explosive Release Units); these were fired electrically to throw a bomb clear of the new high-speed aircraft. Before connecting up each unit, it was tested with a sensitive No Volts Tester so that there was no immediate risk of explosion. Once aboard *Victorious* the N.V. Testers alarmingly showed at least 24 volts on occasions when they were used and the warning flags started to wave. The experts were then called in and we were assured that all was well, and that this was merely a harmless low current static charge. Later this was found not to be the case and much effort was applied to solve the Radhaz (Radio Hazards) problem, which arose because the circuit wiring acted as a receiving aerial to many of the radio and radar frequencies emitted by the ship and, equally but at less close range, at air stations. There were ultimately a number of accidents on other ships, but in the meantime care was taken to power down the numerous radio aerials and radars, which bristled from the sides and island on *Victorious*, whenever aircraft were operating on deck.

Size and weight mattered; the Scimitar could not be manhandled and a variety of specialised aircraft handling gears were eventually introduced to simplify the task of moving the Scimitar and its successors in the limited space on a carrier, so that by 1966 our new 4 wheel drive and steer aircraft tractor was a revelation to the R.A.F. However for the moment standard tractors and later specially designed powered trolleys were used on *Victorious* and there were numerous collisions with the ship's structure and with other aircraft. Both our ground crew and the aircraft handlers were careful to monitor each movement but the space was so limited that it was not possible to set absolute rules on minimum safety clearance and it was all down to judgement and experience, which took time to acquire. When the call went up for "Brakes" the response time made the difference between a small clearance and a "prang", but the Scimitar had momentum and did not react at once; it simply ate chocks and, after all the old slatted chocks had been destroyed, we were issued with new solid ones. Naturally ship movement was a factor and this caused major damage to an aircraft being moved one night on the flight deck; however Scimitars were not the only casualties and on one glorious occasion Jumbo, the aircraft emergency lifting mobile crane, disappeared overboard during heeling trials. Generally the damage was to a protruding part of the aircraft such as the tip of a tail plane, but often the moulded plastic drop tanks were clobbered and this required a major clean up if fuel was spilled before the tank could be drained. Once the aircraft had finally been positioned it was lashed down to ringbolts in the deck with wire strops under tension to prevent further movement; these were doubled in bad weather, and mobility in the hangar was very restricted.

Probably the least attractive feature of the Scimitar was its fuel system. Feeding the twin Avon's needed a lot of kerosene, and this was fitted into integral wing tanks as well as in the fuselage, and in addition there were the wing drop tanks and provision for flight refuelling. A special valve allowed fuel to be jettisoned in emergency via the appropriately nicknamed "Donkey's Plonk" beneath under the rear fuselage. A mass of valves and pipes were needed to supply both engines, to balance the weight of fuel distributed across the aircraft and to prevent air being drawn from empty tanks and the system was electrically operated. All these features are now common but were then novel and gave trouble. The Capacitor type fuel gauge elements fitted in the wing tanks were also a major headache; in theory these were rugged and did not need servicing so they were buried away deep inside the wings. However the extreme vibration from our newest aircraft dealt with that, and in addition to allowing bits of P.R.C. (Protective Rubber Compound) and "Supermarine" debris to find their way inside, it caused some units to partially break up. First the tank was drained and then an electrician attempted to replace the capacitor unit; we reckoned that the ideal person would have a six foot arm with four universal joints, and, lacking such a person, each job tended to be a collective effort as several men and myself had a go. With the new unit in place and checked, the access panel had to be fitted and resealed with P.R.C. before refuelling and checking for leaks. P.R.C. was a two part compound with a short shelf life, it was forever in short supply and the subject of priority store demands, but for all the P.R.C. used the Scimitar leaked fuel from every pore. Fuel even managed to enter an apparently sealed Pitot/Static line on an aircraft during the I.F.T.U. phase. As a result of fuel leaks, and a similar problem with hydraulic fluid, each aircraft spent its hangar time surrounded by drip trays and sawdust or proprietary absorption granules, which had to be spread over the deck to absorb the spillage and in an attempt to lessen the risk of slipping; it was a lost cause and the granules were also in short supply due to the high usage. The only saving grace was that for the first time the aircraft was "pressure refuelled" and could be drained by the same method thus reducing time and further risk of spillage.

Early in the development of the Scimitar much effort had been put into strengthening the structure to reduce the damage due to the vibration from the engines, one can only guess what disasters might otherwise have happened, but as supplied to us the problem was far from solved. Heat and vibration caused cracking of the tail-pipes and the titanium shields and several pipes were ejected rearwards and hit part of the tailplane. The fitters spent a lot of time crawling up the pipes and checking for cracks using "Ardrox" dye. Heat was transferred into the radio bay between the engines and, despite a cold air unit, the equipment became overheated and failed; finally the vibration was so severe that it was rare for any of the aircraft's external lights to be working after night flying. At particular risk was the tail light, which was fitted in the conical tip of the tail plane; a variety of different schemes were tried including some low voltage lamps, but even the light fittings themselves disintegrated. Most of our electronic gear was still controlled by thermionic valves, and therefore continued to suffer from shock and vibration but we now found some equipment worked best under the rough treatment given during deck operations; one of these was the Servo-pot a key component of the jet pipe temperature indicating system.. It sat above the spring back catapult hook, and a quick pull and release of that item often worked wonders. Ashore or afloat some part of the Scimitar was never happy.

The aircraft as a whole was becoming more of a "system" where the trade divisions of the engineering team could no longer apply and we had of necessity to work more closely together. It was therefore not unusual when I was sent to Hal-Far with a crew to repair an aircraft with tail-pipe damage that had been diverted to Malta with a full bomb load. This should have been a quick operation since we had done it so many times before, although it would have been easier still had not the fittings intended to simplify engine removal been omitted as an economy. As usual once the station armourers had unloaded the bombs the station reverted again to its "Happy Valley" mode and we were left to get on with it. As the last screws were being replaced in the engine panels one of my "Chiefs" dropped one into the Turbine Cooling Air Intake; this led to an annular space around the turbine from which there was no accessible exit, and all our attempts to extract the screw failed. Had we left it in position it might have created a hot spot and caused engine failure, so an engine change was required. Once again we took it apart and finally on completion late one evening took the plane out for a test run but no sooner had it started when I saw sparks from the exhaust and we switched off at once. Some foreign object had been sucked into the intake and damaged the engine. F.O.D. (Foreign Object Damage) was an ever-present danger with jet aircraft, as witness the recent case of the French Concorde, but not if the airfield had been given proper attention. So that was another "black mark" for Hal-Far, and we finally returned to the ship after another engine change. Fortunately on this occasion we had done no damage to the fire-wire elements which surrounded the engine bay and were very vulnerable and regularly flashed up a Fire Warning on the C.W.P. (Central Warning Panel) which was another innovation on the Scimitar

This was one of two visits to Hal-Far with problem Scimitars; on one occasion I returned by Whirlwind, and offered a go at flying the chopper I found it did perfectly well without my assistance, in fact a great deal better. On the other visit I returned aboard in the back of an A.E.W. Skyraider for my only arrested landing; it was a very soft landing indeed. Skyraiders were our lifeline in bringing mail and urgent stores to us wherever we were during this cruise.

The engine starting on a Scimitar was yet another first, and instead of using cartridges or electric motors it used low pressure air supplied off board by a Turbomeca Palouste Gas Turbine. Ashore we had a large wheeled trolley unit, but aboard a streamlined pod with retractable wheels was used, and this contained in its rear end an assembly of hoses and connectors to link the air supply to each engine in turn. The Palouste pod was the size of a drop tank and could be mounted on one of the bomb pylons under the wing whenever it was needed to operate ashore from an airfield without this facility. Our planners in choosing this system must have used a lot of imagination as it was virtually impossible to start another aircraft or indeed the parent aircraft with the starter mounted on an aircraft. 803 Sqdn. Line Book at one time contained some elegant cartoons by Lt. John Beard, in which the pilot eventually disappears down his own engine intake while attempting to start his own engine, but the attached cartoon is an original. Evidently the choice of this starter had been dictated by the need for a new approach for the new generation of powerful engines on Naval aircraft; on the R.A.F. Canberras a cartridge the size of a 4.5 inch shell was used, but the Hunter used I.P.N. (Iso Propyl Nitrate) a high energy mono–fuel which required careful handling. This fuel was carried in a tank on the Hunter, which then could operate away from base. However the Navy considered it too dangerous for shipboard stowage. Later however I.P.N. was used on Wessex and the fuel kept in one gallon cans stored in easily jettisonable stowages at the edge of the flight deck.

When 803 first joined *Victorious* the starter pod and several other external stores had not been given flight clearance by Boscombe Down, and when in a "knock for knock" encounter the *Victorious'* catapult damaged the tail skid on the C.O's Scimitar, and the skid damaged the catapult, the damaged aircraft and its chum was diverted to a French N.A.T.O. airfield at Oran. Lacking any suitable starting system, the A.E.O. was flown ashore by Skyraider, and then the ship had to close the shore and land a ground crew and a Palouste by ship's boat. After repairs the ship had to put to sea to recover the aircraft and then return inshore to recover the ground crew and starter.

Another first was the Interim Dynamic Reference System based on the M.R.G. Mk 1 (Master Reference Gyro). This was the first element of the Integrated Flight Reference System under O.R.946 (Operational Requirement), which was later fully installed in the Buccaneer and Lightning; the Sea Vixen only had the M.R.G. The objective of the new system was to reduce the proliferation of gyroscopes and instruments, with similar functions, that were fitted in the increasingly complex systems such as Radar, Sighting systems and Stabilisation. With the M.R.G. all demands for Heading and Attitude could be supplied from a single unit. However once again theory failed in practice. In trials conducted at Farnborough the Meteor trials aircraft had not attempted the manoeuvres normal in a "Scimitar", and, due to a fundamental weakness in design, the vertical gyro quickly toppled and gave false attitude readings. In the event our M.R.G.'s had an M.T.B.F. (Mean Time Between Failure) of <10 hours and we led a hand to mouth existence as the ship's spares were quickly used and panic signals were sent to U.K.

In principle some repairs were possible on board, and a little clean room had been set aside on *Victorious* solely for the M.R.G. although it was not possible to carry out full testing at sea; out of concern for the occupants the Dockyard had put a glass window into a 3 to 4 inch armour plate bulkhead to prevent claustrophobia! The M.R.G. was a sealed unit in a two-part aluminium case about 10 inches in diameter, joined and sealed with lead/tin solder to contain a mixture of helium and nitrogen to aid heat dissipation and to resist corrosion. Separating the two halves needed a lot of heat using a 500 watt iron, so that even if a repair was feasible then if the heat had damaged the tinning it might still not be possible to re-tin the aluminium and reseal the canister. Priority replacements were picked up straight from the production line and flown out by R.A.F. Hastings transports packed in "hairlock" and sealed in enormous cylindrical drums. On arrival in Malta they were rolled down the ramps and brought to *Victorious* for testing, and, since they had no gimbal locking system, most had been damaged in transit and were promptly repacked and returned to U.K.

With the examples given above it can be seen that Colin and I had little relaxation at sea; our routine was an unvarying 84 hour week of 12 hours a night until the flying programme stopped and the ship went into port. We ate our lunch at midnight in the ratings' forward dining hall, missed any mess entertainment, and had our daytime rest interrupted by the crash and roar of landing Scimitars. My single cabin was midships aft and the deck head was the armoured flight deck so I got the full treatment. It was nonetheless an improvement on *Eagle* except in very heavy weather, which was infrequent; in heavy weather the bows and stern were subject to violent movements, and on one thankfully rare occasion I watched as a mug was hurled up out of its holder, seemed to be suspended in mid-air, and then crashed to the deck. Usually the flying programme was of about fourteen days' duration, and it took all of that time to adapt to night working, so I was most amused many years later to read that a funded scientific study had proved what we already knew from experience. As I recall the only compensation was being awake and on deck before dawn as we sailed up the Norwegian Fiords on the way to Oslo later in the commission.

On night shift we normally finished after the first launch and following a debrief on the night's work, but we also did day work on occasion, and seeing off a flight of Scimitars was an energetic exercise. As each was started the Palouste starter was manoeuvred to another aircraft and the first aircraft would taxi forward. By the time all were started the first two were on the catapult and the combination of wind speed, ship speed, and hot paraffin jet blast frustrated our efforts to move around to clear the deck for the following aircraft. It required the joint efforts of all present to lay low over each starter and heave it into the cover of the Island. On *Eagle* we had only been issued with rubber earplugs for protection against noise, but now we received full ear defenders and proper flight deck clothing and the engineers were also equipped with headsets, which enabled us to communicate with an aircraft and with flying control via the flight deck magnetic loop system. This was a big help, but the downside was that all the gear was on my permanent loan list.

When the aircraft returned, it was as usual a case of interpreting the pilot's scrawl in the U/S section of the Form 700 and trying to obtain a more detailed statement before making a snap judgement as to how to juggle both the U/S and S aircraft between the flight deck and hangar in the best sequence and to deploy the ground crews to work on them. The returning pilots were tired, keen to get out of their flying clothing and get debriefed so their responses were often pretty cryptic and we had to best guess what had actually happened. Similarly the ground crew rarely wrote a detailed account of the most difficult remedial or diagnostic tasks because at the end of their shift they had had enough for the day. This all meant that the real reason for a problem was often never discovered, and the problem was then repeated or transferred to another aircraft in a defective but apparently serviceable component when repair by replacement was used to speed up the rectification process. The task of the Maintenance Data Recorder was to compile statistics for use in forward planning, but their job was negated by poor data entries. Some years later when I was tasked to investigate a large database of maintenance records, the words "tested and no fault found" appeared so often that it was pointless to continue. I was told by a friend in industry, as recently as 2000, that he had the same result using R.A.F. records, so it is obvious that human nature always takes the easy way.

The ship also embarked a Work Study team, who dogged our every move and asked all sorts of questions designed to help them find ways of simplifying our task. Unlike the majority of similar studies where one

A Bit of a "Tiff"

ended up getting the results that you had wanted to implement all along but were not permitted to try, this team actually made some original proposals and they proved helpful in organising our maintenance. The ideas had a general application to all Squadrons but were not fully adopted, so that in 1965 when I joined the Buccaneer 2 I.F.T.U. the unit was committed to learning the same lessons all over again from scratch.

As always our planes were full of hazards for the unwary and even experience did not stop men getting gashed by one of the little triangular U.H.F. aerials under each Scimitar; all were very aware of the dangers of moving surfaces during ground functional tests on jacks and precautions were taken, but despite this one of my P.O.'s was trapped and injured by the large hydraulic dive brake aft of the tail pipe. The ship could also take its toll and did so very effectively when a J.B.D. (Jet Blast Deflector) was raised beneath Ted Anson's (later Vice-Admiral) aircraft. A J.B.D. was fitted behind each catapult and was a large steel plate hydraulically raised to deflect the hot jet gases upward away from the flight deck; it did considerable damage to the underside of the fuselage for which no spares were held. Repair was left until we returned to Portsmouth and a retard party was left aboard while the remainder returned to Lossiemouth. By good fortune I was i/c this party, which was split into two; the first half including myself went on leave while the rest stripped down the aircraft making it ready for the replacement items when I returned from leave. At this point our good friend "Murphy" lent a hand in the form of the ship's hangar party; their sole task at this time was to keep the hangar clean, and this meant getting everything portable out of their way because they were not blessed with high intelligence. For this very reason my men had carefully stowed the serviceable items removed into the large dustbins we normally used for fuel waste and rags, so the hangar party simply dumped the lot into Pompey Harbour where they still remain. On my return from leave I had to rush off down to Vickers at Swindon, identify the missing items from a parts catalogue which we did not hold on board and arrange for them to be sent to the ship. So far so good but "Murphy" hadn't finished with us and managed to have Vickers send port instead of starboard spares, which naturally were useless. The situation was resolved but the work was incomplete by the time we went to sea again. More black looks from Geoffrey!

After a while the problem with overheating in the radio bay was to be resolved by modifications; the first of these, a convoluted assembly of pipes, fed cooling air directly to each of the affected units and the second involved replacing the I.F. (Intermediate Frequency) strips in the T.R.1934/5 radios. The job was far too lengthy to be carried out during a normal flying period, but an opportunity presented itself after we left Gibraltar and before the aircraft flew off to Lossiemouth. The A.E.O. and A.L.O. had returned separately to U.K. and I geared up the ground crew and radio workshops to do the job during the two or three days available. The work proceeded as planned and the aircraft were in all respects ready to launch when my Chief Radio Electrician told me that there was a potential problem with the radio modification. Evidently the Sea Venoms of 893 Sqdn. had also carried out the I.F. strip modification and had found that it was then impossible to communicate at short range. With minutes to go before launch I rushed to the Bridge and explained the problem, and our Scimitars flew in stream to Lossiemouth since they could not intercommunicate while in formation; en route the radios gave an excellent performance at long range. On arrival at Lossiemouth the modifications were removed until a new workable scheme was provided.

In yet another case of inadequate checking of modifications, we were required to replace the soft rubber hoses supplying the Pitot/Static lines in the wing fold joint. The existing rubber hoses suffered under constant attack by kerosene and hydraulic fluid, and the new material was impervious to these fluids. The first aircraft to be fitted was one that I was servicing on detachment at Lee-on-Solent; we found the hose slightly larger in diameter than the original and also stiffer but it checked out on test, and we called in a test pilot from Fleetlands to do a test flight when our work was completed. He spread the wings and took off, only to find that he had no Airspeed or Altimeter readings and was diverted at once to a safe emergency landing at R.A.F. Thorney Island. I hopped across by "chopper" and the crew followed with the Palouste by lorry. We found that the reduced clearance and stiff tubing had caused kinking as the wings were spread so it was back to the old and off with the new to make the plane serviceable, and I had to raise the A21 Defect report to go with the pilot's A25 Accident report.

On board the pattern of work did not leave much time for jollification and aircrew avoided alcohol during the flying programme, but on one occasion I helped members of 893 Squadron load a Sea Venom tail plane into their C.O.'s cabin; it filled the cabin completely and he was not amused. On another occasion a couple of their pilots dressed up as officers' stewards and proceeded to make mayhem on the Cabin Flat, I was well tricked by this and attempted to apprehend them before I realised what was going on.

Of course our life was not all hard labour and, following the notion that all work and no play makes Jack a dull boy, our Lordships of the Grey Funnel Line had arranged for us to visit a number of interesting places

A Bit of a "Tiff"

starting with the Mediterranean, that happy hunting ground for Jolly Jack. Despite interruptions caused by flying during which four Scimitars gave an impromptu flypast for Winston Churchill at Gibraltar, we did visit Gibraltar again, but this time toured the Rock, saw the apes and after visiting the Royal Engineers' M.T. workshop deep inside the Rock, where they were busy skimming brake drums, we were only a little concerned that our brakes would work as we careered downhill in an open top Army lorry. I remain amazed at the labour and skill required to create the network of galleries and gun positions before the arrival of modern machinery. Rigor wanted to go to La Linea for a haircut for some reason, so we went into Spain and he duly got his short back and sides, after which we repaired to a little bar where a succession of glasses of Bristol Cream washed down the freebie bar snacks very effectively at a cost of just 35 pesetas. This was exactly the sum in small change that I had left over from a visit three years earlier and our trip to the tobacconist before crossing the border had been unnecessary. One never used the official exchange rate since the tobacconists were always better value. Later we returned to Spain and spent a day at a horse race meeting and visited the Hotel Reina Christina; this elegant establishment was sited on the shore facing Gibraltar and had an excellent floorshow of Spanish dancers. Back in Gibraltar on a later visit we called in to a hostelry near the airfield, which was a magnet for most of the ship's company due to a number of female dancers; neither very professional and certainly not undressed they nonetheless filled the need for the audience. In such a small town it was difficult to avoid meeting our lads if they were on a pub crawl; we needed to tread a careful line and keep a clear head since their objective was then usually to get us well and truly sozzled and tell us a few home truths, but such "ad lib" parties were often good for morale.

From Gibraltar to Malta now rather less busy than in 1956; at least a new Wardroom had now been built at Hal-Far and when I was dealing with our rogue aircraft I was quartered in a very spacious cabin with a high ceiling; ideal in hot weather but rather cold in November. Each cabin had wired in Rediffusion, which proved a surprise when I was woken very early by the theme tune of Radio Malta i.e. Ave Maria. The main gate was now decorated by one of the 897 Sqdn. Seahawks salvaged from the Genoa crash. Then on to Toulon, where the Scimitars operated out of the French Naval Air Station at Hyeres, and created a deep impression on the French hangar; as the Scimitar was jacked up the hangar floor sank beneath it. However the French got their own back when their unstabilised ground power supplies did nasty things to our fuel gauge systems. *Victorious* was berthed close to the French carrier *Arromanches* and our C.P.O.'s were invited across for drinks which included a liberal supply of Pernod; it was inevitable that one of my men would get into trouble and I had to collect Johnny Fisher after he had been swinging from the hammock racks and generally creating mayhem. Johnny was one of my contemporaries from Newcastle and had a propensity for skatishness. Back aboard *Victorious* I had him confined to his mess before I went off to duty at Hyeres; this was not entirely successful but his messmates managed to prevent any charges being brought against him.

Using schoolboy French, I succeeded during a day off in hiring a little Renault Dauphine by phone from an address I had tried to use three years earlier and had it delivered to the Dockyard gate. Three other engineers and I took ourselves on a tour to Aix-en-Provence, Nice, and St Raphael. We had to replace a headlight, which failed as we were driving round the hairpin bends on the coast road back to Toulon at night and I successfully negotiated the rush hour the following morning and found the garage to return the car, but the indicator switch snapped off as I indicated a left turn across the road and cost me 100 francs for the privilege because my French wasn't up to negotiation with "Madame".

When we left Toulon some French Naval officers joined the ship for the trip back to Malta and to see us in operation. When we anchored in Marsaxlokk bay the French visitors and Rigor M., who claimed some urgent business ashore, left quickly by ship's boat and equally quickly returned alongside just in time to stop the boat from sinking. In true Navy Lark fashion somebody unknown had failed to replace the bilge plugs; it took a long time to lift the boat clear while the water slowly drained out. No doubt this created a good impression with our visitors! Although my records do not give a date and place I seem to recall that *Victorious* managed to savage the lighthouse on the jetty at another Mediterranean port when the ship left, possibly due to the large overhang of the angled deck; we always enjoyed these misadventures.

After Toulon with the Scimitars again in trouble, some were disembarked to Hal-Far while the ship continued to Messina. With little to do on the grounded aircraft Colin and I took a party on a very successful long hike into the hills. We also hired a car and took ourselves to see Taormina, and joined a trip by Hydrofoil across the Straits of Messina (Scylla and Charybdis) to Reggio and on to the ski resort of Gambari. *Victorious* was actually able to lay alongside the harbour at Messina, and, since this was virtually in the town itself, the ship became a big attraction on an open day, so much so that police had to be called in to prevent trouble as the waiting visitors grew impatient at the long queue and charged the brow, and the ship was then closed to visitors.

From Messina where I had managed to buy some presents for my children, we sailed towards Malta, where our Sea Venoms of 893 Sqdn. successfully fired Firestreak guided missiles for the first time against a pilotless Firefly target drone from Hal-Far. We spent Christmas 1958 at Malta and the ship was well decorated by lights in the form of a Christmas tree on the mainmast.

I also seem to recall a lethal rum punch in our Sqdn. Chiefs' Mess. During one visit to Malta several of my lads had been taking the "mickey" out of a Maltese taxi driver and had pinched his cap and chucked it around between them. In due course the driver had whistled up his mates and a scrap ensued during which an Electrician's Mate had been well done over and ended up with a broken jaw, which he well deserved. The Maltese police charged him with stealing the driver's cap among other things, and I had to go with him to court in Valetta. While we were waiting the court had dealt with a neighbourly dispute; no sooner had the participants left the courtroom than they started all over again in the waiting room. In our case the proceedings were conducted in Maltese and our participation was severely limited as my lad had his jaw wired together and could only whistle through his front teeth. Eventually his Maltese solicitor negotiated a deal; my man would apologise and pay for a new cap. This he did and everyone went away happy.

We returned to U.K. on 14th January 1959, and Margaret, Richard and Barbara joined the ship at Spithead with about 1000 relatives for the passage into Portsmouth. They were able to see where I worked and to visit my cabin and so were well pleased. At a different stay in Portsmouth we attended a Mess Ball and Margaret was highly amused to find that the "heads" nearest the wardroom, marked "Ladies only", had been so sandwiched in during the reconstruction that they were in effect raised on a plinth and access for our elegantly dressed ladies could only be achieved by backing into the doorway.

In spring 1959, when the Sqdn. re-embarked, the ship carried out a number of flying exercises in the Western Mediterranean and in the English Channel. Four Scimitars were landed at Gibraltar for flying training, only to find that the hose end connecting the starter to the aircraft was missing; starting was possible only by the Deputy A.E.O. and his team holding the open end of the hot hose to the aircraft and holding on like grim death. During this period a Scimitar, with a deck hook fault, landed into the barrier; the system had now been proved to be effective in stopping the aircraft safely but in doing so had cut right through the leading edge of the wing and stopped only when it reached the main spar. The nylon appeared to be a solid mass of aluminium when it was removed. On this occasion the pilot was unhurt but lost his life later in a sequence of events that led to an accident. In all, during fifteen months on the unit, we lost three pilots and four aircraft but it would be fair to say that these were random events, for which no single deficiency of design or operation could be held responsible.

Don Titford our A.E.O. had left us when we returned in January and was replaced by Ollie Greenhalgh who was an entirely different character; Don was tall, intelligent and unflappable, while Ollie was a short dark northerner who called a spade a spade and believed in a practical approach, preferably with a hammer. Ollie was an expert Aeromodeller, had flown his models in pre-war competitions and was fond of making very unconventional ornithopters. He had earlier gained some notoriety by flying a model Swordfish c/w torpedo during a Taranto Night dinner. In his retirement he used to demonstrate his models at Royal Aeronautical Society meetings. When in due course Rigor M. also left there was another personality shift; Laurie W. was tall, slender, wore horn-rimmed spectacles, and was far less sure of himself. Laurie was a sort of grown-up wartime radio mechanic, lacking only the boots and pocket edition of Omar Khayyam. Really he was unsuited to the hustle bustle of squadron life, particularly of a Scimitar squadron. My memories of the unit during Flight Deck Operations, after the arrival of Ollie and Laurie, are of Ollie whacking home a reluctant Wing-fold Locking Pin indicator with his hide faced hammer just before launch, while Laurie peered owl-like through his steamed up spectacles.

The ship continued its travels with a trip around U.K. from Portsmouth via Torquay with more flying exercises and Exercise Shop Window when the Fleet demonstrated its capabilities to an invited audience including foreign military observers and the Press. Visiting aircraft included the Sea Vixen in the process of working up and the N.A.39 (Buccaneer prototype) representing the future beyond the Scimitar. We then spent ten days in Rosyth, where a local group entertained us with Scottish Dancing on the Flight Deck. While we were there, we had two Norwegian submarines alongside and their officers messed with us for the period; they formed part of the force, which was to take part in Exercise Fairwind in the North Sea before we called into Aarhus. Aarhus had an interesting reconstructed old town forming a living museum of life in Denmark several centuries before; I do not know if it was the first of its type, but similar living museums are now to be found in many places including U.K. Colin and I called on the Norwegian submariners at Aarhus, and before leaving for an evening in town decided that their old British diesel submarine was far too cramped for comfort. Denmark unlike Norway, which was to be our next destination, had no inhibitions about alcohol. We were introduced to the delights of beer with Aquavit chasers, and not surprisingly the

A Bit of a "Tiff"

Norwegians made the most of the opportunity as they had while visiting *Victorious*.

Oslo our next port of call held a lot of interest, from the modern Olympic Ski-Jump at Holmenkollen, to the Thor Heyerdahl "Kontiki" raft and the Viking Ships. The Norwegian Folk Museum with its 12th century "stave" church and old wooden buildings was another worthwhile visit, as was the Frogner Park with its array of sculptures by Gustav Vigeland depicting human existence from birth to death. This lifetime work was mostly of the human nude and the scale of the undertaking was beyond belief.

While our travels were highly entertaining, I always regretted that my family were unable to enjoy them with me. Partly from cost, but mainly because of the high risk of cancellation due to the "exingencies of the service", we never risked booking a foreign holiday while I was still serving. However we went to Italy on my retirement leave in 1971, and took Margaret's two maiden cousins from Scotland to Norway in 1973 on their first trip abroad. It was the "Oh my!" when they saw the nudes in Frogner Park that made our trip worthwhile. It was good to be able to share some of my experiences and Margaret enjoyed them very much.

It was during a period in Portsmouth during 1959 that *Victorious* received the first 2000 lb H.E.M.C. Atomic Weapons; during this activity there was strict security and when I happened to notice a fairly scruffy civilian idling in the hangar I concluded that he had some security role. On a later spell in Portsmouth the same person was in attendance, he was a Dockyard Matey doing what they were good at, as well covered by the song only part of which I now recall: -

Dockyard Matey's children sitting on the Dockyard wall
Watching their fathers doing sweet f— all
When they grow up they'll be Dockyard Mateys too
Just like their fathers with f— all to do.

When 803 Sqdn. returned we became the Navy's first nuclear capable strike force. This had several results and the first was that the squadron needed training in the use of the weapon. Normal method of delivery was by the "Long Toss", in which the aircraft pulled up from high speed at low level and the weapon was released automatically by a timer before the aircraft reached the vertical and reversed direction to escape. The Weapon Range at West Freugh near Stranraer had the facility for this training. Rigor M. was very keen on the wilds of West Freugh and always went whenever the Sqdn. deployed for training, leaving me happily holding the fort, often at Portsmouth and within easy reach of my family. Although the real weapon gave a Big Bang, it was not very clear what was the intended target. If it was a ship or fleet of ships then the target had to be identified visually since we had no radar, but if the target was ashore as at West Freugh then the aiming point would need to be offset from an I.P. i.e. a readily identifiable landmark. In an attempt to resolve the first difficulty Rigor M., in conjunction with one of our R.E.A.'s, modified the little ranging radar serving the gun sight. If it worked then a pilot flying at low level would be able to initiate the L.A.B.S. (Low Altitude Bombing System) and launch the weapon at the correct range. First there had to be a practical test, and I was detailed to design a radar reflector giving an echo equivalent to a small ship. Using the only textbook on the subject on the ship, I had a reflector made in workshops and mounted on a raft supplied by our seamen. Come the day and the raft was dropped astern, and was never seen again. That trial was dropped, but the land attack option was achieved when I discovered unused horizontal deflection coils in the new Light Fighter Sight, and provided a control to utilise them. I do not know if the scheme was generally adopted.

When we returned from Oslo we embarked two extra Scimitars bringing our total to twelve (as if we hadn't got enough problems) and sailed for the United States. This was a prestige trip to demonstrate our new capability of which the Scimitar was a major part, if and when it actually flew. Our Flag Officer Aircraft Carriers at this period was Vice-Admiral Charles Evans C.B., C.B.E., D.S.O., D.S.C., who with his blond beard and wartime record as a Naval Aviator was the very epitome of the Yanks' idea of a British Naval officer and would be sure to make a big impression on his own. He was not of course often visible to the common herd but occasionally would be encountered striding in his white bush jacket and almost "Bermuda" style white shorts through the "Burma Road", the long central passageway which held most of the accommodation and galleys and ran from the stern forward one deck level below the flight deck. As the Admiral swept past this busy thoroughfare was brought to a temporary halt.

Prior to entering the U.S. Naval Base at Norfolk, Virginia our aircraft intercepted all eighteen U.S. aircraft sent to attack us, and this set the pace for showing the Yanks how it should be done. After Norfolk things were not so clever for a while as the aircraft on deck had become saturated by continuous heavy rain that crept past cockpit seals. The first day of Exercise Riptide was a disaster and we were again reduced to flying any aircraft available regardless of role; on one launch our unarmed photo-recce planes were launched as interceptors. Quite why a Naval aircraft should suffer from rainwater was never clear, but presumably the designers hadn't planned

A Bit of a "Tiff"

for rain at sea. Once the snags had been cleared we gave a fair account of ourselves in interception and in ground attack, when our low level strikes caused some surprise. Various comments were reported with some amusement but many Americans were astounded that with so much thrust the plane was not supersonic. The Scimitar seemed to them a bit like a Harley-Davidson, big, bluff, and powerful but never a T.T. Racer, since it was able to manage about M=0.97 virtually anywhere it flew, but could not quite make M=1.0. In fact Supermarine planned several developments of the Scimitar each of which would have been fully supersonic, but Naval policy had moved on to low-level strike rather than supersonic interception and all these concepts were cancelled by the selection of the Buccaneer. It was not until the U.S. Phantom F.G.1 arrived in the I.F.T.U. as 700P Flight in 1968 that the F.A.A. went supersonic at last.

At Norfolk, despite being the latest and most advanced British carrier, we were somewhat overawed by the seemingly infinite U.S. military presence, it appeared as if all our Dockyards, Airfields and Barracks could be accommodated on the one site. We were berthed close to the new 60,000 ton U.S.S. *Independence*, which was double our size and, after visiting her hangar, guessed that it could have easily have accommodated the total Scimitar production line of 76 aircraft. This was clearly food for thought to say the least, and even if biggest isn't always best it clearly does matter. During Riptide the U.S. ships fired ship-to-air G.W. at drone targets, a facility that we lacked until the Seaslug entered service.

Naturally hospitality was much in evidence throughout our visit to Norfolk, followed by Boston and New York. At each place we held the usual first night cocktail party and the guests entered the hangar via a replica of Anne Hathaway's cottage. Other quaint Limey attractions were provided such as an operating Cockle, Mussel, and Jellied Eel Stall manned by an officer dressed in traditional Southend barrow boy rig. The Yanks much appreciated these entertainments despite often failing to understand the relevance; obviously and unusually they had not done their homework. Many visitors found that the bread baked aboard *Victorious* was far superior to the local product and quite a lot found its way ashore. In America it was difficult to prevent the Barons from doing the strangling as they pulled out all the stops to give us a good time, and it became our duty to fill the lists for all the entertainment on offer. However it was also most entertaining to observe the differences as we visited each port in turn.

At Norfolk most of the guests were serving U.S. officers and as we British officers queued to bring them into the hangar and see that they were fed and watered, it became clear that our priorities were very different; as quickly as a drink was thrust into their hands they excused themselves.

To be invited to *Victorious* was one thing, but to be seen by their immediate superiors as being present on this important social occasion was more important to their future. So off they went making there way up the U.S. social ladder, and off we went back to the entrance to start again with a new guest. At the end of the evening Colin and I were invited to stay with a recently retired R.A.F. Wing Cdr. and his wife for a thoroughly enjoyable weekend. We saw some historic sites and visited our first out-of-town hypermarket. The high standard of service was something of a culture shock with the goods being delivered to the car, but the sight of steak packed into uniformly square and round pieces with no fat attached bemused me. That is a practice that we have not yet adopted.

At Boston the infamous Tea Party had been long forgotten by all but the Irish policeman who refused us entry to the U.S.S. *Constitution*; the U.S. equivalent to H.M.S. *Victory*. Everything else was sweetness and light. Following orders a very large group of officers were driven by coaches to a Country Club where we were dispersed to various Club hosts for the day. A gracious Colonel Smith and his wife collected Colin and me, fed us lunch and took us sailing on the local equivalent of the Norfolk Broads wearing their son's clothes. In the evening we were driven to an outdoor concert in the grounds of a replica or reconstructed castle. At this point our host excused himself saying that he had already heard the concert, and it was evident that Club Membership carried both an obligation and a privilege to act as hosts when the Club so decided and in this case it had been decided that the visit of *Victorious* was an item of social importance. The number of guests depended upon one's social status, so Colonel Smith got two but others got more or less. On another occasion a coach load of officers spent the day at the seaside residence of the Sears family who were not at home. We were however fed and very amply watered by the butler and staff, and swam in the pool with changing facilities and towels provided.

New York was a very different social scene. At our cocktail party many of the worldly-wise U.S. guests were utterly seduced by the idea of free booze. They bit very firmly and returned every night until we left. Nonetheless we found New York fascinating, saw all the sights, went to the home of a New Zealand Trade Commissioner, and to an official cocktail party. We saw the panorama from the top of the Rockefeller Centre skyscraper, didn't buy the Brooklyn Bridge but visited Maceys where I bought a dress for Barbara, and was amused to find a little old lady – not quite all there – strumming away happily on a piano in the middle of the music department. She was left to get on with it.

On our return to U.K. the ship spent a month in Portsmouth while we all took leave, and then made a quick dash up the North Sea to the Lofoten Islands for Exercise Barefrost in an attempt to test our ability to operate in Arctic conditions; my recollection is that the weather failed to co-operate, but we got a certificate for working north of the Arctic Circle. Then more time off Pompey, Gibraltar, Malta, Marseilles, Gibraltar again and home in time for Christmas. I was now the last of the original group of Squadron Engineers, since Colin had left to join the "Dagger" course at Cranfield.

Colin's replacement, Dave W. was a brash newly out of Manadon Lt.(E) and was a pain in the butt. The C.O. Geoff. Higgs left and was replaced by Lt.-Cdr. (later Captain) Spiv. Leahy. By then most of the original officers and ratings had gone by a progressive process made necessary in part by promotions which caused crowding in the already limited space in the senior ratings' messes. Under new management we visited Hamburg during yet another attempt to find cold weather. The weather was certainly cold and it was snowing but I do not recall any great feats of airmanship or engineering during that time. However we did have a trip to Lubeck and visited a Luftwaffe training camp where we were much impressed by their language school teaching N.A.T.O. English to budding pilots. The beer was good in Hamburg and the entertainment in the bars off Grosse Freiheit lived up to their reputation.

Apart from the periods spent in Pompey and Lee earlier in the commission, it was normal for the whole Squadron ground crew and miscellaneous staff to disembark from *Victorious* and get themselves to Lossiemouth by rail from Portsmouth together with all the ground equipment, stores, publications and interchangeable role equipment not fitted to the aircraft. This made for a lot of hard work because there were at that time no plans for properly designed containers. While the other Squadrons also had a similar problem they had rather less gear and were based much closer to Pompey at Yeovilton or Culdrose. The fun started when we attempted to return the Flight Deck Clothing before leaving. Naturally some had been lost or damaged, and sailors as usual found solutions to the problem by confusing the count and pilfering items already returned; in the end despite new schemes of doing the job and the gallant efforts of our Chiefs the final count would be wrong and had to be accounted for by none other than yours truly.

Apart from the clothing I also volunteered to look after the Air Publications because it was important to keep abreast of the continual changes; we carried with us not only all the Scimitar manuals but also those related to its equipment such as Electrical, Instruments and Radios, which covered every equipment in service as well as the odd item in our aircraft, but in order to keep abreast of changes all had to be kept fully amended, and was nearly a full time job. Typical of the problem was the Modification Manual for Ejection Seats. No doubt with justification, Messrs.

Martin Baker seemed to issue several modifications weekly, and the manual became four thick volumes in no time, although only a small part had any bearing on our aircraft. I hope that new techniques have reduced this difficulty. In any event these publications were also carried with us so that in theory we were self contained and could move independently.

Sometimes our disembarkation would coincide with leave and we would disperse on leave having loaded the kit and stores on to rail wagons. However the Dockyard Rail System and British Rail managed to get that wrong too, and on one occasion the crews returned to Lossiemouth to find that nothing had arrived and the unit had to improvise until the wagons turned up several days later. On our return to U.K. following Exercise Barefrost the aircraft flew direct to Lossiemouth, and the Engineers and ratings were to be taken off by Admiralty tug from Rosyth as we closed Lossiemouth. Our night shift was still asleep when disembarkation was "piped" without warning and the ratings had missed their evening meal by the time they and their gear was assembled. Disembarkation was completed after dark and we arrived at the quayside at Lossiemouth with 180 very disgruntled men. Unloading the gear to the quayside was conducted with "enthusiasm" during which a quantity of some personal and squadron kit disappeared into the sea. More post–mortems, more loss reports, more black marks, but the experiment was never repeated.

The possibility of using R.A.F. Transport Command had not been properly investigated and inter-service rivalry was still very significant, but we had a minor breakthrough when I was required to take a maintenance team to R.A.F. Acklington to service four Scimitars during a Defence Exercise. We flew there and back in an R.A.F. Valetta. In principle disembarked F.A.A. aircraft were part of the Air Defence of Great Britain and we were to take part in a particular exercise, the details of which were as always an operational matter. All I had to do was get the planes flying and then return them serviceable to Lossiemouth afterwards. On arrival, it transpired that the R.A.F. Hunters were parked in readiness, and each was plugged in via its Telebriefing connector to the G.C.I. Radar Station controlling the exercise. Telebriefing allowed the Hunter pilots to be briefed directly prior to take-off, their I.P.N. starter would start the engine and the aircraft taxied away from the quick release connector and took off within seconds. Our Scimitars were fitted with Telebrief but it was not used on ships and we had no means of testing it so it was unproven. I was therefore instructed to attend the pre-exercise briefing so that I could then take a telephone briefing from G.C.I. and relay this to each of our pilots. With some reluctance and even more reluctance from the R.A.F. Security Officer I attended and my worst fears were realised. The exercise assumed total radar jamming and the message I would relay would send our aircraft on a heading and altitude assumed to be the location of the attacking Canberras. My experience, of the very low-fi quality of aircraft radio and the cryptic jargon of aircrew, suggested that I would be sending our planes on a one-way journey through the intense rain and total cloud cover in the area. After some discussion with the C.O. we arranged for a test transmission from the G.C.I. via the Telebrief and the exercise started. As expected the Hunters were airborne and out of sight by the time we got our aircraft started with the Paloustes, and after launch we waited anxiously for their return. They returned having seen nothing of the enemy and one pilot returned with his canopy completely misted over because he had forgotten how to operate the cockpit air conditioning. Return to Lossiemouth required the aircraft to be started before the Paloustes could be loaded on to their pylons for the flight back; it was clumsy and long-winded compared with the Hunters. The Hunter unit had another advantage in that the personnel remained with a Squadron for long periods even when the Squadron was posted overseas. The benefit was that the crews knew their aircraft intimately in a way that we could not because our people moved to entirely new jobs after 12-18 months on a Squadron. Mind you I was personally very relieved when my new appointment came in February 1960 and I left to join R.A.E. Farnborough.

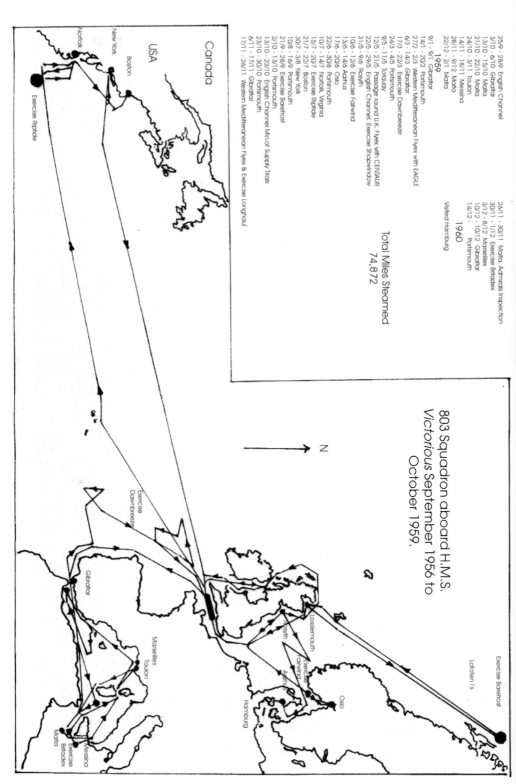

803 Squadron aboard H.M.S.
Victorious September 1956 to
October 1959.

Total Miles Steamed
74,872

1959
25/9 - 28/9 English Channel
3/10 - 6/10 Gibraltar
13/10 - 15/10 Malta
21/10 - 22/10 Malta
24/10 - 3/11 Toulon
14/11 - 18/11 Messina
28/11 - 9/12 Messina
22/12 - 2/1 Malta

1959
9/1 - 9/1 Gibraltar
14/1 - 202 Portsmouth
27/2 - 2/3 Portsmouth
6/3 - 14/3 Gibraltar
17/3 - 22/3 Exercise Dawnbreeze
24/3 - 4/5 Portsmouth
9/5 - 11/5 Torquay
12/5 - 21/5 Passage round U.K. Flyex with CENAUR
22/5 - 29/5 English Channel. Exercise Shopwindow
31/5 - 9/6 Rosyth
10/6 - 12/6 Exercise Fairwind
13/6 - 14/6 Aarhus
17/6 - 20/6 Oslo
22/6 - 30/6 Portsmouth
10/7 - 14/7 Norfolk, Virginia
15/7 - 20/7 Exercise Riptide
21/7 - 22/7 Boston
30/7 - 3/8 New York
10/8 - 16/9 Portsmouth
21/9 - 28/9 Exercise Barefrost
2/10 - 13/10 Portsmouth
13/10 - 23/10 English Channel Min of Supply Trials
23/10 - 30/10 Portsmouth
6/11 - 17/11 Gibraltar
17/11 - 26/11 Western Mediterranean Flyex & Exercise Longhaul

1960
26/11 - 30/11 Malta, Admirals Inspection
30/11 - 1/12 Exercise Britadex
3/12 - 8/12 Marseilles
10/12 - 10/12 Gibraltar
14/12 - Portsmouth

Visited Hamburg

A Bit of a "Tiff"

H.M.S. *Victorious* at Gibraltar. October 1958.

Scimitar XD232 of 803 Squadron during an Open Day at Toulon.
Victoria October 1958.

"Well Chief, I think the Scimitar has made a big impression
on the French!"

A Bit of a "Tiff"

An engineers' outing. Navigating the French countryside from Toulon. *Victorious* October 1958.

"Chiefie, I forgot to put back the bung!"

Victorious alongside at Messina November 1958.

803 Squadron Exped. Messina November 1958.

A Bit of a "Tiff"

803 Squadron Exped. Messina November 1958.

The author in "Ice Cream" rig for entering Harbour. *Victorious.* October 1958.

Victorious lit up for Christmas Malta 1958.

Scimitar landing on *Victorious* 1959.

A Bit of a "Tiff"

Sea Vixen FAW 1 of 700Y Flight during Exercise Shopwindow
Victorious May 1959.

Blackburn NA 39 during deck trials. *Victorious* 1960.

A sequence during Exercise Shopwindow. The Destroyer is
making an attack using its Limbo A.S. Mortars.
"Running in"

"Firing" One of the missiles is circled

A Bit of a "Tiff"

"Exploding"

"A tight fit?" *Victorious* passing under the Forth Bridge June 1959.

Victorious at Oslo June 1959.

"Oh my!"
Frogner Park
Oslo June 1959.

A Bit of a "Tiff"

Flight Deck scene *Victorious*, summer 1959. Note the Firestreak missiles on the Sea Venom and the Palouste Starter to the starboard of each Scimitar.

Sea Venom of 893 Squadron fitted with two Firestreak A-A GW *Victorious* summer 1959.

803 Squadron Scimitar loaded with R.P.'s being taxied to the
Catapult. *Victorious* summer 1959.

Scimitar taxiing toward the Starboard Jet Blast Deflector.
Victorious summer 1959.

A Bit of a "Tiff"

Scimitar ready to launch from Starboard Catapult. *Victorious* summer 1959.

Scimitar at launch from Port Catapult.
Victorious summer 1959.

Scimitar being launched down the Port Catapult.
Victorious summer 1959.

Sea Venom about to launch from Starboard Catapult.
Victorious summer 1959.

A Bit of a "Tiff"

Crowded Deck Park. *Victorious* summer 1959.

Visiting USN Ling-Temco-Voight F8U-1 Crusader from USS *Saratoga*
in background. Off Norfolk Va. *Victorious* summer 1959.

The Empire State
Building from
the Rockefeller Centre,
New York.
Summer 1959.

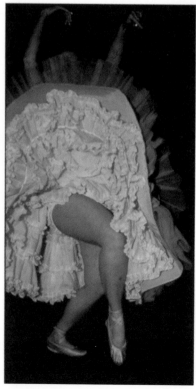

"All work and no play
makes Jack a dull boy"
Gibraltar November 1959.

A Bit of a "Tiff"

A Scimitar Specialist at work.

"Young Blenkinsop was always a bit of a self starter!"

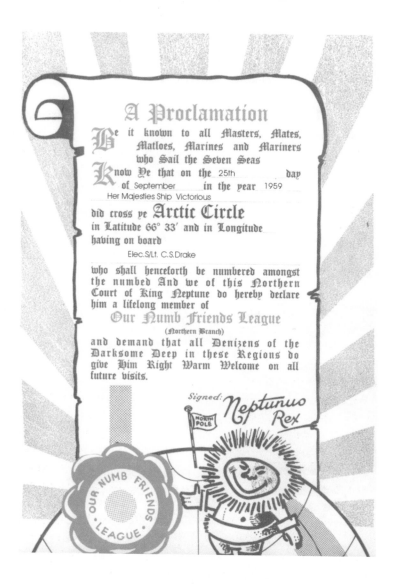

A Proclamation

Be it known to all Masters, Mates, Matloes, Marines and Mariners who Sail the Seven Seas

Know Ye that on the 25th day of September in the year 1959

Her Majesties Ship Victorious

did cross ye **Arctic Circle**

in Latitude 66° 33' and in Longitude having on board

Elec.S/Lt. C.S.Drake

who shall henceforth be numbered amongst the numbed And we of this Northern Court of King Neptune do hereby declare him a lifelong member of

Our Numb Friends League

(Northern Branch)

and demand that all Denizens of the Darksome Deep in these Regions do give Him Right Warm Welcome on all future visits.

Signed: Neptunus Rex

OUR NUMB FRIENDS LEAGUE

"and it was a bleak outlook from the deck of *Victorious* at Hamburg in January 1960."

A Bit of a "Tiff"

Chapter 16 Royal Aircraft Establishment Farnborough

My new appointment was to the Equipment and Trials Section at H.M.S. *Ariel* (Lee-on-Solent) but I was based at the I.A.P. Dept. (Instrument and Photographic) at Farnborough as the R.N. Instrument Project Officer. I had a small team of three E.A.'s (A) to monitor the development of new instruments required for Naval Aircraft and to make proposals for changes, recommend and assist in the development of suitable test equipment, and write servicing schedules for the equipment. We worked alongside the Civilian Scientists and Engineers in the Dept. and with our R.A.F. counterparts from the C.S.D.E. (Central Servicing Development Establishment) at Swanton Morley. Our building overlooked the Ejection Seat Test Rig and our days were punctuated with the bang and shake following each test. The next door main building was Q177 at which I later served as a civilian; at this period it held the all stainless steel Bristol 188 being used to evaluate the effects of heating on aircraft structures at high supersonic speeds. This aircraft was surrounded by batteries of electric heaters while under static test.

After a short handover period I relieved my predecessor Taff. E. and found that his primary task had been the dreaded M.R.G. He and his C.E.A. Buck H. an ex-2nd Rodney, were "wide boys" and made the most of opportunities arising in the job. To some extent our superior at Lee was their example; Reggie B. was a very pleasant entrepreneurial rogue, who was always on the look out for a deal in his spare time but was not actually dishonest. At one stage he bought up old pre-fab. houses at Hayling Island and had them renovated, and another venture was the repair and renovation of old T.V.'s. His father-in-law helped by stripping others into spare parts. However Taff had financed a car on the expenses "earned" from toting M.R.G.'s around the country to meet the constant demands from units like 803 Squadron. Taff was then appointed to D.G.A.(N) (Director General Aircraft Naval) in London and continued his shady deals with contractors, later leaving the service to become a Managing Director in one of the small companies to whom he had been feeding work, and Buck H. joined him. Both had large cars provided by the firm; Taff of course had a Rolls Royce, while Buck had a Jaguar. His dodgy progress came to light at intervals even after I had long retired from the Navy and rumour has it that Taff narrowly escaped justice by moving to Spain.

As I arrived at R.A.E. the M.R.G. was still a No.1 hot problem and monthly progress meetings were held at the contractor's premises in an effort to resolve the unreliability issues. The first introductory meeting was an eye-opener; an expensive lunch at an out of town restaurant was followed with brandy and cigars, until around 3 o'clock the contractors suggested that perhaps they should return to work. After a number of similar "lack-of-progress" meetings, convivial though they were, I decided that I had had enough and left the meetings to others. Finally, somewhat late in the day the Gyro experts from another department in R.A.E. were consulted; they confirmed that the basic design was at fault and could not be corrected. The modifications that we had been discussing would therefore only be palliatives and a new system was needed, until this was introduced then our Squadrons of Scimitars, Sea Vixens, Buccaneer 1's and R.A.F. Lightnings would suffer. One intriguing result of the provision of a centralised instrument system was that a form of independent back-up was needed for the primary instruments in the event of failure. In the case of aircraft attitude then a miniature Artificial Horizon was fitted and an early Sea Vixen was lost when the pilot became disorientated and chose to believe the faulty instrument. Nowadays at least triple redundancy is used in the computerised services supplying the glass cockpit displays and a system of voting determines hopefully the most valid result.

With the M.R.G. left to fester, the primary task was the remainder of the O.R.946 Integrated Flight Instrument System as required for the R.N. Buccaneer and R.A.F. Lightning. Essentially this was based upon a Marconi-Elliott Air Data analogue computer and remote electrical sensors of P-S and S pressure (Pitot and Static). After processing, outputs of Airspeed, Mach No., True Airspeed (T.A.S.), Altitude, and Rate of Climb were sent to new servo-driven strip display cockpit instruments, but more importantly to the Autopilot and Strike Sight in the Buccaneer. During our work we found that the T.A.S. output to Strike Sight could not be adequately tested and R.A.E. then evaluated the accuracy of this signal and concluded that gross errors were possible. When I reported this to D.G.A. (N) no action was taken, but it was to have considerable implication to the bombing accuracy of the Buccaneer as I found to my cost much later.

An entirely new range of 1st and 2nd line test equipment was needed and when I found that the intended P/S test set already planned was no more accurate than the equipment being tested then I sought a new mercury Manometer to act as a transfer standard at 2nd line after calibration at the National Physical Laboratory. After evaluation of several alternatives we recommended the purchase of a U.S. servo-driven system licensed to Bryan's Aeroquipment of Mitcham; a far cry from their little hand-pump device based upon the captured German design, and also from the standard Manometer used at N.P.L. Whereas our new instrument had a $1/2$ inch diameter column of mercury, the N.P.L. one had a 4 inch diameter column, was measured by an optical bench and the whole was temperature controlled. It was extremely instructive to see how N.P.L. worked to set up their standards for different physical functions.

Apart from our periodic progress reports to E&T Section we were happily not involved in the normal Naval routine at H.M.S. *Ariel*, so no extra duties or nauseating parades. Day to day activities were at my discretion as required to meet various extra tasks as they were sent to me, and as time passed I had dealings with virtually every manufacturer of aircraft instruments and cameras in U.K. and spent a lot of time on the road. With the Buccaneer 1 about to enter service, we spent time with Blackburn Aircraft Co. at Brough and at their test airfield at Holme-on-Spalding Moor evaluating our new kit in association with the company and with the Buccaneer R.N. Special Maintenance Party (S.M.P.), and later visited 700Z flight when it was formed at Lossiemouth. At Brough we were accommodated in the old Flying Club where the food was good but the rooms as cold as charity. Much time was also spent at Marconi-Elliott's at Rochester Airfield and one Saturday afternoon my C.E.A. and I were the only two people working in the factory.

Although in the early 1960's the aircraft industry was thriving, it was obvious as we went from place to place that most companies were still struggling to work in old and inadequate premises left over from the war and modified on an ad-hoc basis as each new task appeared. There was a great need to invest and change if our industry was to compete. However despite the apparent change of policy arising from the Sandys Defence Review of 1957 many new concepts were being explored, and competition was intense between the large numbers of contractors still in business. One result was that staff were regularly poached on the promise of a better salary, a car and other incentives as each new high tech project created a shortage of expertise. The backwash of this was that, although I did not actually issue contracts or control funds, my recommendations could influence decisions so we were normally assured of hospitality during our visits. It certainly did not influence me, as my belief, based upon the first M.R.G. meeting, was that the better the hospitality the greater the problems that needed to be investigated. An exception to the rule came at Bryan's, where the boss Captain Bryan ran a very democratic "ship". Usually I held meetings with his salesman, who followed standard practice and took us to some high class venue for lunch, but one day Captain Bryan was involved; we were driven to the nearest pub in his large ancient Austin Saloon, given a pint and driven back to the works canteen, where the oilcloth was wiped over and we all sat to eat canteen grub.

At Christmas it was the practice for many firms to arrive at Farnborough with bottles of spirits to be distributed round members of the department. In this Marconi-Elliott was well to the fore and their service reps. serving Blackburn's gained quite a reputation for the amount of booze transported to sustain themselves and guests during their visits. At some point during my time at Farnborough there was an attempt by Government to limit the expenses allowed for hospitality and for a while the contractors drew back a little, but in many cases the contractors' staff benefited directly at the lunches e.g. they would order cigarettes after lunch, in order to pocket all those left over, so they had no incentive to change. Over the years I had my fair share of business lunches and still find it hard to argue the propriety of this in relation to public service employees; compared with the U.S. where any form of gratuity from a contractor is wholly forbidden we seem to be overly relaxed, but our relationship with contractors is at least in part based on personal assessment of each member of the two parties and a lot of mutual respect can be created in an informal setting. As with all things it is the extremes that create the problems.

Prior to my promotion I rarely drank, but with the low cost of duty free drink on board ship (gin and tonic about threepence) I soon got used to drinking without overindulging. I was formally a member of the R.A.F. Officers' Mess at Farnborough, where I had lunch and attended social functions with Margaret. My practice then was to drink only until midnight and then somewhat later to drive home to Fareham on the virtually empty A32. By good fortune I was never stopped, but this was in the days before the "breathalyser"; these days lack of practice and common sense forbids such foolishness. My luck did not however hold one afternoon following a technical briefing and tour of R.A.E. by a newly appointed Naval Attaché; all the Naval officers at Farnborough gathered at lunchtime and for some reason we slurped "Black Velvet" (Guinness and Champagne). By mid-afternoon I was very soporific and decided it was better to go home than to fall asleep at my desk. Taking a nice smooth curve into a corner at Droxford I bashed the rear mudguard of a farm lorry going in the other direction. Sobering up quickly I apologised and agreed to pay for the damage; the Droxford police station was literally just yards away! As it happened my little Austin A35 had already been valued in a part exchange deal for a new Ford Anglia; this was due to be collected at the weekend and I spent the next two days adding small amounts of filler and paint to my damaged offside wing until it looked as good as new and was duly accepted by the garage.

The R.A.F. as the youngest service had some quaint old-fashioned customs, and at Farnborough newly appointed officers were required to leave their "card" on a silver salver in the entrance hall, and there was a formal routine involving the arrival of their families, thus ensuring their place in the social pecking order. Fortunately no one suggested that the Naval officers followed this custom, but certain Mess dinners were an obligation, which even the Navy could not ignore; when on one occasion I was ill and had to cancel I was summoned to the presence of Group Captain Hannafin to explain my absence. He was not impressed with my explanation; evidently sickness was no excuse. The Group Captain was the Senior Officer at Farnborough but not the Mess President and for a Commanding Officer to take such a close interest in mess business would not have happened in the Navy despite its keen interest in tradition. The formality of pre-dinner sherry did not equate with the drill for drinks during the meal; we were seated with our pre-selected bottle of wine stowed beside our chair to be self dispensed as required, very uncouth behaviour! Perhaps other R.A.F. messes were different, but it seemed as if in the absence of the traditions that so bedevil the Army and Navy the R.A.F. had set out to devise some bizarre ones of its own. The social niceties did not appear to include extending a welcome to new arrivals, and on more than one occasion I felt it my duty to bring in and introduce a new R.A.F. arrival who was being ignored.

The R.A.F. Mess was the focal point for much activity during the annual S.B.A.C. Show (Society of British Aircraft Constructors); it provided a convivial viewing area overlooking the main runway and behind the famous Cody Tree for both our families and for invited guests. As a result the Mess funds were well boosted and great efforts were made to run other social events at a loss, in order to avoid having a surplus at the end of each financial year. Any surplus had under R.A.F. rules to be sent to the Central Mess Fund and this was obviously not popular. Besides the social side of the S.B.A.C. show there was obviously much of technical importance in the show which required our attention but even as residents of R.A.E. there was no automatic right of entry to the show site which was always based on the opposite side of the main runway to the control tower. Each department however had a small allocation of tickets, which were used in turn as required for the staff. Similarly the Services were also allocated a small numbers of tickets, but these were like gold dust and it was generally the senior officers who were able to attend. I.A.P. Dept. however had a work site within the show area and it was remarkable how many of our Naval colleagues from other establishments were needed to visit the Tacan Hut during the show week. For us residents it was virtually impossible to work during the show period which started with practice flying several weeks before, and in addition our cars were likely to be "zapped" by the corrosive red or blue dye used to create the spectacular smoke trails by the services flying teams. Well before the Red Arrows the F.A.A. and R.A.F.

competed annually to provide the largest formation aerobatic team with eventually the R.A.F. winning with a vast formation of Hunters. The quantity of unburned dye was considerable and not only our cars but also the local housewives found their washing being stained to their great indignation.

From 1950 onwards I attended many shows at Farnborough until I finally retired in 1986; at the beginning every year brought a new range of British aircraft as the jet era started to make its impact and the prototypes of Hunter, Canberra and V-Bombers appeared; latterly it was the arrival of U.S. and Russian aircraft that held centre stage once the show was International and the British Aircraft Industry reduced in size. In the early days it was the aircraft themselves that were my prime interest but later there was much to learn in the Equipment Exhibition Halls and I would often attend more than once during the show to make business contacts with industry. This was possible because as a project manager I was inundated with invitations; these generally included very generous hospitality in the contractors' chalets, which needed to be accepted with great caution if intending to drive home. On the whole these contacts paid off and gave a broad perspective of the area in which I was involved.

During my time at Farnborough the Department was tasked to investigate the possibility of providing a Head-up Display of basic flying instruments; although a rather simplified system was incorporated into the Buccaneer Strike Sight the prospect of a comprehensive and reliable system seemed a very long way off in 1961. Nowadays, not only is it a routine provision in military aircraft but has been further miniaturised to provide the same service in helmet mounted sighting systems, and the "glass cockpit" head-down displays are multi-function colour, such has been the progress since the arrival of the electronic digital computer which was still a dream in those days. As it happened, Marconi-Elliott was then developing 'Verdan', the first airborne digital computer for the T.S.R.2 and I later attended a short introductory course at Rochester on the technique. I became uncomfortably aware of how rapidly aircraft technology was moving; with a theoretical background stuck in 1943, the emphasis on transistors, integrated circuits, digital computing and beyond left me well out of date. The Navy was not aiming to bring me up to date, so I had to do my own thing. First attempt at a quick introduction to transistors by an R.A.E. expert showed that the only way to proceed was to attend a civilian college, but that option was no more tenable at Farnborough than it had been during earlier appointments due to the location, pressure of work, and constant duty travel, plus the daily forty miles each way to my home.

Without Naval duties I was able for the first time to plan a decent summer holiday during this appointment and we decided to go to the Norfolk Broads. We had just read *The art of coarse sailing* by Richard Gordon so the perils of actual sailing were only too apparent and we opted for a motor-cruiser. Having failed to take a complete toolkit with me my ingenuity was put to the test on the first day when the fresh water pump was found disconnected from its pipe and pumped water into the galley. Fixing that with a penknife and a nail file we sailed on and tied up for the night and achieved a 30-degree list in the small hours as the tide went out. My "navigator" directed us into an eel set later in the trip and we were towed out with the cooling inlet clogged with mud. This I could not fix and I proceeded toward Hickling Broad at idling speed to maintain the engine temperature just below the "red" mark, but once in the Broad could not make headway against the wind and I opened the throttle. The 1000 c.c. Austin engine then reached and passed the "red" mark and began to work on happily as a diesel when the ignition was switched off, at which point I turned off the fuel tap and muffled the air intake, before throwing out the anchor and awaiting rescue. The return journey was equally exciting and we only damaged the windscreen a little as we just scraped under Potter Heigham Bridge at high tide. Our last evening was spent tied up in a small stream off the River Yare in a rainstorm; as I closed down for the night I discovered that we were filling up with water through the prop shaft bearing. All through the holiday I had dutifully given the grease cap a turn each day, but now I found that the grease was solid and had not penetrated to the bearing. We were saved from a nightlong vigil at the bilge pump by wrapping the shaft with greased knitting wool from Margaret's bag. We had had a really good holiday!

In 1962 I was finally promoted to Lieutenant; after years of good reports I had begun to wonder if my name had been lost, but no, it had just reached the top of the pile, and the good news was followed up by an appointment to H.M.S. *Ariel* in the Training Department. Perhaps this would at last provide the chance to improve my education!

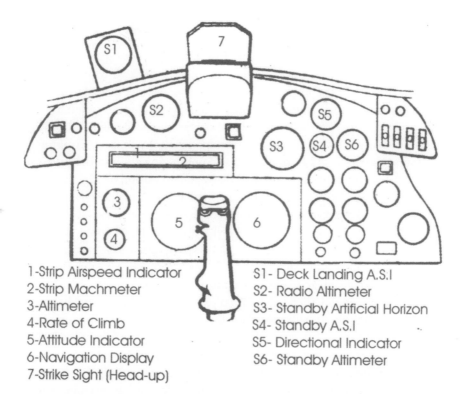

1-Strip Airspeed Indicator
2-Strip Machmeter
3-Altimeter
4-Rate of Climb
5-Attitude Indicator
6-Navigation Display
7-Strike Sight (Head-up)

S1- Deck Landing A.S.I
S2- Radio Altimeter
S3- Standby Artificial Horizon
S4- Standby A.S.I
S5- Directional Indicator
S6- Standby Altimeter

1-4 fed by Analogue Air Data Computer, 5 and 6 fed by Master
Reference Gyro and Fluxgate Compass all part of the OR946
Integrated Flight Instrument System
7 fed as above plus Blue Parrot Radar
Standby instruments are all independent units

THE PILOTS MAIN FLYING DISPLAY ON THE BUCCANEER 1

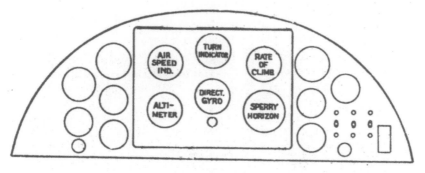

A typical wartime cockpit
centred around the six air
driven instruments of the
Blind Flying Panel and the
P4 Compass read from
above.

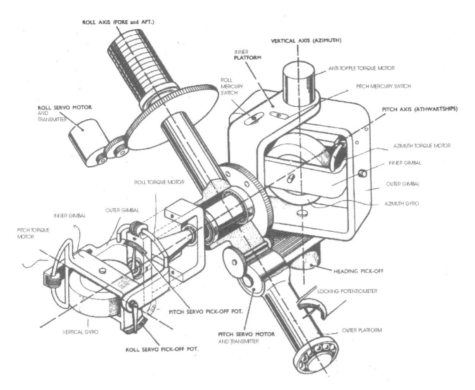

A schematic diagram of the Master Reference Gyro Mk1
showing the principal components.

Officers of the Equipment and Trials Section. Lee-on-Solent 1962.

Chapter 17 H.M.S. *Ariel* Lee-on-Solent

At Lee I found myself i/c the Electrical Equipment Group with my overall boss Rigor Mortimer formerly of 803 Squadron. Rigor was responsive to my ideas for improvements in the training and I was also able to get partial day release for an H.N.C. course at Portsmouth College of Technology. For the next two years this course kept me hard at work in my spare time to the partial exclusion of my family and I duly passed. Interestingly the course was mainly composed of young trainees from industry, with just a handful of mature students like myself, one of whom was another Lieut. (S.D). from *Collingwood*. During the two years it was very noticeable that, just like the Mechanicians that had recently been introduced into the Navy, it was the mature students who were the most dedicated. The content of the course was directly of value to my daily work, as was my recent experience at Farnborough, since by now the Buccaneer systems were being taught at *Ariel*. As a career officer and family man I was anxious to make the best use of my experience and qualifications and I was therefore miffed to find that an ex-Apprentice several years my junior had left the service as a C.P.O, had obtained similar qualifications while a civilian, and had then been re-entered on the Supplementary List and promoted to Lt-Cdr. My own application to transfer under this scheme was not however accepted.

At around this time the R.N. trained a number of Army Air Corps engineers and it was refreshing to hear their ideas on aircraft. Basically they viewed their helicopters as airborne jeeps, requiring them to be simple and reliable; their idea of ground equipment was that it should survive being dropped from a lorry at 30 m.p.h. and having a .303 bullet fired into it. We required our kit to be sailor proof and this also was a very challenging requirement. In many ways the F.A.A. and A.A.C. were well matched in our philosophy, and the Army preferred and appreciated the can-do approach we offered, particularly in operational zones such as Borneo, rather than the service offered by the R.A.F. However I wonder how the Army views the maintenance problems of its new and highly sophisticated Apache Longbow attack helicopters, although I have no doubt that R.E.M.E. engineers will as always do a good job.

During this time I found many basic deficiencies with the training and where possible corrected them, often with the help of specially made training aids. This was particularly the case with gyroscopes and compasses. It was evident that many of our ex-C.E.L. civilian instructors were instructing only to provide answers to previously observed exam questions and not to impart a full understanding of the subject. At the lowest level of instruction i.e. E.M.'s and L.E.M.'s it was often very difficult to provide meaningful questions without exposing this loophole.

A Compass Swing was required routinely every three months on our aircraft and also whenever a major equipment change took place. This could not be carried out at sea and as a result there were times when a plane had operational restrictions imposed until a Swing had been carried out. Often the quick solution was to fly two aircraft ashore so that the pilots could give their aircraft a quick engine running "Swing" at the end of the non-duty runway using a hand-held Medium Landing Compass, and the quality of these Swings was highly questionable. However no effective training was given to our Engineers either, although the latest scheme for Compass Swinging was based on a Fourier analysis of the test results obtained by a very accurate Watts Datum Compass and would produce superior results if carried out carefully, and certainly not on the end of the non-duty runway. I therefore developed a classroom training aid that enabled a full swing to be demonstrated and errors corrected and followed up by investigating the Buccaneer system using a little test box I had built to enable part of the servo loop to be adjusted accurately. It was fortunate that in due course I was able to put my knowledge to use, but it took some four years before I was in a position ultimately to change the policy on Compass Swinging.

Generally it did not fall to me to give lectures and this suited me fine, but occasionally a small group of officers would come in and then I had no option. However looking into the future I was told to get up to speed on Inertial Navigation and prepare instructional material. As a result I visited A.C.O. Slough (Admiralty Compass Observatory) to see S.I.N.S. (Ships Inertial Navigation System), to Ferranti to see the monster created for the T.S.R.2 and to Marconi-Elliott's to see their system intended for the Jaguar. There were no samples to be had, but by chance there was an opportunity to visit a Ministry of Supply Depot at Ampthill near Bedford, where a colleague and I rummaged through a veritable Aladdin's cave of surplus gear and returned with a lorry load of useful equipment for training. I secured a wide selection of I.N. units from the recently cancelled Army "Blue Water" missile programme; with these, and a lot of I.N. brochures and technical papers from the Buccaneer 3 Project Officer, I was able, with our "Schoolie" (schoolmaster), to give a quick short course to visiting Senior Officers. The sensitivity of the Accelerometers was a surprise, and in demonstrations while they were mounted on a bench it was found that merely walking around the classroom was enough to ensure they gave full-scale deflection. When later I worked with A.C.O. Slough the main building was surrounded by a water filled moat and the S.I.N.S. system was able to detect the movement in the building caused by changes in the water level. The Buccaneer 3 did not of course mature and the problem of initial alignment of the Inertial Platform on a ship at sea, although much investigated, was not resolved so far as R.N. aircraft were concerned during my time in the service.

As usual, back with the Navy, I took my turn as O.O.D. (Officer of the Day) at Lee; this duty started at 1100 with the rum issue and completed the following morning after colours. Rum issue was an education; first move was to obtain the keys to the rum store (Spirit Room) and open up, attended by the Leading Supply Assistant Storeman. This gentleman began to look agitated by the time he arrived at the store, as the door was opened and the heady fumes of rum emerged he began to turn puce, and by the time the issue was complete he was sweating profusely. The neat rum required for the day was determined from a list collected by the duty P.O. and, after carefully measuring the level of spirit already in the barrel, the required quantity was pumped by a copper hand pump into copper measuring jugs and then decanted into a wooden "Barrico" (oval barrel). This was then secured by a brass hasp and padlock to which only the O.O.D. had the key.

With the neat rum measured out for distribution to the C&P.O.'s messes, the next task was the preparation of the Grog (rum and water) for the ratings. At *Ariel* the total allocation for each mess was collected in a Rum "Fanny" by a duty or volunteer member and returned to the mess for consumption, but the mixing of rum with water and the actual distribution was carried out in the Annex to the main dining hall using the traditional rum tub carrying the words "God bless the Queen" in brass letters. Mixing the Grog was an art, since in decanting the liquid to open containers there was certain to be spillage; it was not practical to extract the last dregs from the tub and therefore some additional water had to be added. It did not fall to either the Storeman or Duty P.O. to provide water. This was done, not altogether altruistically, by one or two ratings who were always first in the queue; payback time arrived when their mess was called and by careful sleight of hand the Storeman would contrive to pour extra Grog past the various calibrated copper measures into the favoured individual's "Fanny." O.K. I stopped that and the issue carried on more accurately albeit with reluctance. However even before that another game was being played when the "Barrico" was unlocked and inverted over the Rum tub; on the face of it, it seemed reasonable that the oval shape should be rocked over the tub to ensure it was empty, but it was yet another scam. Rocking vigorously ensured that some rum would always be retained in the "Barrico", and when the O.O.D. replaced the wooden bung and locked the hasp he may well have assumed that the "Barrico" was both empty and secure until the next day. However Jolly Jack had obviously found that the slight clearance between the bung and the hasp was enough to ease back the bung and allow the retained rum to be emptied out when the O.O.D. had long departed. So we put paid to that little trick as well! The final act in the drama was ditching the "gash" (remains) down the nearest drain; the quantity to be ditched depended on how much allowance had been made for spillage and how accurate the issue had been, sometimes it was quite a lot but it would not keep fresh for long once mixed with water anyway. Rumour had it that the drain outside the rum store at a certain Naval Airfield in Northern Ireland was the cleanest in the country; this was because a very clean tin can was placed beneath it to catch the gash for later removal. One had to be very alert to the tricks that were played by our men.

The O.O.D. was on duty at the Main Gate outside working hours and slept in the duty cabin to keep an eye on the Main Gate sentries and await the next disaster. By that time many of the rules that had so irked me as a rating had been relaxed, and off-duty sailors wore civilian clothing of all descriptions; only their I.D. Cards distinguished them from the Duty Civilian Stoker. Problems always arose when a coach load of guests arrived for a station function and the question of having each guest personally checked in was always a matter of doubt. Presumably all doubt was removed once the I.R.A. got to work. Sometimes we were involved in an incident of some kind, and on one occasion I had to deal with the attempted suicide of a C.P.O. with marital problems. Another evening I received a telephone call after midnight from a Two and a Half (Lt Cdr) Schoolie living in the wardroom. "My bed has fallen through the floor." My response was brief, "So what do you expect me to do about that? Goodnight."

Once again the Navy Lark arrived back at the flagpole, when the Duty Hand, having lowered the Ensign at sunset, had dropped the upper cleat and this under the weight of the halyards had disappeared irretrievably to the top of the mast. I had the greatest sympathy having passed that way myself, and I could only laugh my socks off. We had no colours the following morning and the Dockyard Riggers had to be called in to re-rig the ropes.

At work the Cold War and various spy scandals had increased concern about security and individuals received positive vetting for some sensitive posts but for the most part this did not impact on daily activities until I received a C.P.O. whose documents were endorsed "No access to Classified Material". He was thus unemployable in even the simplest role in my department, and I looked into the reason for the ban. It transpired that he had stared to drink heavily following a marital problem and this had been reported. He was then reckoned a security risk, but because there had been no follow up action it seemed that he would be branded forever. After I had investigated I found that he had resolved his personal problems and my recommendation that his security rating be restored was accepted.

With my children growing older our little bungalow was too small and we looked for something more suitable, particularly as we wanted to escape from the estate where every other family had a service connection. In 1964 Margaret found a vacant building plot in Shirrell Heath near Wickham and I designed a new bungalow and had it built. Our new place was in an un-adopted lane between two bungalows and by the time the foundations were laid, the nearest bungalow had changed hands, and when we visited the site, Jean, very obviously a "Naval Officer's Wife" who had just moved in, greeted us. That was not quite what we had wanted but at least Margaret would have company while I was away and Barbara had four children of a similar age. Jean's husband was a General List Lt-Cdr. Torpedo specialist and we did not meet for quite a while.

My stint at *Ariel* completed in October 1964 when I joined a course of Electrical Officers to be cross trained in Airframe and Engine subjects at H.M.S. *Condor* at Arbroath; not a very arduous course since it had come a few years too late as anyone with squadron experience would have testified and we were already familiar with the subjects. However as far as I was concerned it had a direct bearing on my next appointment, which was to join the Buccaneer 2 I.F.T.U. due to form shortly at Lossiemouth, and I spent part of the last few months of 1964 at Brough learning about the Buccaneer with my fellow engineers from the I.F.T.U.

As the pattern of earlier I.F.T.U.'s went, it would convert to being the first Buccaneer 2 Squadron when its task was complete and we would then expect to go to sea. On the face of it even the appointer had got it about right based upon my previous experience, and the I.F.T.U. was reckoned to be a plum job, probably good for my career if not for my health, but at least the first Squadron was likely to have a good tour at sea in compensation. With Margaret and Barbara now settled in and Richard a boarder at Peter Symonds in Winchester it would clearly be wrong to move north for a few short months before I was again at sea, moreover Margaret had no stairs to climb as would have been the case in a hiring or married quarter and we had a lot to do in the house and garden. So we accepted our separation gracefully. Back to Lossiemouth!

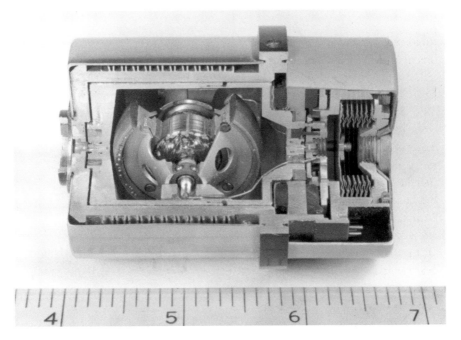

A sectioned Inertial Navigation Gyro. Three of these were fitted to a stable platform. Author's training notes.

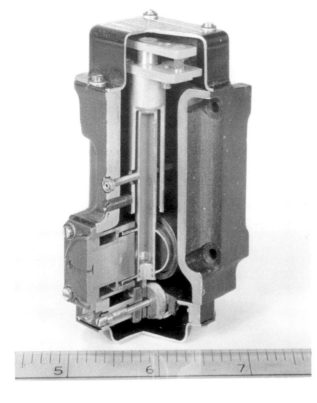

A sectioned Inertial Navigation Accelerometer. Three of these were required on each stable platform. Author's training notes.

The stable platform of a typical Inertial Navigation System. The gimbals allowed the stable elements to remain aligned to the chosen axes when the vehicle moved.
Author's notes.

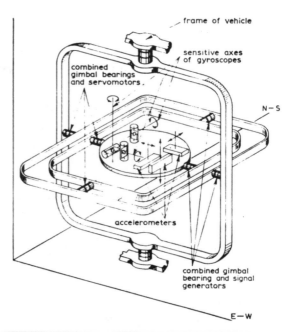

"and about time too."

A Bit of a "Tiff"

Chapter 18 700B Flight, 801 Squadron, 736B Flight Lossiemouth

I joined Lossiemouth in January 1965 and the I.F.T.U. was commissioned as 700B Flight in April when the aircraft arrived. Cdr. Freddie Mills commanded the unit and there were four Engineers. The A.E.O. Lt.-Cdr. Keith Steel, the A.L.O. Lt.-Cdr. Don Ross, who was also a qualified observer, myself as A/A.L.O., and Eddie Day, as A/A.E.O. We also had a Supply S/Lt to handle the Augmented Logistic Support from Industry and Naval Store Depots during the I.F.T.U. period. We eventually mustered eight Buccaneers and operated a single Hunter T8B, which was largely used as a hack aircraft and had an intermittent problem with its undercarriage that always seemed to arise when it was operated away from base.

The Buccaneer 1 had been in service since March 1961 and although most onboard systems on the Buccaneer 2 were the same or marginally improved, the primary difference was that twin R.R. Spey twin shaft turbofan engines of 11,100 lb. thrust were fitted in place of the D.H. Gyron Juniors which gave only 7,100 lbs. Whereas the Buccaneer 1 was basically underpowered, the new engines gave greatly improved performances in range and load carrying ability. Range increased from 1,730 to 2,300 miles and loaded weight from 45,000 to 62,000 lbs in the final variants. This meant that new and additional weapons and other equipment could be carried, although initially this did not apply to the Naval versions as operated by 700B. The ultimate version was the R.A.F.'s Buccaneer 2B and this model, partly made up from converted ex-Navy 2's, well proved the validity of Naval thinking in the late 1950's; in R.A.F. service the Buccaneer showed the U.S. a thing or two during the Red Flag Exercises in Nevada, but unfortunately the contour following during overland flying gave rise to a lot of negative "g" and this greatly increased the Airframe fatigue in this immensely strong aircraft, which had been stressed for positive "g" in Naval operations; after several accidents some aircraft were scrapped and others reworked and strengthened. Despite this setback the Buccaneers of Nos. 12 and 208 Squadrons R.A.F served effectively during the Gulf War of 1991 and the last unit was not retired until 1994.

Obviously the aircraft was far more complex than the Scimitar and still took a lot of effort to maintain, but it had rather fewer of the problems found on the Scimitar. It did not for example leak fuel and hydraulic fluid and the fuel balancing system was based upon calibrated pump chambers all driven by a common shaft, which avoided the earlier snags with electrical systems. We still needed to work a modified shift system, and surprisingly after the pain of 803 Sqdn. and the work-study exercise on *Victorious*, the recommendations made had not been passed on or adopted as a formal policy. Since my colleagues had not been briefed and lacked similar experience they determined to find their own solutions, so some things could have been made easier. In the event however we worked well together.

Some things had changed at Lossiemouth but for the time being we were still using the ancient wartime wooden huts and wardroom; these buildings were literally falling to pieces and the corridors so rotten and sunk that it was impossible to turn a corner standing upright. In compensation however the mess was pretty congenial because the cabins were so uncomfortable. At the Squadron hangar we now found that tea and coffee machines had been installed, so that there was no longer a mad rush for the N.A.A.F.I. wagon on its somewhat unpredictable progress round the airfield. What a good idea! It did not turn out as intended of course, because calls for ground-crew were now frequently delayed with the excuse "they're just finishing/starting their coffee, sir". As always Jolly Jack found ways of circumventing the best of plans.

Our unit operated the Tool Control System, which had been introduced with the Buccaneer 1. Every aircraft had its own toolkit and remained unserviceable until every last item in the kit had been accounted for and signed in. It was intended to prevent aircraft accidents through tools being left in vulnerable locations and in this it was successful. However even with care and experience the odd item, particularly spanner sockets, would go adrift and much time was lost searching for them. Sometimes the missing item would be found in the overalls of off-duty ground crew, but never as I recall in the aircraft. In my view the real benefit for the servicing lay in always having an appropriate tool for the job, rather than having to depend upon what could be found or adapted in the rather less well designed personal toolkits used previously.

The I.F.T.U. identified a number of technical problems and we received support from the Blackburn Technical representative on site. One of the first snags involved the undercarriage locking indicator, all attempts to adjust the micro-switches controlling this system failed and eventually I found that the springs in the new ice-break micro-switches were stronger than the brackets on which they were mounted. These bent at each attempt to make adjustment and had then to be strengthened. This minor oversight in the drawing office caused a real nuisance until resolved. However one problem never quite resolved was that of Tail plane Trim Runaway. In the Mk 1 a defect in the thumb operated Trim switch on the multi function control column caused the Tail plane Trim Actuator on the all-moving Tail plane to run to the end of its travel and obviously this caused control

A Bit of a "Tiff"

problems. The Trim switch was again suspect when similar problems arose on the Mk2 but the switch was now a different design and was not the cause. Following several reported incidents, the next aircraft involved was placed in quarantine until representatives from Blackburns and from the Naval Accident Investigation Unit arrived. My colleague, Fred Allford of A.I.U. and I then took the aircraft apart in an effort to find any fault at all and failed. At one point after midnight the overload trip on the Avometer we were using popped out, and did so repeatedly, suggesting that we had found the problem. We decided to leave further investigation until morning but back at my cabin I worried the problem to a conclusion; one of us had been holding the long wire and in doing so had inadvertently completed a 24 volt circuit through our body. The electrical resistance of a human body was low enough to pass current sufficient to trip the Avometer. The unconfirmed conclusion of our investigation was that the trim had occurred through pilot error caused by his instinctive grip on the control column; the problem did not recur, at least during my time on the unit.

A further problem, which appeared to be pilot inexperience, prevented the aircraft taking off; the airflow over the high set tail plane could be masked if the nose was raised too high. On one occasion I took a crew out to the far end of the duty runway to attend an aircraft that had failed to get airborne for this reason and during our spell there, while other aircraft were noisily taking off past us, we were being dive bombed by a flock of Terns whose nesting site we had disturbed; they were quite unconcerned by the planes. Again this difficulty was overcome with experience, but I cannot recall hearing of a similar problem on the Mk1. At sea the aircraft was launched from the catapult in a nose up attitude and again there was some initial difficulty; after trials by the Naval unit from Boscombe Down, during which the test pilot ditched a "Buccaneer" on launch, the recommended procedure was for the Buccaneer to be launched "hands-off". This allowed the aircraft to take its natural flight attitude and the pilot took over the controls after the plane was airborne. Needless to say this idea did not come naturally to our pilots, but it worked and was then standard procedure.

One oddity arose from the need periodically to clean the burners in the Spey combustion chambers, and the Rolls Royce solution was to ingest crushed walnut shells; and it worked. The mind boggles at the idea of cracking open millions of walnuts to clean Spey engines! This novel solution did not sit comfortably with the ever-present danger of ingesting foreign objects from around the aircraft, nor of the risk of bird strikes, which was a real threat to aircraft at Lossiemouth and particularly to the Buccaneer whose main role was to fly at low level. In fact all aircraft were routinely tested during development by firing a defrosted frozen chicken at the windscreen and into the engines. Nonetheless a big bird could do a lot of damage and since Lossiemouth had a large seabird population Air Traffic Control did its best to chase them off. Various methods were used, including firing signal cartridges, playing recordings of seagulls in distress and operating trained kestrels. All these schemes certainly got the birds airborne for a while but they very quickly returned and were just as likely to take to the air the next time an aircraft passed by, so it was a constant battle as Lossiemouth at that time had a very high level of aircraft movements, many of them due to the need for A.D.D.L.'s (Airfield Dummy Deck Landings). In addition to surviving bird strikes, our Buccaneers survived the erosion caused by flying to the newly erupted volcano at Surtsey off Iceland. With the extended range of the Mk2 the volcano was conveniently sited for a navigation exercise as well as for sightseeing, and our high speed tourists returned with their leading edges and nose cones well sand blasted. In fact we were very lucky not to suffer more serious damage as later occurred when airliners over-flying Mt. St Helens in the U.S. found their hydraulic systems damaged by the abrasive dust.

Although the Buccaneer was very well equipped with Radio Navigation aids, including Tacan and Doppler, it was still necessary to have an accurate Magnetic Compass, and this continued to require routine Compass Swings at three month intervals. As usual this was very inconvenient even at an air station. The Compass Base at Lossiemouth had no power supply and since the Buccaneer required a 3 phase 115 volt supply it could initially only have a Compass Swing with its engines running, since the use of a ground power supply rig so close to the aircraft would introduce errors. As a result I designed a relay trolley, which enabled power to be supplied from a safe distance, and had this constructed in station workshops. In truly democratic fashion the E.A. who did the work then received a financial award for my invention under the Herbert Lott Prize Fund. In earlier posts I had designed several items, which included a counting device for the Typex crypto machine, a jig enabling Gyro Gunsights to be removed and reinstalled without re-harmonisation, and a Pitot-Static pipeline connector which enabled the Blind Flying Panel to be removed and replaced without risking cross connection, as occasionally occurred. I received an award for only one of these so there was no great surprise, nor was reward expected, since with the power supply it was now possible to carry out full "Fourier" Compass Swings; true these took longer but I was able to prove conclusively that the engine running swings carried out by the pilots were merely changing the manually introduced errors of each earlier swing to a new set of errors around the true setting, which had not changed. Regretfully it was not feasible to change the Naval servicing policy from just my experience, but at least our aircraft had properly corrected compasses. In the event my next appointment after Lossiemouth was to N.A.M.D.U. (Naval Air Maintenance Development Unit) and I was then able to assemble the facts and implement a change of policy enabling the Compass Swing intervals to be greatly extended.

The Sperry Rotorace Gyro had replaced my old pet hate, the M.R.G., in the Buccaneer 2. This was very reliable and accurate as a Heading Reference, and eventually in 1985 the R.A.F. S2B's finally received an Inertial Navigation System as had been the intention had the Buccaneer 3 been introduced.

Almost certainly the major problems arose with the complex (for that time) weapon system. In this system radar targeting data from the Blue Parrot monopulse nose mounted radar, together with flight data from the I.F.I.S. (Integrated Flight Reference System) were assembled and processed in the analogue computer forming the Strike Sight. The resulting signals were used to provide steering commands to the pilot on his Head-up Display and release commands for the weapons. In its strike role the Buccaneer 2 was equipped to carry either two WE177 Tactical Nuclear Weapons (the Mk1 only carried the 2000 lb H.E.M.C. Nuclear weapon), or, until fitted for guided weapons, up to 8 x 1000 lb conventional bombs or unguided rockets. In due course the four wing pylons were fitted to take Triple Ejector Racks, and with these fitted the bomb load was increased to 16,000 lbs of which only four of the 1000 lb bombs were carried in the Bomb Bay. When faults occurred in this system there was no means of comprehensively testing the system as a whole, and tracing the signal path through the system literally required the circuit diagrams of each individual unit to be laid out conveniently to the aircraft. If one was lucky then the signal was traced back and forward through the circuits and arrived at the key spot. This was a long-winded process and as normal the short cut was to exchange the items under suspicion for tested spares. The suspect items were then put into the pipeline for testing in the appropriate station workshop but, since the workshop test equipment did not replicate the aircraft installation then they were usually returned labelled "unit tested and found serviceable, no fault found". They then ended up in another aircraft and the defect reappeared again. Our efforts to maintain the crucial Radar system were aided by the dedication of our C.R.E.A. Anderson who spent many off-duty hours back in the hangar, and I was pleased to recommend him for an award under the honours system, which I have always thought much abused. However on this occasion it worked and he received an award.

To add to our woes, our weapon systems were fitted or partly fitted with a number of Naval Service Modifications (N.S.M.'s), the details of which were not fully recorded and which were still largely under development by their instigator. The background to these modifications was the emphasis on the conventional weapon role, rather than the tactical nuclear role. The latter role did not require the same precision delivery needed for conventional weapons, but in fact the system was not optimised for conventional weapons. During a tour with a Buccaneer 1 squadron Lt.-Cdr. Peter Walwyn, who was an Electrical Engineer as well as a qualified Buccaneer Observer, had noted the deficiencies and had devised new bombing techniques, which involved a number of changes to the system. The ideas were good and Peter was appointed into a post, which in effect gave him the opportunity to pursue his ideas, and our aircraft were destined to be his test beds. This was singularly unfortunate as we already had our hands full proving the Buccaneer 2 in the short period allotted to the I.F.T.U. before we were converted to being the first operational Buccaneer unit as 801 Squadron. The work required to validate the new concepts was in my view far more appropriate for a team from Farnborough/Boscombe Down and the contractor who could dedicate all their resources to the study. In the event the number of N.S.M.'s reached double figures, it became impossible to keep track of the details without proper documentation and the only people aware of the state of play were Peter and his tame R.E.A. in the Radio Workshops. Peter spent only part of his time at Lossiemouth and when he was there he was likely to be found in the workshops with Avometer and soldering iron tweaking yet another improvement. I personally had not the time to follow up what was happening and left them to get on with it since I had no power to change the rules. However it was evident that one of the problems faced in improving the accuracy was the inherent errors in the T.A.S. (True Airspeed) signal to Strike Sight, which I had reported to D.G.A. (N) in 1962, but had been ignored.

On the domestic front, and barely in time to stop the wartime huts from rotting completely, we moved into a brand new brick built wardroom in mid 1965. Almost at once a colleague attempted to take a bath one Saturday afternoon and the hot tap came off in his hand as he turned it on. A geyser of scalding water poured out, and after he called for my help, we finally succeeded in refitting the tap and turning it off. Because no provision had been made for sluices to drain away any spillage, and because there was no accessible stop cock, the upper corridor was well and truly flooded, damaging both the carpet and the wood block inlaid flooring which had then to be replaced.

H.R.H. Princess Alexandra formally opened the Mess on 19th July.

This fulfilled a promise made some time previously when her aircraft had been diverted to Lossiemouth during her honeymoon. A formal lunch in the Mess was followed by a full-scale parade on the airfield while the Princess drove slowly past. I remember that I stood swaying in front of my Division thoroughly at peace and enjoying myself as the lunch and champagne did their work. The new Mess was positively palatial by comparison with any other station at which I had served, but we should have been warned by past experience; no sooner did the Navy get its stations properly equipped than they tended to be closed or transferred to the R.A.F. The cosiness of the Mess however disappeared as people did their own thing in the comfort of their cabins, so much so that it was rare to see or hear your neighbours. Not quite as quiet as needed however because the block was built in a U-shape and received and amplified the noise of Buccaneer engines to a point that denied relaxation at night.

For entirely practical reasons I had made the choice of leaving my family in the south but life without them was very unattractive after nearly five years with them in shore appointments and I had never been attracted to the monastic life. I was now forty and apart from a few Married Officers in a similar position to myself, the majority of livers-in were young aircrew, who with flying pay and sports cars were not exactly in my league for company. The local scene around Lossiemouth and Elgin had little attraction with or without a car for a bird of passage like myself and I felt progressively lonelier. I busied myself with my photography using the cabin as a darkroom and consoled myself that I would shortly be at sea with the Squadron not in the expectation of more relaxation but at least pulling together as a unit. With all of us literally in the same boat and the periodic run ashore, hopefully in some interesting foreign place, the "spirit" of a Squadron was usually very high.

In the meantime, when duties made it possible I took any opportunity to fly south to Lee-on-Solent on the Northern Clipper on a Friday, returning on a Monday. This twice-weekly service carried personnel, stores and official mail from the Headquarters at Lee to the Air Stations at Belfast, Abbotsinch, Arbroath, and Lossiemouth using Sea Devons or latterly Sea Herons of 781 Squadron. A Southern service covered the units in the West Country. Invariably en route to Belfast the Irish Sea would be totally covered in cloud and I noticed that as we approached Ireland the pilot started to let down until the sea was clearly visible, he then inched to port until the shore line and groups of white painted houses could be seen. Continuing along the shore we then saw the runway dead ahead and as we landed a large airfield radar could be seen operating on the Short Bros Site. On one trip we were delayed at Belfast and in passing I commented to our pilot that the radar must be a great help in the normally rotten visibility. "Oh," he said, "we can't use that, it belongs to Shorts! What we do is drop down until we can see the sea, then we inch to port until we see the shoreline etc—." This was known as flying by the seat of one's pants and I was much impressed as the approaches to both Belfast and Abbotsinch were littered with buildings and Dockyard cranes.

On one trip the wind was so strong that we were forced to refuel on the Isle of Man, were then diverted to R.A.F. Ballykelly rather than Belfast, and had lunch while we waited for passengers to motor from Belfast, who were then embarked complete with "sick bags" for the onward journey. As always over the Cairngorms the fuselage rattled with ice being shed from the propellers; after we arrived at Lossiemouth it appeared that all other airfields had been closed due to the gales and we were the only aircraft airborne. On another trip south, as we climbed steeply out of Lossiemouth, petrol could be seen streaming out of the starboard wing. It was impossible for the passengers to reach the cockpit during the climb to advise the pilot, so we were much relieved when at last the loss of fuel was detected on the cockpit instruments and we levelled off and diverted to Arbroath for refuelling and to re-secure the filler cap.

As always the junior Squadron Air Engineers were placed on the Station Duty Engineer roster despite normally working far longer hours than the Station staff. My working week normally included Sundays! However on arrival at Lossiemouth we were not allowed to go to our appointed role until we had read and signed for the Air Engineering Standing Orders. This massive tome was nothing less than a potted history of every incident that had ever occurred on the station and the orders that had been written to prevent a recurrence. It was impossible to read in one day and to remain legal one needed to virtually carry one around on every duty. Inevitably I was responsible for yet another Standing Order.

Lossiemouth was a Master Diversion Airfield open twenty-four hours a day; this was a source of prestige to the R.N. Once, bad weather resulted in the diversion of an R.A.F. transport when I was on duty; I was informed by Air Traffic, who had as usual arranged accommodation for the occupants, and I detailed our Duty Crew to attend but declined to do so myself since it was quite unnecessary to supervise wheeling out an aircraft access ladder. As expected there were no problems. Not a good enough reason! So I was included in the history of Lossiemouth.

One day, on duty, my rounds included a hangar containing the Scimitars of a flight refuelling unit; still working, but battered, they were as ever parked over drip trays aligned in the shape of a Scimitar brimming with kerosene and hydraulic fluid. Nothing had changed! Lossiemouth was visited by many non-R.N. aircraft in transit and these included U.S. Northrop F5 fighters en route to Turkey, and U.S.N. Douglas RB66 Electronic Surveillance planes on their way to or from Russian airspace. Duty crew or not our U.S. allies kept us firmly at arm's length with armed guards from their aircraft.

A rather similar situation arose whenever the Royal Andover flew in to drop or pick up Prince Charles from Gordonstoun. I have little doubt that the rule that kept our duty crew hidden from sight less they offended the Royal eyes was entirely dreamt up by our hierarchy, but there was much merriment when one day our Captain went to greet Prince Charles as he entered the airfield by the side gate from Gordonstoun. Captain Kirke appeared as a fairly stiff and formal individual who had little time for engineers; on his occasional visits to the mess he was always ensconced with the aircrew. The side gate to Gordonstoun was normally locked and a sailor was detailed to fetch the key when it was needed for Prince Charles. On this occasion both the Royal car and our Captain arrived early, but the duty sailor arrived spot on time as required. We were greatly exercised by the thought of both parties parked on opposite sides of the gate awaiting the sailor, and without the ability to tear him off a strip for being late. There was probably a new Standing Order for that.

Rather surprisingly, on many occasions a pre-planned arrival by a U.S. aircraft was cancelled when their fuel allocation had been used. The strict application of financial controls seemed at odds with their military expenditure in other respects. Our fuel bill was raised in winter by the battle to keep the airfield open. At the first sign of frost or snow our snow-blow machines were out on the runways back and forth to remove the slightest hint of glazed moisture. This kept the runways open but the hard-standings were left until last and we found it difficult to move our aircraft up the slight incline from the hangar to the flight line. Our snow-blow machines were nothing more than a redundant Derwent, Goblin or Ghost jet engine mounted on a trailer carrying a large steel tank of kerosene and this contraption with a control cabin was towed slowly up and down the runways by a tractor. The operators of this device were of course all the Air Engineers, who took turns throughout the day and night as long as the weather was inclement. Fuelling was carried out by hose after crawling on top of the tank. As there was no heating in the cab we needed to wear our greatcoats at the very least, since our stores did not provide cold weather clothing, and my coat remained "ponging" of kerosene until well after I retired. I still wonder how the Russians manage in their winter; is there something that we do not know?

700B Flight finished its task on 30th September and reformed as 801

Squadron on October 14th, still with our original aircraft and most staff but our Commanding Officer was now Lt.-Cdr. J. de Winton, who had earlier had 809 Sqdn. with Buccaneer 1's. We also lost our Supply Officer. On the 160th Anniversary of Trafalgar the C.O. flew over Trafalgar Square in a ceremonial flypast at low-level. At a later stage an Observer Lt.-Cdr. Mike Clapp became C.O. and in 1982 as Commodore Amphibious Warfare he played a key role during the Falklands operations.

801 Squadron was one of the oldest F.A.A. units, having been formed out of 401 flight in 1933 and had served almost continuously ever since; before the war it had variously operated with Flycatchers, Nimrods and Ospreys, but by 1939 it received Skuas and later briefly Rocs and served, firstly on *Furious* and then on *Ark Royal* during 1940. During this period it served in Norway, covered the Dunkirk evacuation, later Oran, Cagliari and Elmas. As the second F.A.A. unit to receive Sea Hurricanes it served on *Argus* and *Eagle* during the Malta convoys Harpoon and Pedestal. In 1942 it converted to Seafires and retained these until the end of the war on *Furious* in the Mediterranean, and later on *Implacable* in the Pacific. Post war it received Sea Hornets and flew from *Indomitable*, then Sea Furies from *Glory*, followed by Seahawks from *Bulwark* and *Centaur*. In 1963 it had operated Buccaneers Mk1 from Ark Royal. With the Buccaneer S.Mk2 it operated from both *Victorious* and later *Hermes*. Well after my retirement 801 Squadron converted to Sea Harriers and served on each of the Invincible Class carriers.

The Buccaneer S50's of the South African Air Force had joined 700B at Lossiemouth during their conversion training and these left Lossiemouth on 27th October. These Buccaneers had different weapons, carried double size overload fuel tanks, and were fitted with Bristol-Siddley auxiliary rocket engines to improve take-off performance from hot high airfields. The S.A.A.F. had placed an order for sixteen aircraft, one of which crashed en-route to South Africa, but plans to acquire fourteen others were thwarted by U.K. Government opposition to the supply of arms to South Africa. This was the only export sale, although with the cancellation of both the T.S.R.2 and F111K, the extra build for the R.A.F. in addition to the converted R.N. aircraft brought the total number of Buccaneers of all Marks built to 173. By then however it was becoming clear that the high cost of developing military aircraft in U.K. solely on the basis of R.A.F./ R.N. requirements was unsupportable. Despite many innovative and original proposals from our much reduced aircraft industry, collaborative international projects are now routine, and have introduced many delays and difficulties while reducing, hopefully, the unit cost of each aircraft purchased. It is worth noting that even the earliest work on the Hawker

A Bit of a "Tiff"

P1127 was supported by the American Mutual Weapons Development Programme, and later as the P1127 Kestrel by the Tri-Nation Trials Unit. The G.R.5 Harrier and its successors are the result of joint work by the U.S. McDonnell Douglas and British Aerospace. All our major military aircraft programmes are now partnerships e.g. from the Jaguar, Tornado, Eurofighter and now the future U.S. Joint Strike Fighter, which is being part funded by U.K. and with inputs from U.K. contractors. Helicopters have followed a similar pattern in the Lynx and Merlin.

There have in the past been fundamental differences between the R.A.F. and F.A.A. in many areas including Trade Structures and Servicing Policies. These differences were to result in the cancellation of the Hawker Siddley P1154 Supersonic V/STOL project, the fuselage of which was under construction at Brough in 1964; among the R.N. doubts about the project was possible incompatibility with operations on our conventional fixed wing carriers. In the event these were then scrapped and both R.A.F. and R.N. Harriers now operate from our three Invincible Class Carriers although the need for R.A.F. units to serve at sea has not much impressed long serving R.A.F. types who have been used to better things. I must record that the success of the Harrier on carriers was very much dependent upon the ski-jump invented by Lt.-Cdr. Doug Taylor, who was not just an exceptional Naval Air Engineer, but also an ex-Apprentice! This fact is seldom mentioned, nor is the degree of initial opposition to his ideas.

Although initially it was amusing also to note the intention to form a joint R.A.F. Harrier/R.N. Sea Harrier force at R.A.F. Wittering, in recent weeks it has been stated that the Sea Harriers will be phased out in 2006 leaving the already diminished fleet without adequate fighter cover for six years at least until the aircraft that emerges from the U.S./U.K. Joint Strike Fighter programme enters service, and once again throwing doubt upon the ineptitude of our planners and political masters who seem once again to have forgotten lessons learned the hard way by our servicemen.

However to return to the past; 801 Squadron carried on working prior to going to sea on *Victorious* as the first operational Buccaneer unit and continued the Weapon Trials but without a conclusion. In January 1966 we were joined at Lossiemouth by 809 Squadron, which was formed as the second Buccaneer unit under Lt.-Cdr. Lyn Middleton.

During this period four aircraft of 801 Squadron were sent to R.A.F. Cranwell to take part in Exercise "Unison"; this exercise was held at intervals, and aircraft of the R.A.F and R.N. demonstrated their capabilities to Senior Officers of the British and Allied services. Our role was to provide Low Level Photo-reconnaissance using a new Camera Installation. This system was fitted into the Bomb Bay and was a vast improvement on the dreadful

Camera nose of the Scimitar. In the event our aircraft performed well. I took a small party to service and maintain the aircraft, but our arrival at Cranwell was not auspicious, as being Wednesday the whole of the Airfield services were closed down for the weekly sports day. This only confirmed the already low opinion of "Crabs" held by most Naval men. (For the uninitiated the term "Crab" derives from the colour of R.A.F. uniforms which resembles Naval Grey paint or "Crabfat" with which our ships are painted.) When our Buccaneers arrived there was some doubt whether the hangar floor would sustain our weight, but with that resolved our Aircraft Handlers stowed our aircraft away while the "Crabs" were still mucking around with theirs; we had the advantage of the then brand new four wheel drive and steer deck-handling tractor. As expected, our small team worked exceptionally well and pulled together far more effectively than was normally the case in the larger groups at Lossiemouth, and we still managed to go out in the evenings for beer and skittles at local pubs. On the last day all flying was to cease during a final conference, and on the flight line a U.S. RF 4E Phantom was anxious to get away but could not start up or align his Inertial Navigation System without a suitable Ground Power Supply. The R.A.F. had nothing, and our unit was incompatible with the U.S. wiring despite so-called common standards within N.A.T.O.; I solved this by a quick prod into the relay on our trolley, and off he went! At that point I felt I had finally redeemed R.N. professional honour after our dismal performance at Acklington with the Scimitar.

Back in Hampshire there were problems with our Naval neighbour. During my Xmas leave in 1965 Margaret and I attended a New Year party with friends in Fareham; our children remained at home and, although they were old enough to look after themselves, it was arranged that our neighbour Jean would look in to them at some point. In the middle of our celebrations we received a call from Jean, "Malcolm has thrown us out of the car on Portsea Island Bridge, and intends to go home and commit suicide." Malcolm had expected to be promoted to Commander in the New Year promotion list, but had not made it. Apparently this had been his last chance, and having been passed over for promotion this was a great loss of prestige. Anyway, end of party, off I went to check on the state of play at home. All was well, he didn't fulfil his intention, and I returned to the party. In the months that followed, Malcolm's behaviour became increasingly odd, and his children often stayed in our house for safety. Margaret became deeply involved and I could not help from Lossiemouth. In the end I instructed Margaret that on the next occasion when there was a disturbance, she was to phone the Duty Medical Officer at Haslar and report the problem. Inevitably this happened and willy-nilly Malcolm

A Bit of a "Tiff"

was whisked off to the R.N. Mental Hospital at Netley. You can guess the outcome; he was eventually discharged with his "pink chit" and was promoted to Commander. Wish I'd thought of that!

As the time approached for the Squadron to join *Victorious*, trials were needed to calibrate the ship's catapults and arrestor gear for our new and heavier aircraft. I was again sent with a small party to *Victorious* for these trials, having first weighed the aircraft and calibrated their fuel systems. I was also to take with me a young General List Lieut. (L) for his experience. We joined the ship at Portland, or more accurately in Weymouth Bay to save time; in the very rough weather our M.F.V. lost most of its bridge and upperworks while trying to come alongside. I doubt if saving time was that important! The trials were carried out without a hitch at various A.U.W.'s (All Up Weights) using different fuel states and bomb loads. At the conclusion of the trial I was given a signal advising me that I was reappointed to 736B flight at Lossiemouth. My young learner would now take my place on 801 Squadron. In modern jargon I was gobsmacked!

On my return to Lossiemouth I complained and sought to reverse the decision, but it was made clear that my work, dedication and experience were to take second place to the young man's career. The only sop to my aggravation was that I could now expect to remain at Lossiemouth for another two and a half years; clearly that did not suit me under any circumstances, but at no stage was it suggested that my experience was seen as an important contribution to the new unit. I had no gripe against the young man, we got on well and I met him at various times in future posts; he married into a Naval family and eventually rose to Captain but clearly he was not a high-flier.

736 Squadron was the operational conversion unit for Buccaneers at Lossiemouth, and the formation of 736B flight was intended to provide a similar function for the Buccaneer 2, but also to operate as a Buccaneer Weapons Trials unit to continue the still incomplete work started using 700B and 801 Squadrons. The unit had been cobbled together in great haste in the few days while I had been on *Victorious*, and the ground crew were assembled from the least wanted and most inexperienced men dumped from various other units at Lossiemouth. My A.E.O. fell into a similar category, being an idle chinless wonder also from a Naval family. My cup, already well filled, overflowed when the command structure became clear. This small unit had two C.O.'s and two Senior Observers, each with competing interests. The weapons trials continued as before with intermittent visits from our tame "boffin", and in between the conversion flying took place but for which the weapons system was irrelevant. The Buccaneer 2 then became a popular aircraft for the C.O. to buzz around

with at weekend Air Displays, so we had our work cut out trying to meet the demands, but without the incentive that applied in a front-line unit. One day the C.O. landed from a non-operational flight and said "Oh, by the way there's a problem with the Autopilot, but I'm not putting it into the Form 700." This was unacceptable and I placed the aircraft u/s myself, and we then spent several days tracing and rectifying a potentially dangerous defect. Needless to say I had a stand up battle with the C.O. on this issue. It was obvious that I was in a no-win situation with the competing requirements and I had no support from my Cdr. (L); in the words of the well known service phrase I was "fed up, f——— up and far from home" so I continued pushing for a new appointment.

My complaints finally bore fruit when it was suddenly found possible for me to exchange appointments with another officer who wished to remain at Lossiemouth, God bless him! His appointment was to join N.A.M.D.U. at Lee-on-Solent. Before I left gratefully for Lee, Admiral Gibson visited Lossiemouth and explained the future cutbacks in the Fleet Air Arm. We were to lose our fixed wing aircraft and the large Fleet Carriers including the projected 50,000 ton C.V.A.01. He then promised that the last guns had not been fired in the battle for the Aircraft Carriers!

Writing this in 2002 the last guns have yet to be fired, since despite the valuable service given by the "Invincible" Class Carriers, whose function deviously changed from Through-Deck Cruiser, to Command Cruiser equipped only with Sea King Anti-Submarine Helicopters and eventually to the Light Carrier carrying both helicopters and Harriers only just in time to save the Falklands, nonetheless our two new 50,000 ton Fleet Carriers and a new generation of fixed-wing aircraft have not yet arrived and are not due in service until 2012 assuming no political change of heart.

However in 1966 I was more than ever convinced that I had no future in the Navy and would seek retirement as soon as possible. I thankfully left Lossiemouth in August 1966. My flimsy did not reflect my battles with the system, so presumably I was not considered incompetent, just another pawn to be shuffled around at whim!

Postscript – It has recently been announced that the Lockheed–Martin contender for the J.S.F. is to be procured in its STOVL version for both the R.N. and R.A.F. as the F35 and is now called the J.C.A. (Joint Combat Aircraft). Some 150 will be bought by U.K. The U.S. Marines are expected also to have the STOVL version and U.K. plans may yet be thwarted if the much larger U.S. Marine order is not confirmed.

Since the U.K. aircraft will operate as a joint unit succeeding the

Harrier force it may after all the years of controversially different Trade structures and Servicing policy force the adoption of a common system and make for better relations and greater efficiency.

The decision as to which of the two contending contractors will build the two CVF 50,000 ton carriers is also imminent although it will be 2012 before the first is in service. They will each carry up to 50 F35's but the crucial choice of an Airborne Early Warning vehicle now known as Maritime Airborne Surveillance and Control system has yet to be made. In the tortuous path of Aircraft Development and Procurement the nine years remaining before it needs to be in service is a remarkably short time particularly as some of the choices may influence the design of the Carriers and because the U.K. requirement is so limited it seems very unlikely that such a system will be designed and built in the U.K. In all probability once again we will have to look across the Atlantic for a solution.

After all the years of hedging it does seem that eventually the Fleet Air Arm may be properly equipped for its job! Good luck chums!

700B Flight. Lossiemouth April 1965. Author's collection.

Buccaneer 2's of 700B in formation. Spring 1965.
Author's collection.

A Bit of a "Tiff"

801 Squadron Commissioning Ceremony. Lossimouth. 14th October 1965. Author's collection.

Buccaneer 2 of 801 Squadron over Trafalgar Square. Trafalgar Day 21st October 1965. Courtesy Ian McDonald (Photographs) Ltd.

700B's Hunter T8. Clearly still u/s. Lossiemouth 1965.

Buccaneer of 801 Squadron in the Hangar of *Victorious* during Deck Trials. Spring 1966.

A Bit of a "Tiff"

Refuelling on 801 Squadron Buccaneer 2 during Deck Trials on
Victorious. Spring 1966.

Buccaneer 2 XN977 landing during Deck Trials. Spring 1966.

Buccaneer 2 being lined up on the Port Catapult. Deck Trials
Victorious. Spring 1966.

"being tensioned
up prior to launch."

A Bit of a "Tiff"

"launch."

"airborne."

Victorious's planeguard Wessex on a very misty day during Deck Trials. Spring 1966.

R.F.A. Orangeleaf refuelling *Victorious* during Deck Trials. Spring 1966.

A Bit of a "Tiff"

U.S. Northrop F5 (Freedom Fighter) in transit through Lossiemouth 1966.

801 Squadron lined up ready to leave for *Victorious*. June 1966.
Nearest A/C carries a Flight Refuelling Pod and is connected to a
Palouste Starter nearside and an Electrical Supply Rig beyond.

H(RH) Hour at Lossiemouth.

A Bit of a "Tiff"

Chapter 19 H.M.S. *Ariel* Lee-on-Solent

As soon as I left Lossiemouth I started looking to the future and within a few weeks answered an advertisement for an Inertial Navigation Engineer to work for the New Zealand Air Registration Board. At my interview I was instantly accepted and asked if I could fly out within the next month. Regrettably the Navy had no intention of releasing its grappling irons that quickly and I had to refuse, somewhat to the relief of my teenaged children.

However I still had the bit between my teeth and pulled out all the stops for a civilian career. The first thing was to gain C.Eng. (Chartered Engineer) status and for this I took and passed two further H.N.C. subjects at Evening Classes, only to find that a new regulation required documentary evidence of basic education equivalent to O and A levels. This was tricky, since although my education in and out of the Navy covered the subjects I could not obtain the evidence, nor would my boss agree to my attending Day Release to redo the subjects. This was yet another cause for a gripe as I was allowed routinely to authorise Day Release for my Senior Ratings and this matter remained outstanding until my last appointment.

As soon as the terms for early retirement were announced I put my name down, and waited and waited and waited. During the long wait I was kept very busy with a wide variety of tasks at N.A.M.D.U., later changed to N.A.T.E.C. (Naval Aircraft Technical Evaluation Centre), to which I had been appointed as Electrical Appraisals Officer. These included investigating a scheme for on-board Compass Swinging; this opened the way for my plan to revise the swinging procedures and intervals, which was accepted. I visited Blackburns in pursuit of answers to the reason for "no fault found" reports on the Buccaneer. Blackburns had installed an early Maintenance Data computer system on which they recorded all defects in the field, but as is well known computers only work with good data. In this case the reason for "rubbish in = rubbish out" was something that I fully understood; tired engineers do not write good essays! I was also involved with a scheme by Rolls Royce to introduce Time/Temperature Recorders into our aircraft to monitor Engine Health; a visit to their plant in Derby meant retrieving my car, with difficulty, from what appeared to be the largest car park I had yet encountered.

Probably the most far-reaching activity was on the apparently mundane subject of aircraft wiring and connectors. I have already mentioned several different systems used in earlier aircraft and over the years our aircraft had many different systems installed, partly the result of the continued use of older equipment in new aircraft, and now each aircraft contained upwards of forty different types/makes of connectors (plugs and sockets). Each of these covered a range of permutations arising from different pin numbers, orientation, cable size and fittings and mounting arrangements. Logistically this was a nightmare even with the old Plessey Mk4 which had all soldered connections, and these still appeared, but the majority now followed U.S. practice and used U.S.Mil Standard items with crimped fittings i.e. the wires were secured into the connector pins by compressing the outer shell in a plier mounted special die. With such a system, the resulting electrical joint was only reliable if the correct die had been used; there were dozens of these because each manufacturer required a different set, but up until 1966 no concerted effort had been made to rationalise the systems, to educate the maintainers, or to provide the correct tools. I conducted a service wide survey on this subject and the returns showed great ignorance to the point where there was concern about aircraft safety. It was clear that a radical overhaul was needed.

Over the period, I had three C.P.O.'s working almost full time researching the subject, and in addition to sending them into the field to educate the masses, I introduced specific ranges of the correct tools incorporated into the tool control system for each unit and an entirely new range of technical publications to cover all aspects of the subject. However I was unable to persuade D.G.A. (N) to replace the obsolete pre-war plug and socket that connected light series bomb carriers, also a pre war design, to the aircraft. These had just two pins, and a single 6 B.A. screw held the two part plastic moulding together. In theory a keyway prevented mis-mating the two halves, but in the heat of last minute arming up on the flight line the armourers just pushed harder and often succeeded in reversing the connection. As a result at regular intervals one of our aircraft would drop its practice bombs accidentally on the way to the bombing range; this arose because the pins supplying the fusing and bomb release circuits had been interchanged. Fusing was the first step in preparation for releasing a bomb and was sometimes carried out before arriving at the bombing range. It certainly happened during my time on Buccaneers. D.G.A (N) also refused to modify the connector from the Palouste Starter to the aircraft. There was great pressure on all concerned during start up on deck and the connector was routinely thrown to the deck and damaged. This reluctance to act was astonishing since it was clear that just those two connectors were responsible for most reported connector problems.

The work now included liaison with our opposite numbers at C.S.D.E. (Central Servicing Development Establishment) at R.A.F. Swanton Morley, Army Aviation at Middle Wallop, and the specialists at the Ministry of Aviation and Industry. Intriguingly at Warton where the Jaguar was being built, we found that the airframe was built in two halves and the French half, with typical Gallic disdain for anything American, was built using French made Mil–C–26482 connectors. These were electrically interchangeable with the U.S./British made equivalent but were based on a different sequence of cable sizes and cable core "lay". As a result the U.S./British spares and tooling could not be used safely to repair the French built half of R.A.F. Jaguar aircraft.

Work with the R.A.F. and Army led to the achievement of a common standard for a new design in collaboration with the M.o.A. Project office. This was based upon the U.S.Mil–C–26482 range but produced in this country. The choice was not without controversy as we in N.A.M.D.U. preferred an alternative with a number of better features, but this was a game played for big financial stakes and industry had a few games to play. The salesmen from each firm used to call on us regularly with examples of their products, and were active in denigrating their rival's products e.g. deliberately displaying degraded examples of such items in the vain hope that we might be taken in. We were well able to see through their tricks and ignored them, but evidently the R.A.F. did not and we had to concede defeat in the interest of commonality, but it was a very dirty business! We were also asked to assess the suitability of a flat printed wiring scheme being developed by the Ministry of Aviation and, after looking also at a similar scheme being used on the Army "Clansman" radio system, decided to recommend cancellation due to the impracticality of making repairs or modifications and because no provision had been made to link it into existing equipment.

The imminent arrival of the Phantom raised several issues and my experience at Cranwell enabled me to make positive recommendations for the Ground Power Supply, which had not been recognised by the S.M.P. (Special Maintenance Party) who had been based for some time in the U.S. The wiring system was another problem since it was based upon the "wire bundle". Literally the wires (cables) were wrapped into bundles using several different types of adhesive tape, and each bundle ended at a connector which had no metal end fitting but was back filled with one of several different types of compound dependent upon the application e.g. High Temperature. This system saved weight but the materials were not readily available to us and my team had to seek and evaluate the alternatives, and test the procedures for using them in repair work. As an example we tested many tape samples in conjunction with the Scientific Lab. at R.N.A.Y. Fleetlands; the resulting best product was a cheap Japanese tape. Long after this the U.S. Navy Phantoms suffered great problems when their tape adhesives dissolved in the hot and humid climate of Vietnam but I have no knowledge of similar problems in U.K. service.

Our task also included evaluating the then fairly new heat-shrink insulation material, which was a boon providing the heat source was properly controlled. Samples acquired at that time are still viable and I have only recently used a section for an emergency repair at home.

The environment aboard ship led to different practices for caring for Naval aircraft, in particular there was constant concern to provide anti-corrosion protection against salt water, e.g. as far as possible components containing magnesium were eliminated. For reasons not specified the R.A.F. and F.A.A. aircraft had different paint schemes, one used only acrylic, the other epoxy resin, but in the event this did not solve our problems and several squadrons serving in the Far East had the vulnerable areas refinished by a local contractor using a superior material. We did not make general provision for fresh water wash down on our carriers, which might have helped, and on *Victorious* when an exercise assumed we had been contaminated by nuclear fall-out we were ordered to wash down the Scimitars using mops and buckets. Needless to say the mechanics had no protective clothing in which to carry out the decontamination. However by the late 60's the F.A.A. discovered WD-40 and this suddenly became the panacea for all corrosion issues, and during my time at Lee there were regular reports of problems arising due to the over enthusiastic use of this material; these included men slipping off a mainplane, aircrew safety equipment becoming saturated by WD-40 sprayed inside the cockpit, and some plastic components being damaged by the solvent. I do not believe that apart from issuing warning instructions it was ever possible to define "how much was enough" in such a way as to make the use of WD-40 "sailor proof". I wonder how the R.A.F. has adapted to the salty environment now that their Harriers are going to sea!

As in earlier jobs there was great satisfaction in making decisions that had long-term benefits, but as usual Nelson occasionally interfered. One of my key men had a Mongol daughter and needed at intervals to take her to Great Ormond Street. Usually this presented no problem but one routine visit had been planned for the Monday following our return from summer leave. This fell within normal rules covering compassionate cases and I had no hesitation in forwarding a request for special leave with my recommendation to the Commander. To my astonishment the Commander refused this. I failed to see how anyone could be so insensitive in his position but perhaps I should have known better, as I had met many such in the past! A little lateral thinking solved the problem, and I sent him on duty to London, complete with a Railway Warrant.

On duty as before, doing Officer-of-the-Day duty during a leave period when I was to take late leave, the perennial Rum Issue gave me food for thought. Just a small number of sailors remained on camp for essential duties and some of these were unable to attend the midday issue. It was the practice therefore to issue neat rum to all who were available at midday and for the balance to be held in the O.O.D.'s safe in the Guardroom and issued individually when the remainder came off duty. At all these issues the neat rum was consumed on the spot after a measure of water had been added by the rating, but this was the first time that I had witnessed Grog being consumed at the point of issue, and I was therefore shocked to see one Leading Hand actually trembling in anticipation; after drinking his ration the trembling ceased and I had words with him about his problem. If I had doubts before, then it was now clear to me that rum had no place in the modern Navy. In fact it was abolished finally about a year before I retired. The bottled rum held in the O.O.D's safe, was often not collected when an individual didn't think it worth the effort of going to the Guardroom. Before turning in for the night the O.O.D ditched the balance by pouring it down the sink, where its passing was readily apparent to all and sundry and who, of course, bemoaned the loss. Well not quite a total loss, as I sometimes had a wee sip first! The only other item in the safe was just as lethal – the D.C.I. (Defence Council Instruction) on the action to be taken in the event of a suspected homosexual offence. It was required reading for the O.O.D. and considering the explicit detail I was very pleased not to have the misfortune ever to encounter such an incident.

"Meanwhile back at the ranch" – I had been unable to make any progress in the still new house or the garden during my absence at Lossiemouth; in spring 1965 I had attacked the garden and laid a land drain from an overflow I knocked into the cesspit, and then attempted to sort out the overgrown tangle of weeds and brambles. Borrowing a rotovator from Freddie Mills, who lived nearby, I drove into this pile, but it bit back fiercely; the brambles wound round the tines and picked up balls of the glutinous clay that formed our garden until both the engine and I stalled. Attempting to haul the machine out I pulled my back and needed treatment at Lee. Thereafter gardening was deferred until the one day each year when the soil was neither saturated nor rock hard. This did not occur again until I had returned to Lee, and eventually I had my lawns and a vegetable patch as intended. Planned D.I.Y. included built in wardrobes, and a couple of rooms in the loft with a staircase from the hall, and these kept me busy for some time. The smaller of the two rooms was my darkroom, in which I also stored my homemade wine, and both rooms had ceilings plastered with stippled Artex.

The strawberry wine proved to be very drinkable after I had sorted out the pink foam all over the ceiling when it blew its cork off. Downstairs my honey beer experiment went violently wrong overnight and only the screw top remained, with minute particles of glass scattered all over and chunks removed from the plaster. Undeterred I made a strong brew of ordinary beer, but miscounted the water content. The result was delightful when I opened the first bottle; one half pint was followed by just two more before I was totally drunk and violently ill. Homemade beer was off the agenda for a long while.

Barbara was now of an age to go riding, and a knowledgeable friend in the village attended the New Forest pony sale at Beaulieu and on our behalf bought a "yearling", which arrived late one night. "Zak" came out off the horsebox at a trot and my limited understanding of ponies took another knock. I had thought he would be a deal smaller. Anyway he was led away down the garden and into our neighbour's field through a gate I had created, and we retired to bed to await the morning and admire our purchase. Morning came rather too early when we awoke to the clip clop of Zak going up the drive, and I rushed out in pyjamas to catch him. I succeeded in this after being dragged through the strawberry bed and I returned him to the field and raised the gate by another bar. The following morning was similar but this time I was too late and he disappeared into Hampshire on his way back home to the New Forest. With two cars Margaret and I searched the lanes to no avail and returned home for breakfast to contemplate out next move. O.K. we'll call the Police! "No problem Sir, it's always happening." Sure enough we had a call within the hour, a local farmer had found him and had detained him in his field. Off we went to collect him and walk him home for about three miles. We did very well, safely crossing a busy road, until we reached some heath land, at this point Zak saw a dog ahead and took off in chase; Barbara dropped off at once and I stayed until I went through a gorse bush. After that Zak was happy to go quietly home to his field and I raised the gate rather higher. The next step was two hundred yards of barbed wire and fifty oak posts. In no time flat he munched his way through an acre of lush grass in addition to the food we provided and then proceeded to clear all the overgrown brambles between him and our lawn until one day with a shrug he joined us on the other side. More wire and posts! Until then I had not fully understood the pressure applied by a horses hoof on the soil, and I spent a lot of time throwing bricks and rubble at the area around his gate in an effort to reduce the muddy quagmire he created. All to no avail! We had Zak for several years and had many more problems, until in the end Barbara had outgrown her enthusiasm and we sold him.

We didn't repeat the experiment but we have been "doggy" people for most of our marriage and following a couple of mongrels went from

A Bit of a "Tiff"

Corgis to Cairns, and in 2002 have two second hand Border terriers who rule our lives but give me the exercise that hopefully is keeping me fit. Our dogs have all had normal doggie names unlike the dog of a Lt-Cdr. friend in the village, who was called "Commander"; the owner loved to tell enquirers that he had always wanted to kick a Commander up the backside. Until now we have had a cat also but the busy roads make our present home unsafe. During our stay at Shirrell Heath however our cat kept very busy bringing live and unwelcome gifts to our bedroom at night. We saved several, including a mole, which then repaid our kindness by bringing back his chums and digging up the lawn.

Next-door neighbours finally divorced when Malcolm found an alternative while based in London, and Jean remarried and divorced twice since then. For a time she and Margaret ran a playschool at home and when she moved Margaret continued in the village hall in Swanmore. Jean's replacement next door was an ex-naval family but rather less volatile. The very successful playgroup is still running under new leaders, but when we later moved ourselves Margaret ran the Opportunity Group for handicapped children in Winchester for several years.

Richard gained a lot of "O" levels at Peter Symonds as a boarder, but with my impending retirement he was able to go to Fareham Grammar and live at home with us. He had found the restrictions of boarding somewhat excessive, and I knew how he felt! We now experienced the dubious pleasures of teenage motorcyclist friends appearing at inconvenient times, before higher education and a serious girlfriend arrived. Now fifty he is now reliving his youth and rides a very powerful machine. When Richard passed his driving test he was of course anxious to use one of our cars and at a time when long hair was beginning to be fashionable it seemed to me that use of a car and short hair was a fair "quid pro quo". Of course I was indoctrinated by my service life but eventually I had to concede that it was just a passing fashion and accepted the inevitable. Richard also achieved something that I had not when he flew solo in a glider during a Cadet Force Camp at R.A.F. Swanton Morley, but his future did not lay in the services and eventually he became an accountant.

At this remove I do not recall when I had my application for retirement confirmed, but I left for my next appointment on 6th December 1968 knowing that it would be the last, but still not knowing when I would actually retire. With the move from Lossiemouth, and living with my family again I was far less stressed and could wait a bit longer as I completed my preparations for a civilian life.

Officers of the Naval Aircraft Technical Evaluation Centre Lee-on-Solent 1968.

Chapter 20 Director General Aircraft (Navy)

In December 1968 I joined the staff in D.G.A.(N) in the Old Admiralty Building in London to serve as the Electrical Engineer in the Air Armament Section. Arriving at the building one certainly became aware of the history associated with the building from the general appearance of the entrance hall with its pictures, an old black lacquered sedan chair stowed in a corner, and the demeanour of the uniformed civilian hall porter. I had no reason or opportunity to explore the building in detail but the basement for example held a rifle range which could be accessed internally, but also via a side entrance near Admiralty Arch, where one passed under masses of pipes and communication cables reminiscent of a major warship. I won a small trophy in a shooting competition while I was there. The basement of the building also contained paper archives and with the help of the staff Schoolie Commander I settled down there one day and routed out from many dusty A.F.O.'s all the syllabi and exam results from 1941 to 1953 that supported my educational attainments. With that data and supporting endorsements from Rear-Admiral Holt as D.G.A. (N) and two Captains, I applied to the Institution of Electrical and Radio Engineers and gained C.Eng. and M.I.E.R E. status. So I had achieved my first objective at least.

In my last job I now found could use my experience to advantage, no longer was it the case of "them down at D.G.A. (N)" against "us slaving at the coalface"; I was now one of them and my word carried the weight of Admiralty. It was now possible to override opinions given by senior members of M.o.A. when required. I did so at the Nuclear Weapons clearance meeting for the Sea King, but failed at a meeting on the much simpler R.N. Gazelle helicopter. This machine was designed and built in France and its wiring installation was contrary to our practice and experience, such that moisture ingress would result in inadvertent firing of an explosive device. The French simply said, "Non, no change, our system remains as we supply it". It would be up to us to modify it after delivery! It was amusing to observe the difference between the Navy and R.A.F. when there were joint project meetings. They usually brought several Wing Commanders plus supporting Sqdn. Leaders while we usually had only a Lt-Cdr. and a Lieut. However we did not lose out in an argument.

Quite a lot of our work at that time was involved in clearing up the snags found during the *Torrey Canyon* disaster. Our Buccaneers formed part of the task force attempting to destroy the ship and its cargo of fuel oil after it had been wrecked. The results were not as good as expected due to weapon defects and these had to be investigated and put right.

I was able to write two Naval Staff Requirements as evidence of my passing. The first of these was for a Lockable Master Armament Safety Switch to be used as part of our Tool Control Procedure and which would minimise the risk of the accidental weapon firing that I had several times encountered. I do not know whether this is now used on Naval Aircraft, but I saw it being manufactured by Dowty's in Gloucester in the late 1970's for Army Lynx helicopters. The second N.S.R. was for a new adaptable Light Stores Carrier to replace the ancient device then still in use after forty years. The requirement included all the features that were absent from the old kit, and I felt that I had now struck a blow for future generations of Air Engineers.

Working in London had its disadvantages of course, because at that time the "X" Factor pay scheme had yet to be devised and since there was no service accommodation in London we had either to commute from home or find something suitably cheap in town. It did not seem practical to commute from Shirrell Heath and my pay would not stretch to other than squalid digs in town. In the end the solution was found in the Nuffield Officers' Club in Eaton Square. This originally palatial building sat in a row of similar rather posh buildings, most of which had a Rolls parked outside with dents from the London traffic. Internally the club had been much adapted to provide a number of single, two and three bedroom cabins sub-dividing the original large rooms, and most cabins had a small section of the original ornate moulding on one wall and disappearing through the partition to its neighbour. It was not possible to take permanent accommodation in the Club, nor could you choose your room or room-mate. It was normal to book a week in advance and then cancel if duty took us elsewhere. In the event that this failed for some reason, then some of my colleagues went to the Salvation Army Hostel at Paddington, but I never had to resort to that. In fact it was reputed to be very comfortable and welcoming. Meals at the club were to a very high standard and were served by some very genteel ladies and young students at fixed times, and of course this could be a disadvantage if work or entertainment made you late.

In practice, as most of the staff at D.G.A. (N) were civilian, the clock watching to catch the train home had developed to a high order but for those Naval officers staying in town there was a question of how to entertain themselves. Commanders and above had the funds to make hay in the social scene; those that did so often ended with a broken marriage. The rest found themselves with a lot of time on their hands, and for many, like a colleague and I in the section, the remedy was to work late. There was always something to do, and we could often achieve more when it was quiet. Back at the Club our roommates were often Staff Officers for a very Senior Officer, and they returned very late; as their boss also had nowhere else to go; when he stayed behind so did his Staff Officer.

When D.G.A (N) moved to Golden Cross House in the block adjacent to South Africa House, we were rather separated from the rest of the Naval teams in London, but my chum and I were gratified on several evenings while working late, to receive a visit from Admiral Le Fanu. He appeared alone without warning, said, "I'm Le Fanu", and proceeded to ask us how we were getting on. This was a gentleman who set an example that many others could and should have followed, but it was the first time during my career that a Senior Officer had taken the trouble to give me the time of day. I was very much impressed but regrettably Admiral Le Fanu died suddenly soon after. As a contrast, I should mention the case of a S/Lt Air Engineer appointed to D.G.A.(N) about a year before me. He was the only S/Lt in his department, which contained mostly civilians, and his boss was a Commander (L), an Australian with a typically brisk manner. His approach didn't cut much ice with the civilian staff, so he turned his attention on "Subby", who evidently found the going too tough and was seen to walk up the steps of the Old Admiralty Building, stop, shake his head and walk away. He was retired shortly afterward.

For the most part however our evenings, once we started back to the club, involved firstly a visit to the nearest pub. Often we would find others from work already there, and the evening progressed until at last the group broke up and we made our way back to the club finding a meal somewhere en route. One of our favourites was an Italian Restaurant in Shepherds Market, where one evening Gp. Capt. Leonard Cheshire V.C. was a fellow diner. After a while I became very familiar with most of London from Trafalgar Square to Soho and Chelsea and used to recognise well-known faces from among the crowds. Not normally a serious beer drinker, I developed the skill to survive periodic visits to the Gents; in London these were always down very steep steps to the cellar. A very risky experience! London pubs were however unwelcoming places, particularly in Chelsea at the end of Eaton Square. On only one occasion did anybody attempt to hold a conversation, he turned out to be a lonely laird from Lossiemouth down in London on business. This was the era of flower power and hippies, who seemed to spread all over Piccadilly at night and peer out from under the deckchairs stacked in St. James Park as we walked to work in the morning. We also became used to seeing bag ladies and the cardboard box dwellers sleeping in the semi warmth of the warm air outlets from buildings. The many attractions of London do not include a welcome to the mentally ill and impoverished!

As usual in a Naval unit it was customary to hold an annual official Cocktail Party at which our guests were people from organisations with whom we worked throughout the year. As an indication of the basically different rationale of our Admiralty Civilians, they of course attended with gusto but did not contribute to the cost in any way. As far as the Armament section were concerned, immediately following the party the G.W. (Guided Weapon) team began preparations for the next one. They filled their filing cabinets with home made wine and late at night one could hear a steady bubbling from the cabinets as the fermentation process continued very efficiently in the permanently centrally heated offices.

When D.G.A.(N) Rear-Admiral J. Holt retired a farewell dinner was held in H.M.S. *President*; this is the H.Q's of the R.N.V.R. and is permanently berthed alongside the Embankment. For this occasion we all attended in our uniform, which was a rare event when serving in London. Quite what purpose was served in officers working in civilian clothes was never explained; at Farnborough we wore uniform while working alongside the civilian engineers and scientists and I only discovered the distinction when I travelled from Farnborough to D.G.A.(N) one day as a S/Lt. and found myself incorrectly dressed.

I looked for ways to further prepare for retirement, and since the accommodation issue ruled out private study I enrolled in an M.B.A. course at the Regent St. Polytech. To enter this very popular evening course all entrants were selected following an I.Q. test, which I took with some trepidation since most applicants were clearly much younger. Having completed the tests quickly I was assured that my marbles were still intact and I passed easily. On the first evening, a great mass of people gathered to form several classes, all were unknown to me, but as we sorted ourselves out I found that the only three people to whom I could possibly relate were my immediate neighbours. These were a G.P.O. engineer, a British Airports Authority engineer, and a scientist from R.A.E. now working in London. I have remained intrigued by the process that determines personal relationships but have as yet no answers.

I learned many things during the course but probably the most significant was one word – "Sorry". For the past thirty years the word appeared to have been omitted from use in the Navy; after all the Naval Discipline Act only required obedience. Although my course work on Personnel Management was otherwise spot on, the need for an apology when appropriate was evidently crucial in the outside world, and I have never forgotten. Circumstances determined that I would not complete the course but taken together with my service experience and a number of pre-retirement Extra Mural courses taken at Bristol University this

A Bit of a "Tiff"

enabled me to become a M.B.I.M. (Member of the British Institute of Management). I was now as prepared as I could be for the outside world.

I eventually received notice of my retirement on 31st July 1971 and had given some thought as to what I would like to do. Essentially I wanted to use my experience and qualifications in a new non-military enterprise, preferably one that had a social dimension. Teaching seemed one of these, and I felt I had a lot to offer. The first setback came one morning at Bristol University when my group were gathered for coffee in an annex. From across the corridor came sounds of music, singing and thumping noises. Eventually the noise ceased and the occupants emerged, a very mixed bunch including a bearded priest and a nun. Enquiries revealed that this was a class of trainee teachers, and they were in the middle of a session of Musical Movement with Religious Instruction. Teaching now looked like a "no go" area as I have absolutely no leanings to or talent for histrionics.

More appropriately I also attended a course for Computer System Analysts. In subsequent years I was deeply involved in activities for which computers were an essential but never had to put my training into practice. It is only since the decision to start this book that I have owned or used a computer and of course their capabilities are light years beyond those being used in 1971.

Later I attended a Pre-Retirement Course in London; a lot of interesting people talking about the perils of being a sub-postmaster and the problems of running a small-holding or bed and breakfast accommodation, which evidently appealed to a few officers. Other speakers were businessmen, another was a senior member of the I.L.E.A. (Inner London Education Authority) talking about teaching, and we were given tips on preparing a C.V. The course ended with a personal interview following one of the clever selection tests designed to reveal latent abilities. Although the test revealed no new insight to my character or abilities (the "rubbish in = rubbish out" syndrome again), at my interview with the I.L.E.A. man he waxed enthusiastically about the opportunities on offer if only I would arrange to join I.L.E.A. Cynic that I am, it took me just a short walk to the nearest Underground station to see all the snags he hadn't mentioned.

Finally the press announced a severe shortage of Maths and Science Teachers. Well this could be the chance I'd been waiting for, and I had an interview at King Alfred's Teacher Training College at Winchester, where evidently they would have been happier had I been offering English, Arts, or Social Studies. In retrospect they did me a good turn as it is now obvious to me that I would not have survived the social manipulation, political correctness, and lack of discipline in schools today.

In the end I accepted that in all probability I would have to revert to some management role in engineering. I sent out lots of C.V.'s and it was no surprise that the positive replies came from companies involved with military work. I rejected a job with Plessey on the National Air Traffic Computer at West Drayton in favour of a post as a Senior Engineer with Marconi at Portsmouth Airport, which would start a little before the end of my terminal leave. So I was never unemployed.

During 1969 I attended a conference of Air Ordnance Officers at Seafield Park, thus returning to the place where I joined up in 1941. I retired in June 1971 to take my terminal leave and left with no regrets after thirty years' service.

The Air Ordnance Engineers Officers' Conference. Seafield Park 1969.

Chapter 21   R.N. Reflections

Even before I started this chapter I realised that it would be the most difficult to write, since I needed to summarise my feelings of the Navy over a thirty year period which ended thirty years ago, and much has changed for the better since then. I also needed to put into perspective the criticisms made in earlier chapters, which, although true, take on a different aspect when read without any personal experience to back them up. I recall reading an account of the Great Mutiny and I was appalled by the brutality of the sailor's life in 1797. In later reading I began to understand that brutal though it was, the lot of most poor folk in England at the time was barely any better and often rather worse.

Readers will of course form their own ideas about my own defects of which there are many, that is your privilege, and you will do this on the basis of your own experience and standards, but please read on. I have learned a lot in just writing this chapter perhaps you also will do the same.

I have already explained why I joined up, and I took early retirement, as I no longer wished to live apart from my family, or suffer the restrictions, or the frustrations in my career. On the positive side, the Navy had given me a basic training and motivation, vast experience in engineering and man management, travel to foreign places (excluding Scotland and Wales), and I had certainly grown up from the naïve little lad who had joined up thirty years earlier.

So what made a naval career different from any other job and why would anyone join up? Was it the uniform? Not very likely in these days of "woolly pullies" and beret, and where uniform is rarely if ever worn ashore, but in 1941 the nation wore uniform of one description or another, some more shapeless than others, and most were uncomfortable, but at least Naval uniform carried the cachet of a long tradition and could be worn with a swagger.

Was it patriotism? Certainly this was the case before conscription; afterwards perhaps if a choice was available, then the prospect of life confined to a wobbling noisy steel box may have seemed marginally more attractive than life in a muddy foxhole as a soldier. Post-war, different motivations must have been at work.

Training for a career, a secure job plus adventure and foreign travel would have been important. Undoubtedly the initial training was an excellent start, but I felt that insufficient effort was then put in to further education as technical advances were made. I do know however that my Senior Observer at Lossiemouth had attended a Specialist Navigators' Course with the R.A.F. and his notes on the operation and errors in the

Buccaneer Instrument System were far more detailed technically than any course given at H.M.S. *Ariel*. In fact it was only due to my H.N.C. studies that the notes were intelligible. One bright star lost to the Navy was a young Leading Electrician who served under me at Ford. At the time he was one among many and my main memory of him at that time was of a cheerful chap who played football. In about 1970 I was asked to provide a reference when he was being vetted for a post at Farnborough as a civilian engineer. By 1986 when I finally retired from work, he was Chief Engineer for a major armaments company. The Navy lost out in failing to keep its men better educated, and at the time many on the lower deck believed that an educated sailor was seen as a threat to the officers who had been given a degree course, and moreover would make the sailor less likely to continue a Naval career if he was qualified to take a better job as a civilian. Although I personally I believe in the principle of self help, the very nature of Naval life strongly denied the opportunity to many otherwise willing and able people. So I am pleased to know that nowadays Artificer entrants are able to achieve H.N.D. status as a formal part of their training.

A career? Well, during my time, the lower deck career stopped at C.P.O. and those who aspired to the wardroom reached a ceiling at Lt.-Cdr. The first promotion to Commander from the F.A.A. Special Duties List came in 1970. Frank Cook an Air Ordnance Officer was from first Rodney Division, and his promotion gave him just one short job in the rank prior to retirement. Frank was a chum with whom I shared many long evenings in London at D.G.A. (N), and he died shortly after he retired. Careers were seen to be the prerogative for the General List Officer and it seemed that the rest of the Navy was designed to be the stepping stones for these people on their way to the top, whatever the abilities of the individuals concerned. However no one denied this treatment for the true high flyers who were sufficiently rare to be immediately obvious. Job security took a knock with the 1967 Defence Review, but before that it was possible to soldier along for years doing as little as possible and many did just that, and also made sure they found a good excuse never to go to sea.

However it was as difficult to obtain the release of a sailor with prospects in civilian life, as it was to eject a real skate. In both cases a disgruntled unhappy man was unlikely to be an efficient one and could be a bad influence on others. Again a more enlightened approach seems to apply currently.

Adventure? Well there was of course a kick from knowing that your job was different to the majority of civilians, a sort of one up-manship macho concept. This was however not truly justified for the majority of sailors either. On a carrier, only our Aircrew could be said to be in the firing line at war or in peacetime; while the rest of us potential targets for bombs and torpedoes, however important in sending our fliers airborne, fell under the N.A.A.F.I. motto : -

"They also serve who only stand and wait."

The opportunity to demonstrate true grit or any other feat akin to bravery, arrives only by chance in the lives of most of us. In the lottery of life I, like many others, served without ever seeing the enemy. I do know I have a strong survival instinct but no idea how I would have coped in extreme conditions. Just as it is today, others faced dangers that I did not, and they had my admiration.

Foreign travel? Well that certainly was a good reason. The range and variety of places visited under the auspices of the Grey Funnel Line were and still are enormous. I travelled a lot in my next career but nothing compares with the first sight of a new place as seen from a ship approaching the shore.

Coming from a Naval family certainly influenced some to join up, but this only worked to the advantage of General List Officers; they had in effect joined an exclusive club, of which their fathers were members of the board.

Glamour? The picture of a life based on a "girl in every port", and "all the nice girls love a sailor", doesn't quite fit reality. The girls readily available in ports around the world are not especially nice, and despite being away from home and very sexually frustrated, most sailors are far more cautious and faithful than fiction proposes. Just possibly, this idea stems from pre-war when long overseas postings to the China Station would have tempted a saint. In wartime, relaxed morals affected not just sailors, but they were hard pushed to make headway with British servicewomen, who often fell into the category of "Officers for the use of". I cannot imagine any great change now that females serve at sea, but as always – "Where there's a will there's a way!"

Tradition? Well that has been a mixed blessing. The Navy seemed to use tradition to avoid the necessity of accepting change. However while the Army uses Regimental tradition as an inspiration to keep morale high, this has not been possible with the Navy since sailors do not serve continuously with the same ship or unit.

The cry used to be – "The last ship is the best ship". The truth of that is simply that sailors love to spin a line, and talking about their experiences in a previous ship allows free expression of both the good, as well as the bad times; usually the bad times tend to be forgotten. In fact only two events in Naval history are routinely commemorated; these are of course – "Trafalgar", and for the Fleet Air Arm – "Taranto". No great emphasis was ever made during training of our "Glorious Naval Tradition", so it is to be

A Bit of a "Tiff"

supposed that the inspiration for such irrational uses of "traditional routine", as mentioned earlier in my text, derived solely as an excuse to make the name of the officer who dragged it out of its resting place in history. For the sailor it was a considerable irritant, even when so many other irritants were still in force due to the war and its after effects.

A caring service? It is true that the Divisional Officer scheme in the Navy was far superior to any commercial organisation, until post-war such large companies as I.B.M. showed industry how to look after and inspire loyalty in their employees. Certainly, as a C.P.O. when my need was greatest the Navy came up trumps and that decided me to continue serving once I had qualified for Branch List. The caring side of the Navy goes hand in hand with Naval discipline. Another hoary old saying goes, "A tight (disciplined) ship is a happy ship". The question arises - what sort of discipline and is it applied fairly and logically? That it was not always the case is obvious from some earlier examples and apart from indicating the personal defects of the officers concerned, it also suggests that the Navy had failed to understand the change in the nature of the new generation of sailors who were better educated and could think for themselves. Indeed the Navy depended upon everyone using their intelligence at work, so how could they be expected to accept rather pointless orders without question?

Self-evidently people joined the Navy for reasons as varied as the individuals themselves, and some of them were misfits. In my experience I had a Leading Electrician whose reading matter was the Amateur Poultry Breeder, somehow he was doing a job for which he had no interest whatever. Other Mechanics sat around, waiting for the planes to return, reading kids' comics, like *Beano*. I also had an ex-Apprentice E.A.4 (A) who never went ashore from the ship, and had to be obliged to do so; he clearly didn't fit the pattern. When I joined, one was either fit and suitable for the job or not, but later the selection procedure included aptitude tests devised by psychologists, and a colleague told me the following tale of his time at a New Entry establishment. A particular new entry had taken his aptitude tests, which included fitting a selection of irregular wooden shapes into a rectangular tray. This he did with such speed that the psychologists rated him a "genius". It was only when this assessment was reviewed that it was discovered that the young man had been a packer in a biscuit factory!

So who were my shipmates and what were their characters? In my view they were a cross-section of our society in every respect, although during the war the variety was a great deal broader, and I served with barrow boys and fashion designers; they certainly had no plans for a future career in the Navy, but with the minimum of training did an excellent job, when the motivation was present. I do not believe in the notion of the stereotypical British sailor, as in "Hearts of oak are our ships, jolly tars are our men"; at all ranks and levels the Navy is manned by individuals each with their own agenda, and since service in a particular ship is never continuous, then the "family" of men (and now women) who form a ship's company change their allegiance at every move. They tend to become indistinguishable from their civilian neighbours once they come ashore, but usually their drive and initiative marks them out from the man in the street. Often the young career officer straight out of Naval College, arrives full of his own "p— and importance" and has the raw edges knocked out of him by contact with the Chief and Petty Officers and Ratings. Only when this has happened is he able to form viable working teams from the very diverse staff that are within his care; it is only then that the British sailor is at his best.

During my service I was privileged, at all levels, to meet many real gentlemen, some intelligent and educated, but there were also snobs and bullies and the nature of the system allowed some of these to thrive. There were also wimps, the thoughtful, the uncaring, and the ignorant, energetic and bone idle, honest men, liars and cheats, rogues and vagabonds, family men and adulterers, genii and idiots, and of course alcoholics.

This strange mixture of people is the essence of the Navy; it works well when it is well led, has a sense of purpose, and is very much better in smaller rather than in larger units, and when removed from the distraction of family life. That does not mean that the family is forgotten, but rather that work becomes a diversion to compensate for its absence. If these factors are absent then the rule is :-

"Sod you Jack, I'm all right."

One thing that however is pretty universal is the sailor's perverse sense of humour. They tend to chuckle at their own and others' misfortunes, and on occasions when po-faced civilians are completely flummoxed. In the days when cinemas were widely attended, I always knew that sailors were present when guffaws arose at wholly inappropriate times.

I did not expect to find the same companionship in civilian life, so that would be the feature of Naval life that I would most miss, but there would be other benefits and new problems to face. With such a regular movement of jobs and people it was going to be difficult to maintain contact with many of my colleagues, so I am lucky still to have several old chums with whom I share a good laugh in my dotage. When occasionally I meet someone I haven't seen for years we then pick up where we left off years before, but as for the Navy in 1971 it was a case of "been there, done that", and time to move on.

Chapter 22   R.N. retired

Part 1 D/Space

Following an enjoyable holiday in Italy with Margaret and Barbara, I had barely joined Marconi in July 1971 when I had a call from Freddie Allford. He was now the F.A.A. Employment Liaison Officer and suggested that I might apply for a post available in the Space Dept. of MoD/P.E. (Ministry of Defence/ Procurement Executive). Although the pay and hours at Marconi were acceptable, my role as Engineering Finance Officer (i.e. Bean Counter) for the various Sea Dart Test Equipment projects, appeared to have no great future or an absorbing technical role, and I therefore applied to MoD/PE, was accepted and started work in London as a P.T.O.2 (Professional and Technological Officer) late Sept 1971 in the Directorate of Space where the short experience of MoD accounting procedures at Marconi proved very useful.

At that time, and for many years after, it was common for MoD contracts to be charged on a Cost Plus Profits basis and this was open to abuse, having no incentive for a contractor to work efficiently. The alternative was for a Fixed Price Contract, which was negotiated at the outset and could only be increased under strict rules. This system was fairly new and of course was not popular with contractors, but the Sea Dart Test Equipment was being built under both types of contract, and I soon found that the Manager of the Fixed Price contract was able to shunt his excess expenditure to the other contract by simply directing his staff, using common services at the plant, to book time to the other contract. In these instances I was able to correct the records and MoD were none the wiser, any more than they were when I found errors in my own cost records, which were due in part to periodic faults in the Swiss made Electro-Mechanical Calculator. This was the era when the first Electronic Calculators were only just coming into general use, and Marconi had not yet invested in such luxuries, at least for MoD contracts; instead the motor, shafts and levers of my calculator whirred and rattled, and occasionally ran amok to produce impossible answers. With that experience in mind I purchased a Sinclair Oxford Scientific Calculator in London for the princely sum of £25, and it is still working although several times larger than the slim-line calculators now available at a fraction of the cost.

My new job was in Space 2 as a Project Officer for the Skylark Sounding Rocket working from Prospect House in New Oxford Street. Skylark was the largest of three U.K. Sounding Rockets, and had 44 cm diameter solid fuel motors. It was the only remaining U.K. Space Rocket following the recent cancellation of the "Black Arrow", which had successfully launched the "Prospero" satellite in October 1971, but of course was not intended to enter orbit, merely to take scientific payloads to high altitude. Skylark was actually a collection of units assembled as required by various scientific bodies, primarily the S.R.C. (Scientific Research Council), for particular experiments. Several different bodies funded the Skylark according to their needs and programmes, but as each component required for the forecast programmes had a different production lead time, some years in the case of the rocket motors, this tended to increase the stockpile as insurance. There was thus difficulty in matching user demands to the available budget funds; with a little thought I devised a formula which solved the overspend at the expense of a reduction in work by the main contractor, who was not best pleased. By 1971 the Skylark programme, which had been designed by R.A.E. Farnborough, had been running successfully since 1956. It and its smaller less powerful Petrel and Skua partners had established a good record in research in the upper atmosphere, being both relatively cheap, easy to prepare and with a 87% reliability. Many of the 270 firings to date had been conducted at Woomera but later work was also carried out in Sweden and in Sardinia under the E.S.R.O. (European Space Research Organisation) programme. All of these had been fired from fixed launch facilities but by 1970 a mobile launcher had been tested which gave opportunities to use Skylark in many other locations. With the most powerful of the series of Booster and Sustainer Motors a Skylark could reach altitudes of up to 400 km before falling back to earth.

Simply monitoring the supply of bits and pieces hardly qualified as a highly technical job even if it did involve a lot of chasing around, but Farnborough as the Technical Authority had seen a need for Skylark to be used for Earth Resource Sensing and this saved me from boredom. I arrived as the programme started. The objective was to release an attitude stabilised payload bay containing one rather dated but still useful F24 reconnaissance camera, and a standard commercially available Hasselblad camera. These two cameras were programmed to take photographs of the ground during the short period when at the top of the ballistic trajectory; the payload body was rotated around the vertical axis in six steps of 60 degrees, so that the photographs covered some 500,000 sq.kms. The payload was then recovered by parachute. Since the object of the programme was to assess the vegetable and mineral resources in the target area the F24 used a black and white panchromatic film with a range of special filters and the Hasselblad a special false colour infra-red film. Both cameras were therefore sensitive to radiation over a band appropriate to the materials being studied; this made them stand out from their background on the resulting images.

A Bit of a "Tiff"

Critical to the success of the programme was the ability to relate the photographic images with what was actually on the ground. The Ground Truth studies were to be conducted by a team of scientists from the University of Reading under contract, and I became involved in their activities e.g. from funding a supply of picks and shovels, to arranging with the Army Air Corps to fly a scientist in a helicopter over a test site. Neither the Navy nor R.A.F. were prepared to co-operate.

The first trial was successfully carried out using Skylark SL 1081 at Woomera in March 1972 and although the exercise was being conducted in collaboration with the Australian C.S.I.R.O. (Scientific and Industrial Research Organisation) there was great panic when the Aussies initially refused to release the films for processing, because the images included areas of the Woomera weapons testing range. I had to rush over to St Giles Court and raise an urgent signal to secure their release before the extreme temperatures damaged the infrared film.

The next step involved firing two Skylarks SL1181 and 1182 over the wheat fields of Argentina, where the ability to assess the potential yield was very important commercially. For this purpose Farnborough set about making a transportable launcher, and most of the extensive resources of the workshops were employed on this task. The basis of the launcher was a pair of guide rails elevated by screw jacks from a base mounting structure. These rails were initially chosen from a length of second hand railway track, but the workshop was unable to divide them lengthwise because of the work hardening caused by the passage of trains, and new rail had to be ordered. "Shades of the recent Hatfield rail disaster!"

The programme was carried out as planned, but was not continued thereafter. It was no surprise to me since, by the time the U.K. got into the Earth Resources business, the U.S. had already demonstrated the principles on Apollo 9, and were forging ahead on the specialised Earth Resources satellite series starting with ERTS "A". Arguably the spacing of over-flights by a satellite left large time gaps in coverage of areas of interest, which could easily be obscured by cloud cover on successive passes. Skylark was intended to exploit this potential problem but it was undeniable that the idea of launching and recovering a large ballistic vehicle over even the wide open wheat fields of Argentina was unlikely to appeal to anyone beneath its flight path. Nowadays the supply of satellite imagery is a very commercial enterprise.

The U.K. Space programme changed direction about this time as we got out of the large and very expensive launch vehicle business and took a fairly minor role in the European Space Programme. U.K. work has since concentrated on satellites, their payloads and space technology. Just as with the case of aircraft it has been necessary to join collaborative international programmes.

Skylark had only one minor role in military affairs, when some of the booster motors were procured for use during re-entry tests of the multiple warheads being developed for Polaris under the Chevaline programme.

The job in Space 2 was the beginning of a fifteen year second career in the Civil Service, and it was quite different to the Navy; the most noticeable change was the general lack of formality, first names only and no "Sir" this and "Sir" that. However there were some deep divisions lurking in the background; in particular these related to the role, pay and status of the Executive, Professional/Technical, and Scientific classes. Essentially, the Executive class were the overall Policy Makers and Administrators with a direct line to the mandarins at the top of the Civil Service; as such they looked down on lesser mortals even when they had no detailed knowledge of the subject under discussion, and were capable of using their ultimate control of finance and contractual matters to impede the progress of the technical and scientific tasks. Oddly often the most inflexible and difficult were junior female Executive Officers. The Executive class succeeded in awarding themselves relatively higher pay than the remainder and appeared to move insidiously toward elevating it to one grade above their notional equals in other classes. At the bottom of the pay structure were the scientists, who were rightly aggrieved at getting less than anyone else of equal rank. This anomalous situation has been rectified since my retirement, but it was a source of discontent at the time; somehow the scientists were believed to be so keen on their subjects that they had no real interest in money, and although this was certainly very far from the truth, there was a hint of unrealism in their optimistic forecasts of work.

The Executive class often claimed, with some justification, that the cost and time estimates given by scientists were one third, and by engineers one half of the ultimate project cost and time. However they themselves were not guiltless in the inflexible world of Defence Votes and Annual Budgets. Each year when the estimates had been pruned, juggled and finally approved, the April beginning of a financial year allowed a flood of work to be started, and even allowing for obstructions and delays it was usual for new work to be frozen within two to three months when the bean counters forecast an overspend. The lean period ended in September or October when they now forecast an underspend and demanded an instant response; this then allowed one or two pet projects to be slipped in unnoticed but so late in the financial year that the actual bills started to appear at the beginning of the next financial year and the stop-start cycle continued. Delays by contracts branches and contractors in negotiating final contract payments further exacerbated the problem, and although an underspend could not be carried forward to the next year nonetheless the bills still had to be paid eventually, usually when it was least convenient.

During much of my time the Contracts and University Agreements that I let were based upon experience of the past or known expertise of a company or team, but in some cases Government policy directed that all work, say that involving lasers, would be confined to a few specified contractors, so that their expertise would be maintained in that field. In that way a feeling of mutual self-confidence was achieved but to the critics this arrangement was altogether too cosy; it certainly did not encourage contractors to use their own funds or to exercise restraint with public funds. The progressive introduction of both fixed price contracts, competitive tendering, and performance incentives and penalties was a shock to the system as a whole, and although it is now the norm, it invariably resulted in extremely long delays, and much frustration. Companies used to generous public funds for research also began to question whether being paid to undertake research for MoD was likely to result in any benefit to their core manufacturing business; since scientists are expensive to employ they might be better used to create a new commercial product for their employer, and in some cases I received a point blank refusal to do MoD work. As a taxpayer I could hardly complain and I embraced the new policy as often as was convenient, but there were occasions when it did not suit and then I needed all my skills to beat the system. In fact it was a challenge that suited me well

From the start of my job in London I had been commuting daily from Winchester; this meant a long day and the journey up to town was invariably standing room only, followed by a charge across Hungerford Bridge among the solid procession of other worker ants. In this procession there was always someone who walked swinging his umbrella ostentatiously back and forth to the peril of those behind, so I was very "chuffed" one morning when my shoe trapped a brolly swinging aft and neatly removed the ferrule. The owner looked a little surprised but didn't comment. I was never able to repeat that success. On the morning that the I.R.A. bombed the Westminster Hall I was just passing the National Theatre when the explosion took place and I saw the cloud of smoke from across the Thames. Commuting had some benefits, as a Civil Servant my routine at work was much more relaxed and allowed easy access to the shops in Oxford Street, Charing Cross Road and Tottenham Court Road. Once properly programmed it was possible also to achieve some useful reading during the journey and of course to catch up on lost sleep if all else failed. The reverse journey was usually rather better, and I was now a clock-watcher in order to catch my train. Routinely I joined several other fellow travellers to form an orderly queue around the predicted point on the platform where our carriage was expected to stop; this was marked out on the white paint by a line scratched into it by the "brolly" of a retired colonel. Periodically our organisation was disrupted by a particular little old lady going home after a day's shopping. She would have made an excellent scrum half as she charged head down for the door and, gentlemen that we were, she was first inside. Another elderly couple also caused amusement; on their days out they carried lots of shopping bags which they distributed along the length of the compartment and spent their journey walking up and down to check them.

In the winter of 1971 it became clear that my fourteen mile drive to and from Winchester along the winding and very slippery back roads would eventually result in an accident, and that if, as seemed likely, I was now to be a commuter for years then we would have to move closer to a station. We now found a new Georgian style house in Winchester from which I could walk to and from the station; this was a super house but we soon came to realise that we were not townies; the three "C's" of Winchester (College, County and Church, but not forgetting Commuters) stamped upon it a style we did not embrace. Even walking our dogs required a three-mile drive to Farley Mount.

When we moved in an Admiral's son from Alverstoke helped me in clearing up the builder's rubble in my garden. He was attending the same Art course as Barbara. He arrived with long hair and a studded belt and was very helpful; Barbara visited his family, who were also very pleasant and for a while I contemplated the future with an Admiral as an in-law but I was spared that when Barbara dumped him. An earlier boyfriend didn't survive the course either; Barbara returned one evening to tell us that his father kept Siberian tigers and we remained highly sceptical until she was taken to visit his parents and to see the tigers. Dad owned Marwell Zoo!

As usual "Sod's Law" stepped in again, and no sooner were we installed at Winchester than Richard was married and Barbara moved on to Harrow Art College, so we were now rattling around in our large four-bedroom house. We felt sympathy for local students looking for housing after Barbara's experience in Harrow, but our brief experience with two girl students was uncomfortable and survived less than two terms. Almost at once we received a call from Kent, Mum was ill and Dad, who was wholly undomesticated, could not cope. My cars could have driven that route automatically, and once again we travelled to Bearsted and brought them back to live with

A Bit of a "Tiff"

us. It was evident that they could no longer live in Bearsted and we helped them sell their house; Richard and I moved their belongings down to Winchester and neatly filled the hired van, firstly with the furniture and then with the contents of Dad's shed. This of course included many tools and large pieces of timber, but finally we were left with some boxes of rusty nails, some off-cuts of wood, and some paintbrushes soaking in creosote. At this point we had no more space in the van and had to discard them. As was inevitable, once Dad had been rehabilitated, by doing various little jobs in the garage, he complained at the items we had left behind. However he made several very good pieces of equipment for the handicapped children at the Opportunity Group, which Margaret was running in Winchester. Margaret also nursed and rehabilitated Mum, who was not an easy person to cope with, and as both my parents became fit, it was obvious that they could not adapt to living with us or with the new environment. After several traumas they decided they would be able to return to their home ground but in different accommodation. After eighteen months with us they bought a small flat in Maidstone and returned to familiar surroundings and friends. Dad survived just one year; Mum continued to live there until 1986.

The stairs in our house were very hard going for Margaret, particularly because of her caring for Mum, and we had begun to look around for bungalow accommodation capable of taking all of us. The decision of my parents to move back to Kent gave us rather greater choice and we moved to a very large modern bungalow in Ropley. This was to be our home for the next twenty-one years and was conveniently close to Alton station, which being a terminus gave a guaranteed seat and allowed a good nap on the way home, without fear of overshooting the station.

In Winchester I had first overcome my fear of heights when I needed to decorate the outside of the house, and so after moving to Ropley I had no qualms in taking three weeks of my annual leave to renovate the exterior of the bungalow which had a high pitched roof. All went well in the fine hot weather until on the final day I mounted the ladder, which slipped and I ended up in hospital with a broken collarbone. Perhaps my instincts were right after all!

I had by 1972 changed my job on promotion, and was now working in D.R.A.S.A. (Directorate of Research, Space, Avionics and Air Traffic) based in the Adelphi close to Shell Mex House, which was rather more convenient to Waterloo station.

Chapter 22 R.N. Retired

Part 2 D.R.A.S.A.

D.R.A.S.A. (Directorate of Research Avionics, Space and Air Traffic) had been established during one of the periodic changes in MoD/PE, in an attempt to co-ordinate the research needs of all three Armed Services and Civil Aviation. Other Directorates had been established similarly covering other specialist fields. Studies had shown the need for a proper proportion of total project costs to be allocated separately for Research, Development and Production, and that it was unsound and costly to move into Development, or Production until Research had removed uncertainty and risk in the technical plans. Many costly failures bore witness to the truth of that principle. The future was also to be based upon the Customer/Contractor relationship between the Service customer and D.R.A.S.A. as their contractor, between us and the Research Establishments and of course our civilian contractors. This was a complex relationship in which D.R.A.S.A. was piggy in the middle. Since most of the programmes were inherently long term, then I had to monitor to a conclusion those I had inherited. This might not always be satisfactory and a decision not to continue was usually bound to upset some or all of the participants. This happened quite quickly when after a year attempting to measure the size of water droplets with a laser, a PhD student we were employing had only succeeded in evaporating the droplets. This result was not altogether surprising. The financial sponsor of the work had been abolished in a departmental shake up, it was impossible to make a case for the work to continue with another sponsor and I cancelled the study. Shortly the University Chancellor contacted the Chief Scientist complaining at the cancellation, but my explanation was supported. There were obviously pitfalls in this new job!

New tasks arrived from different sources; for example the general objectives arose at various discussions regularly held by the Research Directors, the Customers, Industry and the Scientific Community. Thereafter it was up to the individuals in our directorate to work out a suitable research programme; usually this was done in collaboration with a research establishment already active in the field, and then we had to persuade the "customers" to allocate funds. In some cases no less than four funding sources contributed to my projects, some committed to pay for a percentage of the whole cost, while others paid just a small fixed sum. The risks inherent with research meant that each project that failed reduced the chance of a customer coming back for more, and there were many failures. Perhaps the most difficult customer branch was the D.T.I. (Department of Trade and Industry), despite its remit to assist British industry. In the face of many notorious and costly failures with high profile projects D.T.I. appeared to impose so many rules that it would have been easier to go to a commercial bank. Fortunately once committed most of our customers took only a passing interest in progress. Our remit was broad and if there appeared to be a gap in the coverage of our specialist subject, then it was possible to make a case and start a new activity.

My responsibility covered initially the Air Traffic field of Environmental Factors. These included High Integrity I.L.S. (Instrument Landing System), Visibility (i.e. Lighting and Fog measurement), and Wind (e.g. Wake Turbulence, Clear Air Turbulence, Windshear, and Building Turbulence). You may now be wondering how I could suddenly be a specialist in these obscure subjects. First requirement was to do some pretty intensive reading, not only of books held in the St Giles Court library, but also by accessing the wide range of reports from both British and foreign sources held in the Defence Research Information Centre (D.R.I.C.), and last but by no means least the U.S. *Aviation Week and Space Technology* (A.W.S.T.) magazine, and the *New Scientist*. In fact, because the subject matter was so far ahead of current knowledge there were few real experts with hands-on experience and at headquarters they would have been wasted, so our job was to rationalise the options on basic principles and logic. Advice was taken from the Research Establishments, not only Farnborough and Bedford, but also Malvern, and the Met Office at Bracknell, but it was Farnborough and Bedford that provided the Technical Authority for our Extra-Mural Contracts, since they either required such work to support their own Intra-Mural Studies, or had specific expertise in the subject. From their point of view had the staff and funds been available they would have preferred to undertake all research internally, but they were certainly "effort limited" as the establishments got ever smaller. This meant that relations with these groups were very amiable as we funded the contracts, but it did not suit their Directors, who wished to manage their own funds. In due course the London based Research Directorates were absorbed back into the Establishments in 1978. At that time this change seemed a retrograde step, since it removed an element of the oversight that had been provided, and allowed a return to the somewhat incestuous ways of old. That system has also changed since my retirement with the introduction of the D.E.R.A. (Defence Evaluation and Research Agency) giving the Administrators further chances to meddle.

The problem in overseeing research work is that without repeating the work, it is often difficult to detect flaws in the results until they become glaringly obvious and at that point the preceding work may have all been nugatory. Of course a negative result is always possible in any event and has to be accepted, just as the work may be totally negated by some new concept or requirement that overtakes the work in hand.

One case, in which I played only a minor role, was a study of a High Integrity I.L.S. (Instrument Landing System). I.L.S. had been developed from the pre-war German Lorenz Beam System by the B.L.E.U. (Blind Landing Experimental Unit) at Bedford. This system enables suitably equipped aircraft to land automatically in low visibility; I.L.S. or its successor M.L.S (Microwave L.S.) is now used routinely at all the world's major airports, but in the 1970's only a few aircraft and airports were equipped as experience was building up and the safety limits gradually extended. One limitation was that bogus signals to a landing aircraft could occur from reflections due to other aircraft or objects in the vicinity; H.I.I.L.S. was intended to eliminate the bogus signals, and without this then the landing separation distance might have to be extended. As I arrived in the job, the contractor had been unable to find a solution after some months of study; he therefore held a "brain storming" session internally and produced a number of new ideas. These were submitted to D.R.A.S.A. at a meeting chaired by my Asst. Director and one scheme using a working demonstration rig was accepted as the basis for further work to produce a full prototype. This work proceeded, but as it did so the results not only failed to improve when using high-grade electronic components, but also actually got worse. Farnborough was then finally obliged to consult their Mathematicians and they, after working through the contractor's theory, concluded that the assumptions were faulty. The basis for the scheme was a mathematical series in which it had been assumed that all terms after the third were negligible and could be ignored. This not unusual assumption was in fact wholly wrong in this instance; the values of subsequent terms increased and negated the theory. I then chaired the meeting at which the contract was cancelled.

I had only a watching brief on the subject of Airfield Lighting; this work was run by a small team at Bedford, who had previously run the Naval unit for Carrier trials. It was therefore not surprising that their new glide-slope indicator lights should bear resemblance to the system of landing aids used on carriers. At that time, and probably still ongoing, groups of experts from N.A.T.O. countries held regular meetings to exchange ideas and to promote standardisation of equipment and facilities. This was a very chummy arrangement, which, once started, carried the participants on trips to the different countries in turn. On one such "jolly", the lighting group went to Denmark, and finding themselves in Copenhagen, availed themselves of the local entertainment at a live sex show. No doubt this would not have been of any great import to those of us remaining in U.K., but the audience, which naturally included an R.N. Commander, were obliged to watch the performance by standing on benches; the performance ceased abruptly when the audience fell off the bench and the male entertainer could not subsequently rise to the occasion. This tale went the rounds very quickly.

Environmental Factors studies were considered crucial to Civil Aviation; I had inherited a number of contracts and in each case British weather proved as unco-operative as usual. In the case of fog, a range had been established on the Isle of Wight at which a number of lasers of different frequencies were attempting to measure fog density. If this work proved successful then it was hoped that a system focused up the glide path on airfields would give aircraft critical information on runway visibility. Current provision was based upon a small number of "transmissometers", similar to those now used on motorways; these gave the fog density only at a few feet above the runway in say three fixed locations, and this was clearly of limited value since the cockpit of any aircraft was many feet higher than the equipment. Aircraft using the I.L.S. system were graded as to their ability to land in low visibility e.g. a Category 3C aircraft could land automatically in zero visibility, but less well equipped aircraft were only permitted to continue to a landing if the runway lights could be seen at the "decision height" given in their type clearance. A more reliable indicator of visibility was obviously desirable. Obviously everything depended upon fog appearing whenever the equipment was ready to measure it and of course it did not do so, so there was much fruitless waiting despite the best forecasts. Such data as was collected was transmitted for processing to the U.S. but there was a massive glitch when the basement room containing the contractor's data equipment was flooded. Finally it was decided that not only was the test site unsuitable but that "sea fog" had different properties from that encountered on airfields! I made a case for the removal of the equipment to Farnborough on the evidence supplied by the P.S.O. (Principal Scientific Officer) as Technical Authority, and C.A.A. funded the new range. Eventually results started to arrive from the occasional fog and appeared to confirm that we were indeed measuring fog density. The P.S.O. decided to emigrate to New Zealand at this critical point and his successor took one look at the results and declared them useless. The theoretical basis for his views could not be faulted and since it was no longer possible to confront the original sponsor with this evidence this contract was also closed.

The only on-going task on wind was to measure wind speed, direction and temperature at intervals up to 1000 ft on two television masts sited in the very different terrain at Lichfield and Mendlesham. Two contractors were employed, one of whom supplied the data monitoring stations, and the other supplied the services of an ex R.A.F. Meteor pilot, who was happy to climb up the masts to install the instruments in the early mornings when the transmitters were switched off. Twenty-four hour T.V. had not yet been introduced! Before the programme started it had been an assumption that wind speed would not exceed the capability of the special propeller anemometers, (I think 90 knots) and that the probability of a lightning strike on a mast was no more than one in the course of the study. We did eventually get our results, rather later than intended after two lightning strikes and a gale that stripped off all the instruments. I have to hope that the work added some tiny scrap of useful information, but like all our research work, the final report ended in the D.R.I.C. archives. Although I found these records very useful, in fact many people in M.o.D did not use them or were unaware of their existence and continued their own studies unaware of the possibility of re-inventing the wheel.

Wind was however a red-hot issue as a result of a number of accidents due to turbulence, and the U.S. had very many programmes covering all the recognised problems. We had just two minor studies; in one of these Birmingham University was tasked to study the detection and measurement of wake turbulence using acoustics. As always the difficulty was to generate routinely and maintain the phenomena for sufficient time to perform the measurement. After many snags, during which we investigated the use of a test tower at Aston Down where the rotor head of the Fairey Rotodyne had been installed for noise measurements, the best result came from mounting an aerofoil section on the roof of our researcher's Jaguar and this produced an adequate vortex during a high speed run. I had to go back to basic aerodynamics before I was assured that the lift produced would not destabilise the car, but I cannot remember how we resolved the question of his insurance. The other line was the use of a laser, following an earlier demonstration by Malvern.

Wake turbulence is created when the low-pressure air above a wing meets the high-pressure air beneath the wing at each wing tip, and especially on swept wing aircraft this results in two powerful vortices having energy equivalent to the total lift on the aircraft. These vortices do not readily disperse or break up although they will drift in a crosswind. They can be seen at altitude as vapour trails but at runway level are normally invisible, however a smaller aircraft entering the vortex of say a "Jumbo" weighing 400 tons would be seriously disturbed, and crashes had occurred. For this reason landing separation distances were extended to maintain adequate safe margins between aircraft, particularly if a small aircraft was following a "Jumbo".

Our objective was to develop the tools to study vortices and hopefully to provide advice or suggest operational gear to assist Air Traffic controllers. The first move was to try our experimental kit in the field, and this required me to convince the British Airports Authority that our small CO_2 laser was safe; this achieved we proceeded to install both the laser and an acoustic device at the end of a runway at Heathrow. The trial demonstrated a capability but we now had to provide more suitable gear for full trials. The requirement outlined by the scientist at Bedford was not in the form of a Specification that could be offered to possible contractors, but eventually a satisfactory document was produced when he moved to a new job and his replacement Bill Britten was very helpful. We went out to tender and chose to develop a trailer mounted system in which a single 10w CO_2 laser was sequentially directed through telescopes to measure the airspeed of particles passing through a defined volume of space. The resulting device looked like a multi barrelled rocket launcher.

With this work in hand we now had reason to visit fellow workers in the U.S. and I arranged a fourteen day visit for myself and the P.S.O. from Bedford, and also an Assistant Director and his deputy from C.A.A. During our tour in May 1976 we visited the F.A.A. and N.A.S.A. in Washington, the National Transportations Systems Center in Boston, the Wave Propagation Laboratory in Boulder, installations at Chicago O'Hare Airport and N.A.S.A.'s Marshall Space Flight Center at Huntsville. It was impossible not to be impressed by the sheer scale of the U.S. work but contrary to popular opinion in U.K., this multiple attack on the various problems was not overkill, because in many cases the experience gained, from even a programme that was not ultimately adopted operationally, was used in a later related activity. In other words there was considerable "spin-off". I was also impressed that despite the scale of their resources they were willing to use very low tech. solutions if appropriate. As one example a ground based laser anemometer built by N.A.S.A. was fitted into an old bread van, and used cling film as the window protecting the laser optics. At Chicago elements of their experimental Vortex Advisory System used the pressure switches from domestic washing machines, but had each unit protected electronically from lightning strikes. Our hosts planned to give us a quick tour of Chicago but their plan failed when we met a solid traffic block of all six lanes of the highway from the airport to Chicago following an accident. The Americans were welcoming hosts and anxious to share information. At Huntsville as well as visiting the Space Museum, which was open to the general public and showed examples of every vehicle in their programme as well as a small piece of "Moon Rock", we were taken on a tour of the N.A.S.A. Space facility including the flotation chamber used to provide weightless acclimatisation for astronauts. We had gained the impression that our tour was a privileged visit, but then found coach loads of schoolchildren on the same tour; the principle of "freedom of information" was certainly a world apart from the closed doors back in U.K.

We had travelled to the U.S. courtesy of the regular R.A.F. VC10 flight from Brize Norton; these had rear-facing seats for safety, no alcohol, and seating and boarding was strictly controlled by rank. Arriving back at Brize Norton, leaving the aircraft was similarly controlled and so was access to baggage retrieval, at least in theory, but after watching this in action for a few minutes I gave us instant promotion and walked on through.

Back at work I sought the advice of experts at Farnborough as to how we might protect our equipment against lightning strikes when it was installed at Bedford. Quick as a flash, they had no advice to offer! So we proceeded without such protection and in the end had an array of propeller anemometers, an acoustic system and the laser system all linked up to a trailer containing a "Digital" (™) PDP11 computer on the airfield at Bedford. This did not go without the usual hitch as the laser system was running late; on the day during which I had phoned the Managing Director of the company to complain, the trailer was damaged by fire due supposedly to the laser being left focused on an inflammable screen. At last the gear was installed when once again there was a gale that damaged the shutters protecting the laser telescopes, and no sooner was this repaired than lightning hit Bedford and induced current in the connecting cables destroyed the computer. Against the odds however the array of sensors produced the results expected, so this had been one success among many failures. Our contractor did his best to derive some commercial benefit from his laser system, but in the end our system remained a one off research tool, and like so many similar MoD activities once the original task had been completed there was neither the staff nor funds to develop or maintain the equipment and I have no doubt that it ended on the airfield junkyard.

Our next objective was to build an airborne Laser Anemometer with which we might pursue several areas of concern. The first of these was C.A.T. (Clear Air Turbulence); C.A.T. arises from temperature inversions in the atmosphere and can cause severe disturbance to any aircraft flying into it but there was no method of reliably forecasting the likelihood of it arising in any particular area. I believe that even now the best forecasts arise from reports by aircraft having already flown through such turbulence. In 1976 aircraft were not yet designed to cope with the stresses of a C.A.T.

encounter, and some had certainly been damaged and passengers injured. I understand that the controls of later aircraft are better able to respond. The effect is similar to flying in the turbulence due to a mountain, and this has caused several fatal accidents. The long-term hope was that an airborne laser might detect turbulence sufficiently far ahead of the flight path to allow a change of course, perhaps to modify the flight controls, or just simply to get passengers seated and strapped in. This was really a long-term prospect and the more urgent need was for a means of detecting Windshear, which had already caused several fatal accidents to passenger aircraft in the U.S. Windshear is a phenomena in the area of a thunderstorm and aircraft in the vicinity may suddenly encounter large and often very localised wind changes, and sometimes severe downdrafts. The effect on an aircraft landing or taking off is to induce high sink rates which if uncorrected in time can lead and has led to a fatal crash. Various ideas were then current and one need was for a means of measuring true airspeed ahead of the aircraft. Our proposed Laser Anemometer offered such a solution.

The complex programme I initiated used the resources of R.R.E. Malvern and R.A.E. Bedford plus three contractors to build the L.A.T.A.S. (Laser True Airspeed System) and install it into the H.S.125 at Bedford for flight trials. This was successfully completed in 1980, although by that time I had moved on. The ultimate hope was for such an installation to be a standard fit on commercial aircraft, but despite other countries developing similar equipment, commercial pressures led to other solutions.

The engineering of the laser installation was arranged by Ted Whitely (Lt.-Cdr. R.N.rtd.) who was one of the first entry of Naval Air Apprentices and had trained at R.A.F. Halton. During one visit I met Capt. Geoff. Higgs at that time the O.C. Flying at Bedford. Another visitor that day was Ollie Greenhalgh who had come up to give a talk and demonstration of his flying models to the local branch of the R.Ae.S.

One final environmental task required us to assess the risks to aircraft arising from turbulence caused by the third "Jumbo" hangar planned for Heathrow. This time we found a small team of experts at Bristol University, who carried out our study in their wind tunnel.

I had for some time been also involved in the business of navigation, this was certainly a subject of which I had some knowledge, and in due course it became my full time task working with the Navigation Department at Farnborough, the Admiralty Compass Observatory (A.C.O.) at Slough and later with the F.V.R.E. (Fighting Vehicle Research Establishment) at Chobham. At the outset the business was mundane; Farnborough was still pursuing a "dry-tuned" gyro, was monitoring Loran and Omega radio navigation aid signals, and monitoring a research student investigating methods of using hardening alloys of aluminium for use in gyros. Perhaps the most urgent of all was a search for an alternative resin bonded fibre material to that currently used to form the bearing cages in the miniature ball races of the Aircraft Inertial Navigation system gyros built under licence in U.K. The facts were that the material then used was machined from .375 inch diameter rod imported from the U.S. and its manufacture had ceased. The U.K. requirement was so small that perhaps just a length of a few feet would have satisfied all known requirements for years to come had it been available, but because it had been specially chosen for its apparently unique ability to retain just the precise amount of lubricant, then finding an alternative was critical to the provision and maintenance of R.A.F. I.N. systems. This was not the first occasion when the small U.K. demand for specialised material was insufficient to justify commercial production, and it continues today.

A.C.O. had many irons in the fire, but were, so far as my involvement was concerned, deeply into improvements to materials and techniques used to make the very precise gas-bearings used in S.I.N.S. (Ships Inertial Navigation Systems). A gas bearing used plain journal bearings machined to optical tolerances, and the clearance between the shaft and the outer bearing was so small that in normal circumstances the two halves would wring together like a gauge plate. In practice the precision machining was modified by hand in a very skilled lapping process that reduced the risk of wringing and a minute quantity of lubricant applied that would be absorbed into the surface but would be insufficient to unbalance the gyro. In operation, with the gyro rotating, the virtually frictionless gas layer that existed between them separated the two halves of the bearing. If the gyro stopped then the two halves would almost certainly wring together and destroy the bearing; for this reason all the gyros in use and their spares were maintained running in a temperature-controlled environment.

The direction of the current research was to better understand the gas-bearing, by searching for new lubricants, new and exotic ceramic bearing materials and to understand the process by which the lubricants were absorbed and desorbed into the various bearing materials. In the course of this work a very innocuous and unclassified study was launched with Sheffield University, and soon after one routine progress meeting the local "pinko" newspaper carried an article reporting that the university was working on nuclear missiles. This bit of deliberately creative reporting caused some consternation down in London until the truth emerged.

The other major task was to develop a new very high precision cylindrical grinding machine to manufacture the gas-bearings. The work had been let to the industrial element of a university, which had already successfully supplied a surface grinder for the same purpose. The university offered among its many courses one very well publicised course on Management, but this had evidently not filtered across to the team responsible for the grinder, and as a result every successive perfectly prepared financial return showed alarming cost increases on this cost–plus contract. This was not acceptable, and I organised a conference to be chaired by my Assistant Director to examine the case for continuing. The representatives of industry and the MoD branch concerned with industrial machinery did not support the need for the grinder, and the contractor currently responsible for gyro manufacture stated that it could not be used in their organisation, but in a typical compromise no one present was willing to suggest cancellation. The work therefore continued but a fixed price was negotiated and when even this was insufficient the university was persuaded to fund the balance to completion. The design used optical measurement and digital computer controls, and stability was achieved by mounting units on large slabs of specially imported granite. Initially the mounting was by studs secured into blind holes with Araldite, and, surprise surprise, after I had questioned this scheme, tests showed that the Araldite was flexible, and holes were then drilled all the way through the granite blocks. The machine was undoubtedly an advance on the Swiss machines which were the universally used for similar purposes, and was probably the most precise machine of its kind in the world, but in fact it was never adopted for its original role and found a new niche in A.C.O.

A.C.O. had one contractor studying the Ring Laser Gyro as a possible alternative to the conventional rotating rotor gyro. Such devices had already been developed in the U.S. for use in weapons where high rates of rotation were normal, and offered a rugged construction well suited to military use, coupled with the ability to use them in a strapped down mode using digital computers and thus to remove the mechanical platform used in conventional I.N. systems. The fly in the ointment was that the contra rotating laser beams locked at low rotation rates and unless this problem could be solved then the system could not be used to provide accurate navigation as required by aircraft and ships. The U.K. contractor had over a period failed to find a solution, and as a result the contract ceased. Almost at once it was reported, in the journal A.W.S.T. that at least two American companies had solved the problem, in one case by the fairly simple method of giving a controlled "dither" around the sensitive axis. With this in mind I now became project officer for the U.K. Laser Gyro programme. We started with three separate studies and followed up by a competition for a demonstration programme, plus further work to develop strap down navigation. This work was focused on the aircraft application since the extra order of accuracy needed by ships would not have been feasible at this early stage.

Further surprises were in store when A.W.S.T. reported U.S. plans for "Navstar" the Global Positioning System (G.P.S.), once again we devised a programme involving Farnborough and a contractor working to provide British equipment, once negotiations with the U.S. had released key information to us.

I then launched a U.K. programme using pattern recognition techniques to navigate using I.R. imaging, as opposed to Tercom in which height contours are stored for similar purposes. Both techniques were used in the early U.S. cruise missiles, the latter for long range navigation in association with I.N. and the former for terminal homing. T.V. images of the weapons turning at road junctions in Baghdad showed their effectiveness. Later weapons use G.P.S.

It was somewhat ironic that I flunked a board for a post in D. Science (R.A.F) at about this time, during which I remarked, accurately but inappropriately, that our best research programmes came straight out of A.W.S.T. From my experience it was obvious that the lack of resources and limited internal demand left the U.K. in a position where were continually striving to keep up with the U.S. despite the undoubted ability of our scientists and engineers. In the 70's much was made of the improvements that had been made in U.K. to license built equipment from the U.S. and the pity was that while we concentrated our energies on the improvements, the U.S. was racing ahead to new ideas, which caught us napping.

The Army had little activity in the field of navigation, just a small number of modified aircraft I.N. systems were available, and most tanks had a system based on a magnetic compass, which was clearly not ideal in the steel casing of a battle tank. On the other hand our main battle tank of the period was unlikely ever to get lost since it was expected only to cover a few miles before it broke down. However the need for a north seeker was identified and I arranged and ran a contract for such a device. The purpose of this kit was to enable a mortar platoon in the new FV432 troop carrier to "shoot and scoot" from a previously surveyed site in northern Germany. The philosophy of the time denied the possibility of any advance into uncharted territory across the "Iron Curtain". I was much relieved to hear that in the nick of time the Army had finally purchased hand-held G.P.S in the build-up to the Gulf War. Otherwise I wonder how they would have managed in the desert.

Other tasks included the development of a dry tuned gyro for the

A Bit of a "Tiff"

Naval M.A.I.N.S. (Medium Accuracy I.N.S.) and a rather smaller gyro for an aircraft Attitude and Heading Reference System, but it was the Laser Gyro that had great interest. Very many new techniques were involved; the ring was formed from a block of special low expansion glass and ultrasonic diamond drills were used to form a triangular path forming the lasing cavity. At each corner a mirror was fitted to complete the lasing circuit, but these were no ordinary mirrors, each had multiple metallic coatings to produce almost 100% reflectance, which alone would ensure "lasing". At the time the most precise mirrors were produced in that most unlikely location, the little state of Liechtenstein, and duly a delegation went there from Farnborough, but I never discovered how this expertise had emerged in the first place. I believe that the only other significant product is false teeth, in which Liechtenstein has almost a monopoly.

By 1978 I qualified for promotion to Principal, for which I had to secure a new posting, and the combined efforts of the Directors of Research Establishments had finally borne fruit and this meant the abolition of D.R.A.S.A. and similar H.Q. Research branches; henceforth all Extramural Research would be managed internally by the absorption of the London based staff into the Research Establishments. It was not a move that I welcomed, but after a brief spell in the Navigation Dept. I found a post on promotion in E.P. Dept. (Engineering Physics) at Farnborough.

Chapter 22 R.N. Retired

Part 3 E.P. Department R.A.E. Farnborough

At E.P. Dept. (Engineering Physics) I headed a small electrical engineering cell dealing with Extra Mural Research (E.P./X.R.) under an Assistant Director. This was a role ripe for change from its conception as the scientists saw full control of research funding within their grasp, and did their best to obstruct a more rational approach to managing the work. Both the mechanical and electrical aspects of the departmental work showed it to be a department that had lost its way; it had evidently been formed from the remnants of the old Electrical Dept. and a similar Mechanical Engineering team to undertake a variety of miscellaneous tasks which did not fall naturally into the other specialist groups at R.A.E. As in London, the role of E.P./X.R. was to initiate, fund and monitor Extra Mural Research with Industry and Universities on behalf of the Head of E.P. Dept.

It is not entirely unfair to say that the working atmosphere had much of a university air and that management skills, and particularly man management, did not figure high on the qualifications of the scientific staff, so it was very difficult to introduce the idea that a research contract could and should be treated like any other contract, with a prepared and costed plan to tackle the investigation, or that just maybe the contractor, who in many cases was being paid to do work in support of his own future projects, might actually put in some funds of his own. In many cases the scientists were actively hostile to any idea that would limit their freedom to throw £50K at a favoured contractor and tell him in effect to go away and see what happened. It had always to be recognised that the advancement of a scientist was determined by his ability to worry an important and obscure subject to death and then to produce a learned treatise on the subject, which gained him status among his peers. Each new paper was a benchmark in his career and was a perfectly logical notion provided that the end result was timely and relevant to the main objectives. It followed that it was with the utmost difficulty that new ideas could be introduced and one needed to be a professional psychologist to counter the objections, which ranged from N.I.H. (Not Invented Here), to, following a pause for reflection, "Oh yes I thought of that years ago".

The range of subjects tackled in the Department meant that it included individuals with a wide range of expertise, some of them very queer fish indeed. One of these, "Ollie", headed one of the three working groups and ranked with my Asst. Director but he was so objectionable to all he encountered that he should never have been placed in a managerial role. The other two at his level were reasonable men but lacked drive and my own A.D., also from Farnborough, never supported his staff in any controversy. His two outside interests were model railways and sailing on the ponds at Frensham, so a duty trip with him provided a very limited range of conversation. Another character was "Tex"; this larger than life bearded scientist drove an Army style Land Rover and dressed as Fidel Castro, complete at one stage with pistol. He claimed some linkage with the S.A.S. but, whether or not this was true, he did in fact devise a new form of "abseiling gear" and also a compressed air line-throwing gun for rescue purposes. In all he did he ignored any attempt to limit his freedom.

The secretary to my A.D. was a mature genteel lady working for the first time due to reduced circumstances, but she drove a Rolls-Royce Reg. No. NPH 2L, which she was obliged to retain owing to a long running family dispute over ownership. The car carried the family crest dating back to the crusades, and she drove into Farnborough without the usual security checks applying to mere mortals with Fords. Occasionally the XR group would go out for lunch or drinks in the Rolls, and the sight of petrol pouring into a seemingly bottomless fuel tank at a garage was more than enough to convince me that such a monster had no future.

By the 1970's MoD/P.E. did not design and control every last nut, bolt and fitting on a military aircraft as had been the case of D.T.D. and S.D.M.'s as described in an earlier chapter. Instead the incorporation of any particular bright idea from Farnborough into a weapon system or aircraft depended upon it being sold, firstly to the service customer, but also to the contractor, and in an era of more competitive tendering the ideas could be rejected on commercial grounds to avoid the risks associated with underdeveloped items. This occurred in the case of some solid state power switches, which had some potential for use in the control of rotor blade de-icing on the Westland EH101 Merlin, and it also occurred in the case of a new efficient fuel pump motor. This motor had been the baby of one individual for many years and when he proudly presented his brainchild to a routine meeting with aircraft industry engineers, he was mortified to be told that everything needed by industry was readily available on the commercial market.

As before a considerable number of activities were ongoing when we took up our posts and they continued to occupy effort. The collection of data on bird strikes and the assessment of bird populations in the vicinity of airfields was one typical task; M.A.F.F. were funded to collect and examine bird corpses. Difficult to see an end or even a satisfactory outcome on that; it had been going on for years and from my experience at Lossiemouth birds liked the open space and relatively undisturbed life at airfields and would continue to live there whatever action was taken against them.

Another similar task used expertise at the Atomic Energy Authority at Harwell, who had been contracted for years to study lightning. The facilities available at Harwell enabled them to produce a handbook to guide aircraft designers on the problems of protecting against lightning, to provide a consultancy service and to test various measures. At the time the use of carbon fibre composites added a new requirement and the work also seemed to have no logical end.

Lightning at one stage took a back seat when static electricity reared its head. R.A.F. rescue helicopters were deploying crewmen directly to the deck of vessels in distress and the considerable static charge built up by the rotors discharged through the crewmen. Once discharged the static recharged immediately so that care was needed not to repeat the performance, e.g. in attempting to help the distressed crewman. A suit incorporating a metallic weave was one proposal to protect the crewman, but I was pleased to know that the R.N. employed a different technique and were not affected. It is very easy to dismiss static electricity as of little account but the R.A.F. had recently lost a Pembroke aircraft when fuel was being drained from the high mounted engine into a plastic bucket. When at length the static charge, created by the fuel dropping several feet, had built up sufficiently it flashed over and caused a fire. It has also fired weapons and destroyed electronic equipment.

Farnborough had had a big role in developing carbon fibre composites for aircraft use but in the mid 1970's no British aircraft used carbon fibre structures. E.P. Dept. however was still deeply involved in investigating the practical and theoretical electrical properties of the material; the reason of course was that the airframe provided the earth return path for all electrical circuits, and electrical continuity was required between all the separate components comprising the airframe. At one point it was not known how effective even the current generation of all metal aircraft were in that respect, until I arranged for a team to visit R.N.A.Y. Fleetlands to conduct measurements. Whatever deep understanding we still lacked on the matter the French had already built a carbon fibre fuel tank in the fin of the Airbus and McDonnell Douglas were planning the new Harrier GR5 with an advanced resin bonded material. It was hard not to feel that once again we were lagging.

Also looking ahead to next generation aircraft the role of E.P. was trying to devise efficiency improvements in such basic equipment as electrical generation systems. In principle such improvements would save weight, and in a knock on effect lead to more fuel or payload capacity or, more favoured in some circles, make for a smaller, lighter and more manoeuvrable aircraft. In isolation it was not of earth shattering consequence and there were no guarantees that any ideas would be incorporated in a new design even if by chance it happened to be British built.

Helicopter icing/de-icing was another area of activity and the objective was the Westland EH 101 Merlin. The prime candidate system was for a series of electrically heated strips on each blade, each of these to be heated in a computer controlled sequence. It is my understanding that such a system is now in use but it is worth remembering that this was taking place twenty years before the first Merlin entered service. I strongly supported that work, which included a new and novel icing-detector.

The Mechanical engineering group had work on active undercarriage systems to help operations on unprepared airfield surfaces, but one of their major tasks was the development of Thixotropic safe aircraft fuel. This was a collaborative programme with the U.S. and U.K. and involved a major oil company. Success would, it was hoped, reduce the risk of disastrous fires on large commercial aircraft but carried the high potential cost of converting the worldwide fuel supply network and also the aircraft themselves, which needed the means to convert the gelled fuel to a liquid form for use in the standard fuel burners. Storage of the new fuel was a problem since it broke down with time, and therefore needed to be made up and pumped in shortly prior to flight. All in all it looked an unlikely solution, but the work continued, partly due to the U.S/U.K. agreement. The activity was I believe finally wound up when a full-scale crash test was held in the U.S. In the test a Convair 990 four engine commercial aircraft was converted for remote control in the U.S. and deliberately crashed. In the event the aircraft was slightly misaligned with its intended crash zone, and the resulting fire was at least as spectacular as any before it when seen on T.V. Protagonists claimed partial success but were not convincing.

Among the new work that I initiated was a contracted study to determine the means of protecting aircraft electronic systems against Radiation and Electromagnetic Pulses due to nuclear explosions and to prepare a guidebook for the aircraft industry. Up to that time only lip service had been paid to that subject.

Finally however I made a breakthrough and persuaded the group to start work on computer controlled Aircraft Utility systems. Contracts placed with both B.Ae. and Smiths Industries enabled both firms to develop the techniques used in the Eurofighter and other aircraft. The everyday use of computers may suggest that the solutions were easy but in fact the need to demonstrate reliable operation in all flight conditions and after battle damage was a quite different ball game.

After all the battles with our colleagues it was finally the blunt instrument of a Moratorium on new Defence expenditure that finally gave the X.R. group some credibility. Until then our spending had followed the pattern reported in Part 2 but now it stopped entirely for a period; even ongoing construction work ceased when the workers ran out of welding rod and using this, plus the threat of no work without co-operation, both our scientists and the contractors came to heel; the latter even agreed to joint funding which stretched our limited funds a bit further. Only a direct appeal to the Minister gave any relief in any specific case, and I did in fact succeed in one such appeal. During this major hiccup, my A.D. did one important job by devising a scheme of probability for calculating our expenditure and budget forecasts. The new forecasting system was accurate within a few percent but required effort to maintain that system was only available when, during the Moratorium, we had no other work.

As usual in the Civil Service, no sooner had we achieved some success than there were rumours of change. I had been seeking a new post for some time but while I didn't see eye to eye with my boss he refused to release me. On the day that the new scheme was announced, all those who did not fit the new plans received personal letters from the Director R.A.E. advising them that they should seek a post outside Farnborough. I received my letter with great satisfaction and took it along to show my boss who looked up and said glumly "I've got one too". As a Farnborough based scientist his new posting was to run the Air Publications team that was just moving to Glasgow, hardly a plum job. The Director R.A.E. had finally recovered complete control of his finances, and the X.R. groups were abolished. For my part I had found the work and environment unrewarding and was glad of a move.

After some chasing around I took a post in D.T.GW. (Directorate of Trials Guided Weapons) based at Fleetbank House in London after just three years at Farnborough.

A Bit of a "Tiff"

Chapter 22 R.N. Retired

Part 4 D.T.G.W.

D.T.G.W. (Directorate of Trials Guided Weapons) was responsible for the development, procurement and support of airborne target systems for all three armed services, as well as providing the same service for trials of guided weapons by MoD/PE and its contractors. In another masterpiece of organisation however it did not have responsibility for the trials or the ranges at which they were carried out; the actual trials or practice firings were arranged by the user branch in conjunction with the Superintendent of the range who was responsible to the Head of Instrumentation and Trials (I.T.) Dept. at Farnborough. Neither the User Branches nor I.T. Dept. were financially responsible directly for target material consumed during trials although D.T.G.W received his funding via allocation from the Services Votes, and as a result users had no incentive to seek more cost effective solutions. Such rationing of certain expensive resources was a function of D.T.G.W. officers who used their best judgement as for example during some urgent trials carried out at the time of the Falklands War. Similarly D.T.G.W. did not influence the policies by which the service users trained their "weaponeers", although a live firing against a target was in fact only one aspect of the total weapon development and service operational assessment and training package in which computer simulation and modelling played their part.

The majority of our work was focused at targets used at the main weapon range in Cardigan Bay, and the Supt. Aberporth was also responsible for the airfield at Llanbedr from which a contractor operated various aircraft and targets that we supplied. Needless to say the contractor was not under D.T.G.W. control and was almost a law unto himself, since, while it was possible for Farnborough at intervals to put the contract to competitive tender, the staff could only be transferred to a new contractor because they alone had experience and their skills were not readily available in that part of Wales. The potential cost of redundancies was another deterrent. It was apparent that the organisation was designed to ensure conflict and create a power struggle between the contenders.

My role as T.G.W.2 under A.D/T.G.W. carried the bulk of departmental work, although I later shed some of the projects to concentrate on certain key tasks. At the outset I was custodian for 3 Canberras (T.T.), the last two surviving Meteor U16's, 1 Meteor T7, around 20 Jindivik Mk 103 target drones, all based at Llanbedr, plus a total of 23 Sea Vixen F.A.W.2 at different locations and in different states of repair, which were being converted to unmanned operation. I was also responsible for procuring Northrop Chukar 2 and Shelduck drones for the R.N. as well as developing and procuring Electronic Augmentation systems and Towed Targets. Compared with my earlier posts in London this was a very busy one since the work had a direct impact on operational trials and required a lot of travel in U.K. and abroad. I even held one contract meeting at my home in an effort to keep the momentum going while I was recovering from an operation. Business lunches in London were of course a regular feature of life, and since Fleetbank House was just off Fleet Street, I found two particular hostelries very acceptable; the first was the well-known and old Cheshire Cheese, whose speciality was steak and kidney pie with onions, and the second was the Cellars, situated under a railway arch by Blackfriars Station. Despite reservations about these lunches we did in fact achieve results.

The very idea of a Sea Vixen drone gave me food for thought, and when within a few days of my arrival I received a call from the Lt.-Col. i/c the Rapier Project asking when he could expect to use it for live firing, I dropped all else and started probing. I found that the project was still under development although it had been promised to users for months, moreover production had been authorised ahead of completion of development without receiving Safety and Acceptance Clearance by the Range Authority at Aberporth. Aberporth was adamant that it was unacceptable to operate such a heavy and high speed aircraft within Rapier range of the range head at Aberporth, as the fallout due to a missile hit or an accident was a serious risk to the facility, and it was obvious that there had been insufficient consultation at the outset. I then ordered an inspection of all the Sea Vixens and found that many were little more than wrecks when they had been discarded by the R.N. in 1972 e.g. one had its tail booms sawn off. The cost assumptions were therefore hopelessly incorrect as each successive aircraft would need greater corrective work. On the evidence I proposed cancellation of all but two development aircraft to be used solely with a safety pilot for operator training and not as a target; this was welcomed by the head of I.T. Dept. at R.A.E. and I went ahead as planned. One of these aircraft XP924 is now the only "airworthy" Sea Vixen and has been seen in many flying displays since it was retired from MoD in 1991 and is now called "Foxy Lady" for the benefit of the Airshow enthusiasts. However, it was still necessary to determine how any future Full Scale Drone, including Sea Vixen, could be accepted at Aberporth, and my doubts centred initially on the appalling record of reliability of the M.R.G. (see Chap 16), which still formed the basis of the Sea Vixen Drone Control system; surviving records showed that the best M.T.B.F. (Mean

Time between Failure) figure ever achieved for the M.R.G. was thirty-six hours. The original proposal for the project did not address the key issues and it was necessary to launch a new study to determine the criteria on which the reliability of any future full-scale target aircraft could be assessed before acceptance at Llanbedr. After a lot of searching we adapted the technique used by C.A.A. for civil aircraft. Given a full reliability assessment of any aircraft then it was possible to predict how many flights could take place annually before an airfield accident occurred. When applied to the Sea Vixen Drone the probability of failure in drone flight was found to be too high to allow any useful flying to be achieved. The M.R.G. was certainly a major factor and although changes in design could have been made these would not have been cost-effective. The continuing demands from weapon project offices ensured that I continued the search for a replacement for the Sea Vixen despite reservations as to the utility of a full-scale drone either in weapon development or in service training. All available evidence showed that future "threat" aircraft and missiles would have "signatures" very much smaller than any target we could procure; nor could we expect to find any suitable airframes in U.K. since our military aircraft production with the exception of the Hunter was so small and whenever these were taken out of service any having remaining life were at once sold abroad. The Hunter would however have made an ideal target drone having the advantage of simplicity but this was not to be.

Evidence of a new broom in post then led Hd.I.T. Dept. to suggest that perhaps the stock of Jindivik was too high and that it was time to reduce the planned procurement of a new Jindivik Mk104 currently being developed in Australia, and to begin to look for a replacement. During the early development of British Guided Weapons, firstly ex-Naval Fireflies and then large numbers of Meteors were converted to a drone role to become U15 and U16's and both Fireflies and Meteors and a small number of Canberras were also used by the Royal Navy out of Malta in G.W. firings. They were progressively destroyed during trials and without any similar simple low cost aircraft available in large numbers for conversion then the Jindivik was developed in Australia using a U.K. drone control system and a Rolls Royce Viper engine. This had been the mainstay of later work, originally in the wide-open spaces of the Woomera range but latterly flying out of Llanbedr. Llanbedr had been built in 1939 and post war was used by manned target tugs for anti-aircraft training but the first pilotless drone sortie from Llanbedr took place on 3rd February 1954 using a Firefly. Jindivik operations from Llanbedr commenced in 1960.

Jindivik had a wingspan of 19 ft. 3 ins and an overall length of 28 ft. 9 ins and in fact a manned variant called Pika had flown in Australia. It was a very capable aircraft with a max. cruising speed of 564 mph and because of its simplicity was reliable, but it was fitted with a drone control without system redundancy and, with the exception of radio signal failure, would fail following a single fault. It took off from the Llanbedr runway by means of a trolley and landed on a skid, so that the Llanbedr runway had a special high friction surface. Although ideal in a location such as Woomera it was much less mobile than later zero launched targets and could not easily be adapted for air launch. As an early high-speed jet powered target it was costly and comparable with the US. Republic Firebee, which had been largely replaced by smaller cheaper targets such as the Chukar. Directional control for trolley borne take-off was directed by a man stationed behind it on the runway and skid landing was by two runway controllers, one controlling pitch and the other heading, but after take-off control was passed to a control room which took its commands remotely from the range head at Aberporth. The actual controls were rheostats and switches; there was limited feedback from the aircraft and no plotting board. Essentially the system was little different from that used on the pre-war Queen Bee and, although it worked, even a model aircraft enthusiast had a more ergonomic set up. The evident need to preserve these expensive machines led naturally to the Jindivik becoming merely a Target Tug, which launched towed bodies carrying either flares or radar transponders; these were intended to cause a missile to home onto the towed body and preserve the Jindivik. This was in fact highly successful and the 40 Jindivik Mk104 now planned would last forever and deny the introduction of a newer and more cost effective target.

U.K. and Australia jointly funded development of the Jindivik Mk104 under a "Heads of Agreement" negotiated by our Executive Officer, and as usual gave most of the rights to Australia. The aircraft was to have a higher performance than its predecessor and was to be fitted with a new digital flight control system being developed in U.K. for it and Sea Vixen. Once again I found that production of parts had been authorised years ahead of development trials, but in the event I cancelled twenty-five of the forty planned, leaving just fifteen already part built for delivery in due course. It was supposed that Australia would buy the new model also, but only the R.A.N. used the Jindivik out of Jervis Bay and had no intention of acquiring any more. Meetings were held at six-month intervals in Australia and my A.D. attended these, taking with him my Jindivik Project Officer. I declined these trips since only two people were permitted to attend and he had most need. Australia by then had caught the British disease, in which the trade unions ruled the roost, and every monthly return showed an increase in the development cost, but we were no nearer to establishing the intended fixed price for each of the fifteen production aircraft. By 1984 I could no longer ignore the issue and finally went out myself, replacing my A.D. who was a very nice chap but no match for the Aussies, and in the face of yet another delay declared my intention to stay put until a price had been offered and agreed. This had the desired effect. Meantime in a quick tour round the production line I identified a dozen manufacturing defects, which should have been picked up by the local Inspectorate, and I could feel my "Bloody awkward Pom" label growing larger by the day. More problems were to follow the arrival in U.K. of the first deliveries to Llanbedr although by then we had brought an Australian over to oversee the introduction. His arrival, although welcome technically was a blow to our contractor's staff who found he was receiving roughly twice their salary. No wonder Jindivik was so expensive!

My trip to Oz satisfied my curiosity about the country, which had been pestering me since I first volunteered for the R.A.N. in 1948, and then missed the Far East cruise on *Victorious* when I left 801 Squadron in 1965. In three weeks I spent time in various establishments, at Sydney where I met several ex R.N. chums (now R.A.N.) and following established practise stopped work for beer and sandwiches on the day of the Melbourne Cup race, Jervis Bay where the R.A.N. Jindiviks were flown from an airfield having a problem with kangaroos on the runway, Melbourne where I visited the historic gold mining town of Ballarat and bought a fire opal for Margaret, Canberra, and Adelaide where I found time for a weekend with distant relations. On the return journey home I paid for a stopover at Singapore, again fulfilling an omission in my travelling when *Empress* had failed to make the trip in 1945. The modern city was a far cry from what it had been in 1945 but I did see the "Raffles" hotel and visited the notorious Changi jail. I also took the opportunity of buying a ruby ring in anticipation of our wedding anniversary; when this arrived I had been long retired and we spent the Christmas at a private hotel in Devon. On arrival the first fellow guest to whom we were introduced was Admiral Lord Hill-Norton; my alarm was entirely misplaced and he and Lady Hill-Norton entertained us with reminiscences particularly of time working with Earl Mountbatten and of the decision to cancel the Navy rum issue. I was at the time reading *Red Storm Rising* by Tom Clancy and the Admiral confirmed the accuracy of the scenario postulated in the book.

Well before the Mk104 had even flown in Australia, there were problems with the existing model. The first indication came when I was told that during the months of July, August and September the expensive Radar Towed bodies were jettisoned before landing because of the high risk of their falling on to holiday makers on the nearby beach. The loss of these units was unacceptable since they were normally recovered, trailing behind the aircraft on landing, and though battered were repairable. The main runway at Llanbedr ran parallel with the foreshore and public access could be prevented during operations but the approaches at either end were not MoD property and over the years one end had been developed into a yachting marina, while the other end was an extensive holiday caravan park. The potential for an accident was obvious and the policy seemed a sensible precaution, but that did not explain why the towed bodies were falling off. After some probing I arranged for a video camera to be fitted to a Jindivik and recorded the towed bodies in flight. The results were alarming; they were almost wholly unstable in any departure from level flight. After further investigation it appeared that the design had been produced at Llanbedr at a time when a MoD/P.E. engineer from Farnborough was in charge and allowed to make local modifications. As a result there were no proper design studies and the manufactured product was badly made. It took a long time to establish a new standard, and to prove it by flight trials, and as it was clear that there was no longer any expert in MoD/P.E who understood the complex dynamics of towed bodies I contracted a university to advise us; it was fortunate that they had previously studied the dynamics of long towed Sonar Arrays for the Navy.

The next drama arose when the local M.P. for Llanbedr asked a Parliamentary Question about the safety of Drone Target operations at the airfield and I was called upon to draft the official reply. As I was well aware of the limited safety features of Jindivik, I sought to establish their reliability as compared with manned aircraft, which were considered acceptable. This proved impossible since Jindivik failures per flying hour over time remained markedly higher than even the worst record of service aircraft, while the civilian aircraft were obviously even more reliable. In the end, and since at the height of the cold war any interruption in the programme would have dire consequences, I merely reported that Jindivik had successfully flown "X" sorties without accident. Almost immediately a Jindivik was lost on the range, the next year another, and on the following year one crashed on the beach during landing and it was only by good fortune and bad weather that it missed hitting holiday makers in the area. This warranted a full board of enquiry, during which I established that the sequence of events was due to the loss or more likely the omission of a 1/8th inch steel shear pin. In normal operation when the flaps were lowered during the landing approach, the landing skid was also lowered. At touch down the skid sheared the pin and cut off the fuel supply to the engine; with no pin there was no fuel once the flaps were lowered and the aircraft crashed. The remedy for this particular incident was to make a steeper landing approach so that when the flaps were lowered an engine failure still allowed a safe landing on the airfield but I remained unhappy at the general lack of safety features and continued a search for an alternative.

By this time I needed to find a Jindivik replacement, a Full Scale Drone replacing the Sea Vixens and a high-speed air-to-air gunnery target for the R.A.F. The prospect of supporting a purely British development of any of these items was largely ruled out on cost grounds in view of the small numbers involved. I therefore took my requirements abroad. One such trip was to visit the N.A.T.O. range in Crete, where Northrop flew Chukar 2's in a very slick operation. Following that I was finally able to persuade Aberporth to re-admit Chukar to the range head, and we purchased some as a temporary measure complete with towed bodies, and also fitted and tested a small battery of decoy flares as used on R.A.F. aircraft. Aberporth reluctance to accept Chukar was due to a failure of one of the two R.A.T.O.G. motors during an earlier test, with the result that Chukar gave a catherine wheel like performance on the launch pad. The particular advantage of zero-length R.A.T.O.G. launched targets such as Chukar was that they were easily transportable and did not require either a special runway or skilled controllers for take-off and landing. Apart from U.K. and Australia only the U.S. and Sweden had briefly operated Jindivik and the rest of the world adopted targets like Chukar, as did the Royal Navy. The British Army also adopted a similarly sized small target developed in U.K. for use on its ranges. The U.K. agent for Northrop had arranged the trip to Crete and when we returned by British Airways our pilot was an ex- R.N. pilot I had known on *Victorious*. My travelling companion, an ex-Army N.C.O. returned carrying an expended rocket casing through the Customs at Heathrow without being stopped. The casing was intended as an ashtray and since it probably still contained unburned rocket fuel the consequences had he been caught might have been alarming.

During another trip I took two R.A.F. Sqdn. Ldrs. to Dornier at Friedrichshafen and Munich to assess the suitability of a high-speed gunnery target in use by the Luftwaffe. Our objective was for use with Tornado F3 but it emerged that this was physically impossible on the F3 and that the training policy of the two services was wholly different. However we had arrived at Munich just in time to attend the Autumn Beer Fest, which was much enjoyed.

A visit to Aerospatiale in Paris to inspect their small target drones found the item of most interest still under development and under funded, which was sad as it incorporated many good ideas. As usual the U.K. agent who had arranged the visit entertained us. His brief for the evening out was simple "I'm taking you for dinner to a little restaurant in Montmartre and after that everything is downhill." This turned out to be literally true as we faced a very long walk back down to our hotel, but in the moral sense also. As a result we visited a number of bars with topless young ladies and drank quite a lot of beer; with bedtime approaching I remained with our host while my A.D. and a scientist from Farnborough walked back. My intention was to join him in a taxi to avoid the long walk; instead we continued our perambulation through the low life around the Moulin Rouge. I rather assume I cramped his style because when at last we took a taxi to the hotel he was no sooner out of it than he had flagged down a cruising "lady" and disappeared with her. He was not seen again until the following morning.

Back in London sex again reared its ugly head. In common with other offices in London, our staff disappeared to the four corners of the Home Counties at the end of the day and we had no communal social activity so that it was not easy to appreciate the interests and peccadilloes of the individuals. Thus it was a surprise when one of my junior officers failed to report for work having been arrested for the indecent assault of the son of a foreign diplomat in London. I went into top gear and contacted our Security Officer remembering the prime concerns during vetting in my Naval career; I was due for another surprise because the response was "we're not too concerned about homosexuals, we have several 3 star Officers (i.e. Flag Rank) on our books and provided they keep us advised of their current boyfriend then we're happy". It later emerged that my man was also currently involved with the valet to the Japanese Ambassador. The police charged him and he later went to court but of course in the meantime he returned to work as usual to the outrage of his line manager who refused at first to work with him. He was a Boy Scout leader and this made him rather sensitive on this issue. In the event I gave both a lecture and life returned to normal.

The Falklands War kept us busy when the Navy needed targets during its preparation. The thought crossed my mind that I was still liable for recall, and I checked the uniforms mouldering away in my tin trunk, only to find that ten years of home cooking and a desk job had done its worst and only my cap and flight deck beret fitted. Knowing that the Sea Harriers lacked protection against missile attack I offered D.N.A.W. our Jindivik towed-body decoys but my offer was refused; however I have learned that a similar system has now been developed. I therefore watched events unfolding on T.V. and pondered the policies that had removed the large Fleet Carrier from our Fleet.. It seems unlikely that a war would have ever started if they had been still operating. It was equally intriguing that had the Argentinians risked operating their Super Etendards and Skyhawks at sea it would have been from an ex-R.N. Light Fleet Carrier the "5 de Mayo".

The major search for new targets started in the U.S. when I went with my Director, the Head of I.T. Dept R.A.E. and one of his staff on a tour of all the major establishments. For economy the party split for the first week and I travelled with Hd.I.T.Dept. a dour Lancastrian, who was nicknamed "Chuckles" by his staff. At one point we visited Holloman A.F.B. to see their QF86 drones and were invited to inspect the cockpit. I had just placed my clipboard on the mainplane when a dust-devil whipped it open and removed all my papers. These were last seen at 2-300 feet heading across America, clearly not a cause for humour, and I imagined all my notes had gone, but by luck they were safe and only blank H.M.S.O. stationery had got airborne. The visit confirmed all I had read in A.W.S.T; the U.S. services had many full scale and sub-scale targets in use and under development and their drone control systems were far more advanced than ours, enabling formations of target aircraft to be operated as one example. With the vast areas in New Mexico available for ranges it was possible to carry out work that was impractical in the confined area of Cardigan Bay, and despite this their full-scale drones had two dissimilar controls and incorporated a self-recovery mode for safety. Additionally the drones were only flown unmanned from a dedicated airstrip on the range itself. It made the Llanbedr operation look very basic.

One weekend we were in Wichita to visit Beech and were flown to the Ike Eisenhower home and museum, and followed that, after visiting the Naval Weapons Center at China Lake, by driving into Death Valley prior to visiting the Northrop works in Los Angeles. We had declined an offer to take in Disneyland by common agreement. The positive outcome of the visit was an offer from the U.S.A.F. to release between 24-30 F100 aircraft for our programme. The QF100 was in the final stages of a development programme for drone conversion to replace the QF86. On the morning of our final day we visited the U.S.A.F. in the Pentagon and I received a request to attend a presentation by a contractor. A U.S.A.F. major was also to attend and duly I was collected and taken by car for a late working lunch in the contractor's lecture theatre; the lunch was only sandwiches and soft drinks, but the strict rules prevented the major from attending until lunch was over. A far cry from our practice in U.K!

I later revisited twice in pursuit of the QF100; on the first trip it was for a detailed discussion at Phoenix and Albuquerque with Sperry, who was the development contractor, and latterly to U.S.A.F. Davis Monthan and Sacramento. At Davis Monthan, literally hundreds of redundant aircraft were stored in the dry desert air to await conversion, rework or scrap including several hundred F100's; at Sacramento we had detailed discussions on documentation and airworthiness standards of the aircraft. We took in a visit with our hosts to Caesar's Palace at Lake Tahoe and unsurprisingly, despite being given a handful of dollars at the door, none of our party took home any winnings. One American appeared at one stage to be doing well, but left minus $200. We cash limited Brits. carefully avoided losing once the initial kitty had gone.

Returning home I began preparing a detailed specification for the U.K. QF100 and set up a contract for a new drone control system to replace the antique one at Llanbedr. We had a visit from Sperry to inspect our existing facilities and using our new criteria we were able to determine that it would be feasible to operate a restricted drone flying programme; however even with all the improvements over the Sea Vixen the QF100 would not have been given carte-blanche for everyday use. At that point the intended choice of Sperry to do the preparation and conversion went to the wall; the U.S. had decided to limit the production by Sperry to a small initial batch once development was complete, and since the contract gave all rights of design to the U.S.A.F. then the remainder were to be put to competitive tender. The winner turned out to be a small operator who used largely cheap Mexican labour against which Sperry could not compete. My Director then decided that U.K. had also to go to competition, and this opened up many different choices all of which delayed and complicated the issue. I no longer had time to devote to the task and proposed that a new section be set up to deal solely with Full Scale Drone and Jindivik. This was agreed and I devoted my last two years to Electronic systems but in the end no full-scale drone was ever built for U.K.

Our three Canberras suddenly needed new wing spars and as each aircraft was equipped to launch Stiletto Supersonic targets as well as towing Rushton and Low Level Height Keeping targets, we had a major problem maintaining the service during conversion. Similarly our two Meteors U16 had virtually exhausted their fatigue life, they were no longer used as targets but for operator training and the T7 was useful both as a hack and as a chase aircraft. We had no replacements in view. In general, service aircraft were retired when they had little fatigue life remaining and any good ones like Hunters found a ready market abroad, so there were few choices. The struggle for power between Farnborough and D.T.G.W. continued, and in the middle there were no policy decisions on any of the new items that we appeared to need in the long term.

The search for a high speed towed Air to Air Gunnery Target for the R.A.F. had started when our existing contractor had a series of failures during trials of a target they had been developing prior to my arrival; in the end the contract could not continue and as mentioned above I started to look for an alternative. No longer was it permissible to buy a ready made design off the shelf since there was a range of contenders on the market, and we now had to go out to competitive tender against a proper specification. Getting a requirement from our chums in MOD (R.A.F) proved a major stumbling block, they certainly needed something better than the existing 180 knot or so drogue or banner but could not establish what aircraft would tow it since this could not be done on the Tornado F3, nor could the several departments involved agree the speed and range at which the gunnery engagement would take place, and because those factors determined the size and type of target required then we made very slow progress. We even had a problem deciding what colour to be used. Rather surprisingly the solution used by the F.A.A. many years before was not acceptable. The Navy had had two schemes; one attached a banner to the deck hook fitting where the hook had been replaced by an electrically operated bomb release slip, and the other snatched a Dart target from the ground by flying the aircraft with an extended deck hook arm to catch a line erected between two poles. I would have thought that the Dart using a similar arrangement would have been a marked improvement on the old banners and drogues, but the customer did not agree.

The problem with targets across the board was that an acceptable compromise had to be reached between absolute realism, in which the threat aircraft or missiles were faithfully replicated in accurate wartime scenarios, and cost and safety both to the weapon platform and to the weapons range. The limited space available on U.K. ranges was one major restriction compared with the U.S. but even the fairly low cost towed targets had safety implications and restricted the permitted firing zone, so that some scenarios such as a frontal or rear attack were unusable. I had watched T.V. footage of the Falklands and it was clear that some weapons were being used in engagements for which the operators had no experience due to range restrictions. I had at one time watched a Jindivik being attacked at Llanbedr by a Q.R.A. (Quick Reaction Alert) Phantom; on this occasion the Jindivik was being flown at a speed and steady attitude that would have seemed pedestrian to a Spitfire. The Navy of course had some advantage in using safety areas on the high seas, but even here the potential for hazarding the ship was real when defending against long towed targets representing anti-ship weapons like Exocet. No doubt the arguments continue to the present time.

Having relinquished Full Scale Drone and Jindivik my work now centred on equipment to prove new Guided Weapons. It soon became clear that our existing targets had never been calibrated either for their I.R. (Infra Red) signature, nor for their Radar Cross section, in fact the whole set up seemed entirely ad hoc. I started up new programmes and made some surprising discoveries, which required a rethink on the whole basis of target requirements. I planned to do this in house but retired before it was started. The other major programme was based upon the stated need by the A.S.R.A.A.M. (Advanced Short Range Air to Air Missile) project office for a very accurate Miss Distance Indicator. In conjunction with Farnborough I set up a package of measures, which included "impulse" radar, a high-speed modification to the existing Wretar 180 degree fish-eye camera developed at Woomera, and a video camera. These would all be fitted for evaluation to the last Meteor U16 WK800, which would end its days as a live target. The probable result of a hit would be the loss of all data and so we also started a contract on data compression to allow the data to be quickly downloaded. Special measures were also needed to encrypt the results and to protect them against interception. The system trial was to be conducted at Shoeburyness using the last Meteor T7 and for this trial I acquired a batch of 120mm tank shells, which would be fired past the grounded aircraft. Shoeburyness was well known for a high probability of lightning, but this time I was well prepared and I arranged the purchase of special instruments to detect the change in static charge which precedes lightning, thus enabling the equipment to be switched off and protected. This was a multi-million pound programme, and I was glad to hear from my successor that it had been entirely successful. It appears that the two Meteor U16's, one of which, WK800, was expected to be destroyed in the trial but survived, have continued flying presumably with a fatigue life extension. The impulse radar system developed by our contractor has been highly successful worldwide. The A.S.R.A.A.M. programme was bedevilled by delays partly because it was a joint programme with Germany who had different ideas and could never obtain approval for funds. It is my understanding that A.S.R.A.A.M. was test fired in the U.S. very many years later in the absence of a U.K. full-scale drone. In one of the coincidences of life one of the contractor's engineers conducting the conversion of WK800 was "Chirper" Finch who was in the next bed-space to me at Rosyth in 1941 and whom I had not seen since we left Newcastle in 1943.

I should have retired in 1985 when I reached 60, but stayed just one year longer at one grade down. I could have stayed on until 65 in the lower grade, but by then change was in the air and it was no longer worth the hassle of the daily commuter run. At different stages I had experienced several rail strikes and each had made the travelling less attractive. I declined an opportunity to continue in work with one of my contractors as I foresaw that the climate for military business was reducing and I have no regret at my decision.

Skylark Sounding Rocket
on the R.A.E.
transportable launcher.
S.B.A.C. Show
Farnborough 1972.

"comparisons may be
odious but -!"
Apollo Saturn 1 Space
Rocket topped by the
manned capsule.
Huntsville, Alabama
1976.

A Bit of a "Tiff"

The five Main Thrust Nozzles of the Apollo Saturn V Moon Rocket. Colleague Bill Britten from R.A.E. Bedford gives an idea of the size. Huntsville 1976.

A Bit of a "Tiff"

The Apollo Moon Lander, Huntsville 1976.

It may not look much but this is a piece of Moon rock. Huntsville 1976.

The "Spirit of St Louis" of Charles Lindbergh at the National Aerospace Museum Washington 1976.

The Bell X15 reached M=6.04 in 1961 and 314,750 ft in 1962. Huntsville 1976.

A Bit of a "Tiff"

The Scanning Laser Anemometer before installation in its trailer.

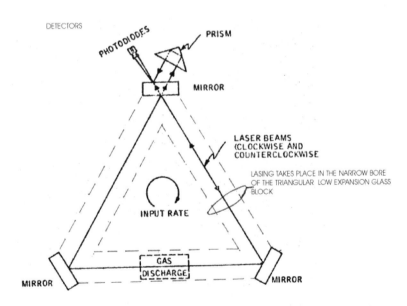

An outline of the elements of a single axis laser gyro. A practical Strapped Down I.N. System requires 3 Laser Gyros and 3 Accelerometers mounted orthogonally and permanently aligned with the vehicle axes. A Computer is then used to continuously calculate the attitude and position of the vehicle relative to its starting point.

ROYAL AIRCRAFT ESTABLISHMENT

21st Anniversary of First
Pilotless Target Drone Sortie
RAE Llanbedr
3rd February 1975

FAIREY FIREFLY U.8 1954

JINDIVIK 103B
ROLLS-ROYCE/BRISTOL VIPER Mk.201
2,500 LB.S.T. TURBOJET
MAX CRUISING SPEED
564 MPH

Flown on 3rd February, 1975, in Canberra PR.3 WE146 — modified to carry Stiletto supersonic target on wing pylons — on its last operational sortie. 'Shepherd' to Jindivik Mk. 103B A92-612 operating with 41 Squadron Phantoms on the Aberporth Range. Range call-sign 'Firefly'. Pilot Sqn Ldr D. E. Betts. Flight time 38 mins.

Officer in Charge
Royal Aircraft
Establishment
Llanbedr, Gwynedd

A Souvenir flown in a Canberra from R.A.E. Llanbedr and acquired at the Jindivik 25th Anniversary Dinner on 25th April 1985.

A Jindivik taking off on its trolley at Llanbedr. It is carrying a towed target beneath the wing. The black fairings at the wingtips hold cameras to record the missile engagement. Author's collection.

A Bit of a "Tiff"

Meteor U16 WK800 on test flight before modification to carry Impulse Radar Miss Distance Equipment in 1986. A retirement gift from members of the project team.

Sea Vixen DMk3 XP924 after retirement from Llanbedr, but still painted in the red and yellow target colours, flying at Yeovilton on 29th September 2001 during a reunion. Photograph is the copyright of and by courtesy of Lionel A. Smith.

Preparation of a Chukar 2 target aircraft at the Northrop managed target facility in Crete 1984.

Chukar launch-pad viewed from the control blockhouse. Crete 1984.

A Bit of a "Tiff"

Chukar 2 at launch - both RATOG motors firing. Crete 1984.

Chukar 2 Floating in the sea after its mission.

"Bell helicopter used to fish the Chukar from the sea and...

... drop it on to a water bed for a wash down
and re-use the following day."

A Bit of a "Tiff"

Stationery over New Mexico.

"From here it's all downhill!"

Photographed in 1984 during a stopover from Australia, this emotive mural in the Chapel of Changi Jail, Singapore was painted by a British Prisoner of War during World War II. It seems to me to have a bearing on most human endeavour, including that described in this book and is therefore a fitting final picture.

A Bit of a "Tiff"

Postscript

I settled down to retirement with a will, building up my workshop and enabling me to tackle most D.I.Y. jobs in wood or metal, and thus to pursue my creative instincts as a cabinet maker, silversmith and jewellery maker, and ceramic sculptor and of course not forgetting gardening, while Margaret continued with her hobbies of spinning, embroidery and fine lace. I had almost forgotten my last job when in 1990 I had a call from a younger ex-colleague who had worked for me and had left for private employment. He had set up a small company with an ex-R.N. Commander with whom I had also worked and they had just won a contract to undertake the investigation I had proposed before my retirement. Would I find it perhaps amusing to work with them as a consultant?

It took just a moment to agree that it would be amusing, and I spent the next year doing for real money what lack of effort had prevented me from doing at D.T.G.W. My real satisfaction was to be able to prove that my concern about the suitability of our targets was justified and this was re-emphasised when during the study some data was released on the minimal radar signature of the U.S. Stealth aircraft and I was able to access Intelligence data on Russian aircraft. That achieved, I doubted that the importance of our findings would receive acceptance in the gelatinous organisation of MoD. and in the post Cold-War climate which had just started. Events seem to have proved this cynical view and I understand that the report eventually was binned when another of the regular reorganisations took place; the Jindivik continues in service with a further eighteen of an updated version, the Mk104-900, but the improvements in the control system have continued. The Australian Navy has never purchased more Jindiviks but continues using their Mk103's with towed decoys, but Australia has evidently also purchased a variant of the Beech MQM 107 which is a much more modern vehicle similar in concept to the older Chukar.

I had been involved with computing in one form or another during the whole of my career, and had planned the general use of personal computers in D.T.G.W. although at the time it was impracticable due to the lack of a training programme and staff to undertake the initial transfer of data. By 1990 they were in use as I had planned and my colleagues urged me to buy one for my work, but I resisted on the grounds that they could perform no useful role at home, could not do the cooking, washing up or the gardening, and my pensions did not warrant a computer to calculate my budget. Needless to say the moment I decided to write this book I had to eat my words!

I would like to write that in retirement I found some vital role in the local community like many of my peers. My first attempt as Community Adviser for our village under the auspices of the Hampshire Emergency Planning Office came at the time of the Lockerbie disaster, Welsh floods and the first Great Storm in the south. Lockerbie pointed up the shortcomings in failing initially to involve the local community, but in my contacts with the police and fire service the professionals were jealous of "amateur" involvement, even when they carried out a specially arranged disaster exercise in the village. When the storm hit the village, many were without power for up to ten days and fallen trees cut off parts of the extended village. Despite their willingness to participate in the scheme, when they were needed my erstwhile supporters had disappeared. Even the Chairman of the Parish Council was working unconcernedly in his garden when I called on his elderly neighbour to deliver paraffin for their heating. Time for a new role and I joined a retired Air Commodore in working with R.E.M.A.P. This national organisation was set up to use the skills of mainly retired engineers in order to produce specially designed or adapted equipment to aid disabled people. We spent a lot of time working to quickly provide two unique items asked for by medical staff in Winchester, only to find that neither were now required. The originator of each request had moved on in the short interval and their replacement had different ideas. In the end I found that apathy was the death to most public activities, and I helped only those who I knew needed assistance. Unsurprisingly these have tended to be elderly ladies like the two separate people who flooded their bathrooms and had to be bailed out

Looking back I feel I have had an interesting and at times controversial career, a few worthwhile successes and certainly some failures. I cannot claim to have participated in earth shattering events, nor have I made miraculous scientific discoveries, but I am proud to have been involved in many activities and believe I made a positive contribution.

"To travel hopefully is a better thing than to arrive,
and the true success is to labour."

Robert Louis Stevenson

Quod erat demonstrandum

Dear Reader,

You will appreciate that the content of "A bit of a Tiff" was set in stone quite a long time before actual publication and my own errors and omissions plus those added by the printer appear in the printed version. This seems to be normal experience and it is only normally possible to make corrections in a reprint. It would be somewhat optimistic for me to expect that to happen in this book and, although this was never a complete history of the Fleet Air Arm or even of Air Artificer Apprentices, now that more information has come to light I will try in this Corrigendum to put things right. My apologies to those of you who like myself have a knack for spotting a missing rivet at a thousand paces and gain satisfaction from reporting your findings as I know that's part of the fun.

Here goes then.

Page i... finally met Graham Bebbington at Clayton Hall on 4th July 2003. The picture of this event is on the inside back cover. It was at Graham's initiative that the memorial bench was installed and unveiled.

Page 9 line 6 to read... would *be* a two mile

Page 13... caption should read.. Granddad Drake.. the word slipped over the page

Page 47... line 16 should read... *seventy eight*... to align with the delayed publication date.

Page 61... fig 2 has been amended on the basis of three articles in the Fisgard Association website and is reproduced as a separate sheet. Between them they form the best chronological record of the Air Artificer entries that I have found for this formative period. Nonetheless there are still a few inconsistencies but since my record deals solely with training of boy entries trained at Newcastle-under-Lyme then that is all that is included. I am indeed most grateful for the work of J.F. O'Reilly RAF Halton (Naval Wing 1938-1942), of J.W. Gibbs (Series 2 1948) and of Tom Hollands (Keppel 1944). It is now most difficult not only to trace individuals with the experience of that era but the memory to back it up. Sadly I am writing in the wake of an announcement that the days of the Air Artificer are over and that in future Technicians will take their place in the style of and trained with their Royal Air Force equivalents as a joint service activity. We are now consigned to history.

Page 66... upper caption to read *Horley* not Homey

Page 79... 3rd line from bottom.. Neither the Oxford or the Anson had an inertia starter for their low powered 350 hp Cheetah engines but had a "wanking handle" geared directly to the engine. Starting was still an energetic activity.

Pages 84 & 85... the caption "The Lysanders were still there in 1944" should appear with the top cartoon on page 85

Page 191... lower caption to read starboard *brow* not bow

Page 212... lower caption "in" should read "*In*"

Page 294... 12th line from bottom should read "*state board*", as anyone from the FAA will know

Page 363... Postscript –no change but as ever the procurement process meanders on with accusations of delays, technical difficulties, and cost rises. It was ever thus!

Page 415... while the announced intention was to use a Convair CV990 I understand that in fact it was a Boeing 707 that was used. An observant reader told me of this error.

Page 438... top photo caption should read M.D.500 helicopter

Page 442... I do now have a vital community role after all. Since Margaret has Alzheimer's and I am her carer I have started up a local Alzheimer's Support Group and it is going from strength to strength. Three of my customers are retired Senior Naval Officers.

Best Wishes

Bill Drake at Bishops Waltham – September 2004

Figure 2. Newcastle trained Naval Air Apprentice (Boy) Entries

Division	Trade	Entered	Basic Training	To Newcastle	Notes	Passed out
1st Rodney	O / L	Jan 1939 Victory	RAF Cosford/Halton Caledonia and Daedalus II (Lympne)	Oct. 1940 / May 1940	Mis 1941 to Caledonia	Dec 1941
1st Benbow	O / L	Aug 1939 Victory	RAF Cosford/Halton Caledonia and Daedalus II (Lympne)	Oct. 1940 / May 1940		June 1942
1st Grenville	O / L#	Jan 1940 Chatham	RAF Halton Daedalus II (Lympne)	May 1940		Dec 1942
1st Anson	O / L	Sept 1940 Puckpool IoW	RAF Halton Daedalus II (Newcastle)	Dec. 1940 / Oct. 1940		June 1943
2nd Rodney	A/E/L/O	Mar 1941 Seafield Park	Caledonia	Jan. 1942		Dec 1943
2nd Benbow	A/E/L/O	Sept 1941 Seafield Park	O & E Fisgard A & E Caledonia	Sept. 1942		June 1944
2nd Grenville	A/E/L/O	Jan 1942 Seafield Park	Caledonia	Jan. 1943		Dec 1944
2nd Anson	A/E/L/O	July 1942 Seafield Park	O & E Fisgard A & E Caledonia	Sept. 1943	Last to pass out as single trade Air Fitters	June 1945
Hood	A/E/L/O	Jan 1943 Seafield Park	O & E Fisgard A & E Caledonia	Jan. 1944	1st cross trained to pass out as Air Artificers A/E and L/O	Dec 1945
Raleigh	A/E/L/O	Aug 1943 Seafield Park	O & E Fisgard A & E Caledonia	June 1944	Completed training at Kestrel on closure of Newcastle in Dec 1945 and passed out Dec 1946	
Effingham	A/E/L/O	Jan 1944 Seafield Park	Caledonia	Jan. 1945	Sent to Condor at Arbroath in Dec 1945	
Keppel	A/E/L/O	Aug 1944 Daedalus III (Bedhampton)	O & E Fisgard A & E Caledonia	June 1945		

Freddie Allford remembers being marched into Chatham Dockyard to welcome home *Ajax* and *Achilles* after the Battle of the River Plate which took place on 13th Dec. 1939.

N.B. In principle the entries and departures should have been at regular six monthly intervals following the pattern of the Civil Service Examinations but there are inconsistencies in each of the records so far seen. At this remove it is difficult to determine the exact dates and the variations are believed to be due to the available training and accommodation slots at RAF Halton, RAF Cosford, *Caledonia* and *Fisgard*. The 1st Anson delay was probably caused by bombing of Lee-on-Solent and shows problems faced in wartime conditions.

Bibliography

In the course of writing I have been at pains to check my memory and records against other sources, particularly the books listed below, all but three of which I have in my collection. I commend them all to readers who wish for more information.

Current Books:-

Ship without Water (The story of H.M.S. *Daedalus II*) – by Graham Bebbington – Churnet Valley Books

Jackspeak – A guide to British Naval Slang and Usage – by Rick Jolly & TUGG – Palamanando Press

Aircraft Carriers of the Royal and Commonwealth Navies – by David Hobbs – Greenhill

The Aircraft Carrier Story 1908-1945 – by Guy Robbins – Cassell

British Naval Aircraft – by Thetford – Putnam

Supermarine Aircraft since 1914 – by Andrews and Morgan – Naval Institute Press

Blackburn Aircraft since 1909 – by Jackson – Naval Institute Press

Vickers Aircraft since 1908 – by Andrews and Morgan – Putnam

The British Fighter since 1912 – by Mason – Putnam

Aircraft of the Royal Air Force since 1918 – by Thetford – Putnam

JANE'S Fighting Aircraft of World War II – Bracken Books

The Fleet Air Arm – by Reginald Longstaff – Robert Hale Ltd

The Fleet Air Arm in Camera 1912-1996 – by Roger Hayward – Sutton Publishing

Wings over Suez – by Brian Cull with David Nicolle & Schlomo Aloni – Grub Street

Fighting Cockpits 1914-2000 – by L.F.E. Coombs – Airlife

Kent's Own (The history of 500 County of Kent Squadron Royal Auxiliary Air Force) – by Robin J. Brooks – Meresborough Books

Wings Over Kent – Kent Aviation Historic and Research Society – Meresborough Books

Joe – the Autobiography of a Trenchard Brat – By Wing Commander Joe Northrop DSO DFC AFC PFF – Square One Publications

The Fleet Air Arm Handbook 1939-1945 – By David Wragg – Sutton Publishing

Printed 1935-1969:-

The Complete Book of Aviation – by S/Ldr C.G. Burges – Pitman

Sea Flyers – by C.G. Grey – Faber and Faber

Britannia has Wings – by Sir Archibald Hurd – Hutchison

Hell's Corner 1940 – by H.R.P. Boorman – The Kent Messenger

The Fleet Air Arm – prepared for the Admiralty by the Ministry of Information – H.M.S.O. Cost 1s 6d in 1943. (A reprint is again available)

Into Wind (A History of Naval Flying) – by Hugh Popham – Hamish Hamilton

The Link Trainer – by Molloy – Newnes – 7s 6d in 1941

The Gyroscope and its Applications – by Martin Davis – Hutchinson Scientific – 1946

Scientific Instruments – by H.J. Cooper – Hutchinson Scientific – 1946

Published for their Ships' Companies: -

H.M.S. *Eagle* 1955-56 Commission
H.M.S. *Victorious* 1958-59